APPROACHES TO THOUGHT

MERRILL'S
INTERNATIONAL PSYCHOLOGY
SERIES

Under the Editorship of

DONALD B. LINDSLEY
University of California at Los Angeles

ARTHUR W. MELTON
University of Michigan

and

ROBERT M. GAGNÉ
University of California at Berkeley

APPROACHES
TO
THOUGHT

Edited by

JAMES F. VOSS

University of Pittsburgh

A *Symposium of*
THE LEARNING RESEARCH AND DEVELOPMENT CENTER
University of Pittsburgh

CHARLES E. MERRILL PUBLISHING COMPANY

Columbus, Ohio   *A Bell & Howell Company*

This volume is a collection of papers prepared for a symposium made possible through financial support provided under a contract with the Personnel and Training Branch, Psychological Sciences Division, Office of Naval Research.

Standard Book Number: 675-09553-0
Library of Congress Catalog Card Number: 69-14309

1 2 3 4 5 6 7 8 9 10 – 73 72 71 70 69 68

PRINTED IN THE UNITED STATES OF AMERICA

PREFACE

This book began with a conference held at the University of Pittsburgh in October, 1966. The intent of this conference was to shed new light on the research area of thought through the varied approaches of the participants. These approaches to the study of thought and the discussions which follow constitute the chapters of this book.

In the invitation which was sent to the participants, a point was proposed regarding the nature of the conference and, on the whole, this point was adhered to in the conference presentations. Specifically, the conference was to provide an opportunity for individuals to discuss or speculate on the issue of how their general research interests could be relevant to the study of thinking. It was not meant to imply by this requirement that the conference should be regarded as anti-empirical; instead, it was felt that the participants had ample opportunity to report their own research via the usual methods of journals and books and that a conference such as this should present an opportunity for them to say what they ordinarily would not put into typical research reports.

The selection of thinking as the subject for this conference was due to a number of factors, foremost of which was the observation that in many areas of study, organismic factors were receiving more and more attention as determiners of behavior. Since the 1940's, it seems that emphasis has been changing from the externally presented stimulus as the major cause of behavior to the role of factors within the organism as a primary cause of behavior. Such a claim could be documented; e.g., by reviewing recent work in conditioning, verbal learning, concept learning, and computer simulation. With this shift of emphasis, it is apparent that the concept of thought increases in importance.

No attempt was made to present a definition of thought to the conference participants prior to the conference sessions. At first glance, it would seem that if a conference on thought is to be held, then the definition of thought should be provided. Such a definition was not specified, however, for two reasons: first, the term "thought" has been used in numerous ways, and it was considered both presumptuous and limiting to indicate what thought is; second, it was hoped that one outcome of the conference would be to reach agreement on the general nature of thought or even a specific definition of the term. As the reader will find, however, the latter result was not forthcoming. Nevertheless, the conference did provide an opportunity for people of diverse interests to converge upon a topic of common concern. I am sure that it was stimulating for all the participants to encounter views from outside their own immediate research areas. I hope that the reader will find the papers similarly thought-provoking.

J.F.V.

ACKNOWLEDGMENTS

The conference "Approaches to Thought" was sponsored by the Office of Naval Research and the Learning Research and Development Center of the University of Pittsburgh. An expression of appreciation is offered to those of ONR and LRDC who made this conference possible.

A special expression of appreciation is offered to Mary Louise Marino of the LRDC staff who spent much time and effort in making the conference arrangements. Catherine Miller, the typist of the manuscript, also is thanked for her extensive effort.

An expression of gratitude is expressed to assistants Mimi Cohen, Wilson Judd, Judy Petrich, Dick Popp, and Barbara Watts whose notes provided the basis of the account of the conference discussions.

TABLE OF CONTENTS

ix

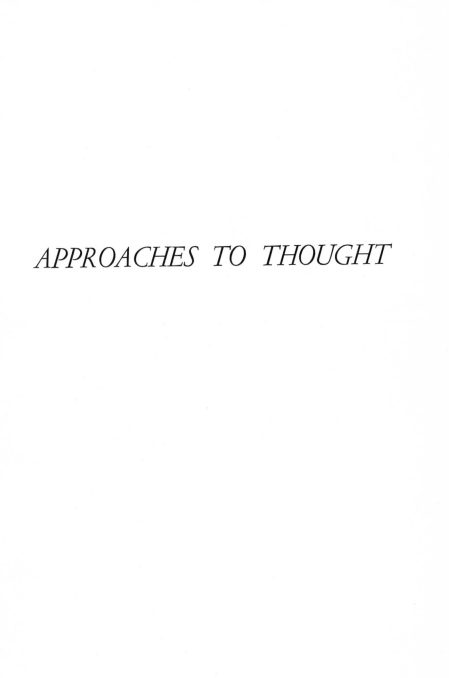

APPROACHES TO THOUGHT

1

PERCEPTION AND THOUGHT: AN INFORMATION-PROCESSING ANALYSIS[1]

RALPH NORMAN HABER
University of Rochester

While this discussion should apply to all aspects of the interaction between perceptual and thought processes, it is concerned primarily with thought processes that arise directly as a result of perceptual stimulation, especially those involved in solving the problem of what it is that was just perceived. This has been a central problem in the study of recognition processes, as clearly exemplified by Bruner's work (especially 1957), but it is only now coming to be appreciated that all perceptual behavior is inseparably related to more general thought processes, and vice versa.

Perception and thought must be considered on a continuum of cognitive activity. They are mutually interdependent and cannot be separated except by arbitrary rules of momentary expediency. Further, to

[1] This paper was prepared with the assistance of research support from the United States Public Health Service (MH 10753; MH 03244) and the National Science Foundation (GB 2909).

I want to thank Naomi Weisstein for her perceptive comments on an earlier draft, and my graduate students at the University of Rochester who have offered many critical suggestions and improvements.

understand how these processes function and interact, they should be subjected to an information-processing analysis rather than be viewed as static structural systems. Such an analysis makes it clear that a proper explication of thought processes must begin with perceptual behavior, just as thought cannot prosper in the absence of stimulation. Equally as important, it is not possible to understand perception without understanding the whole range of cognitive activity.

At this point, some basic definitions are needed. "Perceptual" here refers to all those processes concerned with the translation of stimulus energy falling on a receptor surface (limited to visual for this discussion) into the reports of experience, responses to that stimulation, and memory persisting beyond the termination of that stimulation. "Perceptual experience" is a label for the perceiver's report of what he says the stimulus looks like. This experience may be reported as an introspection, or the perceiver may be required to follow specific rules and to use specific categories of report, as Postman (1963) discusses for the analysis of the introspective-like reports. As I have indicated elsewhere (e.g., Haber, 1966), reports of what the perceiver says he has seen when a stimulus appears provide crucial data for any theory of perception. All too often, we attempt to find out something about perception by only asking what the perceiver thinks was presented, rather than asking him what, in fact, he does see.

The terms "detection," "reaction time," "recognition," and "identification" are defined in the typical ways—realizing, of course, that many methodological variations exist, some of which intrude into theoretical interpretations. Memory, or in this case "perceptual memory," is a report by the perceiver of a stimulus which is no longer impinging on the receptor surface. In this sense, most laboratory experiments of detection, recognition, or identification demand reports of perceptual memory, since the effective stimulus has ended by the time the report is given. It is, of course, for this reason that many memory processes cannot be isolated from perceptual ones. The term "perceptual response" is used to apply generally to all of the above categories indiscriminately.

Processing models are not new to psychology (for example, Freud's personality development and motivational theories can be considered *energy*-processing models since they are concerned explicitly with the transformation, fixation, and investment of psychic energy). However, it has only been in the last decade or so that the greatest development of *information*-processing models in cognitive activities has taken place and such analysis has been performed, especially with sensory and perceptual systems and behavior. Reitman (1965) has provided an excellent review and discussion of these advances in thinking and problem solving, and Broadbent (1965a) briefly has indicated how this approach has been applied to perceptual processing.

Several trends have combined in this new direction—most notably those of microgenetic interests in temporal processes in vision; the application of communication theory in psychology, especially when viewing sensation-perception as a communication system; and some theoretical analyses based upon information theory and computer models as they apply to vision. Equally as important, information-processing language permits us to talk about sensory-perceptual processes in a common vocabulary. As Broadbent (1965a) points out so clearly, one great impasse has been trying to relate spectral energy falling upon specific receptors on the one hand, to the experience of perceiving red on the other. Information-processing analysis attempts to look for correlations between contents of the stimulus and contents of the responses measured at various times after the stimulation begins. By examining these correlations, some notions can be gained of the properties of the flow of information in the nervous system, especially regarding the content of that information at any given point. It is not immediately concerned (though it can be ultimately) with the specific physiological-neurological units or with the energy distribution of the information flowing through the nervous system.

What is assumed is that if the appropriate operations could be devised, it should be possible to sample and examine the contents of stimulation at every point in time and at every level in the nervous system. Comparing those samples over time and location with the original stimulus and with the perceiver's responses (be they description of his perceptual experience, or his detection, recognition, reaction time, identification, or other discrete responses), would indicate the nature of the processing of that stimulus into perceptual experience and responses. This is analogous to what a verbal learning theorist does when he analyzes the changes in the contents of memory over time since initial memorization (e.g., Waugh and Norman, 1965). He then attempts to make statements about the reorganization of memorial processes as a result of time, limited capacity of retention, interference, and other competing demands upon cognitive activity.

It has been only very recently that such attempts as this have been made for the study of perception itself, and for the translation of stimulation into experience, response, and memory. One of the purposes of this discussion is to demonstrate the utility of looking at processing of sensory information as it acts upon and is transformed by the nervous system.

Assumptions of an Information-Processing Viewpoint

Several basic assumptions have governed the processing approach. A perceptual response is assumed not to be an immediate consequence of stimulation, but rather one which has gone through a number of stages or processes, each of which takes time to organize or transverse. Further, it is assumed that this processing is limited by the capacities of the information-handling channels, the information content of the stimulus, and the prior experiences and condition of the perceiver. In addition, it is assumed that perceptual processes cannot be studied or analyzed independent of memorial ones, since recoding and preservation of information occurs at all stages of information processing.

These assumptions apply to the typical laboratory recognition or identification situation in which the stimulus is on view for a relatively short time and the responses to it occur at a time when the perceiver cannot refer back to the stimulus. Moreover, these same assumptions can be applied to the situation in which the stimulus continues in view. In addition, problems arising from eye-movement scanning, from temporal summation, and from updating of processing arising from the continued presence of the stimulus have to be taken into account in ways that are elaborations and extensions of the assumptions being presented.

Before discussing these assumptions in detail, a theoretical concern regarding methodology must be underlined. Many experiments have reported effects that are consistent with a process analysis, but are little more than suggestive because of the many possible alternative interpretations of their results. Garner, Hake, and Eriksen (1956) elaborated the concept of a converging operation specifically to limit interpretations of experimental results. They argue that for every possible potential mechanism process or model that might be used to explain an empirical result, it is necessary to provide some operation in the experiment that will differentiate that mechanism from all others.

A processing approach such as the one being proposed here requires very careful attention to converging operations. For example, whenever it is proposed that a process occurs between time t_0 and time t_1 (or locus L_0, and locus L_1), it is required not only that a measure of the information content be made at both t_0 and t_1, but also that some additional manipulation or measure be taken "to converge" on the changes observed between t_0 and t_1. For example, finding an information loss between t_0 and t_1 is open to many interpretations, such as interference, fading trace, selective encoding, and probably others. However, a post-stimulus sampling cue introduced at various intervals of time between t_0 and t_1 could provide information about the time course of the loss of content. Hence, post-stimulus sampling is one converging operation. Manipulating the stimulus content could provide another converging operation. For example, if two sets of stimuli were used, one composed of items known to be prone to interference, and another known to be resistant to interference, and no differential loss between the two sets of stimuli occurred between time t_0 and t_1, then this converging operation would suggest that interference was probably *not* involved in the process accounting for the loss. Without these two converging operations, and probably several others as well, merely reporting the loss from t_0 to t_1 indicates relatively little about the underlying process. It is for this reason that information-processing analyses cannot usually be applied to old data. If the converging operations were not included at the time the data were collected, it is usually impossible to differentiate possible interpretations or processes. Nor are such analyses often applicable to data collected for other reasons or within the context of other points of view.

The first assumption, that of the non-immediacy of perceptual responses arising from stimulation, has important and far-reaching implications. Until quite recently, perception, as an end product of sensation, was considered to be immediate (which was one of the several reasons James Gibson, 1959, objected to using these two concepts when he thought that one would do). Gestalt theory also did much to advance this immediacy view. And, of course, nearly all introspection of percepts arising from stimulation supports immediacy because rarely can one have any sense of a time lag or of stages taking time. However, failing to be aware of elapsed time does not prove that time does not pass. It has taken rather elaborate experiments to demonstrate that the "sense of immediacy" means only that short durations of time are difficult to discriminate.

Microgenetic theory (see Flavell and Draguns, 1957, for a general review) has argued for a temporal developmental process of each percept of a stimulus, characterized primarily by a growing clarity over the first few hundred milliseconds after the onset of stimulation. However, while microgenetic theorists speak of stages, they usually imply continuous processes of growth rather than qualitatively different operations being performed on the percept. Kaswan and Young (1963) have reported recent work which also suggests a quantitative growth of contours, which until clear, makes it difficult for the subject to distinguish fine detail. But, since provision is not made to separate slow, continuous growth from distinct operations, it may be that the basic microgenetic theory can be subsumed under information-processing analyses. Werner and his co-workers at Clark University have been most influential in arguing for and demonstrating this form of non-immediacy of perception. Their model has not been as productive as it could be, primarily because it fails to provide very many operations to examine the changes occurring between stimulation and response. Such operations help make it possible for information-processing anal-yses to make far more rapid advances.

One facet of the first assumption of information-processing analyses is that the total time from stimulus onset to the occurrence of a percep-tual response can be divided into intervals, with each interval charac-terized by a different operation. Using this assumption, we can create a block design of these intervals, labeling each block according to its operation, connecting the blocks to suggest the order in which the operations are performed, and paralleling the blocks to suggest opera-tions that are simultaneously performed. Then we can begin a careful program of experimentation derived from aspects of this design: Have the intervals been divided up correctly? Are the order of operations correct? Is the overall organization of the processing of information correct? Such questions and the experiments derived from them repre-sent the crux of information-processing analyses. A number of models have been constructed using such block designs, most notably those of Broadbent (1958), Sperling (1963), and Melton (1963).

The second assumption, regarding limited information-handling capacities, is also an important one. The problem of limited channel capacity has been clear in the study of perception for most of the his-tory of experimental psychology; e.g., concepts such as selective atten-tion and immediate memory span. The nervous system is apparently just not large enough to maintain all aspects of stimulation perma-nently. What this fact suggests for information-processing analyses is that we should look for instances in which recoding of information takes place—recoding generally in such a way that some of the con-tent is maintained more explicitly at the expense of the other aspects which are dropped out. The points in time at which the recoding occurs should be particularly important ones in the study of informa-tion processing; it is not surprising that most information-processing models refer to these points almost exclusively.

Boynton (1961) has argued that whenever channel capacity for visual information is exceeded, temporal information is sacrificed in favor of retention of spatial characteristics. While he is concerned with peripheral neural encoding mechanisms, his comments suggest operations by which the encoding and recoding processes could be studied and manipulated. Pollack (e.g., 1964) has been pursuing such an approach for several years.

The third assumption underlying an information-processing analysis concerns the commonality of perception and memory. This theoretical assumption has grown out of an important methodological controversy affecting the design and interpretation of perceptual experiments: How is it possible to conclude whether or not a particular independent variable affected perception when the subject must use a response indicator, drawing primarily on his memory, to report what he thinks he saw? This concern is whether independent variables are affecting perception directly, or whether their effects are being mediated entirely by changes in the indicator system being employed by the subject. Thus, for example, when high-frequency words are perceived more readily than low-frequency words, it could be because frequent words produce clearer percepts. On the other hand, given the same adequacy of the percept with high- or low-frequency words, superior perception of the former occurs because it is easier to guess the word (Eriksen, 1962); it requires less information to fill in part-cues (Guthrie and Weiner, 1966); or lower criteria for reporting frequent words are employed (Broadbent, 1967). Each of these latter alternatives suggests an effect of word frequency acting upon the type of report required that is quite independent of any perceptual effect. Garner, Hake, and Eriksen (1956) were the first to see this issue most clearly. Many others, of course, have made this distinction in the course of interpreting individual experiments (e.g., Eriksen, 1958, 1960, 1962; Goldiamond, 1958; Haber, 1967), but it is frequently doubtful that the point has entirely struck home.

Perceivers, obviously, can remember that which is previously seen, but psychologists tend theoretically to isolate the study of the processes that give rise to the perception from those that give rise to the memory. While it is likely that these processes differ, they also share a common antecedent: stimulation; and except in some unusual situations, both *always* occur as a result of stimulation. Thus, not only do we have a percept of stimulation while that stimulation lasts, but we also have a memory of that stimulation and percept persisting for from minutes to decades after the stimulation itself is terminated.

Thus, it is not sufficient merely to worry about whether the response indicator is an unbiased index of the perception. Since (at least in many natural and most research settings) the stimulus is either changed or is no longer present when the response is given, we must also worry about the content and organization that the stimulation has taken in memory. To conclude that a particular response indicator did not give a fair picture of perception also may mean that most of the variance in the experiment was concerned with how the stimulus and percept were translated into memory and not with perception at all (see Haber, 1966, for a detailed discussion of this point). Information-processing analysis makes this distinction quite explicit, since many, if not most, of the operations specified are concerned with recoding or translation. While some of these recodings are designed primarily to permit the information to travel through limited capacity channels, some of them, especially in latter stages, are designed for preservation of the information more permanently. This, of course, is the operation of memory.

I have reviewed these assumptions very briefly to set the stage for more detailed examination of some of the theoretical issues and operations being employed in information-processing approaches to perception and cognitive processes. Before proceeding further, however, a few comments are in order regarding the relevance of physiological and neurological disciplines to the discussion in this paper.

Some Neurological Considerations of Information Processing

Physiological psychologists have a clear referent for stages: the neurological pathways marked off by different levels of synapses. Thus, we find an overriding distinction set up between peripheral and central mechanisms, corresponding usually to events taking place before or after the impulses enter the primary visual cortex. Within the peripheral events, they talk about events occurring at the primary receptor cells, combinations at the bipolar level, the ganglion cell in the optic nerve, and the synapses and crossings at the lateral geniculate body. It is clear from a large mass of research that it takes considerable time for the train of pulses and changes in resting levels to travel from the receptor surface to the visual cortex and beyond. Furthermore, the properties of those trains of pulses may be changed radically from level to level.

This discussion, however, will not be concerned with information processing at the strictly neuro-physiological level. Stages here do not imply the different pathways, synapses, and centers that are involved in the neural transmission of impulses. Such stages may or may not correspond to those stages in an information-processing analysis.

But a more interesting side of the question involves the physiological correlates of information itself. It has been argued that we can talk about information impinging on the retina only insofar as we have a model or theory which gives the transfer function for such stimulus energies falling on the retina to be transformed into information. The most common and most developed of such models is one which considers patterns of active and inactive cells on the retina as the information in the stimulus. Nearly all theories of pattern recognizers (e.g., Rosenblatt, 1957; Uhr, 1963) use such a model quite effectively. Recently, however, quite different models have been suggested, following evidence that receptor fields of cells in the retina are arranged in such a way that impulses will arise from them only when the shape, or orientation, or movement of the stimulus energy corresponds to that specific arrangement of cells. Hubel and Wiesel (e.g., 1962) have provided the best documentation on this, although numerous publications have now supported this kind of very peripheral information processing.

Before formally discussing the principal converging operations used in information-processing analyses of perception, it would be well to consider the different theoretical attacks and methodological procedures that have been employed to study one specific aspect of this problem.

Parallel and Serial Processing

One important facet of information-processing analyses is often phrased in terms of asking whether information is transferred through stages in parallel or in serial order. In a typical visual stimulus, where the information is concentrated on or near the fovea, that information is seen at a glance. This can be thought of as being received in parallel —in that a large number of retinal units are stimulated simultaneously. However, it is possible to inquire whether these parallel inputs are also being processed in parallel, or whether some mechanism treats them sequentially in a serial order. For example, Sperling (1963) has argued that arrays of letters are stored in a visual short-term storage lasting several hundred milliseconds, after which they fade and all information is lost. However, during that time the contents of that storage are being translated item-by-item into a more permanent memory. He finds on that basis of several converging operations that the rate of serial processing of individual letters is about ten milliseconds per letter. Broadbent (1958) used an auditory task to show that if a string of different digits arrived simultaneously to the two ears, the subject will report all of the ones from one ear and then report those from the other ear. This formulation suggests that while we may think we can pay attention to two conversations simultaneously (in parallel), we actually listen to one and then to the other (in serial). It also suggests that a short-term storage is needed to hold those items whose report is delayed.

On the other hand, there is some evidence that doing two or three things at once takes no longer than doing one, thus suggesting that parallel operations are being performed. Neisser (1963), showed that it takes no longer to search for two items in a list than for one, implying that the two operations are combined and done in parallel. More will be said about his research design when reaction time as a converging operation is discussed.

The interpretation of reading skills is also usually viewed as a parallel process, such that each fixation brings in a block of information that is handled as a unit. This view has led to the prediction that if larger block sizes are acted upon with fewer fixations thereby occurring, then reading speed could go up without sacrifice to comprehension. This position seems to be true up to a point, as attested to by the success of speed-reading programs; cf. Miller (1956); Poulton (1962). But, of course, without any converging operation on what happens during each fixation, such evidence can be no more than suggestive of major parallel operations.

As another example of the serial-parallel distinction, evidence with respect to the duration of stimulation needed for correct recognition as a function of stimulus content has been considered relevant. If it is true that a linear increase in duration is needed for correct recognition as a function of increases in stimulus information, serial item-by-item processing might be indicated. A parallel process might produce a step function, with no decrease in accuracy occurring as content increases up to a point, after which too many items would be present for a single parallel operation.

The evidence for recognition tasks generally supports the linear (serial) relationship between accuracy and information content. I have verified this in my laboratory when the number of letters in the stimulus array is increased. Weisstein (1966), in a task in which only one item is selected for report, showed that as the number of items displayed increases, the probability of correct recognition decreases. The result is somewhat confounded by the fact that the arrow telling the subject which item to report also produced some masking, but probably not sufficient to invalidate this particular conclusion. Hake (1957), and Estes and Taylor (1966), also report similar data.

However, evidence from counting tasks, in which the subject is asked to count the number of items in a briefly presented display, generally shows a step function (Hunter and Sigler, 1940; Cheatham and White, 1952; Averbach, 1963), with the first step occurring as items increase beyond five, to eight per presentation. Further steps for each two to three items added were found by White (1963). This suggests that small groups of items can be taken in at a glance and counted in parallel, but as further items are presented, additional counting steps are added serially.

These last results suggest the difficulty of simply using the correlation between information content of the stimulus and response accuracy as an index of serial or parallel processes. Longer processing time may be needed with more complex stimuli because more serial operations are needed or because a single parallel operation has to be performed over and over again serially. Weisstein (1964, 1966) has discussed this point carefully, and has argued that a converging operation; i.e., some other index over and above response accuracy alone, must be used before the correlation between information and accuracy can be interpreted in terms of information processing successfully.

As a different type of example of serial versus parallel processing, duration of presentation can be reduced without loss in accuracy if the items combine together to form a meaningful or familiar larger whole, as when letters form words. This would suggest that individual items can be processed as a group somewhat simultaneously. If the items are processed serially at a given rate and then synthesized, how could this latter combination permit a more rapid processing of the items to occur before the synthesis? Some theorists have argued that this is a response rather than a perceptual effect. For example, Eriksen (1958) has argued that perception is unaffected by meaning, but rather the perceiver is able to remember the items better or fill in a partial perception if they spell a word for him. I have attempted to refute this argument in a series of experiments on word recognition processes (Haber, 1965, 1966; Haber and Hershenson, 1965; Haber and Hillman, 1966; Hershenson and Haber, 1965) where I have suggested that meaning is capable of acting upon the process of perceptual experience directly, rather than being mediated indirectly by response or memory effects. To the extent that this argument is correct, the recognition of meaning must be occurring at somewhat the same time as the perception in the individual items, and that this recognition of a superordinate meaning can be considered as parallel to that of the individual items.

Conversely, several lines of evidence exist which imply that when sequential items are presented at high rates of speed, the order in which they came in often cannot be reported correctly even when the names of the individual items are successfully reproduced (Crossman, 1960). This finding would suggest that item identification and order reconstruction are distinct processes, and are serial, in the sense that it takes longer to do both than only to identify the items regardless of order. Kolers and Katzman (1966) have carried this line of thought one step further, with evidence to suggest that in addition to the separation of item and order information, there are certain rates at which the subject can reproduce the items in the correct order without always being able to name the familiar word the items spell. This result implies that synthesis of meaning is an even further serial process occurring after item and order information is extracted.

The serial-parallel distinction is illustrative of the theoretical fertility of information-processing analyses of perceptual and cognitive processes and of the importance of converging operations in the research designs used in the manipulations. As has already been indicated, without such converging operations, it is nearly impossible to make justifiable statements about processing.

Three Converging Operations: Reaction Time, Backward Masking, and Post-Stimulus Sampling

The three principal research designs that have been employed to examine these kinds of temporal information processes in perception are those using reaction time, backward masking, and post-stimulus sampling.

Unfortunately, the reaction-time procedures, while vitally concerned with serial-parallel distinctions in decision making (see Lindsay and Lindsay, 1966 for a brief review), have not been used consistently to study perceptual components. For example, in one typical reaction-time design (Neisser, 1963), the subject is required to scan a large number of items, looking for a critical characteristic. When located or determined, he responds as rapidly as possible. Dividing reaction time into the number of items scanned, number of critical items presented, or other stimulus variables yields various estimates of decision time per item. This measure then can be considered as a function of the number and characteristics of the items, the subject's strategy, his expectations, and the like. While this procedure often has great relevance to an explication of decision processes, the perceptual aspects are not clearly represented. The amount of time each item is stimulating the subject is not controlled, nor is his scanning behavior itself; i.e., how many items are observed at one time, how many fixations are made per item, how fast is the scanning rate, and so forth. In some research, however, scanning behavior is recorded; e.g., Gould and Schaffer

(1965). Such tasks also involve relatively long search times so that multiple fixations are possible, thereby confounding eye movements with decision-making. While it is possible to divide the total search time by the number of items being searched to arrive at a decision time per item, no converging operation is provided to show that in fact the decision time actually corresponds to the time it takes to decide whether an item is critical. It is possible that items may be searched in groups (parallel), a decision made, and then the next group taken, and so forth (serial). It is this lack of a converging operation that makes it difficult to draw conclusions with any confidence from research in this area using a search procedure. Sternberg's recent work (1966, 1967) has done much to remove some of these objections, however.

The problem specifically with the reaction-time research with respect to the perceptual components of an information-processing analysis, is that it has yet been unable to separate the different processes that eventually result in a decision to respond. For example, several experiments have reported (e.g., Neisser, 1963) that it takes longer to process the elements of each item when the task is to respond if the item does not contain a critical element, than to respond when it does contain a critical element. A number of hypotheses are available to explain this, some stressing processing steps after the elements are clearly perceived, some stressing differential discriminability of the elements themselves, and some stressing different strategies the perceiver is using, especially whether he is processing more than is necessary. What is needed in order to separate more of these hypotheses, is to specify the stimulus characteristics that are being processed—template matching, hierarchical testing of element by element, etc.—and to separate out registration of the stimulus, processing of a short-term visual storage, and decisions about whether the items require a response. Such delineations could be made by controlling the exposure duration in a scanning task. While it is obvious that most of the time is needed to make decisions, no one knows how much of it is needed to view the stimulus itself. If such viewing time interacts with the other variables, then the processing steps will become more apparent.

A second major converging operation has been the use of backward masking. It is relevant since it suggests that a later stimulus interferes with the processing of one that came before it. Crawford (1947) showed that a masking flash coming after a test stimulus will elevate the threshold for the latter up to one log unit, depending upon the luminance and the time between the target and mask. He thought that this effect could be due to the overtaking of neural impulses somewhere in the visual system. His interpretation has some credence, since this type of masking effect generally occurs only when the masking stimulus is of greater area and intensity, thereby producing a shorter latency of response. Donchin, Wicke, and Lindsley (1963) have shown with evoked potentials in humans, that this type of masking effect occurs before the visual cortex, and Donchin (1966), using recording electrodes in the optic tract of cats, obtained results suggesting that the masking effect occurs before that point. Thus, in those studies in which the masking flash is usually one of high intensity and often considerably larger in area than the target, a peripheral mechanism is suggested to explain the elevation of the threshold of the test spot by the subsequent masking flash.

There is, however, a large body of literature on metacontrast effects (see Raab, 1963; Alpern, 1952) in which backward masking-like effects are found, but under circumstances in which the masking stimulus is not a large, bright flash, but rather a figure with adjacent contours to the target stimulus. Thus, Werner (1935) showed elevation of the threshold of a disc when an annulus followed it by the appropriate delay. He interpreted this result as evidence for a microgenetic approach, due to the interference with the slow development of the contour of the disc. Numerous studies have shown this relationship that seems to stress the closeness of the contour between the two stimuli in space, even if different in time. For example, Weisstein and Haber (1965) found a U-shaped masking function for letters when followed by a ring, so that no loss in accuracy of recognition of the letters was observed for either simultaneous or short inter-stimulus intervals, or for very long ones. However, for intermediate intervals, a sharp loss in accuracy occurred. Weisstein (1964) showed that this effect was more pronounced when the shapes of the target and mask fit together most closely; e.g., when an O as compared to a D was masked by a ring.

This type of metacontrast effect cannot be adequately handled in the same way as the Crawford type of backward-masking demonstration. While the time relations are often similar, no requirement is necessary in the former for greater area or greater intensity, but only for adjacent contours. While contour interactions seem to be important, a number of studies have looked for a more general central versus peripheral distinction. The most direct attack has been to demonstrate dichoptic masking, in which the target is shown to one eye and the mask to the other. Evidence strongly indicates at least some if not an entire central interaction. This finding has been shown by Kolers and Rosner (1960), Schiller (1965), and Kinsbourne and Warrington (1962). No one has been able to establish dichoptic masking using the Crawford-type masking paradigm. A second line of evidence in support of primary central involvement comes from studies in which reaction time is used as a converging operation for the effects of masking. When a stimulus is decreased in physical energy, reaction time to its onset is increased proportionately. However, the reaction time to masked stimuli, which appear phenomenally decreased in brightness, if not occluded altogether, is not affected (Fehrer and Raab, 1962; Harrison and Fox, 1966; Schiller and Smith, 1966), thus suggesting that the masking effect must be occurring at some center higher than that mediating reaction time.

The third line of evidence for central determination of masking is derived from data from certain kinds of metacontrast experiments. When the luminances of the target, mask, and adaptation fields are equal, then a U-shape function of masking is found as the time interval between target and mask is increased. Thus, when target and mask appear simultaneously, or the mask follows by less than 15 to 30 milliseconds, no loss in accuracy occurs (as compared to presenting the target alone). Accuracy decreases to a minimum value at an interval of 50 to 100 milliseconds, and then returns to nearly the same level as for the very short intervals. Considerably more will be said about the U-shape function later in this discussion, but its relevance here is that it would be quite difficult to construct a peripheral model of masking to explain this shape, while a model employing a central mechanism could easily handle it.

Backward masking and metacontrast are relevant to information-processing analyses of perception and thought. A number of theorists recently have argued that both backward masking and metacontrast interfere with the processing of visual information by the nervous system. Before examining this argument, however, it is necessary to look at the third principal research design, that of post-stimulus sampling, and at the general concept of short-term visual storage.

The first and most explicit of the models to stress the relationship between information-processing analyses to interference phenomena has been that proposed by Sperling (1963). Discussing his work on short-term visual storage and backward masking, Sperling argues that visual information processing can be thought of as first creating a short-term storage for stimulation lasting a fraction of a second. The content of that store is scanned, items being processed serially, item by item, until the store has either faded away, has been erased by new information, or all of the information has been extracted. Thus, for Sperling, while the store is loaded by parallel inputs of information, it is processed serially. It is unfortunate that Sperling chose to call this storage "short-term memory" because of the already extensive but quite different usage this concept has in studies of verbal learning. In the latter case, it refers to accuracy of recall measured in the first few seconds to minutes after learning (cf. Broadbent, 1965b, for a review of methods). To avoid confusing the verbal and perceptual uses of the term, it will here be referred to as "short-term visual storage."

Evidence for the concept of a short-term visual storage comes primarily from the work of Sperling (1960, 1963, 1966), of Averbach and Coriell (1961), and of Mackworth (1963). The research designs generally have employed post-stimulus sampling. The subject is presented with an array of information. Shortly after the offset of the array, he is shown another stimulus which consists of a marker or indicator telling him which item in the array he should report. This technique is used on the assumption that the probability that the subject can report a single item at any moment is indicative of the percentage of the items of the stimulus available in a short-term visual storage at that moment.

In general, results using this procedure have shown that with post-stimulus sampling of a complex target, the subject is able to report individual items of information that were indicated by a marker for several hundred milliseconds after the termination of the target. Since this accuracy is far higher than that achieved when the subject has to report the entire stimulus, it is further concluded that the subject has this information available in a short-term visual storage for this brief time, but can only demonstrate it if he is asked for only one item at a time. Otherwise, by the time he can organize his memory for all of the items he has to report, some of them are forgotten. Averbach and Coriell found that accuracy of recognition of a single letter as a function of the interstimulus interval between a 16-letter array and an arrow indicator declined gradually for several hundred milliseconds, and then dropped more steeply until reaching the base line of accuracy, equivalent to the percentage accuracy for the subject reporting all 16 letters (immediate memory span). It was this higher accuracy during the first few hundred milliseconds after the stimulus offset which Averbach and Coriell also referred to as a short-term (visual storage) memory.

The relevance of a concept of short-term visual storage to information-processing approaches is obvious. It suggests that an early process is one in which all (or nearly all) of the stimulus information is represented intact. Processing proceeds from that representation, rather than from the stimulus, whether it is present or not, and of course, this provides a device to prolong the effective stimulus by several hundred milliseconds.

Despite the theoretical fertility of this concept, including a remarkable number of references to it, relatively little direct work has continued on the basic demonstration. Mayzner, *et al.* (1964) report at least a partial replication, in that accuracy stayed invariant from 50 to 150 milliseconds of interstimulus interval. Since they did not employ either smaller or larger interstimulus intervals, no further evidence from their work is available. Because Averbach and Coriell found a decay in accuracy over the range of 50 to 150 milliseconds, this was considered by Mayzner to be somewhat negative evidence. However, since Averbach and Coriell used a different array size, visual angle, and probably luminance, it is possible that longer delays would have shown the drop.

Eriksen and Steffy (1964), using a modified forced-choice test, failed to find a short-term visual storage effect. Rather, they found interference at short interstimulus intervals, with accuracy *increasing* to a maximum value after about 100 milliseconds. They argue that the indicator, coming rapidly after the stimulus, produced interference, mediated by brightness summation leading to contrast reduction; cf. Eriksen (1966). Only with delays longer than 100 milliseconds, in which the indicator cannot summate with the luminance of the target, will accuracy of the target be observed. These effects were obtained with dark pre-, post-, and interstimulus interval fields, so that the onset and offset of the target and the indicator represented abrupt shifts in illumination—conditions greatly facilitating luminance summation and generally producing interference of perception. For some reason, Eriksen and Steffy never set up conditions similar to Averbach and Coriell's in which the fields were all at the same luminance. They had a middle condition in which the indicator was a luminous arrow rather than a dark figure on a bright field. Here they found neither interference nor short-term memory—the accuracy was essentially invariant over 700 milliseconds of delay. However, the sudden increase and decrease in the illumination of the target, especially its offset, could begin to contribute to the interference. Thus, the Eriksen and Steffy experiment is probably not related to tests of a short-term visual storage.

Sperling has elaborated his notion of a short-term visual storage extensively, particularly with respect to his information-processing model for visual memory tasks (1963, 1967). He has discussed masking operations in several ways. When specific letters are masked by a ring surrounding them (metacontrast), he views this as interfering with the processing of that item in short-term visual storage, or more explicitly, with the transfer of that item from short-term visual storage to a longer persistence storage. He has also used large masking flashes that are not specific to single items, either of the large intense field such as Crawford used, or a random noise grid with a random pattern of dots or lines, usually at lower overall intensity than the target (Sperling, 1965). In general, he assumes that this masking stimulus effectively halts all processing of short-term visual storage, so that whatever has not yet been transferred is now lost. No mechanism is proposed for how this occurs, though he does use a computer analogy or erasure of the short-term visual storage by subsequent masking stimulus.

Weisstein and Haber (1965) and Weisstein (1966) have used this similar kind of hypothesis, but adapted it to explain the U-shaped function obtained by themselves and others. Thus, simultaneous target and mask or a very short interstimulus interval between them has no effect on accuracy because the processing of the "masked" item has not yet begun. Likewise, very long interstimulus intervals will not interfere with recognition of the "masked" item since it has already been read out of the short-term visual storage, and after that, masking by subsequent non-informational stimuli has no effect. Only at the time when active transfer is underway can the masking interfere with that transfer.

It is clear that this kind of perceptual interference is quite different from the physiological interpretation offered by Crawford, Lindsley, Donchin, and others. I view masking as an interference with transfer of information that is already stably represented in the nervous system as a short-term visual storage. The latter theorists see it as an inhibition of neural transmission on the way to higher centers, presumably long before there is any stable representation of the target established any-where in the nervous system. Viewing a short-term visual storage as a receptor phenomenon, perhaps analogous to an after-image, will not reconcile the two positions. An after-image model will not predict the U-shaped masking functions, since very short interstimulus intervals should produce even greater interference than longer ones. One would need to argue that a second flash, following close upon the heels of the first one, would not disturb the after-image of the first as much as if it were delayed 5 to 100 milliseconds. There seems to be no evidence for this assumption. Further, an after-image storage would suggest that no dichoptic masking would be found—an assumption contrary to data. Thus, while there may be data storage in the receptor or in other peripheral units, such storage does not seem to be the same as a short-term visual storage, nor can such storage be that which is obliterated by masking flashes.

Eriksen, in a number of recent experiments (especially 1966), has questioned the interpretation of masking as an interference with information processing. Basically, he has proposed that masking can best be understood as a brightness summation effect, such that as two stimuli are presented in close conjunction in time, their brightnesses summate in the nervous system, thus effectively reducing the contrast of each. It is this reduction in contrast that would account for threshold elevations or losses of accuracy of recognition. Eriksen's model thus predicts that forward masking would be as effective as backward masking, and that the point of maximum masking should occur with simultaneity of presentation of target and mask. He is able to demonstrate these predictions when the eyes are dark-adapted prior to either target or mask presentation, and when the interstimulus interval also remains dark. However, under somewhat comparable conditions, Schiller and Smith (1965) have found clear asymmetry between forward and backward masking, which raises some doubt as to the adequacy of the luminance-summation contrast model of Eriksen.

Further, when the eyes are light-adapted to the same luminance as the target and mask, as is the interstimulus interval, then the U-shape data already discussed are obtained. Thus, it would appear as if the luminance relationships are crucial (cf. Kolers, 1962), though perhaps not through luminance summation as Eriksen thinks. Eriksen's model clearly would not predict any type of U-shaped function, but only a monotonic function with maximum masking effects occurring at simultaneity of presentation and decreasing as the interval between the target and mask changes in either direction. Some recent data by Kahneman (1966) offer a different type of negative evidence. He found that if a blanking field and a target are presented, far *less* masking is shown if the blanking field is presented simultaneously with the target than if it is delayed by one-tenth of a millisecond after the offset of the target. If the subject is adding the luminance of the blanking flash to the target, and thereby reducing the contrast of the target, introducing any delay, even one this small, would attenuate this effect. This procedure should reduce masking, rather than increase it, as Kahneman found. This finding would imply that interference is occurring in this situation over and beyond any possible contrast reduction caused by luminance summation.

I have lingered on Eriksen's recent work because he has proposed a model to explain these interference phenomena peripherally, without any reference to an information-processing mechanism. For the reasons cited above, however, and because the peripheral models designed to

account for metacontrast are also open to serious objections, I feel that
these peripheral alternatives are not adequate and that central events
must be considered.

Backward masking, metacontrast, and short-term visual storage
(post-stimulus sampling) designs each involve the presentation of two
stimuli, separated by some variable time delay. It is often difficult to
specify the criteria for which a design should be named. An important
distinction between short-term visual storage and the other two procedures concerns whether the second (masking or indicator) stimulus is
informational; e.g., does it tell the subject what it is he is to report?
In masking situations, the second stimulus is usually a brighter flash of
greater area than the target, or it is a patterned stimulus superimposed
over the target or surrounding it. In all of these cases, the subject has
to detect the presence of the stimulus or estimate or match its brightness. However, to complicate the distinction, Averbach and Coriell
(1961), in one of their studies, and Weisstein (1966), and Weisstein and
Haber (1965) used a ring surrounding part of the stimulus as a mask,
so that the masking stimulus both interfered with the recognition of
an item of the target, but also signaled to the subject to attempt to
report that item.

This review of the converging operations of reaction time, backward masking, and post-stimulus sampling has been designed to show
how it is possible to pinpoint transformation stages in the processing
of visual information. In general, the data from the experiments discussed have been used to bolster a particular theoretical point of view
—that is, of the existence of a relatively complete but unstable representation, from which information is extracted to be available for
report, awareness, and subsequent perceptual memory. The emphasis
here has limited the general information-processing approach to only
the early stages of the overall perception-cognition continuum. This
emphasis is perhaps more novel, and less advanced, even though it is
beginning to create excitement and activity among visual scientists and
perception researchers.

Information-processing analyses do not stop here, however, nor
do the models being developed on the basis of new experiments. The
models of Broadbent, Sperling, and Melton are most explicit in looking
beyond these early stages to the processes concerned with filtering or
selective attention, encoding mechanisms, recognition processes, rehearsal or memory maintenance processes, retrieval procedures, and
the like. These other processes in this continuum between sensory registration and perceptual responses are currently receiving increased
experimental interest as well; e.g., the interest in auditory rehearsal

processes, and their interaction with stimuli that have high potential for auditory, visual, or semantic confusibility; the interest in encoding strategies used to encode the content of the stimulus (or more likely the content of the short-term visual storage) into memory; the interest in the differences between long-term and short-term memory (the latter concept as used by verbal learning theorists) as an attempt to look at recoding, interference, and decay effects; or the interest in simulating perceptual and cognitive activities, which demands an explicit information-processing analysis, since the computer program must be specified by discrete operations and stages.

I have not attempted to spell out the details of these latter stages, nor have I even made very concrete all of the implications of the earlier stages. I think our knowledge is changing too fast to do this well. But I am quite convinced that it will be done very soon. My hope, in presenting this line of argument, is that the fertility of an information-processing analysis of perceptual behavior, and the power of converging operations, as for example, reaction time, masking or metacontrast types of interference, or post-stimulus sampling, will become more apparent. If my expectations are correct, the entire field of cognitive processes, which rest so heavily on concepts of perception and thought, will undergo a revolution in the next five years, due primarily to the application of these more recent ways of theorizing about the underlying processes.

In summary, I have attempted to discuss some of the general properties of information-processing analyses as they apply to the handling of visual stimulation. Three basic assumptions were presented: visual experience and responses are not immediate, but are built up as a result of the number of distinct successive and simultaneous operations; processing is limited by the capacities of channels and storage; and encoding and memorial processes cannot be divorced from sensory registration and experiential ones.

Following a discussion of these assumptions, some of the basic research designs in information-processing analyses of visual perception were reviewed, especially those using backward masking and those using post-stimulus sampling. The concepts of short-term visual storage and of interference processes were discussed in detail, both in their own right and in relation to each other, in terms of a number of recent experiments. One theme running through this discussion and review of past work was the distinction between serial as compared to parallel processes. This theme was used both to illustrate information-processing analyses, and to explore in some detail an important theoretical issue being posed and investigated in current research today.

My interest in these phenomena has been most explicitly concerned with the perceptual rather than purely sensory or physiological levels of interpretation. A number of questions need immediate attention, with respect both to short-term visual storage and to masking effects, since these two concepts have been almost inseparably intertwined both theoretically and operationally. Of primary concern is the assumption that masking interferes with the processing of information from a short-term visual store into a more permanent one. This assumption underlies much of the work in the field at the moment, and while it has been used to interpret data, it has, itself, not been explicitly examined. If some converging operations can be used to bolster the validity of these assumptions, then a major theoretical model of information processing can be more seriously advanced.

Perhaps an even more pertinent question concerns the concept of short-term visual storage itself. While the few references discussed do not cover all of the current work, still, relatively little direct research has been done along this line. This, as well as the somewhat contradictory data obtained, certainly makes it necessary to continue a direct examination of the data and their underlying assumptions.

Both short-term visual storage and masking effects have been translated into many different specific experiments. This work, and that being done on other parts of the information-processing analysis of a stimulation-perception-cognition continuum should help maintain the revolution in the field of cognitive processes.

REFERENCES

Alpern, M. Metacontrast: historical introduction. *Amer. J. Ophthalmol.*, 1952, *29*, 631-646.

Averbach, E. The span of apprehension as a function of exposure duration. *J. verb. Learn. verb. Behav.*, 1963, *2*, 60-64.

Averbach, E., and Coriell, A. S. Short-term memory in vision. *Bell Systems Tech. J.*, 1961, *40*, 309-328.

Boynton, R. M. Some temporal factors in vision. In M. R. Rosenblith (Ed.), *Sensory Communication*. New York: Wiley, 1961, 739-755.

Broadbent, D. E. *Perception and Communication*. New York: Pergamon Press, 1958.

Broadbent, D. E. Information processing in the nervous system. *Science*, 1965, *150*, 457-462. (a)

Broadbent, D. E. Techniques in the study of short term memory. *Acta Psychol.*, 1965, *24*, 220-233. (b)

Broadbent, D. E. The word-frequency effect and response bias. *Psychol. Rev.*, 1967, *74*, 1-15.

Bruner, J. S. On perceptual readiness. *Psychol. Rev.*, 1957, *64*, 123-152.

Cheatham, P. G., and White, C. T. Perceived number as a function of flash number and rate. *J. exp. Psychol.*, 1952, *44*, 447-451.

Crawford, B. E. Visual adaptation to brief conditioning stimuli. *Proceedings of the Royal Society*, 1947, *B134*, 282-302.

Crossman, E. R. F. W. Information and serial order in human immediate memory. In C. Cherry (Ed.), *Information Theory*. London: Butterworth, 1960.

Donchin, E. Personal Communication, 1966.

Donchin, E., Wicke, J. D., and Lindsley, D. B. Cortical evoked potentials and perception of paired flashes. *Science*, 1963, *141*, 1285-1286.

Eriksen, C. W. Unconscious processes. In M. R. Jones (Ed.), *Nebraska Symposium on Motivation*. Lincoln: University of Nebraska Press, 1958. Pp. 169-226.

Eriksen, C. W. Discrimination and learning without awareness: a methodological survey and evaluation. *Psychol. Rev.*, 1960, *67*, 279-300.

Eriksen, C. W. Figments, fantasies, and follies: a search for the subconscious mind. In C. W. Eriksen (Ed.), *Behavior and Awareness*. Durham: Duke University Press, 1962. Pp. 3-26.

Eriksen, C. W., and Steffy, R. A. Short-term memory and retroactive interference in visual perception. *J. exp. Psychol.*, 1964, *68*, 423-434.

Eriksen, C. W. Temporal luminance summation in backward and forward masking. *Percept. & Psychophys.*, 1966, *1*, 87-92.

Estes, W. K., and Taylor, H. A. Visual detection in relation to display size and redundancy of critical elements. *Percept. & Psychophys.*, 1966, *1*, 9-16.

Fehrer, E., and Raab, D. Reaction time to stimuli masked by metacontrast. *J. exp. Psychol.*, 1962, *63*, 143-147.

Flavell, J. A., and Draguns, J. A. A microgenetic approach to perception and thought. *Psychol. Bull.*, 1957, *54*, 197-217.

Garner, W. R., Hake, H. W., and Eriksen, C. W. Operationism and the concepts of perception. *Psychol. Rev.*, 1956, *63*, 317-329.

Gibson, J. J. Perception as a function of stimulation. In S. Koch (Ed.), *Psychology: A Study of a Science.* Vol. 1. New York: McGraw-Hill, 1959. Pp. 456-501.

Goldiamond, I. Indicators of perception: I. Subliminal perception, subception, unconscious perception: an analysis in terms of psychophysical indicator methodology. *Psychol. Bull.*, 1958, *55*, 373-411.

Gould, J. D., and Schaffer, A. Eyemovement patterns during visual information processing. *Psychon. Sci.*, 1965, *3*, 317-318.

Guthrie, G., and Wiener, M. Subliminal perception or perception of partial cue with pictorial stimuli. *J. Pers. soc. Psychol.*, 1966, *3*, 619-628.

Haber, R. N. The effect of prior knowledge of the stimulus on word recognition processes. *J. exp. Psychol.*, 1965, *69*, 282-286.

Haber, R. N. The nature of the effect of set on perception. *Psychol. Rev.*, 1966, *73*, 335-351.

Haber, R. N. Repetition as a determinant of perceptual recognitive processes. In J. C. Mott-Smith, W. Wather-Dunn, H. Blum, and P. Lieberman (Eds.), *Symposium on models for the perception of speech and visual form.* Cambridge: MIT Press, 1967. Pp. 202-212.

Haber, R. N., and Hershenson, M. The effects of repeated brief exposures on the growth of a percept. *J. exp. Psychol.*, 1965, *69*, 40-46.

Haber, R. N., and Hillman, E. R. Changes in single letter clarity with repetition. *Percept. & Psychophys.*, 1966, *1*, 347-350.

Hake, H. W. Contributions of psychology to the study of pattern vision. *USAF WADS Technical Report* No. 57-621, 1957.

Harrison, K., and Fox, R. Replication of reaction time to stimuli masked by metacontrast. *J. exp. Psychol.*, 1966, *71*, 162-163.

Hershenson, M., and Haber, R. N. The role of meaning on the perception of briefly exposed words. *Canad. J. Psychol.*, 1965, *19*, 42-46.

Hubel, D. H., and Wiesel, T. N. Receptive fields, binocular interaction and functional architecture in the cat's visual cortex. *J. Physiol.*, 1962, *160*, 106-154.

Hunter, W. S., and Sigler, M. The span of visual discrimination as a function of time and intensity of stimulation. *J. exp. Psychol.*, 1940, *26*, 160-179.

Kahneman, D. Time-intensity reciprocity under various conditions of adaptation and backward masking. *J. exp. Psychol.*, 1966, *71*, 543-549.

Kaswan, J., and Young, S. Stimulus exposure time, brightness, and spatial factors as determinants of visual perception. *J. exp. Psychol.*, 1963, *65*, 113-123.

Kinsbourne, M., and Warrington, E. K. The effect of aftercoming random pattern on the perception of brief visual stimuli. *Quart. J. exp. Psychol.*, 1962, *14*, 223-234.

Kolers, P. A. Intensity and contour effects in visual masking. *Vision Res.*, 1962, *2*, 277-294.

Kolers, P. A., and Rosner, B. S. On visual masking (metacontrast): dichoptic observation. *Amer. J. Psychol.*, 1960, *73*, 2-21.

Kolers, P. A., and Katzman, M. T. Naming sequentially presented letters and words. *Lang. & Speech*, 1966, 84-95.

Lindsay, R. K., and Lindsay, J. M. Reaction time and serial versus parallel information processing. *J. exp. Psychol.*, 1966, *71*, 294-303.

Mackworth, J. F. The duration of the visual image. *Canad. J. Psychol.*, 1963, *17*, 62-81.

Mayzner, M. S., Abrevays, E. L., Frey, R. E., Kaufman, H. G., and Schoenberg, S. M. Short-term memory in vision: a partial replication of the Averbach and Coriell study. *Psychon. Sci.*, 1964, *1*, 225-226.

Melton, A. W. Implications of short-term memory for general theory of memory. *J. verb. Learn. verb. Behav.*, 1963, *2*, 1-21.

Miller, G. A. The magic number seven, plus or minus two. *Psychol. Rev.*, 1956, *63*, 81-97.

Neisser, U. Decision time without reaction time: experiments in visual scanning. *Amer. J. Psychol.*, 1963, *76*, 376-385.

Pollack, I. Interaction of two sources of verbal context in word identification. *Lang. & Speech*, 1964, *7*, 1-12.

Postman, L. Perception and learning. In S. Koch (Ed.), *Psychology: A Study of a Science*, Vol. 5, 1963, 30-113.

Poulton, E. C. Peripheral vision, refractoriness and eye movements in fast oral reading. *Brit. J. Psychol.*, 1962, *53*, 409-419.

Raab, D. H. Backward masking. *Psychol. Bull.*, 1963, *69*, 193-199.

Reitman, W. R. *Cognition and thought: an information-processing approach.* New York: Wiley, 1965.

Rosenblatt, F. The preceptron: a probabilistic model for information storage and organization in the brain. *Psychol. Rev.*, 1958, *65*, 386-407.

Schiller, P. H., and Smith, M. C. Detection in metacontrast. *J. exp. Psychol.*, 1966, *71*, 32-39.

Schiller, P. H. Monoptic and dichoptic visual masking by patterns and flashes. *J. exp. Psychol.*, 1965, *69*, 193-199.

Schiller, P. H., and Smith, M. C. A comparison of forward and backward masking. *Psychon. Sci.*, 1965, *3*, 77-78.

Sperling, G. The information available in brief visual presentations. *Psychol. Monogr.*, 1960, *74*, (11, whole No. 498).

Sperling, G. A model for visual memory tasks. *Hum. Fact.*, 1963, *5*, 19-31.

Sperling, G. Temporal and spatial visual masking. I. Masking by impulse flashes. *J. opt. Soc. Amer.*, 1965, *55*, 541.

Sperling, G. Successive approximations to a model for short term memory. *Proceedings of the Eighteenth International Congress of Psychology—Moscow, 1966.* Amsterdam: North-Holland Publishing Co., 1967.

Uhr, L. "Pattern recognition" computers as models for form perception. *Psychol. Bull.*, 1963, *60*, 40-73.

Waugh, N. C., and Norman, D. A. Primary memory. *Psychol. Rev.*, 1965, *72*, 89-104.

Weisstein, N. Temporal aspects of perceptual systems. Unpublished Ph.D. dissertation, Harvard University, 1964.

Weisstein, N. Backward masking and models of perceptual processing. *J. exp. Psychol.*, 1966, *72*, 232-240.

Weisstein, N. and Haber, R. N. A u-shaped backward masking function in vision. *Psychon. Sci.*, 1965, *2*, 75-76.

Werner, H. Studies in contour: I. quantitative analyses. *Amer. J. Psychol.*, 1935, *47*, 40-64.

White, C. T. Temporal numerosity and the psychological unit of duration. *Psychol. Monogr.*, 1963, *77*, (12, whole No. 575).

PERCEPTION AND COGNITION AS PROCESSING LEVELS [1]

MICHAEL I. POSNER

University of Oregon

As Haber suggests, the time immediately after the presentation of a stimulus is a critical one because of the processes which relate the new input to previously stored information. If perception is viewed as a temporal succession of stages involving storage and transformation, an information-processing language appears to be useful. Moreover, the use of such language points out the commonality between the perceptual processes required for handling new input and the cognitive processes which place more emphasis upon the handling of previously stored information.

There remains a conflict, however, between the older language of perception, in which the percept is thought of as an inspectable object, and the newer information-processing account. In his definition of perception as a process, and in his three basic assumptions, Haber clearly identifies himself with the informational view. Nevertheless, Haber does not seem quite willing to relinquish the inspectionist view of the percept. For example, he suggests that data from reaction-time studies refer more to decisions than to perception per se, as if the percept could be divorced from the decisions which relate the successive stages of processing.

[1] This paper was supported, in part, by NSF Grant GB 3939 to the University of Oregon.

I wish to thank S. W. Keele and W. G. Chase for allowing me to cite their unpublished data. I was fortunate to have the advice of my colleagues R. Hyman, S. W. Keele, and J. Adkins in preparing my comments.

The problem inherent in the view of a percept as a thing is most striking when Haber raises the question of the role of meaning and familiarity in perception. In his studies (Haber, 1967), Haber has argued that the perceptual clarity of a word is affected by its familiarity. The ability of the subject to report letters of the word grows with repetition of the stimulus, and the overall level of his performance is a function of the word's familiarity. This view leads Haber to suggest that familiarity affects perception. It is possible to conclude the reverse as Hochberg (1966) has recently suggested. Hochberg showed that subjects can classify two nonsense words as physically identical just as fast as they can classify two meaningful words. Thus, he concludes that learning and familiarity do not affect perception per se, but rather they affect only storage processes.

If one holds the view of the percept as a thing, then it is paradoxical that it both is and is not affected by familiarity. A processing analysis of the task eliminates the conflict. In order to report the letters in Haber's task, one needs to collect information from the incoming stimulus and must also match it against stored information concerning letters of the alphabet. By its very nature, such a task involves memory; it should be no surprise that highly familiar combinations of letters which obey the organization of English are more readily identified than unfamiliar sequences. Subjects may report easier identification as increased perceptual clarity. This does not require the parallel processing of meaning in any very complex way, as Haber seems to suggest. In Hochberg's task of matching two stimuli, the subject need not identify letters. This task requires only stimulus examination and not memory search (Neisser and Beller, 1965). Both of these tasks involve stages of perception, but since one requires identification and the other does not, it is not surprising that one is affected by familiarity and the other is not.

I would like to turn now to the successive processing stages which Haber outlines. I shall first deal with the problem of whether a visual storage system exists, then with its stability, and finally, with how items are processed from it. In the final section, I shall take up some general issues of how studies of matching may bridge the gap between perceptual and conceptual levels of processing.

Visual Memory System

I believe that Haber is correct in arguing that the results of Eriksen and Steffy do not vitiate the concept of a visual storage system. Moreover, I think it is now possible to explain this quite precisely. In one study, Dr. Steve Keele and William Chase (1967) presented strong evidence that the Eriksen and Steffy (1964) results were due to placing too small a load upon memory. When they used 6 or even 10 binary symbols they found little evidence for forgetting, but when they converted the array to letters and numbers such as used by Averbach and Coriell (1961), they obtained clear forgetting functions even with the luminance conditions which Eriksen used. The use of binary symbols allows subjects to concentrate on the positions of all the symbols of a given type, thus effectively halving the display. The very high retention curves in Eriksen's study indicate that they were not really testing memory at all. For this reason, I agree with Haber's conclusion about the reality of a short-term visual memory system. Just as Eriksen has quite properly warned people interested in memory about the importance of purely perceptual phenomena, it might be proper to warn those working in perception that the memory literature may provide useful data for them.

Loss of Information from Visual Store

We have been conditioned by the work of Sperling (1963) and Averbach and Coriell (1961) to think of visual storage as necessarily being very brief (1 to 2 seconds). For this reason, it has been tempting to propose that visual storage is related to after-image. For conditions in which the stimulus consists of a large number of letters some part of which must be reported later, this appears to be reasonable. However, Haber and Haber (1964) have shown that visual information in the form of eidetic images may persist over quite long periods. In my laboratory, we have been able to show (Posner and Konick, 1966b) that a visual representation of the position of a circle on a line may persist over a long period with sufficient clarity that no loss is obtained in accuracy of reproduction. The verbal reports of the subjects, the high accuracy levels, and the results of verbal and kinesthetic conditions make it clear that subjects were not retaining a verbal encoding of the circle's position. Reproduction of the position of the circle showed no decrement in accuracy over 30 seconds if the subjects were left free to concentrate during the retention interval. As attention was demanded by other activities, however, forgetting increased regularly. There appears, therefore, to be no necessary reason to hold that visual information storage is *always* a short-term affair.

If my analysis is correct, it makes little sense to ask what is the duration of visual storage as if this were a fixed quantity. It seems likely that information may even reach permanent or long-term memory in the form of a visual code. However, it is frequently the case that visual information will either be recoded or lost. If the number of items are few and if they are later to be reproduced in verbal form, the subject may recode all of them into an auditory storage system. Having done this, he need no longer attend to the visual information and it will fade. As the number of items increases, the difficulty of recoding also increases (see next section), and some visual information is lost during the coding process itself. For these reasons, the number of items reported from a visual store must be highly dependent upon the amount of information stored and the task which is demanded of the subject.

It may be possible to distinguish between very brief visual images and more persistent visual codes. Presumably, the former will be more susceptible than the latter to the effects of visual masking and visual confusability. There is, however, some reason to suspect that the duration of even the relatively brief visual image may depend upon the number of stored items. Posner and Konick (1966a) have shown that, for auditory information stored in short-term memory, as the number and similarity of stored items increase, the rate of decay also increases; i.e., decay rate is a function of the degree of interference. This "acid bath" notion might also easily apply to the visual memory system. Thus, even with recoding processes held constant, it might be that the degree of fading of a visual image increases with the amount and similarity of stored information.

Transformations from Store

Haber (1966a) has made important contributions to our knowledge of how information is processed from the visual image. For example, in his earlier work, he showed the critical importance of the type of translation strategy used by the subject in recoding the stimuli. There are three important questions concerning these coding processes. First, what is the nature of the storage codes which follow after the visual image? Second, what limitations are there on the rate of the recoding processes? Finally, does interference with recoding give rise to the metacontrast effects which Haber reports?

Some recent investigators (Sperling, 1963; Mackworth, 1963) have identified recoding from the visual image with inward speech because the recoded material is subject to auditory confusion errors. There can be little doubt that auditory recoding is often involved. However, even with letters, it need not always occur. For example, Chase and Posner (1965) have shown that search of short-term memory for previously presented letters is more affected by visual than by acoustic similarity. Thus, if the subject is required to recognize rather than recall letters, there is little evidence that they are in auditory form. Moreover, in the recent study by Keele and Chase referred to earlier, as the delay between the visual exposure and the probe increased, the probability of visual confusion declined, but the likelihood of auditory confusion errors did not increase. Sperling (1966) has suggested that recoding from visual memory is first into a motor code, and only later, when verbal output is required, into auditory form. Thus, the rather simplified model of visual followed by auditory information storage should be replaced by the concept of a variety of types of memory codes. The codes may have quite different rehearsal characteristics and rates of decay (Posner and Konick, 1966b).

The second question concerns the rate at which recoding takes place. Of course, with different codes this may vary, but Haber raises two important general points. First, are the items translated from one code to another serially or in parallel? Second, can the rate of such recoding processes be described in terms of a limited channel capacity concept? Sperling (1966) suggests, on the basis of his data from letter recall, that translation processes from the visual image to the motor code operate in parallel, but that their rates are systematically related to the item's position within the image. Haber suggests a somewhat similar combination of serial and parallel operations from the metacontrast data of Weisstein (1966). One must also be careful in applying a channel capacity notion to such processes. In the study of discrete reaction-time tasks, it has been shown that the notion of a general human channel capacity is not very meaningful (Posner, 1966a). Different codes, levels of training, and types of transformation give different rates of information transfer. Despite these complications, some lawfulness is emerging from the study of human performance in discrete reaction-time tasks, and these findings may be increasingly useful in helping us to characterize the transformation processes between different memory codes.

Haber uses the U-shaped curve obtained in some backward-masking experiments as evidence that the blanking stimulus interferes with translation processes following visual storage rather than at some earlier stage. While this idea is interesting, I do not believe that it is forced upon us by the data. For example, the blanking stimulus may be having its effect within the visual memory system itself. One cannot be sure that maximal interference between items in memory is a monotonic function of the interval between them, as Haber assumes. Consider the ring as noise and the letter as signal. If they are presented simultaneously at the same intensity and fade together, the signal-to noise ratio is always one. If, however, the noise occurs after the signal has partly faded, the signal-to-noise ratio is less than one and the discrimination becomes more difficult. If the noise is delayed too long, the signal is already recoded and the noise has no effect. In this way, a U-shaped function would relate the interval between signal and mask to the probability of a correct report. The use of the letters D and O as a signal and a ring as mask, would seem to offer considerable opportunity for interference of this type. A converging operation is surely required if Haber is to show that the ring interferes selectively with the recoding process.

Perceptual Matching as a Unit of Cognitive Activity

One aspect which cognitive processes share with perception is the requirement of stimulus matching or recognition. The idea of a comparison process underlies current investigations varying in content from the psychophysiology of habitation to the operation of complex cognitive plans. For example, Sokolov (1963a) suggests that the orienting reflex arises from the failure of a new incoming stimulus to match a stored neural model which is assumed to reflect the parameters of prior stimulation. Miller, Galanter, and Pribram (1960) suggest that cognitive plans are terminated when the feedback arising from the test of a prior operation matches the image of a future goal state. Within the context of perceptual research, the process of matching has always played a prominent role. Psychophysics often involves the requirement that the observer match a variable stimulus to a present (comparative judgment) or stored (absolute judgment) standard. The perceptual identification tasks which Haber has employed also involve matching. In this case, the information extracted from the stimulus must be compared with some stored standards in the process of identifying a letter or word.

The pervasiveness of matching tasks in the experimental laboratory is no accident. The philosopher H. H. Price in his book *Thinking and Experience* points out: "The fundamental intellectual process seems to be the experience of recognition. On this, both thinking and intelligent action depend." The process of recognition forms the necessary link between external stimulation and past experiences represented in memory.

Recently, I have been studying some simple matching tasks which seem to have the potential of bridging the gap between the various levels of recognition involved in perceptual and cognitive operations.

My studies measure the reaction time for subjects to classify a pair of letters as "same" or "different." At the simplest level of processing, the "same" response is based on physical identity (e.g., AA), at the next level on name identity (e.g., Aa), and finally on rule identity (e.g., both vowels). What is particularly interesting about this task is that the identical stimulus-response combination (e.g., AB-"different") may be studied at all three levels of processing. As the depth of processing required for a "same" increases, the response time to respond "different" to AB changes from about 450 to 800 milliseconds.

The use of this paradigm has revealed some important facts about recognition at various levels. For example, we find by switching between letter and Gibson figures that lifetime experience with a form does not aid processes at the first level (physical identity). This is similar to the findings of Hochberg (1966) which I discussed earlier. Moreover, we have also found that the physical identity node and the name identity node are merely two ends of a continuum of time. For example, the letter pair Cc can be matched faster than Aa, but not so fast as the mean of CC and cc. In fact, I have shown previously (Posner, 1964) that the act of matching two nonsense patterns, which have been given the same name in a prior learning task, is a linear function of their perceived similarity. The data on letter pairs indicate that the same relationship holds even after lifetime learning. I hope that these findings indicate that the process of matching can be studied at successive levels which depend less and less on physical correspondence.

The notion of levels or processing becomes a useful experimental tool when it is combined with manipulation of independent variables which might have different effects at the various levels. For example, it has already been shown that visual confusability plays a decreasing role in affecting the rate of processing as the input array shifts from being present in the visual field to being present only in memory (Chase and Posner, 1965; Gibson and Yonas, 1966; Neisser, 1963). Such analyses may give valuable clues as to the coding and operations at each level.

The process of matching is most interesting when the subject is required to recognize a new instance of some familiar category. Clearly, when the child calls his first dachshund "dog," and when the automobile fan labels the 1967 model as a "Ford," the process of matching involves much more than comparison with some single, stored template. In some sense, the subject has managed to match the input against a composite or abstraction of many prior experiences. This type of matching underlies the psychological tasks of concept formation and pattern recognition.

Most analyses of concept identification have had relatively little contact with perceptual research. They analyze concepts into a set of separate dimensions and the rules which govern their combination (Haygood and Bourne, 1965). While this approach is fruitful, it may be far too rational and analytic to serve as a model for the formation of such categories as "dog" and "triangle." For these tasks, it may be more reasonable to think of the subject as storing information about actual objects or exemplars to which he has been exposed.

One approach to this problem is to study meaningful and nonsense patterns which can be distorted by noise (Edmonds and Evans, 1965; Posner, 1964, 1966). It is possible to show lawful, psychophysical relations between the amount of distortion and perceived similarity. Subjects can be taught to classify noisy patterns of this type even when they never see the prototype from which the distortions are made. In one study, distortions of a triangle, the letters M and F, as well as a nonsense shape were used. The less distorted were the patterns from the prototype, the more rapidly the learning took place (Posner, Goldsmith, and Welton, 1967). The patterns at low levels of distortion were quite similar to each other and the patterns became more dissimilar as the distortion increased. In transfer studies, it was shown that subjects who had learned the broad category (high level of distortion) did better in recognizing new patterns which were equidistant from the stored exemplars.

In understanding how the subject uses his experience to recognize new input, it is important to know what information is stored and by what means a match is made between the stored material and the new input. These are, of course, familiar questions to the learning and perception psychologist, and ones which he may find stimulating to encounter in the rarified context of the "cognitive processes."

Recent research has provided a variety of answers to these questions. Pick (1965) has suggested that the subject stores information concerning the set of transformations which a stimulus may undergo in familiar perceptual situations. A new stimulus looks familiar despite distortions because it obeys a lawful transformation which the subject has learned to recognize. This explanation seems to fit her data, but it is less applicable where the transformation is a random noise process rather than a set of familiar operations. Some investigators have suggested the storage of a schema or abstracted central tendency (Edmonds and Evans, 1966). Sokolov (1963) suggests that the subject probes his new stimulus for points which may be in common with stored templates. The subject implicitly calculates the probability that the new instance could arise from each of the stored templates. On the other hand, I have suggested that subjects store only actual instances which they have encountered in their prior learning (Posner, 1966b). The distance of a new stimulus from the exemplars of each category is compared with the intra-category distances. Thus, the subject is able to recognize new input based upon storing only particular instances from his past learning. This view is flexible, since it suggests that instructions in a given experiment may influence the set of exemplars which are used. Thus, the concept of a triangle may be very different when discussing geometry than when evaluating a child's drawing.

Whatever may be the proper resolution of this issue, I believe that the basic point is made. It is quite possible to analyze processes underlying the genesis of an "abstract idea" into components which involve the familiar questions of perception, storage, and transformation presented in Haber's discussion. Of course, new problems arise at each level, but it is comforting that some of the same tools can be carried forward.

REFERENCES

Averbach, E. and Coriell, A. S. Short-term memory in vision. *Bell Systems Tech. J.*, 1961, *40*, 309-328.

Chase, W. G., and Posner, M. I. The effect of auditory and visual confusability of visual and memory search tasks. Paper presented to the Midwest Psychological Association, 1965.

Edmonds, E. M., and Evans, S. H. Schema learning without a prototype. *Psychon. Sci.*, 1966, *5*, 247-248.

Eriksen, C. W., and Steffy, R. A. Short-term memory and retroactive interference in visual perception. *J. exp. Psychol.*, 1964, *68*, 423-434.

Gibson, E. J., and Yonas, A. A developmental study of the effects of visual and auditory interference on a visual scanning task. *Psychon. Sci.*, 1966, *5*, 163-164.

Haber, R. N., and Haber, R. B. Eidetic imagery I: frequency. *Percept. mot. Skills*, 1964, 131-138.

Haber, R. N. Repetition as a determinant of perceptual recognition processes. In J. C. Mott-Smith, W. Wather-Dunn, H. Blum, and P. Lieberman (Eds.), *Symposium on models for the perception of speech and visual form*. Cambridge: MIT Press, 1967. Pp. 202-212.

Haber, R. N. The nature of the effect of set on perception. *Psychol. Rev.*, 1966, *73*, 335-350.

Haygood, R. C., and Bourne, L. E. Attribute and rule-learning aspects of conceptual behavior. *Psychol. Rev.*, 1965, *72*, 175-195.

Hochberg, J. Reading pictures and text: What is learned in perceptual development? Paper presented to the Eighteenth International Congress of Psychology, Moscow, 1966.

Keele, S. W. and Chase, W. Short-term visual storage. *Percept. & Psychophys.*, 1967, *2*, 383-386.

Mackworth, J. F. The duration of the visual image. *Canad. J. Psychol.*, 1963, *17*, 62-81.

Miller, G. A., Galanter, G., Pribram, K. *Plans and the Structure of Behavior*. New York: Holt, 1960.

Neisser, U. Decision time without reaction time. *Amer. J. Psychol.*, 1963, *76*, 358-376.

Neisser, U., and Beller, H. K. Searching through word lists. *Brit. J. Psychol.*, 1965, *56*, 349-358.

Pick, A. D. Improvement of visual and tactual form discrimination. *J. exp. Psychol.*, 1965, *69*, 331-339.

Posner, M. I. Information reduction in the analysis of sequential tasks. *Psychol. Rev.*, 1964, *71*, 491-504.

Posner, M. I. Components of skilled performance. *Science*, 1966, *152*, 1712-1718. (a)

Posner, M. I. An informational analysis of the perception and classification of patterns. Paper presented to the XVIIIth International Congress of Psychology, Moscow, 1966. (b)

Posner, M. I., Goldsmith, R., and Welton, K. E., Jr. Perceived distance and the classification of distorted patterns. *J. exp. Psychol.*, 1967, *73*, 28-38.

Posner, M. I., and Konick, A. F. On the role of interference in short-term retention. *J. exp. Psychol.*, 1966, *72*, 221-231. (a)

Posner, M. I., and Konick, A. F. Short-term retention of visual and kinesthetic information. *J. Organ. Behav. hum. Perform.*, 1966, *1*, 71-86. (b)

Price, H. H. *Thinking and Experience*. London: Hutchinson, 1953.

Sokolov, E. N. *Perception and the Conditioned Reflex*. London: Pergamon Press, 1963. (a)

Sokolov, E. N. A probabilistic model of perception. Translated in *Sov. Psychol. Psychiat.*, 1963, *1*, 28-36. (b)

Sperling, G. A model for visual memory tasks. *Hum. Fact.*, 1963, 5, 19-31.

Sperling, G. Successive approximations to a model for short-term memory. Paper presented to the XVIIIth International Congress of Psychology, Moscow, 1966.

Weisstein, N. Backward masking and models of perceptual processing. *J. exp. Psychol.*, 1966, 72, 232-240.

GENERAL DISCUSSION

POSNER was asked whether he meant to imply that there was no distinction between short-term visual store and memory. He replied that whether such a distinction can be made is uncertain. POSNER did suggest, however, that if there is a distinction, it is not only on the basis of type of content per se.

POSNER also was asked whether a lack of information load is an important variable in short-term visual storage. He replied by indicating that he has data which show a short-term memory effect under conditions of no interference. Thus, he suggested that not only information load is important, but stimulus conditions also must be taken into account.

It was asked whether visual and acoustic coding are simultaneous, or whether the subject must guess which type of response will be required. HABER replied that the problem is one of stimulus selection, and that subjects generally will pay attention to what is asked of them.

It was pointed out that, with respect to interference, there are data which show a release from proactive inhibition effects. More specifically, it has been found that using the Peterson technique, eight consecutive visual presentations produce a proactive inhibition effect, eight consecutive auditory presentations yield a proactive inhibition effect, but alternating visual and auditory presentations yield a complete release from proactive effects. It was indicated that the response in all cases was oral, and that visual and auditory stimuli were to be presented simultaneously to determine whether subjects can shift coding modality in order to reduce interference.

NEWELL commented, "Be sure the subject keeps his eyes open."

KIMBLE observed that it was interesting that latencies of response for different versus same judgment with regard to letters (Posner's data) are latencies of the same order of magnitude as those of simple conditioning versus discrimination problems in classical conditioning; i.e., 450 to 800 milliseconds.

POSNER replied that he did not mean to attach too much significance to the numbers per se. What is important, he indicated, is to specify how subjects go from one stage to another.

It was asked whether pictures with appropriate verbal labels have been used in visual short-term storage tasks. POSNER replied that they have not.

KEPPEL inquired whether subjects usually serve in all conditions of an experiment.

POSNER answered that both designs; i.e., with the experimental conditions occurring between subjects and within subjects, have been used. He further indicated that this procedural variable yields differences, but that the differences are complex and small.

UHR asked whether adaptation of the matching mechanism has been studied by using different degrees of similarity.

POSNER replied that study of this question has shown that there is a continuous function as similarity changes.

2

NEUROPHYSIOLOGY AND THOUGHT: THE NEURAL SUBSTRATES OF THINKING[1]

RICHARD F. THOMPSON

University of California, Irvine

I suspect that the inclusion of a discussion of neurophysiology in a book on thought is something of an afterthought. Indeed, most texts on thinking make little or no mention of neurophysiological processes. This is only fair; neurophysiology texts do not discuss thinking. Such mutual disregard simply reflects our considerable ignorance of the neurophysiological bases of many behavior phenomena, including such fundamental areas as learning and motivation as well as "higher mental processes."

In trying to relate neurophysiological processes to "thinking," I have found an adequate definition of thinking to be a source of some diffi-

---

[1] This paper was supported in part by NIH Research Grant NB-02161 and Research Career Award MH-K-6650.

The initial version of this paper was completed while the author was in the Department of Medical Psychology, University of Oregon Medical School, Portland, Oregon.

culty. Consequently, I was much encouraged by the following passage
from Bertrand Russell's *Analysis of Mind* (1921, pp. 226-227):

> A certain sensory situation produces in us a certain bodily move-
> ment. Sometimes this movement consists in uttering words. Preju-
> dice leads us to suppose that between the sensory stimulus and the
> utterance of the words a process of thought must have intervened,
> but there seems no good reason for such a supposition. Any habitual
> action, such as eating or dressing, may be performed on the appro-
> priate occasion, without any need of thought, and the same seems
> to be true of a painfully large proportion of our talk. What applies
> to uttered speech applies of course equally to the internal speech
> which is not uttered. I remain, therefore, entirely unconvinced that
> there is any such phenomenon as thinking which consists neither of
> images nor of words, or that "ideas" have to be added to sensations
> and images as part of the material out of which mental phenomena
> are built.

It seems clear that neurophysiology has little to contribute to our
understanding of complex human thinking of the sort categorized in
Battig's paper (Chap. 4), in terms of complexity, abstract or symbolic
character, and structure. On the other hand, more general definitions,
such as Bertrand Russell's, or "thinking is perception" (Haber's paper,
Chap. 1), or Hebb's (1949) definition as "some sort of process that is
not fully controlled by environmental stimulation yet cooperates closely
with that stimulation . . . the delay between stimulation and response"
are amenable to discussions in terms of neural processes.

Now that the brain has been readmitted to a status of respectability
in psychology (thanks in part to the efforts of Hebb), the issue of central versus peripheral theories of thinking is largely irrelevant. It would
seem evident that central and peripheral events occur and interact in
all complex behavioral phenomena. The possibility that peripheral
events play a *necessary* role in thinking has been disposed of by the
rather bold experiment of Smith, Brown, Toman, and Goodman (1947),
where a totally paralyzed (curarized) human subject was able to perceive, solve problems, etc., in a normal manner. On the other hand, a
large body of earlier and current research indicates that many types
of "reduced" muscle responses normally accompany instructed thinking
(e.g., Jacobson, 1930; Sokolov, 1963; Luria, 1961; Novikova, 1957). The
extent to which these fractional muscle responses may be epiphenome-
nal remains to be determined. In any event, we now have a wide variety of brain response measures available for comparison with behavioral measures.

The Physiological Basis of Thought

It is perhaps worthwhile to begin our discussion with a few simplified propositions regarding the physical basis of thinking. Thinking is nothing more than brain activity, together with associated receptor and effector events. Brain activity, in turn, is nothing more than interactions among individual nerve cells in the brain. The chief way that a nerve cell can influence other nerve cells is by synaptic actions, and these can be produced only by the neuron firing all-or-none spike discharges. Hence, thinking can be reduced to a pattern of digital events in a physical system.[2]

The general approach used by modern theorists in attempting to relate brain and thinking is well illustrated in a concise discussion by Lashley (1958, pp. 6-8):

1. The billions of neurons in the cerebral network are organized into a large number of systems. Each system consists of the traces of a number of habits or memories . . . . The traces or engramata in any system are more closely connected with one another than with other systems. The [trace] systems are not anatomically separate, and the same neurons, in different permutations, may participate in many systems.

2. Such a trace system may be thrown into a state of tonic activity by an external stimulus which activates one set of traces within it. In the tonic state, the traces of the system are readily excitable and available to recall. Other systems are in abeyance . . . .

3. A [trace] system in tonic activity dominates the brain field, limiting the organization of other systems. It is relatively impervious to unrelated excitation. An intense stimulus, or an emotionally charged one, such as the sound of one's name, may break in, but the great mass of afferent excitations is excluded. This blocking might be either an active inhibition or the preemption of neurons which might otherwise be included in the blocked system. The phenomena of attention demand some such hypothesis.

4. The neurons in a trace system, under tonic activation, exert some mutual facilitation. The tonic state of the whole system is thus built up and maintained . . . .

5. The levels of tonus in the partially activated system may vary. Circuits which have just been fully activated may retain a high

---

[2] For a dissenting view, see the very interesting discussion by Fisher (pp. 73-80).

level of subthreshold activity and thus contribute to the temporal organization evident in the memory span.

6. Fixation in memory is generally possible only when the remembered material forms part of such a dominant system.

Lashley touches on several basic issues common to most physiological theories of thinking, or for that matter, behavior theory in general: learning (Lashley's paragraph 1), motivation (paragraphs 4 and 5), and attention (2 and 3). Before considering these topics, I would like to discuss briefly a more fundamental problem; namely, assumptions about the manner in which neurons interact with one another; i.e., the nature of synaptic transmission.

Mechanisms of Neuron Interaction

At the time when Lashley, Hebb, and others were initially developing "trace system" views of neural organization and thought, it was generally believed the synaptic transmission was electrical, and the only type of event was excitation. (Actually, both excitatory and inhibitory electrical transmission have been found in invertebrates.) Subsequently, it has been demonstrated beyond reasonable doubt that synaptic transmission in the mammalian CNS is *chemical*. The two best known types of synaptic events are postsynaptic excitation and postsynaptic inhibition. In addition, there is rather conclusive evidence for another type of inhibition, presynaptic inhibition. Still more recently, an analogous type of excitatory process, "presynaptic excitation," has been described. Finally, there is very recent evidence favoring still another type of process which might be termed "remote inhibition." Although various types of nonsynaptic processes such as dc field effects and glial cell actions have been suggested as alternative mechanisms controlling neuron activity (see Fisher's discussion pp. 73-80), there is as yet no very compelling evidence for their existence. I would like to take a few minutes to describe the basic types of synaptic processes noted above; they have obvious implications for theories of complex neural function. The extent to which such theories are "central" rather than "conceptual" views of the CNS will depend upon the extent to which the real synaptic events in the brain are used as basic assumptions.

Figure 2-1 summarizes the various types of synaptic processes (see Eccles, 1964, for detailed discussions). Consider first the *postsynaptic excitatory* synapses formed by the nerve terminals a_1 on a neuron.

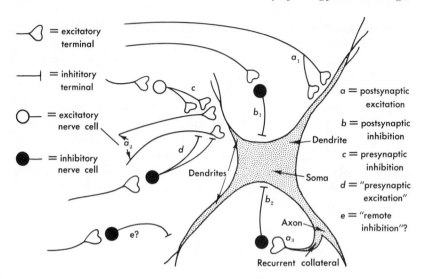

Figure 2-1. Highly schematic drawing of various types of synaptic mechanisms believed to act on the spinal motor neuron.

When an impulse arrives at the terminals, small amounts of an as yet unknown transmitter substance are released to cross the synapses and act on the postsynaptic membrane. This produces a brief shift in the membrane potential of the cell, termed an excitatory postsynaptic potential (EPSP). The normal resting level of the membrane is about −70 mv (millivolts). The EPSP can shift this potential in a *graded* fashion from resting level to spike discharge threshold of about −60 mv. The EPSP is always a depolarization—it shifts the membrane potential toward zero. Figure 2-2 illustrates an EPSP recorded with an intracellular microelectrode from a spinal motor neuron in response to

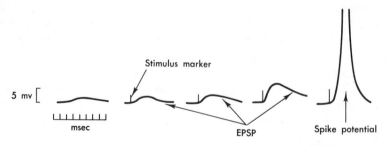

Figure 2-2. EPSP responses of a motor neuron (intracellular microelectrode recording) to increasingly strong activation. (Redrawn and modified from Coombs, Eccles, and Fatt, 1955.)

increasing degrees of excitation (indicated by the stimulus marker). Note that the EPSP is graded—the size of the EPSP reflects the total amount of afferent bombardment of the cell. More specifically, in a case like this where the excitation is produced by one synchronous volley in the afferent nerve, the EPSP amplitude is directly proportional to the number of afferent fibers that synchronously activate the cell membrane. Note the time course of the EPSP—approximately 10 msec. This is a very short duration action. Temporal and spatial summation can occur only with this brief period of time. Actually, most cells are continously bombarded in an asynchronous fashion by excitatory (and inhibitory) synapses. The "resting" level of a given cell could thus be very close to discharge threshold; i.e., it could be partially depolarized in the normal steady state.[3]

Postsynaptic inhibition acts in an analogous but opposite manner to decrease the excitability of the cell. Consider the inhibitory pathway formed by an excitatory synapse on the inhibitory interneuron b_1. Excitation of the interneuron occurs in the same manner as excitation of the large neuron by a_1. However, the inhibitory interneuron, b_1, acts to produce inhibition of the large neuron. When the action potential in b_1 arrives at the synapse on the large neuron, a small amount of an as yet unknown transmitter substance is released. This diffuses across the synapse to act on the postsynaptic membrane of the cell body. However, the cell membrane potential is shifted toward a greater degree of polarization; i.e., the cell membrane becomes hyperpolarized. The actual membrane potential may shift from −70 mv to −73 mv. This is termed the inhibitory postsynaptic potential (IPSP). When an IPSP occurs, an excitatory action that previously depolarized the cell to firing threshold will no longer produce a depolarization sufficient to reach spike threshold. Actually, the combined effects of synchronous EPSPs and IPSPs are not the simple algebraic summation implied by this description—the net outcome depends on the equilibrium potentials of various ion species—but the overall result is approximately so. Examples of IPSPs produced in a spinal motor neuron by increasingly strong volleys in an inhibitory nerve are shown in Fig. 2-3. The IPSP appears to be roughly a mirror image of the EPSP. Note that it grows in a *graded* fashion with increasing stimulus strength. Note also that it has a relatively short time course, approximately 10 msec. An excita-

---

[3] These *synaptic* processes of postsynaptic excitation and inhibition appear to be the types of phenomena referred to by Morrell in the quotation in Fisher's discussion (p. 74).

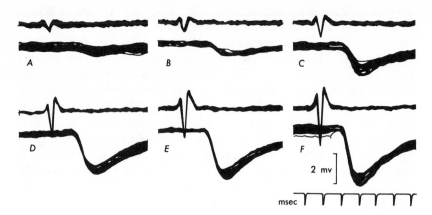

Figure 2-3. A-F: Effect of increasingly strong inhibitory stimulation (response in upper tracing of each pair indicates degree of activation) on a motor neuron IPSP. (From Eccles, 1958.)

tory volley to the cell would be inhibited only if it reached the cell within a few milliseconds of the inhibitory volley. Again, however, this picture holds only for synchronous volleys. The normal state of the CNS involves asynchronous bombardment of cells. Hence, a given cell can have a steady-state excitability level that is reduced below the normal resting membrane potential level by a tonic inhibitory bombardment. A very common arrangement for postsynaptic inhibition in the central nervous system is illustrated by the recurrent inhibitory pathway of a_3-b_2 in Fig. 2-1. A collateral fiber from the axon of the cell branches off (a_3) and has an excitatory synapse on an inhibitory neuron (b_2) which, in turn, acts back on this and neighboring cells to produce postsynaptic inhibition.

Presynaptic inhibition is believed to result from the mechanism schematized by c in Fig. 2-1. Cell c is an excitatory interneuron that synapses on afferent terminal fibers from other cells (a_2) that themselves exert postsynaptic excitation on the neuron. Activation of c produces a partial depolarization of the a_2 terminals. This results in a reduced action potential in the afferent terminals of a_2 (e.g., if the membrane potential has been reduced from -70 mv to -60 mv, an action potential that normally causes the afferent terminal membrane potential to shift by 100 mv will now only produce a shift of 90 mv). This, in turn, appears to result in a reduced release of transmitter substance across excitatory synapses to the cell; a smaller EPSP is induced in the cell. The time course of presynaptic inhibition induced in IA afferent fibers in the spinal cord is illustrated in Fig. 2-4. Note that this effect lasts several hundred milliseconds, considerably longer than post-synaptic excitation and postsynaptic inhibition.

Still more recently, an analogous kind of presynaptic excitatory process has been described in the mammalian CNS (Lundberg and Vyklicky, 1963; Mendell and Wall, 1965). This is tentatively schematized by channel *d* of Fig. 2-1. A conditioning stimulus induces post-

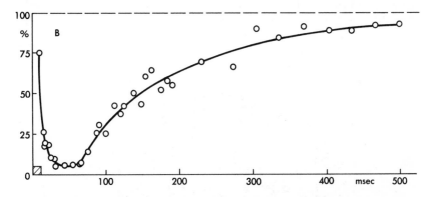

Figure 2-4. Time duration of presynaptic inhibition of monosynaptic reflex discharge in the spinal cord. Hatched bar at origin indicates conditioning stimulus. (From Eccles, Schmidt, and Willis, 1962.)

synaptic inhibition in the afferent terminal fibers. This hyperpolarization results in a greater-than-normal action potential and a consequent increase in the postsynaptic excitatory potential induced in the cell. Finnlly, Granit, Kellerth, and Williams (1964) have described a kind of "remote inhibitory" phenomenon (*e*[1] in Fig. 2-1) that resembles the process first postulated by Frank (1959) to account for the initial observations on presynaptic inhibition (Frank and Fuortes, 1957). In essence, it appears that a postsynaptic inhibitory action may occur remotely on a dendrite such that the excitability of the cell is decreased. However, the membrane potential of the cell body is not altered sufficiently to be seen by a microelectrode in the cell body.

The regional distributions of the various types of synaptic processes described above are of some interest. Postsynaptic excitation and postsynaptic inhibition appear to be ubiquitous; they are found everywhere in the central nervous system. Presynaptic inhibition, on the other hand, is very pronounced in sensory systems, but has not yet been described at the level of the cerebral cortex. "Presynaptic excitation" and "remote inhibition" have as yet been studied only in the spinal cord; possible occurrence in the brain remains to be determined.

The diagram of synaptic endings on a motor neuron shown in Fig. 2-1 is of course highly schematic. The various types of synapses do not generally exist in isolation; e.g., there are probably axoaxonic terminals on most presynaptic excitatory terminals. Furthermore, the cell body and dendrites are covered by an almost continuous layer of synaptic terminals. Figure 2-5 is a more realistic representation of a motor neuron together with the larger synaptic terminals on the cell body. Finally, Fig. 2-6 is a section through the cerebral cortex illustrating the

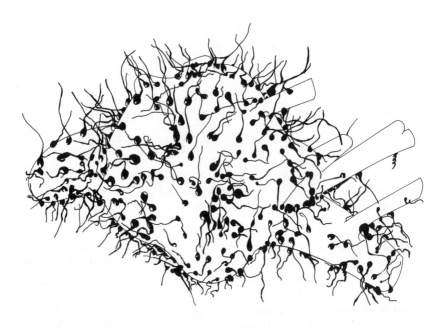

Figure 2-5. Reconstruction of the larger synaptic knobs terminating on a spinal motor neuron. (From Fig. 3, Haggar and Barr, *J. comp. Neurol.*, 93:35.)

packing density of nerve cell bodies, each of which is covered by a continuous layer of synaptic terminals, which, in turn, may have axoaxonic terminals. The system is not simple. It should be clear from this brief survey that no model of brain functioning postulating only excitatory interconnections can succeed in predicting the real complexity of organization and functions of the brain.

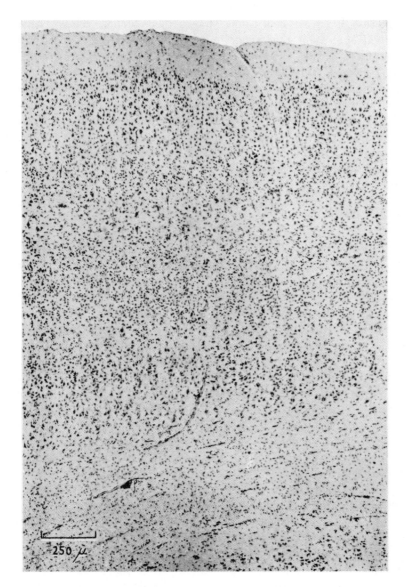

Figure 2-6. A section of visual cortex from a human brain. (From Scholl, 1956.)

Motivation. The physiological basis of motivation has been perhaps the most widely discussed topic in physiological psychology. It would serve little purpose to survey this vast literature here (see reviews by

Lindsley, 1957; McCleary and Moore, 1965; Stellar, 1960). There is general agreement that such brain structures as the hypothalamus, reticular formation, and limbic system are involved in motivated behavior. However, little direct evidence is available concerning the more specific mechanisms of action, and the indirect evidence is somewhat contradictory. To take an example, there is considerable evidence implicating the ascending reticular activating system (ARAS) as a neural substrate of motivation or drive (see Lindsley, 1957). On the other hand, Vierk (1965) has reported that electrical stimulation of the ARAS serves to decrease drive level. I would like to sidestep this important and complex subject and simply take for granted that behavior is motivated—organisms do behave and engage in complex ongoing behaviors that might be termed "thinking."

Attention. Most discussions of thinking emphasize the fact that the thinking organism "attends" to the task; irrelevant external stimuli and endogenous influences are excluded or suppressed. There has been a good deal of recent work on electrophysiological correlates of attention, beginning with the well-known report by Hernãndez-Peon, Scherrer, and Jouvet (1956) that click-evoked brain responses in a cat were reduced when the animal attended to interesting visual stimuli. The suppression or reduction of sensory-evoked responses during attending behavior in animals appears to be nonselective; responses generally tend to be reduced (Horn, 1960). This is particularly true for responses recorded from nonspecific association areas of the cortex (Thompson and Shaw, 1965). On the other hand, the later components of "primary" sensory-evoked responses recorded from the human scalp do appear to be selectively enhanced during selective attention (Davis, 1964; Spong, Haider, and Lindsley, 1965).

Eccles (1964) has suggested that presynaptic inhibition may be the major type of synaptic process mediating the gating of sensory input by the central nervous system. It could thus be the major synaptic process involved in selective attention. Presynaptic inhibitory effects are found throughout the somatic sensory system; for example, from incoming afferent fibers to the thalamus. Anderson, Eccles, and Sears (1964) have shown that electrical stimulation of the sensory motor cortex in the cat induces very pronounced presynaptic inhibition on sensory fibers entering the spinal cord from the body region homologous to the area of cortex stimulated. Interestingly, similar electrical stimulation of the frontal portion of this cortical region mimics both of the "attention" effects on cortical-evoked responses noted above: suppression of the nonspecific association area responses and enhancement of the later components of primary, sensory-evoked responses (Thompson, Denney, and Smith, 1966). A variety of brain regions have been shown to be capable of exerting presynaptic inhibitory control over incoming sensory information (Lundberg, 1964). It may be that processes analogous to "presynaptic excitation" are responsible for the enhancement of primary, sensory-evoked responses during selective attention. There are, of course, many alternative possible mechanisms.

Learning. The nature of the physical changes in the nervous system underlying learning has been perhaps the most crucial issue in theories of complex neural processes. A variety of possibilities ranging from growth of new synaptic knobs to RNA coding and glial cell actions have been suggested for permanent memory storage. At present, there seems to be no convincing evidence regarding these possibilities. Most theorists have felt the necessity of postulating some type of short-term or "active trace" process to maintain activity in the CNS for a few minutes following a learning trial until more permanent traces are laid down (e.g., consolidation hypothesis). In fact, it has recently been suggested that there may be three different time-dependent processes in memory storage, one for immediate memory, one for short-term storage, and one which consolidates slowly and is relatively permanent (McGaugh, 1966).

The time courses of the various synaptic events discussed above are relatively short; probably too short to mediate short-term memory storage. The longest duration effect, presynaptic inhibition, lasts about 500 msec. Postsynaptic inhibition, incidentally, may be of considerably longer duration in the brain than in the spinal cord—up to 100 msec or more. An example of postsynaptic inhibition acting via recurrent collaterals on cells in the ventrobasal complex of the thalamus is shown in Fig. 2-7. When a cell is fired, it induces postsynaptic inhibition back upon itself and neighboring cells. This hyperpolarization lasts about 100 msec. Only after this period of time can the cell be excited again. Since the inhibition also acts on neighboring cells, if the cells are subject to more or less random excitatory bombardment from below, they will have a tendency to get in step; i.e., fire rhythmically at a rate of 10 to 12 per second. This type of mechanism has been postulated to account for the 10- to 12-per second alpha rhythm of the cortex. Alpha waves, incidentally, have been suggested by some theorists as a scanning process involved in thinking (although it has never been clear just who is scanning what). The synaptic hypothesis of recurrent inhibition provided a more parsimonious, albeit less glamorous, interpretation of the alpha rhythm.

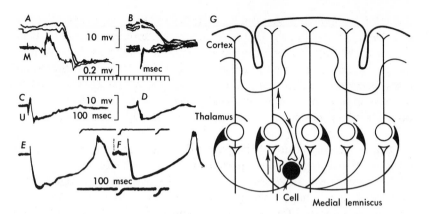

Figure 2-7. A-F: Intracellular records of neurons in the ventro-basel complex of the thalamus. *A* and *C* are evoked by single volleys from the median and ulnar nerves respectively, while *B* and *D-F* are evoked by stimulation of the cortical terminals of the thalamocortical relay cells. Note that *A* and *B* are at much faster sweep speeds than *C-F.* *G* shows diagrammatically the postulated pathways for recurrent inhibition. (From Anderson and Eccles, 1962.)

The "reverberating circuit" first suggested on anatomical grounds by Lorente de Nō (1943), has been the most popular construct to provide short-term memory storage. Although there was much discussion of this construct in succeeding years, no directly relevant physiological data existed. More recently, Verzeano and associates (see Verzeano, 1962; Verzeano and Negishi, 1960) have provided rather compelling evidence for the existence of long-lasting reverberatory activity in neural networks in thalamus and cortex. There are also a variety of other types of relatively long-term changes in excitability that occur in simple neural systems. If a cutaneous nerve of the hind limb of the acute spinal cat is shocked repeatedly, two rather long-term changes in polysyaptic flexion reflex can occur. If the stimulus is weak and given every second or so, the flexion response will decrease markedly (habituation) and will require as long as an hour of no stimulation to recover. (In terms of Hebb's definition, the spinal cord might be said to be thinking during this time.) Alternatively, if the stimulus is given at a much higher frequency or a much stronger intensity for a brief period, the response will increase considerably for a period of several minutes (see Thompson and Spencer, 1966).

An even simpler and more dramatic example is provided by mono-synaptic posttetanic potentiation (PTP). As Lloyd (1949) first showed,

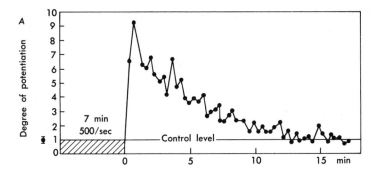

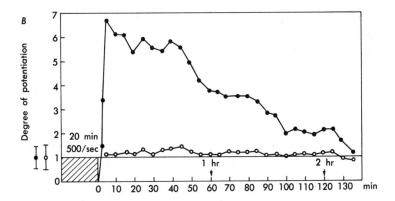

Figure 2-8. Effects of duration of tetanus on duration of mono-synaptic PTP in acute spinal cat. In *A*, the tetanus was given for 7 minutes, and in *B* it was given for 20 minutes. Open circle plot in *B* is response of contralateral control. (From Spencer, personal communication.)

a few seconds of high-frequency stimulation of IA afferent fibers produces a marked enhancement of the monosynaptic reflex which will last for several minutes. Furthermore, the locus of the effect appears to be in the presynaptic afferent fiber terminals (possibly a change in the amount of transmitter substance released). Spencer and Wigdor (1965) have recently shown that if the tetanizing stimulus is given for a period of minutes, rather than seconds, the PTP effect may last more than an hour (see Fig. 2-8). Although a tetanus of 20 minutes duration may seem unphysiological, it must be emphasized that many interneurons fire repetitively in response to single stimulus activation. Hence, a slowly presented stimulus might produce almost continuous tetanic actions in the interneurons which in turn could result in long-lasting PTP. As Spencer and Wigdor note, 20 minutes is the approximate "consolidation time" suggested by drug and ECS experiments.

In sum, there are a variety of long-term changes in the excitability of relatively simple neural systems, many of which do not require the reverberating circuit hypothesis.

Neural Models of Thinking

There are a number of intriguing formal conceptual models of thinking that have been developed at what might be termed the "systems level," ranging from general mechanistic analogs to complex computer programs and mathematical models designed to resemble possible brain systems (e.g., Ashby, 1952; Hovland, 1960; Newell, Shaw, and Simon, 1958; Pribram, Galanter, and Miller, 1960). None of these makes specific assumptions regarding the types of interconnections and interactions that may occur among neurons. Although similarities between the thoughts of these models and the thoughts of the brain are perhaps somewhat formal, it is possible that such models, to the extent that they reproduce human thinking behavior, will impose restraints on the types of system organization that can be postulated to occur in the brain. On the other hand, there are several models whose assumptions are more explicitly neurophysiological. I would like to examine very briefly three such models, Hebb's theory (1949), Milner's modification of it (1957; 1961), and the Perceptron (Rosenblatt, 1959; Block, 1962).

As noted earlier, when Hebb developed his cell assembly construct, the consensus of physiological opinion was in favor of excitatory, electrical synaptic transmission. Consequently, Hebb assumed this type of synaptic interaction among neurons. The probability that a neuron could fire was determined by the number and "strength" of nearly synchronous synaptic excitations, and the extent to which the neuron was refractory or fatigued. Interconnections among cortical neurons were assumed to be random, and some were assumed to be fired by any given adequate stimulus.

As Milner subsequently showed (1957), this constitutes a positive feedback system with no brakes. Once a few cortical neurons are activated by a sensory stimulus, the system will "run free" until all elements are active. In fact, this is just what does happen in the real nervous system when the inhibitory brakes are removed. Strychnine selectively blocks most forms of postsynaptic inhibition in the spinal cord. Following adequate doses of strychnine, the neurons of the spinal cord discharge increasingly until full-scale convulsions develop.

Milner (1957) utilized the same general scheme as Hebb but built in one additional assumption; namely, the occurrence of inhibition mediated by recurrent inhibitory pathways. This assumption permits the system to stabilize at various levels of excitation. Excepting the recurrent inhibitory pathways, that are assumed to act more strongly on neighboring cells than on cells of origin, the excitatory interconnections among cortical neurons are still assumed to be random, as in Hebb's model. Motivation is handled by assuming that the ascending nonspecific system (reticular formation) controls the general level of excitability of the cortical cells. Finally, "set" or direction of response is assumed to be mediated by a kind of "priming " effect. Specifically, "if afferent impulses fall on a cortical cell but do not fire it (because of inhibition or lack of adequate background facilitation) they nevertheless leave the cell with a lower threshold, the effect dying away with a time constant of *many seconds*" (italics added). There is, as yet, no evidence for such a priming process. EPSPs have much too short a time course, and PTP is a change in pre- rather than postsynaptic excitability.

One aspect of Milner's theory that has received further support from more recent work is his hypothesis that recurrent inhibition results from synaptic actions of the inhibitory interneurons on cortical cell bodies. For the type of cell he uses as a prototype—the cortical pyramidal cell—inhibitory synaptic endings appear to predominate on the cell body, and excitatory endings on the dendrites. Since spike initiation occurs at the axon hillock, which is closer to the cell body than the dendrites, inhibition will have a more immediate control over spike initiation than will excitation. This may render unnecessary Milner's assumption that recurrent inhibition from a given cell acts more on a given neighboring cell than on the cell of origin. Eccles (1957) has suggested that recurrent inhibition functions as a generalized damper of neural activity. Although Milner does not, of course, consider presynaptic inhibition or other types of synaptic processes (they were not yet discovered when he wrote), his theory is reasonable and represents a potentially useful base for more formal models.

In a subsequent discussion, Milner (1961) notes the absence of empirical support for his notion of a long-lasting "priming" effect of subthreshold excitation, and proposes an alternative mechanism for short-term storage. In essence, he suggests that when a spike travels to a given afferent terminal knob to induce postsynaptic excitation in a neuron cell body, the excitatory current flow acts backward across other terminal knobs (which he terms "learning" knobs) to increase their excitability. Postsynaptic inhibitory actions would induce parallel inhibitory effects on learning knobs. Again, there seems to be little empirical evidence regarding these possibilities. Interestingly enough, the effects Milner suggests occur in "learning" knobs do, in fact, occur in afferent terminals, but the mechanisms of action are quite different. Decreases in the excitatory actions of terminals are produced by the axoaxonic synapses on the terminals that yield presynaptic inhibition (action of c on a_2 in Fig. 2-1). In like manner, increases in the excitatory actions of afferent terminals can result from presynaptic "excitation" (action of d on a_2 in Fig. 2-1). Again, however, the time courses of these actions, at least in response to very brief stimuli, are less than 0.5 seconds—still too short to subserve short-term storage.

The theoretical development of the Perceptron (Block, 1962; Rosenblatt, 1959) is highly complex, and any kind of adequate exposition is impossible here. Instead of reviewing even the assumptions in any detail, I would like to select just one aspect of the theory; namely, consideration of randomness of interconnections among elements. Without specifying particularly the synaptic processes, the Perceptron assumes both excitatory and inhibitory projections of sensory "points" to "projection" or "association" areas. One model assumes a random environment and a system of randomly connected units. This model does not perform well—it cannot generalize. On the other hand, a "differentiated environment" model, where "each response is associated to a distinct class of 'similar' stimuli" performs much better. Trial-and-error learning, generalization, and simple cognitive sets are all claimed for this model of the Perceptron. In short, it behaves more like a brain if the connections are not assumed to be random. Hebb, Milner, and other theorists, it will be recalled, assume a high degree of randomness among the excitatory interconnections of the cortex.

Coding of Concepts by Single Nerve Cells

The extensive investigations of Hubel and Wiesel have provided a great deal of new information regarding the manner in which the brain codes visual stimuli. The basic response measure used in their experiments is the extracellular spike discharge of single neurons in the cat visual cortex in response to various types of visual stimuli; i.e., the level of analysis that treats the CNS as a system of digital elements.

In the cat, ganglion cells of the retina and geniculate neurons have

simple receptive fields of two types: an "on" center field that is excited
by a light in the center and inhibited by a surround light, and an "off"
center field having the opposite organization. However, at the primary
visual cortex (area 17) no cells were found with these elementary receptive fields. Hubel and Wiesel (1962) subdivided cortical cells into simple and complex in terms of their receptive fields. Simple fields were
those having one or more regions of excitation and inhibition. Thus,
some fields have a central field or line of excitation bounded on both
sides by inhibition, or vice versa (line perceivers?), and others have
adjoining regions of excitation and inhibition (edge perceivers?).

Complex cells in area 17 were not so easily predictable in terms of
regions of excitation and inhibition. An example of one such cell is
shown in Fig. 2-9. This cell responds to a vertical edge with brighter
light *either* to the left (*A-D*) or right (*E-H*), but does not respond to
illumination of the entire area (I) (boundary perceivers?). Another
complex cell is shown in Fig. 2-10. This cell is activated by a black rectangle *if the rectangle is horizontal, but not if it is tilted.* Slow movement of the rectangle down across the receptive field maximally activated the unit (Fig. 2-11). This cell was unresponsive to boundaries or
edges; only a black rectangle approximately one-third degree visual

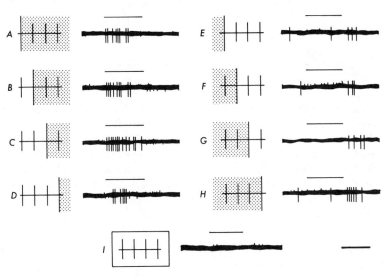

Figure 2-9. A-H: Responses of a cell in area 17 of cat cortex to a
vertical edge in various parts of the receptive field. *A-D,* brighter light
to the left; *E-H,* brighter light to the right; *I,* large rectangle, 10 × 20
degrees, covering entire receptive field. Time, 1 sec. (From Hubel and
Wiesel, 1962.)

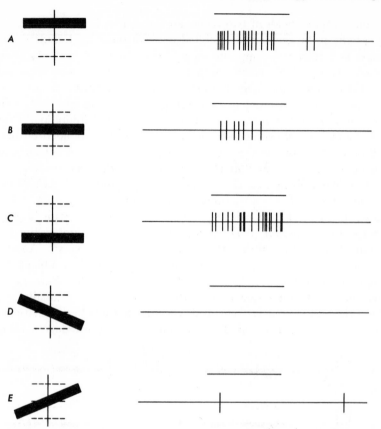

Figure 2-10. Cell activated only by left (contralateral) eye over a field approximately 5 × 5 degrees, situated 10 degrees above and to the left of the area centralis. The cell responded best to a black, horizontal rectangle, 1/3 × 6 degrees, placed anywhere in the receptive field (*A-C*). Tilting the stimulus rendered it ineffective (*D-E*). The black bar was introduced against a light background during periods of 1 sec, indicated by the upper line in each record. (From Hubel and Wiesel, 1962.)

angle wide was effective. (This cell might be called a "slowly descending, horizontal object perceiver.")

In more recent work, Hubel and Wiesel (1965) have extended their investigations to the visual association areas 18 and 19. Cells in area 18 are of two types: complex units resembling such units as those in area 17, and what they term "hypercomplex" cells. In area 19, cells

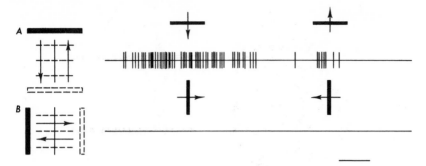

Figure 2-11. Same cell as in Fig. 2-10. Movement of black rectangle 1/3 × 6 degrees back and forth across the receptive field: *A*, horizontally oriented (parallel to receptive field axis); *B*, vertically oriented. Time required to move across the field, 5 sec. Time, 1 sec. (From Hubel and Wiesel, 1962.)

were either "hypercomplex" or "higher-order hypercomplex." In general, these terms mean that the cells respond to increasingly more abstract or specialized aspects of the stimuli.

An example of a hypercomplex cell from area 18 is shown in Figs. 2-12 and 2-13. This cell might well be called a right-angle edge perceiver. It responded most to upward movement of a right-angle edge with dark below and to the right (Fig. 2-12). A right angle was more effective than an acute or obtuse angle (Fig. 2-13). Note that the cell could also be fired, although less well, by an angle edge having dark below and to the left (Fig. 2-13, *G*). Examples of a higher-order hypercomplex cell from area 19 are shown in Figs. 2-14 and 2-15. The cell responds to upward right-angle edges of either left or right orientation moving in any direction through a rather large receptive field in *either* eye. This cell is a general angle perceiver.

These findings have obvious implications for perception. I suspect that they have equally important implications in the analysis of concept formation. To take a specific example, the cell of Figs. 2-14 and 2-15 can be said to respond to or represent the concept of right angularity. The effective stimulus is not to a specific set of receptor cells, but rather results from abstract, relational aspects of the stimulus configuration. (Gestalt psychologists might describe the effect of the stimulus in terms of field interactions, but it is clear that no such fields are required to explain the cell's behavior. The abstract "concept" of angularity that activates the cell is the result of complex, syaptic interactions at various levels of the visual system.)

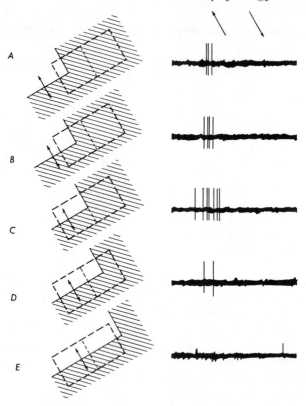

Figure 2-12. Records from a hypercomplex cell in area 18. Stimulation of right (ipsilateral) eye. Receptive field, 2 × 4 degrees indicated by interrupted rectangle. Stimulus consisted of an edge oriented
at 2:00, with dark below, terminated on the right by a second edge
intersecting the first at 90 degrees. *A-C;* up-and-down movement
across varying amounts of the activating portion of the field; *D-E,*
movement across varying amounts of the antagonistic portion. Rate of
movement 4 degrees per second. Each sweep 2 sec. (From Hubel and
Wiesel, 1965.)

I deliberately selected "angle-perceiver" cells as examples because
of Hebb's analysis of how we might learn to perceive or conceive of
angularity (1949, Chap. 5). In Hebb's schema, a brilliant elaboration
of a possible way that the excitatory interactions among nerve cells
could lead to the concept of angularity, he finds it necessary to invoke
not only learned cell assemblies (i.e., Lashley's trace systems), but also
complex combinations of these into "phase sequences." For Hebb,

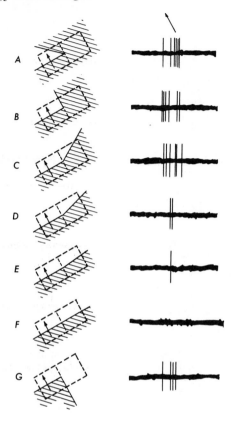

Figure 2-13. Same cell as in Fig. 2-12. Stimulation with two intersecting edges moved up across the receptive field as shown. Inhibition
is maximum when the right (antagonistic) half of the receptive field
is stimulated with an edge having the same orientation as the optimum
edge for the left (activating) half (*F*). Duration of each sweep, 2 sec.
(From Hubel and Wiesel, 1965.)

angularity is represented by enormously complex interaction patterns
among sets of interacting patterns among groups of nerve cells. There
is no individual cellular representation of angularity. The same type
of general organization is implied in Milner's model involving both
excitation and inhibition. To the contrary, Hubel and Wiesel have
shown that single cells do represent the concept of angularity. To put
it another way, complex perceptual and conceptual aspects of stimuli
are coded by individual cells in the visual cortex: lines and edges predominate in area 17 and angles and forms in areas 18 and 19.

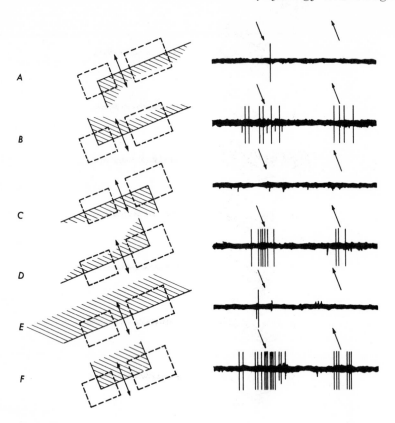

Figure 2-14. Responses of a cell recorded in area 19, right hemi-
sphere. Receptive field 6 degrees from center of gaze. Regions from
which responses were evoked are indicated roughly by the two interrupted rectangles, of which the right was 3 × 4 degrees in size. A
right-angled corner with dark up and to the right (*B*) evoked responses
when moved down or up over the left-hand region; no response was
evoked in the right-hand region. A corner with darkness up and to the
left evoked responses to up-and-down movement only over the right-
hand region (*D*). Little or no response was obtained with corners with
dark below (*A* and *C*), or with unstopped edges (*E*). A tongue (*F*)
combining stimuli *B* and *D*, gave the most powerful responses. Rate
of movement, about 0.5 degrees per second. (From Hubel and Wiesel,
1965.)

Most theorists who have developed brain models for complex perceptual and conceptual phenomena have taken for granted that percepts or concepts are learned. The most elaborate treatment of this is

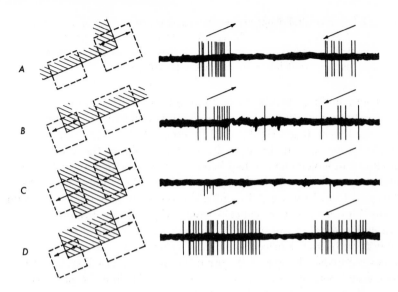

Figure 2-15. Same cell as Fig. 2-14. Responses to movement down
and to the left, and up and to the right, of corners with dark above
(*A* and *B*); failure to respond to an unstopped dark bar (*C*); strong
response to a dark bar stopped below (*D*), combining stimuli *A* and *B*.
Sweep duration, 20 sec. (From Hubel and Wiesel, 1965.)

again by Hebb: the cell assemblies and phase sequences that come to
represent lines and angles are learned during the early development
of the organism. Milner and Rosenblatt make similar assumptions. In
a most important paper, Hubel and Wiesel (1963) investigated the
functional organization of cells in the visual cortex of one- to three-
week kittens whose eyes were still closed. Their results are clear and
conclusive (pp. 999-1000):

> The main result of this study has been to show that much of the
> richness of visual physiology in the cortex of the adult cat, the re-
> ceptive-field organization, binocular interaction, and functional
> architecture . . . is present in very young kittens without visual
> experience. Our conclusion is that the neural connections subserv-
> ing these functions must also be present, in large part, at or near
> the time of birth. . . . These findings were somewhat unexpected
> in view of behavioral observations in very young kittens. . . . They
> appear quite unable to use their eyes at the time of normal eye-
> opening, which usually occurs between the sixth and tenth day.
> Avoidance of objects is seen at the very earliest about 14 days,

while pursuit, following movements, and visual placing appear only
at 20-25 days. . . . Visual acuity, measured by observing opto-
kinetic nystagmus, increases rapidly from the second week and
approaches adult levels by about the fourth week. . . .

These findings would seem to stand in direct contrast to many
observations reporting markedly defective vision in dark-reared animals and man (e.g., Hebb, 1949; Riesen, 1961). Wiesel and Hubel
(1963) reinvestigated this issue by studying cells of the visual cortex
in kittens in which one eye had been deprived of vision at birth or subsequently and for varying periods of time. They found that kittens
deprived from birth for 2-3 months showed extremely defective vision
in the deprived eye. Cortical cells were actively driven from the normal
eye with normal receptive fields, but only one cell out of 84 was at all
influenced by the deprived eye. Thus, visual deprivation at birth produces regressive changes in the organization of the visual system. Complex visual percepts and even concepts are built into the nervous system at birth; they are not learned. Furthermore, they are represented
in the brain by single nerve cells.

The very elegant observations of Hubel and Wiesel suggest many
speculations relating brain organization and complex behavioral phenomena. The categories of stimuli that activate cells fit within the
rubric of operational definitions of *concepts*. Thus, Van de Greer and
Jaspars, in their 1966 review article, state that "S has a concept if he
has a disposition on the basis of which he can make nominal classifi-
catory statements or responses ('this is X, that is not X')." By definition,
then, cells in the visual cortex of the cat have concepts.

Learning to "see" percepts and concepts by young and adult organisms does not involve learning of "perceptual organization," it only
involves learning to respond to the appropriate stimulus configuration.
This, in turn, means responding to the discharges of cells that themselves are organized by built-in circuits to discharge to the various
stimulus configurations. Learning would seem to be much more on the
output side than on the input side.

An attempt to push the notion of single-neuron representation of
concepts obviously breaks down when we consider categories more
abstract than "form." Colors, incidentally (a "concept" often used in
card-sorting concept experiments with human subjects), are coded
rather discretely by single cells in the primary visual cortex (Lennox-
Buchthal, 1962). It is perhaps of significance that color, coded in area
17, is a more rapidly learned concept than form, which is coded in
areas 18 and 19. However, no one has yet described cells that respond

to more abstract categories such as "number." The view adopted here would seem to suggest that such cells may be present.[4]

Actually, it can be shown that individual cells in the CNS code all concepts, "thoughts," or "ideas," no matter how complex. However, the demonstration is somewhat trivial. If it is granted that a particular response is necessary at some point to indicate the appearance of a concept, then it follows that the motor neurons controlling the muscles involved in making the behavioral response will respond uniquely to the concept. In man, it is likely that these motor neurons are, in turn, activated by cells in the motor cortex. Hence, all concepts are represented by single cells in the cortex. This is not a very interesting argument; the crucial point is, of course, the nature of coding processes that intervene in the cortical-subcortical systems between the sensory and motor areas of the cortex. A rather wild speculation might be entertained: a great many "subsets" of concepts are already coded by single cells in the brain as a result of the wiring diagrams present at birth. Much of the concept learning that occurs simply involves learning to respond selectively to activation of the various categories of "concept cells." Although I would not suggest that such a hypothesis be taken literally, a greater emphasis on this type of interpretation may lead to rather different models of CNS functions in complex behavioral phenomena.

In concluding, I would like to return once more to the issue of random versus patterned organization among neurons in the cortex. As we noted earlier, most models assume random interconnections. However, the data reviewed above on the visual cortex suggest the opposite. Actually, there are several levels of patterned organization in most sensory areas of the cortex. Thus, in the visual cortex, there is first the long-known retinotopic projection—the retina is topographically represented on the cortex. At the next level, there is a functional subdivision of each region of retinal projection into columns of cells. Hubel and Wiesel (1962) found discrete columns of cells extending from surface to white matter (at right angles to cortical surface); within each column, the cells all had the same receptive-field axis orientation. Cells having both simple and complex receptive fields were found within any given column. This general type of columnar organization of cortex, incidentally, was first demonstrated by Mountcastle (1957) for the somatic sensory cortex: within each small region of body projection

---

[4] In a research project in the author's laboratories, cells were discovered (October, 1967) in nonspecific association areas of the cerebral cortex that do in fact appear to code "number" concepts. See "Postscript added in proof," pp. 67-68.

there are separate columns of cells, a given column containing cells responsive to only one modality (i.e., touch, deep pressure, joint movement).

Finally, there is the discrete cellular representation of specific or abstract aspects of stimuli. These must result from a highly specific, non-random, patterned organization of cellular elements. Excitatory and inhibitory synaptic interactions among nerve cells are the only mechanisms available. Hence, very specific patterned interconnections must exist to yield the highly individualized and abstract functional characteristics of many cortical neurons. It would seem probable that increased understanding of the neural basis of complex behavioral phenomena is contingent upon a knowledge of the patterns of neural organization rather than upon assumptions of randomness.

POSTSCRIPT ADDED IN PROOF

As noted, cortical cells have been shown to code color and form. It was suggested (pp. 64-65, written in November, 1966) that cortical neurons may someday be found to code even more abstract categories of stimuli or concepts such as "numbers."

In the course of a project devoted to analysis of complex properties of polysensory cells in association cortex of cat, we recently (October, 1967) encountered cells in the suprasylvian gyrus that appear to "count" or code number concepts. The clearest example to date is a "number 7" cell. When a simultaneous compound stimulus (click-light, flash-forepaw shock) was given repetitively at a rate of once per second, the cell fired on the seventh presentation of the stimulus. This effect was highly reliable. In eight separate series of ten stimuli, with rest intervals of at least one minute between each series, the mean stimulus presentation on which the cell first discharged was 7.0. The probability of first discharge as a function of stimulus number in the sequence is plotted in Fig. 2-16. The probability of first discharge is very high for the seventh stimulus, low for the sixth and eighth stimuli, and zero for the remaining stimuli.

It is of some significance that the "7" effect held over a range of interstimulus intervals. The cell tended to fire first on the seventh trial with two-second and four-second interstimulus intervals, as well as with the one-second interval. Since the counting behavior of the cell was independent of the time between stimuli, at least over this limited range, it would seem possible to categorize the cell as coding a number concept. The cell behaved as though it were counting to seven.

While it may seem slightly bizarre to characterize a single neuron as coding a number concept, it is not difficult to conceive of neural mechanisms that might produce the behavior of the cell. If each stimulus induced long-lasting activity in recurrent systems of neurons that had excitatory actions on the cell, and this activity were summative, then the number of stimulus presentations required to fire the cell would be crucial. Furthermore, if the excitatory activity decayed with a slow time course, the effective number of stimuli would tend to be

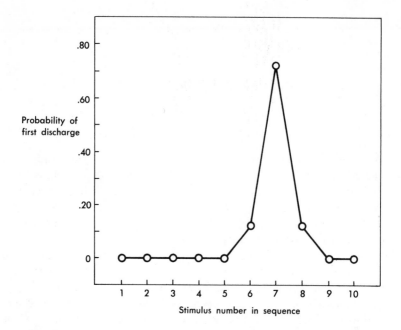

Figure 2-16. Probability of first discharge of a cell in suprasylvian association cortex as a function of stimulus number in a sequence of ten stimuli. The cell behaves as though it were "counting to seven."

independent of interstimulus interval, at least over a given range. The behavior of the cell would simply be a special case of temporal summation.

At the behavioral level, there are situations where response probability increases as a function of number of stimulus presentations. Therefore, it is not unreasonable to suggest that the same may be true for individual neurons in the cerebral cortex. As noted (p. 64), color-coding cells are found in primary visual cortex and form-coding cells in the visual association areas. Now it appears that number-coding cells are present in nonspecific association areas of the cortex. It is possibly relevant that results of human card-sorting experiments rank the relative difficulty of these three concepts in a corresponding order.

REFERENCES

Anderson, P., and Eccles, J. C. Inhibitory phasing of neuronal discharge. *Nature*, 1962, *196*, 645-647.

Anderson, P., Eccles, J. C., and Sears, T. A. Cortically evoked depolarization of primary afferent fibers in the spinal cord. *J. Neurophysiol.*, 1964, *27*, 63-77.

Ashby, W. R. *Design for a brain*. New York: Wiley, 1960.

Block, H. D. The Perceptron: A model for brain functioning. *Rev. mod. Phys.*, Part I, 1962, *34*, 123-135.

Coombs, J. S., Eccles, J. C., and Fatt, P. Excitatory synaptic action in motoneurones. *J. Physiol.*, 1955, *130*, 374-395.

Davis, H. Enhancement of evoked cortical potentials in humans related to a task requiring decision. *Science*, 1964, *145*, 182-183.

Eccles, J. C. *The physiology of nerve cells*. Baltimore: Johns Hopkins Press, 1957.

Eccles, J. C. The behavior of nerve cells. In Ciba Symposium *Neurological basis of behavior*. London: J. and A. Churchill Ltd., 1958. Pp. 28-47.

Eccles, J. C. *The physiology of synapses*. New York: Academic Press Inc., 1964.

Eccles, J. C., Schmidt, R. F., and Willis, W. D. Presynaptic inhibition of the spinal monosynaptic reflex pathway. *J. Physiol.*, 1962, *161*, 282-297.

Frank, K. Basic mechanisms of synaptic transmission in the central nervous system. *I.R.E. Trans: Med. Electron ME-6*, 1959, 85-88.

Frank, K., and Fuortes, M. G. F. Presynaptic and postsynaptic inhibition of monosynaptic reflexes. *Federation Proceedings*, 1957, *16*, 39-40.

Granit, R., Kellerth, J. O., and Williams, T. D. 'Adjacent' and 'remote' postsynaptic inhibition in motoneurons stimulated by muscle stretch. *J. Physiol.*, 1964, *174*, 453-472.

Haggar, R. A., and Barr, M. L. Quantitative data on the size of synaptic end bulbs in the cat's spinal cord. *J. comp. Neurol.*, 1950, *93*, 17-35.

Hebb, D. C. *The Organization of Behavior*. New York: Wiley, 1949.

Hernãndez-Peon, R., Scherrer, H., and Jouvet, M. Modification of electrical activity in cochlear nucleus during "attention" in unanesthetized cats. *Science*, 1956, *123*, 331-332.

Horn, G. Electrical activity of the cerebral cortex of the unanesthetized cat during attentive behavior. *Brain*, 1960, *83*, 57-76.

Hovland, C. I. Computer simulation of thinking. *Amer. Psychol.*, 1960, *15*, 687-693.

Hubel, D. H., and Wiesel, T. N. Receptive fields, binocular interaction and functional architecture in the cat's visual cortex. *J. Physiol.*, 1962, *160*, 106-154.

Hubel, D. H., and Wiesel, T. N. Receptive fields of cells in striate cortex of very young, visually inexperienced kittens. *J. Neurophysiol.*, 1963, *26*, 994-1001.

Hubel, D. H., and Wiesel, T. N. Receptive fields and functional architecture in two nonstriate visual areas (18 and 19) of the cat. *J. Neurophysiol.*, 1965, *28*, 229-289.

Jacobson, E. Electrical measurements of neuromuscular states during mental activities. *Amer. J. Physiol.*, 1931, *97*, 200-209.

Lashley, K. W. Cerebral organization and behavior. In "The brain and human behavior," *Proceedings of the Association for Research on Nervous and Mental Disturbances*, 1958, *39*. Pp. 1-18.

Lennox-Buchthal, M. A. Single units in monkey, cercocebus torquatus atys, cortex with narrow spectral responsiveness. *Vis. Res.*, 1962, *2*, 1-15.

Lindsley, D. B. Psychophysiology and motivation. In M. R. Jones (Ed.), *Nebraska symposium on motivation 1957*. Lincoln: University of Nebraska Press, 1957. Pp. 44-105.

Lloyd, D. P. C. Post-tetanic potentiation of response in monosynaptic reflex pathways of the spinal cord. *J. gen. Physiol.*, 1949, *33*, 147-170.

Lorente de Nō, R. Cerebral cortex: architecture. In J. F. Fulton, *Physiology of the nervous system*. (2nd. ed.) New York: Oxford University Press, 1943. Pp. 274-301.

Lundberg, A. Supraspinal control of transmission in reflex paths to motoneurons and primary afferents. In J. C. Eccles, and J. P. Schade (Eds.), *Progress in brain research, Vol. 12, Physiology of spinal neurons*. New York: Elsevier, 1964. Pp. 197-219.

Lundberg, A., and Vyklicky, L. Brain stem control of reflex paths to primary afferents. *Acta physiol. scandanav.*, 1963, *59*, supplement 213, 19.

Luria, A. R. *The role of speech in the regulation of normal and abnormal behavior*. New York: Liveright, 1961.

McCleary, R. A., and Moore, R. Y. *Subcortical mechanisms of behavior*. New York: Basic Books, 1965.

McGaugh, J. L. Time-dependent processes in memory storage. *Science,* 1966, *153,* 1351-1358.

Mendell, L. M., and Wall, P. D. Presynaptic hyperpolarization: a role for fine afferent fibers. *J. Physiol.,* 1965, *172,* 274-294.

Milner, P. M. The cell assembly: mark II. *Psychol. Rev.,* 1957, 64, 242-252.

Milner, P. M. Learning in neural systems. In *Self-Organizing Systems.* New York: Pergamon Press, 1961. Pp. 190-204.

Mountcastle, V. B. Modality and topographic properties of single neurons of cat's somatic sensory cortex. *J. Neurophysiol.,* 1957, *20,* 408-434.

Newell, A., Shaw, J. C., and Simon, H. A. Elements of a theory of human problem solving. *Psychol. Rev.,* 1958, *65,* 151-166.

Novikova, L. A. Electrophysiological investigation of speech. From N. O'Connor (Ed.), *Recent soviet psychology,* 1961.

Osgood, C. E. A behavioristic analysis of perception and language as cognitive phenomena. In *Contemporary approaches to cognition.* Cambridge, Massachusetts: Harvard University Press, 1957. Pp. 75-118.

Pribram, K. H., Galanter, E. G., and Miller, G. A. *Plans and the structure of behavior.* New York: Holt, 1960.

Riesen, A. H. Stimulation as a requirement for growth and function in behavioral development. In D. W. Fiske, and S. R. Maddi (Eds.), *Functions of varied experience.* Homewood, Illinois: Dorsey Press, 1961. Pp. 57-105.

Rosenblatt, F. The Perceptron: a probabalistic model for information storage and organization in the brain. *Psychol. Rev.,* 1959, *66,* 386-408.

Russell, B. *The analysis of mind.* New York: MacMillan, 1921.

Sholl, D. A. *The organization of the cerebral cortex.* New York: Wiley, 1956.

Smith, S. M., Brown, H. O., Toman, J. E. P., and Goodman, L. S. The lack of cerebral effects of D-Tubocurarine. *Anesthesiology,* 1947, *8,* 1-14.

Sokolov, Y. N. *Perception and the conditioned reflex.* New York: Pergamon Press, 1963.

Spencer, W. A., and Wigdor, R. Ultra-late PTP of monosynaptic reflex responses in cat. *Physiologist,* 1965, *8,* 278.

Spong, P., Haider, M., and Lindsley, D. B. Selective attentiveness and cortical evoked responses to visual and auditory stimuli. *Science*, 1965, *148*, 395-397.

Stellar, E. Drive and motivation. In J. Field (Ed.), *Handbook of physiology. Section 1: Neurophysiology, Vol. III*. Washington, D. C.: American Physiological Society, 1960. Pp. 1501-1527.

Thompson, R. F., Denney, D., and Smith, H. E. Cortical control of specific and nonspecific sensory projections to the cerebral cortex. *Psychon. Sci.*, 1966, *4*, 93-94.

Thompson, R. F., and Shaw, J. A. Behavioral correlates of evoked activity-recorded from association areas of the cerebral cortex. *J. comp. Physiol. Psychol.*, 1965, *60*, 329-339.

Thompson, R. F., and Spencer, W. A. Habituation: a model phenomenon for the study of neuronal substrates of behavior. *Psychol. Rev.*, 1966, *173*, 16-43.

Van de Greer, J. P., and Jaspars, J. M. F. Cognitive functions. *Annu. Rev. Psychol.*, 1966, *17*, 145-176.

Vierk, C. J. Reticular stimulation and generalized drive. *Exp. Neurol.*, 1965, *12*, 109-122.

Wiesel, T. N., and Hubel, D. H. Single cell responses in striate cortex of kittens deprived of vision in one eye. *J. Neurophysiol.*, 1963, *26*, 1003-1017.

PROBLEMS IN THE ANALYSIS OF COMPLEX NEURAL FUNCTION

ALAN E. FISHER

University of Pittsburgh

As a preamble, let me say that I believe we know a little more about the neurophysiological bases of organismic behavior and a little less about the rules governing the functions of individual brain cells than Thompson's opening remarks would suggest. In any event, both of us admit to knowing next to nothing about THOUGHT, and perhaps should be asked to sit at a lower level than those of you who are loath to make such an admission. Scientists studying brain function from the inside out simply haven't even approached a stage in which the investigation of complex thought processes is either reasonable or possible. Instead, they have found it most productive to emphasize the study of neural systems that are highly preorganized, with comparatively inflexible structural and functional characteristics. Thus, information has accumulated rapidly, relative to the functional organization of the input (sensory) and output (motor) systems. In addition, much data are available concerning the anatomical substrate for reinforcement and the neurophysiological mechanisms underlying motivation and emotion. This is not the appropriate place to review such material, but the following sampling of references may be of interest (Nauta, 1963; Olds, 1962; Miller, 1965; Fisher, 1965; Levine and Mullins, 1966; also, see Chaps. 6-11 in Grossman, 1967).

On the molecular side, I do not agree that it is safe to infer that virtually all factors of significance to brain function are synaptic actions following all-or-none spike discharge, and that the processes underlying thinking can be reduced to a pattern of digital events. Such reductionism may be suitable for model building, but there are dangers that the resulting model will explain more about computer function than brain function. In fact, there seems little doubt about the fact that a cell in the brain can be involved in a process or "thought" without responding in an all-or-none manner. One of the most influential and productive scientists in this research area has stated that "a growing body of knowledge suggests that the most significant integrative work of the central nervous system is carried on in graded response elements, elements in which the degree of reaction depends upon stimulus intensity and is not all-or-none, which have no refractory period and in which continuously varying potential changes of either sign occur and mix and algebraically sum" (Morrell, 1961). Whether or not dendritic or glial elements propagate or respond to functionally significant electro-ionic field events in the intact organism remains to be demonstrated. However, there is clear evidence for both facilitatory and inhibitory field effects in experimental preparations. Perhaps the most fascinating findings involve the application of a low-level anodal current to motor cortex. Such extracellular current fields produce no movement patterns unless and until they are accompanied by an external stimulus such as a tone or light. Then, an overt movement may occur, which is appropriate to the function of the stimulated portion of the motor cortex. The exciting finding, however, is that that the *specific* stimulus then *retains* the capacity to elicit the movement pattern for 20 to 30 minutes after the anodal current is terminated (Rusinov, 1953). This is of particular interest because many data suggest that there are several phases or mechanisms involved in the memory process, and that the time course of one of these is approximately 20 minutes.

Morrell has followed up Rusinov's work (Morrell, 1961) and has demonstrated that the anodal current alone does not influence the all-or-none spike discharge rate of individual neurons in the motor cortex, but such neurons respond to a previously neutral stimulus during the anodal stimulation and for 3 to 20 minutes after removal of the anodal stimulation. Thus, a non-digital field effect may impose conditions which promote retention of specific sensory-motor relationships for short periods, and Morrell emphasizes that there is a strong possibility that short-term memory coding may be achieved via other means than preservation of all-or-none spike discharges. Landauer (1964) presents an interesting but untested theory of neural function in which field effects also play a major functional role.

As suggested earlier, there is similar evidence for central inhibitory effects that are basically unrelated to synaptic inhibitory action. Spreading cortical depression (Leao, 1944) is due to a direct current shift across the cortex which apparently involves a chain reaction liberation of potassium ion from cells over an extended field (Morrell, 1961). Albert (1966) has demonstrated both facilitation and inhibition of memory consolidation in the same subjects (rats). A polarizing, anodal current applied to the cortex speeds consolidation or reinstates interrupted consolidation, while a polarizing cathodal current interferes with consolidation. Again, we cannot say as yet that these essentially non-synaptic chemical and electrical field effects have functional significance in the intact organism, but neither can they be excluded from our largely incomplete memory equation. Field theories of neural function have weathered an era of unpopularity, but in my opinion, the mechanisms underlying the phenomena mentioned above hold more promise of being functionally related to learning and memory than, for example, the posttetanic potentiation phenomenon supported by Thompson.

The ubiquitous neuroglial cell also looms as a potential hazard to model builders. Although long relegated to the role of nonfunctional brain bulk, glial cells may soon emerge in a stellar role. In fact, we have had so little success relating thought and memory to nerve cell function, that a few hardy souls are ready to suggest that nerve cells may do the more mundane housekeeping chores, while neuroglia do the thinking (Galambos, 1961). Recent evidence suggests that glial cells move in and out of synaptic regions and may store or impart the structural or chemical changes which underlie learning (Hyden, 1962).

While on the subject of extra-synaptic influences, I would like to emphasize the importance to brain functioning of internal chemical and physical changes. There are not only general effects, such as the influence of calcium ion (controlled by parathyroid hormone) on nerve cell thresholds, but highly specific effects as well. Evidence now strongly supports the concept that internal changes in such factors as osmolarity, blood glucose level, hormone levels, temperature, and even light may be monitored directly by specific receptor neurons in hypothalamic and limbic structures. The major point to be made is that nerve cells not only respond to many non-synaptic influences, but such influences often determine whether synaptic events occurring at other levels will achieve translation into effective action. For instance, infrahuman female sexual behavior is highly dependent on hormone levels, and these levels are monitored by nerve cells in the hypothalamus. Thus, the physiological state of a specific group of cells in a complex system is critical to the functional integrity of the entire system. I think it important to stress that many of the so-called digital units in the brain are highly differentiated, and not simply in terms of complexity of interconnection with similar units. I agree with Thompson that there are many neurons entrusted with "concepts," but the neurons I am discussing are not dependent on their afferent connections for functional specificity. These cells monitor the internal environment, and their responsiveness to non-synaptic events then determines the level of function of complex neural and neuro-endocrine systems.

It is of some interest that Thompson and I can talk about single neurons having concepts from quite different points of view. In the purest sense, I think it is easier to defend such an idea when discussing neurons in which "conceptualization" is independent of afferent connection. It may be a semantic problem only, but it is difficult for me to follow an argument about the complex functions of single neurons when such functions are most probably an outgrowth of interconnection with many neurons at the same and different levels of the central nervous system.

Nevertheless, I should have confessed before now that many of the views expressed by Thompson are exceedingly attractive to me, particularly since both my training and experience lead me to respond favorably to theories emphasizing genetic preorganization of neural systems. I do feel an obligation to play devil's advocate, however, since Dick [Thompson] and I are the only representatives of our discipline contributing to this text. So I hope he will forgive my attempt to present alternate arguments.

Although he is very polite about it, I believe Thompson's major thesis is that Hebb's pioneering theories of CNS function were wrong on virtually every count. Thus, Thompson emphasizes data suggesting that single neurons are capable of highly complex functions, while Hebb emphasized the need for systems of neurons to carry out even simple functions. Thompson stresses the high level of preorganization of brain systems, while Hebb wrote in terms of random connections and the exceedingly gradual onset of perceptual awareness and functional integrity within developing systems of neurons. In a very real sense, Thompson is suggesting a form of racial or species memory, in which nerve cells are provided with genetically coded "concepts" deriving from phylogenetic but not ontogenetic experience. The major task remaining to an organism endowed with such a brain is to interrelate concepts and behavior. In other words, the organism's problem is to learn to attach appropriate responses to his perceptual and conceptual view of the world—not to develop the concepts or percepts in the first place.

I think Thompson is both courageous and correct to etch an alternative position so sharply. The truth will no doubt lie somewhere on middle ground but he, and others of like mind, must offset more than 20 years of homage to an opposing theory.

What are the chief arguments that can be mounted against the kind of brain model Thompson is proposing? First, it is important to make the obvious, but often neglected point that phylogenetic level must be considered as a highly relevant variable. Putting it bluntly, the answers one gets to the questions Thompson is raising may well change as the identity of the experimental organism changes. For instance, it is highly probable that the perceptual "givens" in lower vertebrate forms are more explicit than in higher mammals. Even if one accepts without question the Hubel and Wiesel data that Thompson presents, it is still reasonable to postulate that the cat visual cortex contains some cells whose functions are more flexible and less predetermined than corresponding cells in the frog brain. By the time we get to the human, it is conceivable that preorganization of connections and concommitant percepts is the exception rather than the rule. I believe that Thompson is deliberately betting against this argument, however, and would postulate that humans are as finely tuned to encode (and decode) specific environmental energies as lower organisms. In his theory, the differences between phylogenetic levels would involve the extent to which arbitrary connections to motor pathways are available to the infant organism. The literature contains so many conflicting data on these points that the question certainly remains open.

Since Thompson bases much of his argument on data from Hubel and Wiesel's laboratory, we need to consider the generality of that data and the extent to which it can support Thompson's position.

First, it should be said that there are investigators that do not agree with some of Hubel and Wiesel's data and conclusions. Baumgartner, *et al.* (1965) disagree with the premise that cortical cells never have concentric visual fields. They report many cortical concentric field neurons, indicating a simple projection of retinal events to area 17 without post-retinal integration at lower brain levels. More important, and again in opposition to Hubel and Wiesel's findings, they also report evidence for many simple "on" "off" neurons at the cortical level. They go on to suggest a model in which facilitation and inhibition among adjacent "on" and "off" cortical neurons could provide a basis for perceptual contrast. In other words, cells with simple "on" and "off" concepts could be organized into systems that mediate perception of contrasting forms. They do concede that specialized cells of the types reported by Hubel and Wiesel are probably involved in complex form perception.

The critical question, however, is whether the data Hubel and Wiesel present provide direct evidence against Hebb's theory of brain organization and function. Hebb's major premises were: 1) that relatively undifferentiated, randomly connected neurons are involved in the organization of perception; and 2) that systems of neurons achieve functional integrity only after a prolonged and experientially based period of organization (Hebb, 1949; Hebb, 1959). It is difficult for me to agree that data from adult cats fully negate Hebb's position, since the neuron being tapped at any given moment could still be part of a cell assembly at that cortical level, albeit a much less diffusely organized one than Hebb envisioned. The data on young kittens could be much more crucial, but I do not feel that the evidence is as yet quite as convincing as Thompson obviously does. For instance, virtually all the cells in the visual cortex of naïve cats are much less responsive, only area 17 (primary sensory area) has been studied in such animals, and fewer cells with complex "concepts" have been clearly identified. Hebb, however, did not assume random connections, diffuse conduction, or gradual onset of complex function for area 17, but only for the projection fields beyond it (areas 18, 19, and 20).

Also, Wiesel and Hubel themselves report (1965b) that visually deprived kittens give no behavioral evidence of visual function, even though many cells in area 17 can be shown to respond appropriately and specifically to visual stimuli. Such data would appear to favor Hebb's position, since they suggest that perceptual organization may be required before raw sensory data can be utilized effectively.

In spite of my stated reservations, however, I must avow that the data Hubel and Wiesel present are compelling, and that many of the extrapolations made by Thompson are thought-provoking. It is certainly time to rid the world of the "learning is all" fallacy. In fact, Wiesel and Hubel are now suggesting (1965a, 1965b) that a *lack* of stimulation or disparate stimulation of visual systems during early development can lead to the disruption of preorganized connections and/or of perceptual function. As Thompson indicates, such data cast considerable doubt on the validity of isolation and deprivation studies, traditionally used as a crucial test of the extent to which animal behavior is innate or learned. Thus, the very conditions used to gather crucial behavioral data on preorganization of neural circuits may have effects which mask valid evidence for preorganization and force quite invalid conclusions.

In closing, let me say that I've enjoyed my role of devil's advocate, but in my heart of hearts—or should I say thought of thoughts to insure that *something* related to thinking is connected with neurophysiology in this text (?)—I find much satisfaction in the emergence of the kind of theory Thompson is helping to develop. The high level of preorganization of his "brain child" may be just what is necessary to help it survive.

REFERENCES

Albert, D. J. The effects of polarizing currents on the consolidation of learning. *Neuropsychologia*, 1966, *4*, 65-77.

Baumgartner, G., Brown, J. L., and Schulz, A. Responses of single units of the cat visual system to rectangular stimulus patterns. *J. Neurophysiol.*, 1965, *28*, 1-18.

Fisher, A. E. Chemical stimulation of the brain. *Sci. Amer.*, 1965.

Galambos, R. A glia-neural theory of brain function. *Proceedings of the National Academy of Science.* Washington, D. C.: 1961, *57*, 129-136.

Geiger, R. S. The behavior of adult mammalian brain cells in culture. In Pfeiffer and Smythies (Eds.), *International Review of Neurobiology*, 1963, *5*, 1-51.

Grossman, S. P. *A textbook of physiological psychology.* New York: Wiley, 1967.

Hebb, D. O. *The organization of behavior: a neuropsychological theory.* New York: Wiley, 1949.

Hebb, D. O. A neuropsychological theory. In S. Koch (Ed.), *Psychology: a study of a science.* Vol. 1. New York: McGraw-Hill, 1959. Pp. 622-643.

Hyden, H. The neuron and its glia: a biochemical and functional unit. *Endeavour*, 1962, *21*, 144-155.

Landauer, T. K. Two hypotheses concerning the biochemical basis of memory. *Psychol. Rev.*, 1964, *71*, 167-179.

Leao, A. A. P. Spreading depression of activity in the cerebral cortex. *J. Neurophysiol.*, 1944, *7*, 359-390.

Levine, S., and Mullins, R. F. Hormonal influences on brain organization in infant rats. *Science*, 1966, *152*, 1585-1592.

Miller, N. E. Chemical coding of behavior in the brain. *Science*, 1965, *148*, 328-338.

Morrell, F. Electrophysiological contributions to the neural basis of learning. *Physiol. Rev.*, 1961, *41*, 443-494.

Nauta, W. J. H. Central nervous organization and the endocrine motor system. In Nalbandov (Ed.), *Advances in neuroendocrinology.* Urbana, Illinois: University of Illinois Press. 1963. Pp. 5-21.

Olds, J. Hypothalamic substrates of reward. *Physiol. Rev.*, 1962, *42*, 554-604.

Rusinov, V. S. An electrophysiological analysis of the connective function in the cerebral cortex in the presence of a dominant area. *Communications of the XIX International Physiology Congress*, Montreal, Canada, 1953.

Wiesel, T. N., and Hubel, D. H. Comparison of the effects of unilateral and bilateral eye closure on cortical unit responses in kittens. *J. Neurophysiol.*, 1965, *28*, 1029-1040. (a)

Wiesel, T. N., and Hubel, D. H. Extent of recovery from the effects of visual deprivation in kittens. *J. Neurophysiol.*, 1965, *28*, 1060-1072. (b)

GENERAL DISCUSSION

KIMBLE asked whether it is true that the cat has the neurophysiological mechanism for color vision even though behaviorally he is essentially color-blind. THOMPSON replied that such was the case.

Reference was made to a study in which ducks were reared in monochromatic light and later showed an inability to generalize. From this result, it was pointed out, it seems that generalization ability across colors is a function of experience with varied color.

THOMPSON pointed out that such a deficit could be interpreted in terms of lack of experience with a particular type of response contingency rather than a lack of perceptual experience.

It was indicated by RESTLE that physiologists seem to view learning as building a system out of chaos. However, he pointed out, learning can be viewed as the selection from available structures as opposed to the formation of new structures. Moreover, if the selection view is correct, then the learning versus the genetic problem is not really important because the presence of a particular structure at birth is not evidence against learning.

THOMPSON commented that the physiologist actually is stressing output and saying that the organism is more modifiable on the output rather than the input side.

It was asked by RESTLE whether, if an organism learns to ignore the activity of a certain neuron, the neuron then is on the input or output side.

THOMPSON replied that it is on the input side, but its activity must be connected with a certain response.

FISHER added that the organism must learn to connect integrated sensory patterns with integrated motor patterns.

NEWELL pointed out that a selection position also requires the formation of a connection.

It also was mentioned that the selection process can act in a negative manner; i.e., the organism learns to inhibit or ignore firing in some circuit as the cat seemingly does in color vision.

81

HABER pointed out that Hubel and Wiesel used cats, but work on lower organisms has yielded contradictory data. Moreover, HABER pointed out, complex cells move higher into the cortex as the phylogenetic scale reaches man. Thus, why results are contradictory in lower organisms may be attributable to the existence of more complex cells in the periphery in lower organisms. HABER indicated, furthermore, that primates therefore may show less evidence of built-in concepts.

RESTLE commented that the problem may be that such cells may be more difficult to find in complex organisms because there is a greater total number of total cells.

3

ASSOCIATIVE LEARNING AND THOUGHT: THE NATURE OF AN ASSOCIATION AND ITS RELATION TO THOUGHT[1]

JAMES F. VOSS
University of Pittsburgh

The purpose of this paper is to consider the relationship of associative learning and thought. This topic is one of the oldest in psychology, for the associationistic doctrine has been of importance to the study of thought ever since a description of thought was attempted. Although an historical account of the relation of associationism and thought will not be presented, it should be noted that Humphrey, in his book entitled *Thinking*, summarized the issue by declaring, "It may be said that the history of the psychology of thinking consists largely of an unsuccessful revolt against the doctrine of associationism" (p. 28).

[1] The preparation of this paper was supported by the National Institute of Child Growth and Human Development (00957-03).

The author wishes to thank Drs. Norman Anderson and William Battig for their helpful suggestions.

The thesis of the present paper is that the study of associative learning can make significant contributions to the understanding of thought, but for such contributions to occur, the study of associative learning per se must be developed empirically and theoretically.

The paper consists of three parts: associative learning, thought, and how the area of associative learning may be studied in order to contribute toward a better understanding of the psychology of thought.

Associative Learning

The term *associationism* refers to a theoretical position which states that learning, thought, and possibly other processes may be described and explained by associationistic principles; i.e., the laws of association. The classical associationistic position states that an individual has the tendency to associate two events when these events have occurred in close temporal relation (Law of Contiguity). The associationistic viewpoint also typically states that the more often the events occur in such a contiguous relationship, the stronger the association becomes (Law of Frequency). In addition to the laws of contiguity and frequency, a third law states that as the similarity of the two events increases, the greater is the tendency to associate the events (Law of Similarity). Other associative laws have been stated, but contiguity usually has been regarded as the fundamental law and the laws of frequency and similarity have been considered of extreme importance.

The nature of the events that are said to be associated has varied with the orientation of the writer; ideas, contents of ideas, sensations, images, stimuli, stimuli and responses, and neurons all have been thought to be associated. The fact that associationism has been applied to such a variety of units attests to the pervasiveness and permanence of the doctrine.

Associative learning may be defined as the study of the acquisition of associations. A broader definition also would include the study of the retention of associations and how the acquisition of associations influences the acquisition of new material (transfer).

The experimental method used most frequently in the area of associative learning is the paired-associate paradigm in which an individual is shown a pair of verbal items and must, upon later presentation of one of the items, produce the second item. The paired-associate method, or variations thereof, has been used to study a wide range of issues including whether associations are formed in one trial and whether associations are learned bidirectionally. In addition, the method has been used to study the effect of meaningfulness of verbal material, length of list, stimulus and response intralist similarity, distribution of practice, acquisition of concepts, and other phenomena.

The doctrine of associationism is related to associative learning in that the methodological developments in the latter area have been influenced by the laws of associationism. It is of interest to point out, however, that the relationship of the laws of contiguity and frequency to associative learning is that contiguity and frequency have been *assumed* to be at the base of associative learning. This assumption is attested to by the fact that the paired-associate procedure consists of repeated contiguous presentations of the associations, thus insuring the operation of contiguity and frequency factors. This fact apparently has been taken for granted, for despite the apparent basic nature of associative laws, the laws per se have received little or no experimental attention.

Associative learning and the nature of an association. The study of associative learning naturally presumes that the organism learns an association. *The question:* The nature of that entity, termed "an association," must now be considered more closely. The study of behavior in stimulus-response terms consists of observation of a response change which occurs in conjunction with the presentation of a stimulus. But what of the study of verbal associations in an S-R framework? The experimental paradigm most widely used to study associative learning; i.e., the paired-associate design, lent itself readily to an S-R model because the denotation of stimulus and response is virtually a built-in characteristic of the method. As we now realize, however, considering paired-associate learning in S-R terms constituted an oversimplification. In particular, there appear to be at least three shortcomings within the straightforward S-R model of paired-associate learning.

The first problem is that the item of the pair that is denoted as the stimulus is not necessarily the functional stimulus in the learning of the association (Underwood, 1963). In other words, what the subject is using as the stimulus is not necessarily the stimulus item presented to him. Because of this, there is currently considerable interest in determining what constitutes the functional stimulus.

Finding what constitutes the functional stimulus, however, is a complicated issue. Knowledge of the functional stimuli may only be possible when there is a greater understanding of three factors: the verbal structure of the individual, the aspects of the external stimulus conditions that the individual uses in learning the association, and the relation between these two factors. The question of the role of verbal structure in stimulus selection is reminiscent of a comment made in 1896 by Dewey, ". . . the so-called response is not merely to the stimulus, it is into it" (1896, p. 359).

The relation between associative learning and associative structure warrants further comment at this point. Associative structure may be defined as the inter-relationship of verbal units within the verbal repertoire of the individual (cf. Deese, 1965, p. 1). Such organizational processes have been demonstrated in a number of learning situations. For instance, Bousfield and his colleagues (e.g., Bousfield, 1953) have demonstrated that words related to each other tend to cluster in recall. Tulving (1962) has shown that repeated recall of a list of apparently unrelated words yields increasing sequential consistency of item recall over trials. Finally, Deese's work on inter-item associative strength demonstrated the existence of networks of related words (Deese, 1961). Despite the variety of studies demonstrating associative structure, however, there has been little study on its influence upon the acquisition of paired-associates.

A second problem in the area of associative learning involves use of the term *response*. The word response refers to an action of the subject as well as to the response item itself. Such ambiguity may not produce difficulties if the uses of the term are specified. However, failure to distinguish these two aspects of the situation probably has tended to obscure an important question; namely, what processes are involved in the subject's learning of responses?

Three approaches to the problem of response learning have been made. The first attempt was an emphasis upon response selectivity as a mechanism in which a correct response was acquired by a trial-and-error mechanism; e.g., Melton (1950). The second was the description by Mandler (1954) of response integration. This concept points out the need to consider how a particular unit; e.g., a CVC trigram, is integrated into a functional unit. The third approach was the distinction between response learning and associative learning discussed by Underwood and Schulz (1960). This concept involved emphasis on the learning of the responses of the list as responses per se, and differentiating such learning from the process of associating the responses with the stimuli. However, despite these three highly worthy contributions, the problem remains as to what processes are involved in the acquisition of the response items of the list. Furthermore, it may be suggested that associative learning may be better described as sensory integration in which the two units are integrated into "an association" and the response of the subject is an indicator that such an integration has occurred.

The third deficiency of the S-R description of associative learning follows from the first two issues; namely, if the effective stimulus or stimuli are not specified, and if it is not clear how the subject learns the response items, what then can be said to be associated? In other words, if the stimulus and response processes cannot be readily identified, on what basis can one speak of processes involved in the learning of an association?

The answer to the problem of what is associated probably requires a testable mediation-type model which includes representational processes of the two items of an association. It would seem that such a representational model should provide for the absorption of the items of an association into the repertoire of the individual if the items are unfamiliar to the subject. The model also should provide for the differentiation of items into those that are on the list to be learned and those that are not. Clearly, the study of the mechanism that permits so few extralist intrusions to occur is an interesting and important problem. The model also should describe how, when familiar items are used, the particular association becomes stronger than the remaining associations in which either of the associated items occurs.

Associative learning and associative strength. The study of associative learning involves not only the issue of the nature of an association; it also involves the question of what constitutes associative strength. The term *associative strength* is used to denote a tendency of one verbal unit; e.g., A, to evoke another verbal unit; e.g., B. The term is currently used to depict the number of times a response is given to a stimulus in obtaining group word norms, the position of a particular response in the stimulus-response hierarchy of one individual, and the tendency of a stimulus to evoke the correct response in a paired-associate task.

Despite the widespread usage of the term associative strength, little is understood regarding either the measurement of associative strength or the processes involved in the growth and modifications of associative strength. Two issues raised by the concept of associative strength are now considered: the relative nature of associative strength and the problem of shifts in associative strength.

The first issue, that of the relative nature of associative strength, may be introduced by summarizing the results of an experiment reported by Erdelyi, Watts, and Voss (1964). In this study, a modified paired-associate design was employed in which more than one response was associated with the stimulus. Over 120 trials, the probability of S-R_1 was 0.70 for all conditions. The probability of the competing responses was varied. In one condition, S-R_2 had a probability of occurrence of 0.30. In another condition, S-R_2 had a probability of 0.15 and S-R_3 also had a probability of 0.15. The probability of non-R_1 responses was varied in this manner over six conditions, ranging from the S-R_2 probability of 0.30, to a condition in which a different response occurred on each of the 36 non-S-R_1 trials (probability of each response of 0.0083). In addition, there was one condition in which blanks occurred in place of non-S-R_1 responses. The result of interest is that R_1 anticipation frequency was a function of the non-S-R_1 condition. In particular, as the probability of the non-S-R_1 responses decreased from 0.30 to 0.0083, R_1 anticipations increased. It should be noted that the probability of S-R_1 in all conditions was 0.70 and that there were 84 identical presentations of S-R_1.

But what does this experiment indicate about associative strength? First, S-R_1 frequency was constant over all conditions and, hence, R_1 anticipation should have been constant over all conditions. But this result did not occur. Therefore, it is necessary to conclude that performance is a function of the difference of associative strengths of competing responses. This interpretation, which appears to be quite reasonable, raises the point to be made; namely, that it is virtually not possible at present to specify the associative strength of any given association; instead, it appears that associative strength of one response should be considered as greater than that of other responses associated with the same stimulus.

The distinct possibility that the associative strength of a particular association may not be described in isolation has implications for the study of word norms and for the study of paired-associate learning. With respect to word norms, this notion suggests that two specific responses; e.g., R_i and R_i^1, to two respective stimuli, S and S^1, may not be compared with respect to associative strength because the remaining responses of the distributions of S and S^1 are related to the per cent occurrence of the responses. Thus, the strongest response to S may not be compared in strength to the strongest response to S^1 because the associative strength of each of the strongest responses is a function of the associative strengths of the remaining responses of each respective response distribution.

The relevance of this notion to paired-associate learning is that in the acquisition of a particular paired-associate, a correct response may be thought to occur when the associative strength of the association to be learned is relatively greater than the associative strength of the stimulus and any other item associated with the stimulus (Gibson, 1940). This viewpoint, it should be noted, suggests that a correct associative response is related to a difference threshold, rather than to an absolute threshold of associative strength of the particular association.

The second issue involving the concept of associative strength is the question of how shifts in associative strength take place as a function of task conditions. This general problem has recurred during the history of psychology and a few illustrations now are considered. First, the Wurzburg school of investigators formulated this problem in terms of the relation of the Aufgabe or task and the stimulus presentation. Thus, if the stimuli 9 and 3 were presented, which response of the numbers of 12, 6, 27, and 3 that would occur was determined by the task; i.e., add, subtract, multiply, or divide, respectively? An effect that is quite similar has been demonstrated by Howes and Osgood (1954) who showed that the free-association response to a particular stimulus word varied with the words presented contextually with the stimulus word.

Phrased in another way, the issue is related to the question of response selection in a situation in which a stimulus is associated with a response hierarchy. If stimulus conditions are changed, the response may change. Such a modification rather strongly implies that either the associative strengths of stimulus and the respective responses change, or that associative strength must be considered to be a function of contextual stimulus conditions. In either case, the associative strength of a particular association is contingent upon stimulus conditions and, hence, may not be specified as a fixed magnitude.

Thought

In order to discuss how the study of associative learning may contribute to an understanding of thought processes, it is desirable first to consider how associative processes have been related to thought. A series of viewpoints on the relationship of associationism and thought therefore are presented, with the criteria for selection consisting of recency, diversity, and pertinence to the topic of this paper.

Bartlett (1958) has proposed that thinking essentially is a process of filling in gaps which occur between evidence of information. After discussing his view of thinking, Bartlett states, "More briefly thinking can be defined as: The extension of evidence in accord with that evidence so as to fill up gaps in the evidence: and this is done by moving through a succession of interconnected steps which may be stated at the time, or left till later to be stated" (p. 75). Thus, this position states that an outcome may be known or desired and certain information is available, but how the outcome is reached becomes the subject of thought. Moreover, filling in such gaps involves a sequential process of steps in obtaining the final result. It would seem that this view of thinking suggests that associative processes may be involved in filling in the intervening steps, although it should be pointed out that Bartlett stresses not associative processes, but rather direction and organization in thought.

Miller, Galanter, and Pribram (1960), working within a computer analogy, also have stressed the role of organization and direction in thought processes. Although associative development is not treated in the monograph, it is clear that Miller, *et al.* have the view that associations essentially become the servants of the master plan or intention; e.g., "The intention does not 'stamp in' or 'strengthen' the associations —it merely signifies that the person will search for associations he already has" (p. 129). It also may be noted that another book on thought which was written from the information-processing viewpoint treats associative structure as one aspect of list format. In other words, associations or associational representations constitute one type of structure that exists cognitively (Reitman, 1965, p. 55).

Underwood (1952) presented an orientation for research on thinking which was based squarely on the concept of contiguity. He states, "The basic assumption is that in order for relationships among stimuli to be perceived and acquired, responses to those stimuli must be contiguous" (p. 212). Underwood uses a concept-learning example as an illustration of his view of the role of temporal relations, and indicates that more rapid acquisition of a concept should occur if the instances are placed in relatively close rather than distant temporal proximity.

Underwood also points out that perceptual and symbolic stimulus presentation require consideration, and that problem solution may be a function of those stimulus properties which have greater availability in memory. Thus, if an individual is able to recall relevant properties, problem solution may be more readily obtained than if irrelevant properties are recalled. Again, it is implied that the reason for this difference is that recall of relevant properties will permit appropriate responses to occur contiguously with other responses.

How associations develop into higher-ordered structures was the theme of a paper by Mandler (1954). Emphasis was placed by Mandler upon the importance of the overlearning of associations. Such overlearning, Mandler maintained, produces cognitive structures which may be applied to new situations.

Berlyne (1965), in what he describes as a neoassociationistic approach, examined directed thinking and defined it as "thinking whose function is to convey us to solutions of problems" (p. 19). In his book, Berlyne attempted to take into account the work of Piaget and recent findings of Russian investigators. It is quite difficult to attempt to summarize the role of associationism in Berlyne's work because of the extensive nature of his treatment of associative factors. Certain points made by Berlyne, however, will be summarized here. The first involves his discussion of Russian work; remaining points pertain to his own development of theory.

In discussing the work of Sechenov and more recent Russian investigators, Berlyne points out that Sechenov considered thought as essentially a receptor-adjustment mechanism (pp. 110-112). A description of the process is that a stimulus object or situation occurs, followed by a receptor-adjustment response of the organism which yields a representation of a stimulus object or situation for which the response adjustment is a response. It is further pointed out by Berlyne that more recent Russian work suggests that thought involves a mechanism of search similar to that of a receptor-adjustment of the organism searching for something in its external environment.

Berlyne, in his own theoretical development, holds that stimuli and responses may become associated in three ways: they may be inherited, learned, or developed by mediational processes (p. 28).

Berlyne also emphasizes the role of information rejection. Two ways in which information rejection occurs are by attention, in which the organism's state of arousal is involved, and by abstraction, in which the organism selects certain aspects of the stimulus complex (pp. 39-40).

Berlyne stresses a point not previously mentioned in this paper; namely, that motivational processes play a role in associative learning. Berlyne states, "It is now clear that contiguity alone does not guarantee learning; numerous everyday experiences and experiments on remembering attest that we can perceive two events together or in close succession many times without the thought of one of them evoking the thought of the other. . . . Learning requires, in addition, reinforcing agents. Neither the associationist nor the early behaviorist account of thinking tells us how the associations that carry thinking onward are reinforced" (p. 100).

In summary, Berlyne's neoassociationistic position may be interpreted as one attempt to apply the notion of associationism to thought by expanding the concept of associationism to take into account the importance of factors such as motivation and more complex processes. It also may be mentioned that Mowrer (1960) stressed the role of motivation in relation to symbolic behavior.

Associative Learning and Thought

The purpose of this section is to consider how the study of associative learning may be extended and how such development may be applied to the understanding of thought processes. Four issues are considered.

The study of associative networks. As previously mentioned, one area of research receiving considerable attention in recent years is the study of associative networks. Experimentation involving associative networks consists mainly of the description of the inter-relatedness of verbal units and the study of the verbal response hierarchies of individuals.

The study of verbal networks has demonstrated that semantic organization of words does occur and that there is a degree of commonality between individuals with respect to the associative networks. Deese (1965, pp. 10-20) has pointed out that the existence of highly structured verbal networks poses a problem for the classic associationistic position; namely, that associative strength may develop between verbal items even though a number of contiguous occurrences have not apparently occurred. Deese (1965, pp. 163-167) argues that the associative structure determines the associative strength and in this way, structure may be more important to associative strength than contiguity or frequency.

Considering Deese's point and Berlyne's previously mentioned position, it seems reasonable to state that one contemporary point in the development of associations is that mediational and structural factors increase associative strength as the individual learns conceptual relations, language, etc.

Whether or not the development of associations by semantic and conceptual relationships completely eliminates contiguity as a necessary condition for associative development is, of course, open to question. It is quite possible that whenever a verbal item is presented, the related network or networks of items are aroused, so that the representation of the verbal item occurs contiguously with the related networks. Thus, structure may be important to associative growth, but it may be important because the entire structure may be associated by contiguity. Although model construction is beyond the scope of this paper, it should be pointed out that it is conceivable that a model could be developed which is based upon contiguity; i.e., contiguous occurrences of the representations of verbal items which could handle semantic relations.

A second issue of interest is the problem of how verbal networks may be modified experimentally. Response hierarchies have been studied in such a manner by Maltzman (1960) in his study of originality and creativity; by Bilodeau and his associates, (e.g., Bilodeau, Fox, and Blick, 1963); by Bruder (1966); and by Voss (1965). Of interest, is the finding that training on specific associations of a response hierarchy modifies the position of the responses involved in the training, and that the modification persists over time. In addition, one experiment on the stability of hierarchies (Simpson and Voss, 1967) has yielded results which suggest that individuals use a gating type of control (Bruner, 1957) to regulate which will be termed associates of a particular stimulus.

The study of associative networks and verbal hierarchy relations is of particular interest because of the specific and general effects that may be derived. First, if associative structures have particular characteristics which may be described lawfully, such description probably will be relevant to the understanding of cognitive structure in general. Second, if the development of associative structures is understood more fully, it is quite likely that cognitive development will be understood better.

Analysis of associative laws. As previously mentioned, one area of investigation which has received surprisingly little attention is that of the analysis of associative laws. Some implications of such an analysis are now presented.

Assume that a single paired-associate is presented to a subject for a duration of T seconds, where T is some rate commonly used in paired-associate experiments. If the verbal material is of the traditional type; i.e., CVC trigrams or adjectives, the association quite likely will be acquired in one trial. But if the list is composed of several paired-associates, more trials will be required for the subject to acquire the list. The functional relation, moreover, is probably linear, although there has been little research on a wide range of list lengths since Lyon's monograph (1914). The question of interest to the associationistic position is why a greater frequency of presentation is necessary in order to learn as list length increases.

One reply is that the items of the list interfere with each other and, therefore, a number of presentations is necessary in order for the subject to reduce this interference. Moreover, the interference may take three forms. One source of interference is the lack of item discrimination. This form of interference involves the difficulty of discriminating each item of the list as such (Underwood and Schulz, 1960). A second source of interference is that associative strength may develop between a stimulus item and either another stimulus item of the list, or one of the incorrect responses of the list. A third source of interference is the verbal habits the subject brings into the situation (Coleman, 1963; Garskof and Bryan, 1964). Since acquiring a particular association involves overcoming these three sources of interference, it may be asserted that one function of presentation frequency is to reduce interference from these three sources.

This simple interference-reduction interpretation of frequency raises certain questions. First, the results of some experiments on variation in presentation rate suggest that paired-associate acquisition is a function of total presentation time (Bugelski, 1962; Bugelski and Rickwood, 1963; and Johnson, 1964). In these studies, variation in presentation rate produced acquisition differences; however, when a total time measure was employed, rather than trials to criterion, differences between presentation rates were relatively small. These results raise the question of whether the law of frequency cannot be reduced to the law of contiguity by maintaining that acquisition is a function of total contiguous presentation time for a specific association, regardless of how often it is presented.

The issue of frequency may be extended by considering acquisition of a list of paired-associates from an information-processing viewpoint; e.g., Simon and Feigenbaum (1954). Specifically, as length of list increases, the processing load placed upon the subject increases. Moreover, for a specific duration and list length, it may be assumed that the subject is capable of learning only a specific number of associations on any given trial. Thus, an increase in the frequency of presentation may be required simply because of the additional information presented.

The information-processing viewpoint also would suggest that presentation frequency per se should be important to acquisition because a certain small amount of time is probably needed to store the pairs that are learned on each trial, and any greater duration in the presentation of one pair may produce diminishing returns in degree of storage. Thus, there probably is some critical duration for optimal storage, and this duration may vary as a function of certain parameters.

It seems apparent from the considerations of interference and information processing that the problem of why frequency is an important factor in associative learning is simply not well understood.

Knowledge of the role of contiguity in associative learning is considerably less than that of the frequency role. Contiguity as a law has been assumed; contiguity as a phenomenon has not been studied. Certain fundamental questions exist regarding the reasons contiguity is important; e.g., what is the role of difference of onset time and offset time of each item of an association? And is contiguous duration of presentation of an association of primary importance in acquisition? or are the relative onset and/or offset times of the two items of greater importance?

The law of similarity also is not well understood. Moreover, investigation of similarity has the additional problem of definition in that an operational definition of similarity is more difficult to devise than an operational definition of contiguity or frequency.

The point of this discussion of associative laws is this: if associative laws are to be related to the study of higher processes, it is important to understand why such associative laws function. Such knowledge could contribute toward a better understanding of the higher processes.

Elements and integration. One of the most significant concepts developed in associative learning is that the verbal units which the subject associates involve some form of integration. Moreover, when such integration occurs, the association functions as a unit. This idea was noted by Mandler (1954) and by Underwood and Schulz (1960). As already mentioned, Mandler applied the integration concept to the development of structure by indicating that the overlearning of associations may be an important factor in building cognitive structure (Mandler, 1962).

One of the potentially most beneficial ways of extending associationistic theory would be to develop and apply a two-process view of associationism. The first process would involve the association of units, regardless of what the units might be. The study of associative processes in the verbal area traditionally has employed verbal units as the elements of an association. This emphasis, although not erroneous, certainly is limiting. It is not unreasonable to maintain that associations may be developed at virtually any level; i.e., at a concept level or language level and not only CVC trigrams, adjectives, etc. Moreover, "transformational" responses may be associated which permit the individual to change from one symbolic activity to another (Berlyne, 1965).

The second process, which may occur simultaneously with the first, is that any association which develops forms a unit, which may be used as one part of a higher-ordered association. In other words, an association may function as an entity to become associated with other such entities.

The experimental investigation of higher-ordered associative relations is especially complex for two reasons. The first problem, that of taxonomic inadequacy, is that although there may be agreement on what constitutes a letter, a word, and even a concept, the nomenclature of higher-ordered concepts has not been developed. This issue is obviously important because the question of the associative nature of higher processes probably may not be studied until the higher processes are described adequately.

The second problem is that psychology generally has been inadequate in showing how synthesis occurs; e.g., problem solving may be analyzed into component processes, but to indicate how such processes are put together to solve a problem is, in all probability, a more difficult task. It may be mentioned in this connection that the extension of classical conditioning concepts to paired-associate and serial learning produced research, but such concepts did not yield a satisfactory explanation of these two verbal areas. Similarly, the operant-conditioning framework has not generally been adopted by workers in the verbal area.

Despite these difficulties, knowledge of how associations are developed and integrated into functional units may be a help in understanding thought processes. More specifically, it may be hypothesized that the same process or mechanism may underly associative integration at various levels. If so, then it is clear that knowledge of the integration process could increase understanding of how higher-order thought processes develop from lower-order processes, if indeed they do. Stated another way, the problem is to learn more about how letters are integrated into words, words into phrases and sentences, associations into functional units, and two concepts into one unified concept. Thus, if lawful relations of integration are found, such laws may be applicable at virtually all levels.

To avoid misunderstanding, a distinction should be made regarding the role of associative laws in the integration process. The traditional associationistic position has stated that simple ideas combine to produce complex ideas, and that this action takes place by associative principles. The classical criticism of this notion is, of course, the idea that when two elements combine, they make a new whole with properties not derivable from the elements themselves. In this paper, the question is not whether associative laws provide a sufficient explanation for the emergence of the complex from the simple. The point made here is that the integration process per se may be a general process, and how integration takes place may be an important question regardless of the relation of the properties of the simple and the properties of the complex.

Neural factors in associative learning. The investigation of associative learning generally has been pursued at a behavioral level. Moreover, it may be argued that the research in associative learning specifically and verbal learning in general, although not sterile, has not been characterized by the use of new methods and theoretical conceptions derived from other areas of psychology. Recently, however, the area of verbal learning has been upset by two areas of investigation. First, there has been an increasing interest in the study of language per se, rather than in traditional paired-associate and serial domains; second, computer simulation has placed emphasis upon factors internal to the organism as determiners of behavior, rather than the stimulus events per se. There is, however, another force which is making itself felt in the verbal area. This force is physiological psychology; and the point of contact between the verbal area and physiological area is short-term memory. The apparent focus of the physiological study of short-term memory and verbal learning is the description of the properties of the memory trace. For example, Hebb (1949) presented a position of how trace occurrence may affect neurons and how memory may be related to such changes. Furthermore, physiological study of the memory trace has involved a duoprocess view of reverberating circuits and chemical storage (Gerard, 1963; Morrell, 1961). Behaviorally, Broadbent (1958) and Melton (1963) have been concerned about whether a uniprocess or duoprocess trace mechanism best accounts for the results of studies on memory.

That this apparent close relation of physiological and behavioral psychologists may be of a more general interest than only to the area of memory is suggested by the theorizing of Hebb (1949) with respect to learning and perception, and by the work of Peterson (1966) on the relation of short-term memory and learning. Before going too far afield, however, the point to be made is that the outside and inside of the organism have become increasingly close and, in the future, we may readily find more theorizing in the verbal area in terms of neural factors.

It is interesting to speculate regarding implications a neurological orientation may have for the study of associative learning and thought. First, however, it should be noted that it is not advocated that associative learning should be conceptualized or even discussed in neural terms, but rather that two factors make neurological considerations of interest to the investigators of associative learning and verbal behavior: (1) in short-term memory and possibly other areas such as transfer, there is considerable similarity of interest among physiological and behavioral psychologists such that the results of one area may be pertinent to those of the other area; (2) certain conceptions employed in physiological research may be applicable to the theoretical development of associative learning specifically and verbal behavior in general.

Five points are presented regarding the relevance of the study of physiological psychology to the topic of this paper:

1. The view that behavior involves an external stimulus impinging upon a receptor and a muscular or glandular reaction was the classical view of an S-R behavioral psychology. However, it is apparent that the organism selects the stimulus from the various environmental events, and this selection makes "effective stimulus" a more accurate term than stimulus per se; e.g., Guthrie (1959). Indeed, Wickens' (1963) conference summary stresses a non-S-R orientation which points to selective and mediational processes in the organism. In physiological work, there has been interest in the problem of the blocking of afferent impulses by inhibitory mechanisms of higher centers; cf. Thompson's paper, Chap. 2. Thus, an issue of concern to both areas is how certain externally presented stimuli become more effective than others.

The process of stimulus selection raises an interesting question: Does the organism select certain internal stimuli from those events occurring within the organism? In other words, does not the stimulus selection process apply to events within the organism?

The notion of internal stimulus selection is of interest to the study of associative learning. In general, the law of contiguity in a verbal context has referred to the learning by an individual that the occurrence of one external event typically is related to the occurrence of a second external event. However, if it is maintained that representations of the stimuli are associated, it is reasonable to consider the possibility that the representation of one external stimulus event may be associated with the representation of a stored event (Underwood, 1952). Indeed, contiguous occurrence of two representations may take place when neither involves an externally presented stimulus.

The development of associations which were not presented environmentally to the organism has been referred to, of course, as mediation (Jenkins, 1963; Peters, 1935). In this connection, certain recent attempts to analyze mediational effects produced in a three-stage paradigm have consisted of a breakdown into the components of bidirectional associative learning, transfer, and unlearning (Earhard and Mandler, 1965). Moreover, mediational effects may occur when the mediated items occur contiguously; e.g., in an A-B, B-C, A-C paradigm with an A-B, D-C, A-C control condition, mediation effects may occur only if, during Stage 2, A occurs implicitly when C is either presented or stated implicitly (Morning and Voss, 1964). If more research supports this contention, then contiguity as a principle and even a necessary condition for associative acquisition may be maintained for the mediation type of study.

Earhard and Mandler (1965) suggest that strategies are involved in obtaining mediational effects with familiar verbal material, although it is clear that the independent manipulation of strategies to produce mediational effects is far from being demonstrated conclusively. Moreover, if presentation of one item arouses verbal networks, then, once again, contiguity may be important in the development of associations by mediation.

2. Recent work on the orienting response; e.g., Sokolov (1963) and Maltzman and Raskin (1965) suggests that associative learning may be related to the orienting reaction. The nature of the relation is by no means clear, but the physiological components of the orienting reaction suggest that it may be a matter of attention-like properties which permit an individual to concentrate upon particular events and possibly to discriminate relevant properties of the events. Further research is necessary to determine whether attention-like factors, as measured physiologically, are related to associative learning and to higher processes.

3. One issue of relevance to the study of associative learning is the question of item storage. Because of variability in the nature of the stimulus and in the state of the nervous system upon different occurrences of the same stimulus, it is likely that an externally presented stimulus is not stored identically on all presentations. If storage involves spatial factors, the implication is that repeated occurrences of the same item may not be stored in the identical place. This observation implies that in the repeated presentation of an association of two items, *storage does not consist of making a bond stronger and stronger; instead, what is involved is that the various occurrences of an event produce a distribution of representations of that event.* Moreover, in this view, associative strength is not a measure of the bond strength of two items, but rather a measure of probability of selection from numerous coded representations, with each item encoded many times.

What happens when a response is.to be given to an item presented externally? It seems plausible to suggest that the externally presented item arouses a distribution of coded responses which include multiple representations of the familiar item as well as the coded representations of related items. Thus, the response that occurs may be a function of the distribution of various representations aroused by the stimulus, rather than only one response representation. Or, which response occurs may be a function of which particular coded representation is aroused by the stimulus. In either case, response occurrence would be due to the distribution of aroused representations and so related to the probability that the stimulus will arouse different representations. Also, of course, it is possible that other factors are involved such as the spatial distance between the stimulus event representation and the associated events.

4. Consideration of physiological factors also leads to a somewhat different orientation toward associative learning, if not a completely different interpretation of the area. In paired-associate learning, it would seem that even though the individual is presented with a stimulus and says a response, the presentation is essentially sensory or perceptual in nature. In other words, presentation of an association consists of a perceptual event, and acquisition of the association involves sensory-sensory integration.

One implication of considering associative learning as sensory or perceptual in nature is that perceptual factors may be applied more readily in the analysis of associative learning. Stimulus selectivity is one such aspect already discussed. Murdock's work on short-term retention and signal detection (1965) is another example of the application of perceptual factors to learning.

5. It has been pointed out by Broadbent (1958, pp. 4-5) that one concept employed physiologically but seldom used by behavioral psychologists is the notion of reciprocal inhibition. With respect to associative learning, this concept is likely quite relevant and applicable. Two illustrations of the concept are considered.

First, in verbal networks, it is possible that the arousal or excitation of one network is related to a simultaneous inhibition of networks of other items or networks containing some of the same items as the aroused network. Such an hypothesis may be difficult to test, for virtually simultaneous assessment of hierarchies would be required. Nevertheless, the fact that subjects learning a paired-associate list cannot readily give cultural responses to the list stimuli does support the role of an inhibitory mechanism which may work for networks.

Second, in the acquisition of associations, it is by no means known whether the learning takes place by an excitation process, an inhibition process, both, or neither. More specifically, suppose one association of a list of paired-associates is acquired. Within a framework of interference theory, did this acquisition take place by a growth of associative strength between the items of the association? by a reduction in the associative strength of the items of the association and other items? or by simultaneous occurrence of both processes? Some evidence (Voss, 1967) suggests that acquisition of an association reduces the interference produced by the items of the association in the acquisition of other associations of the list. Thus, a reciprocal-inhibition type of principle may be in operation.

Concluding Comments

As mentioned previously, the topics of associationism and thought have been united for quite some time. This is both reinforcing and disconcerting to people studying associative learning. It is reinforcing because individuals trying to describe thought processes have found recourse to associationistic principles necessary; it is disconcerting because the understanding of associative processes has not progressed to a greater degree. Indeed, it is somewhat disheartening to teach a course, "History and Systems" and come to the realization that relatively little advancement has taken place in the conceptualization of associative processes over the history of psychology. The present paper does not provide a remedy to this situation, but it does suggest that we know very little about associationism and associative learning. Moreover, it implies that a better understanding of associative processes may be beneficial to the understanding of thought.

REFERENCES

Berlyne, D. E. *Structure and direction in thinking.* New York: Wiley, 1963.

Bartlett, F. *Thinking.* New York: Basic Books, 1958.

Bilodeau, E. A., Fox, P. W., and Blick, K. A. Stimulated verbal recall and analysis of sources of recall. *J. verb. Learn. verb. Behav.,* 1963, 2, 422-428.

Bousfield, W. A. The occurrence of clustering in the recall of randomly arranged associates. *J. gen. Psychol.,* 1953, 49, 244-250.

Broadbent, D. E. *Perception and communication.* New York: Pergamon Press, 1958.

Bruder, G. A. Shifts in associative hierarchies over time as a function of paired-associate training. *J. verb. Learn. verb. Behav.,* 1968, 7, 413-416.

Bruner, J. On perceptual readiness. *Psychol. Rev.,* 1957, 64, 123-152.

Bugelski, B. R. Presentation time, total time, and mediation in paired associate learning. *J. exp. Psychol.,* 1962, 63, 409-412.

Bugelski, B. R., and Rickwood, J. Presentation time, total time, and mediation in paired-associate learning: self-pacing. *J. exp. Psychol.,* 1963, 65, 616-617.

Coleman, E. B. The association hierarchy as an indication of extraexperimental interference. *J. verb. Learn. verb. Behav.*, 1963, *2*, 417-421.

Deese, J. From the isolated verbal unit to connected discourse. In C. N. Cofer (Ed.), *Verbal Learning and Verbal Behavior*. New York: McGraw-Hill, 1961. Pp. 11-38.

Deese, J. *The structure of associations in language and thought*. Baltimore: Johns Hopkins, 1965.

Dewey, J. The reflex arc concept in psychology. *Psychol. Rev.*, 1896, *3*, 357-370.

Duncker, K. A qualitative study of productive thinking. *Pedag. Sem.*, 1926, *33*, 642-708.

Earhard, B., and Mandler, G. Mediated associations: paradigms, controls, and mechanisms. *Canad. J. Psychol.*, 1965, *19*, 346-378.

Erdelyi, M., Watts, B., and Voss, J. F. Effect of probability of competing responses in probabilistic verbal acquisition. *J. exp. Psychol.*, 1964, *68*, 323-329.

Garskof, B. E., and Bryan, T. M. Paired-associate learning as a function of the number of pre-experimental associative links. *Psychon. Sci.*, 1964, *1*, 163-164.

Gerard, R. W. The material basis of memory. *J. verb. Learn. verb. Behav.*, 1963, *2*, 22-33.

Gibson, E. A systematic application of the concepts of generalization and differentiation to verbal learning. *Psychol. Rev.*, 1940, *47*, 196-229.

Guthrie, E. R. Association by contiguity. In S. Koch (Ed.), *Psychology: A Study of a Science, 2*. New York: McGraw-Hill, 1959. Pp. 158-195.

Haygood, R. C., and Bourne, L. E., Jr. Attribute- and rule-learning aspects of conceptual behavior. *Psychol. Rev.*, 1965, *72*, 175-195.

Hebb, D. O. *The organization of behavior. A neurophysiological theory*. New York: Wiley, 1949.

Howes, D., and Osgood, C. E. On the combination of associative probabilities in linguistic contexts. *Amer. J. Psychol.*, 1954, *67*, 241-258.

Humphrey, G. *Thinking: An introduction to its experimental psychology*. New York: Wiley, 1951.

Hunt, E. B., Marin, J., and Stone, P. J. *Experiments in induction*. New York: Academic Press, 1966.

Jenkins, J. J. Mediated associations: paradigms and situations. In C. N. Cofer, and B. S. Musgrave (Eds.), New York: McGraw-Hill, 1963. Pp. 210-245.

Johnson, N. F. The functional relationship between amount learned and frequency versus rate versus total time of exposure of verbal materials. *J. verb. Learn. verb. Behav.*, 1964, *3*, 502-504.

Kohler, W. *Gestalt Psychology.* New York: Liveright, 1947.

Lyon, D. O. The relation of length of material to time taken for learning and the optimum distribution of time. *J. educ. Psychol.*, 1914, *5*, 1-9; 85-91; 155-163.

Maltzman, I. On the training of originality. *Psychol. Rev.*, 1960, *67*, 229-242.

Maltzman, I., and Raskin, D. C. Effects of individual differences in the orienting reflex on conditioning and complex processes. *J. exp. Res., Personal.*, 1965, *1*, 1-16.

Mandler, G. Response factors in human learning. *Psychol. Rev.*, 1954, *61*, 235-244.

Mandler, G. From association to structure. *Psychol. Rev.*, 1962, *69*, 415-427.

Mandler, J. M., and Mandler, G. *Thinking: from association to Gestalt.* New York: Wiley, 1964.

Melton, A. W. Learning. In W. S. Munroe (Ed.), *Encyclopedia of Educational Research.* New York: MacMillan, 1950. Pp. 668-690.

Miller, G. A., Galanter, E., and Pribram, K. H. *Plans and the structure of behavior.* New York: Holt, 1960.

Morning, N., and Voss, J. F. Mediation of R_1-R_2 in the acquisition of S-R_1, S-R_2 associations. *J. exp. Psychol.*, 1964, *67*, 67-71.

Morrell, F. Electrophysiological contributions to the neural bases of learning. *Physiol. Rev.*, 1961, *41*, 443-494.

Mowrer, O. H. *Learning theory and the symbolic process.* New York: Wiley, 1960.

Murdock, B. B., Jr. Signal-detection theory and short-term memory. *J. exp. Psychol.*, 1965, *70*, 443-447.

Osgood, C. E. On understanding and creating sentences. *Amer. Psychol.*, 1963, *18*, 735-751.

Peters, H. N. Mediate association. *J. exp. Psychol.*, 1935, *18*, 19-48.

Peterson, L. R. Short-term verbal memory and learning. *Psychol. Rev.*, 1966, *73*, 193-207.

Reitman, W. R. *Cognition and thought.* New York: Wiley, 1965.

Simon, H. A., and Feigenbaum, E. A. An information-processing theory of some effects of similarity, familiarization, and meaningfulness in verbal learning. *J. verb. Learn. verb. Behav.*, 1964, *3*, 385-396.

Simpson, P., and Voss, J. F. The stability of response hierarchies. *J. exp. Psychol.*, 1967, *75*, 170-174.

Sokolov, Y. N. *Perception and the conditioned reflex.* New York: Mac-Millan, 1963.

Tulving, E. Subjective organization in free recall of "unrelated" words. *Psychol. Rev.*, 1962, *69*, 344-354.

Underwood, B. J., and Schulz, R. W. *Meaningfulness and verbal learning.* New York: Lippincott, 1960.

Underwood, B. J. An orientation for research in thinking. *Psychol. Rev.*, 1952, *59*, 209-220.

Underwood, B. J. Stimulus selection in verbal learning. In C. N. Cofer, and B. S. Musgrave (Eds.), *Verbal behavior and learning.* New York: McGraw-Hill, 1963. Pp. 197-216.

Voss, J. F. Shifts in associative hierarchies as a function of associative training. *J. verb. Learn. verb. Behav.*, 1968, *7*, 417-420.

Voss, J. F. Intralist similarity in associative learning. *J. verb. Learn. verb. Behav.*, 1967, *6*, 773-779.

Wertheimer, M. *Productive thinking.* New York: Harper, 1945.

Wickens, D. D. Conference summary. In C. N. Cofer and B. S. Musgrave (Eds.), *Verbal behavior and learning.* New York: McGraw-Hill, 1963. Pp. 374-382.

THINKING AND THE EMPIRICAL STUDY OF ASSOCIATIONS

GEOFFREY KEPPEL

University of California, Berkeley

In his paper, Professor Voss examined the area of associative learning, pointed to some of the theoretical problems which have plagued those who have worried about associative learning, and proposed certain topics of concern which may be relevant to the study of thinking. At the outset, I would like to suggest that the area of associative learning potentially offers methods and procedures which may prove to be extremely useful to the researcher in thinking. Voss seems to have singled out the study of "raw" associative learning, by which I mean the study of the learning of associations from scratch. He indicates that little is known concerning the conditions necessary for this learning or the processes involved in the completion of this learning. He has also identified associative learning with the paired-associate procedure. I feel that such an exclusive identification is not warranted. If it is agreed that the province of verbal learning is the study of the acquisition, maintenance, and utilization of verbal associations, then the study of these habits or associations cannot be limited to a particular method or task. It is true that the paired-associate task has been favored in recent years, but this has been due to the analytical power that it has provided in the study of verbal learning. For example, it is known that meaningfulness and intralist similarity, two variables which greatly influence verbal learning, produce different results when they are manipulated on either the stimulus or response side of a paired-associate list. However, it is also true that investigators have adopted old tasks or invented new ones in order to achieve a greater precision in the estimation of what has been learned. For instance, the method of free recall has been used as a means for assessing the degree of response availability following various numbers of paired-associate trials (cf. Underwood, Runquist, and Schulz, 1959). Similarly, the associative-matching test (e.g., Horowitz, 1962) has been employed to estimate the level of associative learning attained.

With this in mind, I propose to mention several areas of research in verbal learning, in addition to those indicated in Voss's paper, which show some promise of contributing to the investigation of higher mental processes. The first of these might be labeled transformational or coding processes. These terms refer to the study of situations in which the subject may be able to change, transform, or code the original input during acquisition. To the extent that the broad range of behavior which is considered the domain of thinking involves such transformational processes, these studies may be of great relevance. Stimulus selection, which was discussed in Voss's paper, is one of these areas of research. Research in this particular field has indicated that there is a rather high agreement across subjects in the selection of stimulus elements based upon differences in meaningfulness and ordinal position, for example. On the other hand, there is little evidence that such selection is actually beneficial to the subject in paired-associate learning. Furthermore, Postman and Greenbloom (1967) suggest that stimulus selection in a paired-associate experiment where the stimulus term might be a nonsense syllable is not overwhelming and is restricted to the first element of the nonsense syllable. While stimulus selection may not turn out to be an important transformational process affecting rate of associative learning, it is true, as Underwood (1966) has noted, that the study of concept learning is essentially the study of stimulus selection; i.e., it is in the very nature of the concept-learning task that the subject must abstract certain elements from the array of stimuli in order to solve the problem.

A second transformational process which has received some attention in verbal learning is the investigation of the coding of individual response terms. The Underwood-Erlebacher (1965) study is an example of this research. Their approach consisted of the presentation of anagrams in free-recall and paired-associate learning. It was assumed that the anagrams could be easily encoded into their solution words; e.g., BSU into SUB or BUS, but that difficulty would arise in the decoding process; i.e., when the subject must go from the encoded unit, SUB, say, back to the original anagram structure, BSU. This would be especially true when the anagram served as a response term in a paired-associate list. Underwood and Erlebacher attempted to facilitate the decoding process through the use of a consistent decoding rule and this was largely successful, although there was the question of whether this type of coding actually facilitated learning. Additional experiments in this monograph were concerned with stimulus coding in paired-associate learning. These experiments showed that such coding can facilitate learning, but that this facilitation is not great and is dependent upon the use of a relatively simple coding system. Another example of the study of coding processes is the work of Lindley (e.g., 1963) in which encoding and decoding cues were made available during the presentation and testing of single trigrams over short periods of time. The importance of these studies for the present discussion is in the demonstration that experimenter-defined coding systems can be studied and can be shown to influence rate of learning.

Associative coding is another area of research which may be applicable to the study of thinking. One approach is represented by the work of Tulving in free-recall learning (cf. Tulving, 1962). Here the interest is in the structure which the subject imposes upon a set of supposedly "unrelated" words. With paired associates, several techniques have been employed. One approach has consisted of the collection from subjects of reports of associative aids which were presumably used during learning. The Bugelski (1962) study is a good example of this. Martin, Boersma, and Cox (1965) have refined this procedure by developing a rating scale, which represents a wide range of complexity, for the classification of the reported mnemonic aids and have reported high reliability with this scale. The work of Jensen and Rohwer at Berkeley, on the other hand, involves a different approach to the study of associative coding. In their experiments, Jensen and Rohwer (e.g., 1965) asked subjects of varying ages to make up sentences containing the to-be-learned pairs and found that subsequent paired-associate learning was greatly facilitated by this treatment. Interestingly, they also found that serial learning was essentially unaffected. In a later study, Rowher (1966) this time *provided* the subjects with the sentences containing the paired associates. Such a pre-exposure, relative to the usual initial study trial, also produced a sizable increase in paired-associate learning. While it is not clear whether this facilitation results from the subject's use of the specific "coding" sentences during learning, or whether it is due to the demonstration to the subject of the notion of associative aids, these experiments do offer an interesting attempt to study the way in which associations may be formed or coded.

In his paper, Voss indicated that a broader definition of associative learning ". . . also would include the study of associative retention and transfer effects." However, he does not consider any further relevance

of these topics to the study of thinking except in his discussion of associative networks. In my opinion, this is a serious omission. In the design
of a typical experiment in thinking, it has generally been assumed that
the subject has available the individual elements which are necessary
to solve the problem. That is, attention is directed primarily to discovery and recombinational processes. If this is the case, these types of
problems really involve a consideration of the retention and transfer
of what has been previously learned, rather than a concern for the
processes involved in the initial acquisition of these elements. In his
discussion of research on thinking, Underwood (1952) indicated the
important role of memory in the production of stimulus contiguity.
(This point was also made by Voss in a later section of his paper.)
Certainly, variables such as instance contiguity in concept formation,
massed and distributed practice, and delay of informative feedback
are all relevant to a consideration of the extent to which memory is a
basic ingredient in the study of thinking. (A valuable review of this
research has been reported by Dominowski, 1965.)

Equally important, however, is a consideration of the role of transfer in research on thinking. The question of the relevance of transfer
to the study of problem-solving behavior has been discussed by Schulz
(1960). In this paper, Schulz illustrated how various problem-solving
tasks can be viewed as instances of the A-B, A-C transfer paradigm.
On the basis of research in this area of verbal learning, he suggested
further research which might be conducted to test the fruitfulness of
this analysis. In this regard, there is, of course, an extensive literature
on transfer as a function of stimulus and response similarity. This research has been reviewed recently by Martin (1965). There are the
equally obvious studies of mediation which also should have direct
relevance for the study of thinking. Another example of the role of
transfer in thinking is the research concerned with the pre-availability
of critical elements in the solution of certain problem-solving experiments; e.g., the Maier two-string problem. The argument which has
been offered is that the critical elements; e.g., rope-swing-pendulum,
are not available to the subject, but are potentially available. Duncan
(1961), for instance, attempted to raise the availability of these elements by means of an association procedure in which the subject listed
original and unique uses for various objects. Judson, Cofer, and Gelfand (1956) manipulated the pre-availability by providing their subjects with serial lists containing the presumably key words necessary for
solution.

I would like to comment upon some specific points concerning associative learning which Voss considered in his paper. As he indicated,

the classical notion of paired-associate learning which was conceived of in global S-R terms has been rejected. In this context, the experiments demonstrating stimulus selection have already been mentioned. I would like to mention some other developments. The question of bidirectional associations is a current problem. First, there is the issue of whether or not the strengths of the two associations are equal. This is still being debated. But whatever the outcome, the question remains as to the conceptualization of this bidirectionality; e.g., should the conceptualization be in terms of a single association with bidirectional properties? or should it be in terms of two independent associations? In addition to the issue concerning the status of forward and backward associations, there is the contextual association. This refers to an association between nonspecific situational cues and verbal responses which has been especially useful in the study of retroactive inhibition. On the other hand, little is known about its characteristics, properties, or necessary functioning in paired-associate learning.

A second major point is my disagreement with Voss concerning the "thinness" of research concerned with the question of what has been learned in paired-associate learning. Let me give some examples: (a) In the study of response learning, the free-recall test, which is used as an estimate of response availability, has been administered following various numbers of paired-associate trials under conditions of high and low response-term meaningful similarity (Underwood, Runquist, and Schulz, 1959), and high and low response-term meaningfulness and formal similarity (Jung, 1965). We have been experimenting with an anagram-like test in which the subject is presented the sets of letters used in constructing each response term and asked to produce the correct letter order. This procedure has the advantage of providing an assessment of specific response integration which is independent of the learning of the specific elements. (b) In the study of associative learning, many investigators have used an associative-matching test. This procedure is assumed to reduce differences among conditions which might have been attributed to response learning in the usual paired-associate experiment. There have also been attempts to look at the joint operation of response and associative learning during paired-associate learning. Jung (1965), for example, has obtained recall and matching scores from the same subjects, which allows a determination of the status of the two stages of learning from the four possible outcomes of the two tests. Using a different technique, Schwenn (1966) has been able to accurately predict the effect of response-term similarity upon the learning of a paired-associate list from the independent estimates of the facilitative effect of this variable upon free-recall learning and the inhibitory effect of the variable upon associative learning. (c) Finally, there is a small body of research employing the verbal-discrimination task as a prior condition to subsequent paired-associate learning (cf. Spear, Ekstrand, and Underwood, 1964). In verbal discrimination, the subject is generally presented two verbal units, one of which is indicated as correct. The issue in these studies is whether any association develops between the two units which have been presented together during training. Essentially, this procedure represents a test of incidental associative learning since subjects do not report any attempts at learning a connection between the two elements of a verbal-discrimination pair (Keppel, 1966). The evidence indicates that such associative learning does occur, and that it is greater for word pairs than for pairs of nonsense syllables.

In summary, I have tried to supplement Voss's treatment of this topic by indicating various areas of investigation in verbal learning in general, and paired-associate learning in particular, which seem to have some relevance for the study of thinking. Whether these approaches will prove fruitful, obviously, remains to be seen. In the meantime, I agree with Voss that we are in need of research directed at the determination of associative laws and the establishment of the conditions which are necessary for associative learning to occur.

REFERENCES

Bugelski, B. R. Presentation time, total time, and mediation in paired-associate learning. *J. exp. Psychol.*, 1962, *63*, 409-412.

Dominowski, R. L. Role of memory in concept learning. *Psychol. Bull.*, 1965, *63*, 271-280.

Duncan, C. P. Attempts to influence performance on an insight problem. *Psychol. Rep.*, 1961, *9*, 35-42.

Horowitz, L. M. Associative matching and intralist similarity. *Psychol. Rep.*, 1962, *10*, 751-757.

Jensen, A. R., and Rohwer, W. D., Jr. Syntactical mediation of serial and paired-associate learning as a function of age. *Child Developm.*, 1965, *36*, 601-608.

Judson, A. J., Cofer, C. N., and Gelfand, S. Reasoning as an associative process: II. "Direction" in problem solving as a function of prior reinforcement of relevant responses. *Psychol. Rep.*, 1956, *2*, 501-507.

Jung, J. Two stages of paired-associate learning as a function of intra-list-response similarity (IRS) and response meaningfulness (M). *J. exp. Psychol.*, 1965, *70*, 371-378.

Keppel, G. Association by contiguity: Role of response availability. *J. exp. Psychol.*, 1966, *71*, 624-628.

Lindley, R. H. Effects of controlled coding cues in short-term memory. *J. exp. Psychol.*, 1963, *66*, 580-587.

Martin, C. J., Boersma, F. J., and Cox, D. L. A classification of associative strategies in paired-associate learning. *Psychon. Sci.*, 1965, *3*, 455-456.

Martin, D. Transfer of verbal paired associates. *Psychol. Rev.*, 1965, *72*, 327-343.

Postman, L., and Greenbloom, R. Conditions of cue selection in the acquisition of paired-associate lists. *J. exp. Psychol.*, 1967, *73*, 91-100.

Rohwer, W. D., Jr. Constraint, syntax and meaning in paired-associate learning. *J. verb. Learn. verb. Behav.*, 1966, *5*, 541-547.

Schulz, R. W. Problem solving behavior and transfer. *Harvard educ. Rev.*, 1960, *30*, 61-77.

Schwenn, E. The role of intralist meaningful similarity in paired-associate learning: A component analysis. Unpublished masters thesis, Northwestern University, 1966.

Spear, N. E., Ekstrand, B. R., and Underwood, B. J. Association by contiguity. *J. exp. Psychol.*, 1964, *67*, 151-161.

Tulving, E. Subjective organization in free recall of "unrelated" words. *Psychol. Rev.*, 1962, *69*, 344-354.

Underwood, B. J. An orientation for research on thinking. *Psychol. Rev.*, 1952, *59*, 209-220.

Underwood, B. J. Some relationships between concept learning and verbal learning. In H. J. Klausmeier and C. W. Harris (Eds.), *Analyses of concept learning*. New York: Academic Press, 1966. Pp. 51-63.

Underwood, B. J., and Erlebacher, A. H. Studies of coding in verbal learning. *Psychol. Monogr.*, 1965, *79*, No. 13.

Underwood, B. J., Runquist, W. N., and Schulz, R. W. Response learning in paired-associate lists as a function of intralist similarity. *J. exp. Psychol.*, 1959, *58*, 70-78.

GENERAL DISCUSSION

KANFER asked whether interference is a function of the intra-item characteristics of the units to be learned.

VOSS replied that interference may exist within the unit, and one problem in the study of unit integration is to isolate such factors.

UHR pointed out that problems such as those related to functional stimuli and matching could be handled by the computer because of the necessity of defining the stimulus and the structure of it.

ANDERSON asked how such a view would handle the type of data which would relate paired-associate acquisition to sentence structure.

UHR replied that programs currently exist which can build up strokes into letters, letters into words, and words into phrases. Moreover, he added, computer models with various match rules may be developed which take into account similarity factors in stimulus matching. UHR added that computer programs are available which are modeled along S-R constructs.

It was observed that studies which manipulate contextual aspects of the stimulus and studies which manipulate formal properties of the stimulus recognize the problem of stimulus variability, and that this problem is essentially empirical.

SIMON mentioned that information-processing models also include S-R units; therefore, the S-R approach versus the information-processing approach per se is not a substantive issue.

ANDERSON commented that computer models as a term should be outlawed because a "computer" model cannot do anything that a person could not do with a pad and pencil if he is assiduous. In other words, the logical nature of the program has nothing to do with the computer.

112

4

SEQUENTIAL LEARNING AND THOUGHT: AN OVERLOOKED COMMUNALITY [1]

WILLIAM F. BATTIG
University of Colorado

Of all the topics that are related to thought in this text, it is doubtful that any involves a greater resistance to the invocation of complex thought processes than research on sequential learning. Yet, there are several senses in which the typical sequential-learning task potentially represents an exceptionally promising device for the assessment and evaluation of human thought processes. We shall attempt here the two-fold task of: a) discussion of the ways in which sequential-learning research has proceeded in directions incompatible with the study of thought processes, along with some of the reasons underlying this divergence, and b) presentation and defense of the counterproposition that sequential learning has a great deal to offer to the study and understanding of basic types of thought processes. Both positions receive convincing support from recent developments deriving from research on "what is learned in serial learning," since results in this area apparently do not lend themselves to interpretation unless thought processes

---

[1] The preparation of this paper, along with some of the research reported herein, was supported in part by Public Health Service Research Grant HD-01062 from the National Institute of Child Health and Human Development.

are invoked which are far more complex than simple associations of individual items.

Before attempting to document this alleged close relationship between sequential learning and thought processes, it will be necessary to deal briefly with some definitional matters so that at least there will be some clarity as to what is meant in this paper by "sequential learning" and "thought."

There appears to be no explicit operational or conceptual delineation of the term "sequential learning" that differs in any substantial way from the more common term "serial learning" in the psychological literature. Nonetheless, our recent research on what we have called serial learning has indicated quite clearly that serial learning encompasses a wide range of phenomena of major psychological importance. Much of this, unfortunately, has been ignored because of the methodological and theoretical strictures imposed by the limited set of procedures and underlying assumptions currently governing serial-learning research. These limitations have become so strong that they are viewed in many influential quarters as basic standards that no serious investigator of serial learning dare violate. In the hope that it may help to free us from these arbitrary restrictions, the term "sequential learning" will be used here in a somewhat broader sense to refer to any learning task in which more than two elements, units, or items must be learned, and in which the order of occurrence of these elements is part of what is learned. Such a definition, it should be noted, is sufficiently broad to incorporate not only everything that previously has been identified as serial learning, but also to cover such other types of learning tasks as probability learning involving conditional dependencies and certain types of sequential learning taking place in our natural language.

As for "thinking" or "thought," we need not become involved in another detailed discussion of the complexities and ambiguities associated with such concepts, but instead, we can simply refer to a previous provisional definition of thought as activity which is characterized by (1) complexity, (2) occurrence largely at an unobservable or symbolic level, and (3) some degree of systematic organization or structure (Bourne and Battig, 1966).

The Role of Sequential Learning in Thought

One of the few hallmarks of consistency that characterizes virtually all attempts to study and understand human thought has been the recognition that thinking proceeds through several steps or stages that follow one another in an orderly sequential fashion. Thus, for example, creative thought has been described as a sequential four-stage process proceeding from preparation through incubation and illumination to verification (Wallas, 1926), whereas thought in general has been conceptualized as proceeding sequentially from conceptual behavior through problem solving to decision making (Bourne and Battig, 1966). The evidence for sequential progress through several steps or stages becomes even more compelling when one looks analytically at a single type of thought process or a typical task used to study thinking. The behavior involved in successful completion of a thought process, as well as the several preceding attempts at problem-solving behavior that are unsuccessful, can readily be seen to exhibit this predominantly sequential multi-stage character. Moreover, sequential orderliness and consistency with which successive steps follow and depend upon one another represent the main distinguishing characteristics of the efficient concept learner or problem solver. In fact, the development of tasks which permit observation and measurement of behavior at each of the several stages intervening between inception and termination of thinking activity has been judged as one of the most important methodological requirements for the effective study of complex thought processes (Bourne and Battig, 1966).

There is, however, at least one fundamental property of the type of sequential behavior involved in the typical conceptual or problem-solving task that differs considerably from the type of serial-learning task typically employed to study sequential learning. Such tasks usually involve a fixed and unmodifiable set of elements which are arranged in a sequential order that is arbitrary and explicitly avoids any pattern or relationship characterizing elements adjacent to one another. In thought, on the other hand, there is a meaningful pattern to the sequence, such that the preceding element(s) along with the response(s) and outcome(s) associated therewith represent key determinants of what comes next in the sequence. Of course, the use of sequential patterns based upon varying conditional relationships is not unknown in serial-learning research, as illustrated by the work of George Miller and his associates (Miller and Selfridge, 1950) and the sequential probabilistic learning task developed by Voss (1966). While these investigators have been cognizant of the relevance of their techniques to the investigation of thought processes, their actual use of the techniques has been limited primarily to other problems of interest. Moreover, the sequential relationships involved in their work encompass the same kind of arbitrariness that has predominated in other serial-learning tasks.

Except for the studies noted above, along with studies of the role of meaningfulness in serial learning (e.g., Noble, 1952), and some recent investigations wherein the sequential arrangement of items has involved a systematic variation in the degree to which this corresponds with population associative norms or grammatical relationships (e.g., Bernstein, 1964; Bourne and Parker, 1964; Diethorn and Voss, 1967; Epstein, 1961, 1962; Horowitz and Izawa, 1963), the sequential-learning literature has been virtually devoid of investigations involving the meaningful conditional relationships that are predominant in sequential thought processes. However, the markedly different shapes of the serial-position curves for their meaningful English sentences, as contrasted with unrelated serial lists, led Mandler and Mandler (1964) to conclude that entirely different learning and/or memory processes may be involved under the two sets of conditions. At least as much that is germane to the type of conditionality involved in sequential thinking has derived from probability-learning studies involving systematic manipulations of adjacent and/or higher-order sequential probabilities (e.g., Anderson 1960), and their demonstration of such undoubtedly thought-related phenomena as the "gambler's fallacy" (Jarvik, 1951).

To summarize this section, the importance of sequential processes in thought appears indisputable. However, the direct formation of new and arbitrary associations involving a series of elements that allegedly occurs in the typical serial-learning task may have little in common with the sequential learning involved in thought, wherein each element in the sequence appears to serve the function of guiding or determining what comes next. The extent to which fundamentally different processes may be involved can only be determined through systematic comparisons between tasks which vary systematically along the dimension ranging from the completely arbitrary, "rote" sequential arrangements that characterize serial-learning tasks on the one hand, to completely meaningful patterns or relationships on the other.

The Role of Thought in Sequential Learning

Although we may well be in the midst of a revolution in research on sequential learning, the outcome of which will be to place greater emphasis upon its complexity and extensive involvement of thought processes, it will doubtless be many years before the current strong resistance is completely dispelled to the replacement of the currently predominant view of sequential learning as blind, rote associations by a more thought-oriented conceptualization. In any event, an examination of the foundations of the current "anti-thought" view of serial learning may be most illuminating.

As with practically all modern rote-learning research, the current de-emphasis on covert thought processes may be traced back to Ebbinghaus (1913). There is little in Ebbinghaus' writings, however, to suggest that he had any intention of minimizing the role of thought in sequential learning. Rather, he considered his studies of serial learning to represent a means by which thought processes could be brought into the laboratory, controlled, and measured objectively. This original intent somehow got sidetracked by experimenters in serial learning who followed Ebbinghaus and who are primarily responsible for the current de-emphasis on thought processes. The explicit reasons, if any, for this gradual separation of thought from sequential learning have never been specified, and this may well have been quite unintentional. The major milestones in this development (e.g., Hull *et al.*, 1940; McGeoch and Irion, 1951), however, suggest that the behavioristic acceptance of the conditioned reflex as the learned element out of which all complex learning is constituted, along with a shift of research emphasis away from humans toward presumably non-thinking lower animals, may have been the most influential contributors toward the development of a "thoughtless" conceptualization of the serial-learning task.

In any event, the typical serial-learning experiment has been conducted under conditions which maximally discourage either the occurrence of thinking by the subject or its detection by the experimenter. Instructions given prior to serial-learning experiments often have gone so far as to try to prevent subjects from thinking, as evidenced by the following quotation from the instructions used in the Yale laboratory (Hovland, 1938):

> Please do not try to think ahead more than one step at a time, or to count, or make up fanciful connections between the syllables to assist the learning process. Don't try to use any special system in your learning, simply associate each syllable with the next one as the series moves along.

Fortunately, there is evidence that such experimenter-imposed restrictions against thinking subjects are becoming less characteristic of serial-learning instructions (e.g., Runquist, 1966).

But, irrespective of the instructions that he is given, any subject possessing any inclination to employ thought processes while learning a serial list would probably find this to be exceedingly difficult under the serial-anticipation procedure and two-second presentation rate provided by the "standard" conditions. This means that during each two-second presentation of a given item, the subject must simultaneously be trying to perform at least the three functions of (1) anticipating the next item in the list, (2) comparing the currently presented item with the one he anticipated during the presentation of the preceding item, and (3) trying to learn the presented item. Under this confusing combination of simultaneous performance, informative feedback, and learning functions, it should come as no surprise that our typical serial-learning subject would exhibit little if any evidence of thinking. And should he stop responding for a trial or two in order to contemplate and try to figure out some "strategy" for coping with this confusing situation, this is likely to evoke the ire of the experimenter and, perhaps, even lead to his elimination from the experiment due to failure to follow instructions.

In defense of the serial-learning researcher, it should be emphasized that he may have quite legitimate reasons for viewing thought as something to be eliminated and prevented from contaminating the phenomena under investigation, rather than as deserving of investigation in its own right. There are, however, more compelling reasons for objecting to the standard serial-anticipation procedure, inasmuch as it has also been shown to be insufficiently sensitive to the effects on serial learning of manipulated independent variables, as well as productive of slower and less efficient learning than other serial-learning procedures. Battig and Lawrence (1967) report that a *serial-recall* procedure, wherein the subject simply studies the list of items during their actual presentation and subsequently tries to recall the items in order during a series of successive blank intervals that immediately follows list presentation, produces (1) significantly faster serial learning, (2) three times the magnitude of between-groups variance, and (3) one-third as much error variance, as compared with the standard serial-anticipation procedure. The latter two differences from the anticipation procedure are clearly indicative of the greater sensitivity of the serial-recall procedure to the effects of the manipulated independent variables of constant versus varied starting points in the same sequential order from trial to trial, and interlist relationships involving a mirror-image reversal versus a scrambling of the second-list order from that of the first list. Epstein (1962) reported a similar insensitivity of the standard serial-anticipation procedure to the effects of variations of apparent syntactic structure of nonsense materials, as compared with a serial-recall technique involving simultaneous presentation of whole lists varying in syntactic structure. Epstein's interpretation of this greater sensitivity, however, was based upon the whole presentation of the list rather than the recall requirement.

Subsequent experiments using this serial-recall technique have shown that the method permits the simultaneous learning of two or more non-overlapping serial lists or of two different serial orders of the same list (e.g., Battig, 1966b). We have not yet made any direct attempt to investigate the amenability of the serial-recall technique to the operation of thought processes. However, the ways in which serial-recall has been shown to differ from serial-anticipation are entirely consistent with and may turn out to be explicable in terms of the separation of the serial-recall trial into temporally separated learning- and performance-measurement phases, thereby making it possible for the subject to think effectively during serial learning.

This is not to say that the serial-anticipation procedure does not involve thought processes. In fact, it is not at all unlikely that the story here may turn out to be very similar to that described elsewhere (Battig, 1966a) for our research in paired-associate learning processes, wherein we have found it manifestly impossible to prevent subjects from the extensive invocation of a variety of complex coding and conceptual processes, no matter what special precautions are taken to prevent their operation. An examination of some of the recent developments in the still active controversy over "what is learned in serial learning" yields a considerable amount of evidence that can best be interpreted as offering indirect support for the position that thought processes may constitute a significant contribution (perhaps even the major contribution) to whatever is learned under the serial-anticipation procedure. This evidence is necessarily indirect, because the controversy to date has been focused on but three alternative possibilities referred to as (1) *sequential associations* of each item with its immediately preceding and following item, (2) *position associations* between each item and the numerical or temporal representation of its serial position within the list, and (3) *multiple-item sequential association*, whereby each item becomes associated with a cluster of two or more preceding items in the list.

The multitude of experiments over the past few years, intended to decide between these alternative serial-learning processes, have been characterized primarily by inconclusive and sometimes inconsistent results, of which summaries, fortunately, are available elsewhere (Jensen and Rohwer, 1965; Young, 1968). Suffice it to say that the evidence that exists for each of the three alternatives has consisted largely of evidence negative for one or more of its competitors, and that current interpretations have come to involve dual or multiprocess accounts including more than one of the alternatives (Young, 1968), or else some fourth alternative incompatible with any of the aforementioned three (e.g., Jensen and Rohwer, 1965). For purposes of the present discussion, the above version of the multiple-item sequential association process can be ignored, since its initial formulation (Horowitz and Izawa, 1963; Young, 1962) renders most of what is said about sequential associations equally relevant thereto, and the only empirical evidence supporting it (Horowitz and Izawa, 1963) cannot be replicated (Young and Casey, 1964). Thus, the present analysis will be limited to three of the more prominent types of comparisons (serial to paired-associate transfer, transfer between two serial lists, and comparisons of ends and middle of serial lists) intended to put the sequential versus position associations controversy to a definitive empirical test. The conclusion that these comparisons are indicative of the extensive involvement of complex thought processes in sequential learning, it should be noted, is not among the interpretations offered by previous investigators for the puzzling results that currently pervade the serial-learning literature.

Serial to paired-associate transfer. To begin with, there is the extensive research begun by Primoff (1938) and revived by Young (1959) showing little, if any, facilitation of paired-associate learning of pairs of items which were adjacent in a previously learned serial list, whereas there is some facilitation of subsequent serial learning if adjacent items in the serial list had constituted previously learned paired-associate pairs. Young's original interpretation had been that serial learning involved primarily associations of each item with its serial position (position associations) rather than with preceding and following items in the serial list (sequential associations). This interpretation, however, has subsequently been seriously questioned by failures to find substantial facilitation of subsequent paired-associate pairs consisting of items from the serial list paired with numerical representations of their positions in the previous serial list (e.g., Jensen and Rohwer, 1965; Young, Hakes, and Hicks, 1967). Thus, one current view is that there is little commonality between the learning processes typically involved in serial and in paired-associate learning (Jensen and Rohwer, 1965). Consequently, according to the prevalent assumption that paired-associate learning represents the epitomy of rote associations between the two items constituting a given pair, it would have to follow that such associations play little if any role in sequential learning as it develops in the serial anticipation task.

There are, of course, other ways of interpreting these serial to paired-associate transfer results. Our previous arguments for the predominant role of thought processes in paired-associate learning (Battig, 1966a) might even be invoked as support for the opposite conclusion; i.e., that paired-associate and serial learning differ primarily in that the former does involve complex thought processes whereas serial learning does not. At least as plausible, however, would be the position that both paired-associate and serial learning involve extensive thought processes, but that these differ considerably across the two types of tasks. Of course, the limited amount and asymmetry of transfer between serial and paired-associate learning may indicate merely that any processes common to both types of tasks become obscured by the major instructional and procedural differences that exist between them. Supportive of such an interpretation are recent findings indicating a considerable increment in serial to paired-associate facilitation if the subjects have been explicitly instructed prior to the paired-associate task that its pairs consist of adjacent items from the previous serial list (e.g., Jensen, 1962; Postman and Stark, 1967; Shuell and Keppel, 1967). Such instructional effects could equally well be interpreted as demonstrating the invocation of complex relational thought processes that may have developed either during or following the conclusion of serial learning. In any event, the very fact that appropriate instructions can facilitate transfer of previously learned serial associations between adjacent items to a subsequent paired-associate list, inevitably leads to the conclusion that something beyond simple rote associations is involved, taking the form of complex symbolic representations amenable to modification of manipulation by instructions.

Transfer between two serial lists. Partly because the serial to paired-associate transfer experiments described above have suggested fundamental differences between serial and paired-associate tasks as to the type of learning and/or thought processes involved, a preference is developing for transfer comparisons involving exclusively serial lists which are systematically related to one another. However, substantial interlist facilitation has been shown thus far only under conditions where the second list maintains the same serial order as the first list, but involves a different starting point such that each item's absolute serial position is changed. This result has been interpreted as powerful evidence for sequential and against position associations (Rehula, 1960). Somewhat paradoxically, among the strongest evidence *for* position associations has been the demonstration of poorer performance under conditions of a trial-by-trial variation in the starting point within a single serial list than when this starting point is the same on all trials (e.g., Ebenholtz, 1963). This illustration of the vagaries of interpretation of the results of serial transfer comparisons as related to sequential versus position associations offers a convincing demonstration of the complexities and inconsistencies pervading this research, as well as an instance where the inconsistency appears to have escaped investigators in the area.

Other more pronounced interlist variations of the serial order of the same items have almost uniformly shown little or no second-list facilitation, and findings of significant interference in second-list learning have been at least as common, if not more so. Even a mirror-image reversal of the first-list serial order produces no overall facilitation under standard serial-anticipation conditions (Young, Patterson, and Benson, 1963). When only alternating odd or even-numbered items maintain the same positions in both lists, while the positions of the remaining items are unsystematically changed, there is little if any facilitation on the former and considerable interference with the latter (Ebenholtz, 1963; Keppel and Saufley, 1964; Young, 1962). Some facilitation has been found when three adjacent items maintain the same relative positions across both lists, although there was none whatever for three non-adjacent items appearing in the same absolute positions (Battig, Brown, and Schild, 1964).

Thus, although the serial-to-serial transfer comparisons have been somewhat more successful than serial to paired-associate transfer studies in demonstrating differential transfer effects associated with the maintenance of sequential and/or positional arrangements across the two lists, the direction and magnitude of these effects have been far too small and inconsistent to support either sequential or position associations, either alone or in combination, as basic serial-learning processes, much less to differentiate between them. Thus, the conclusion from these studies must be very similar to that deriving from the serial to paired-associate transfer comparisons; namely, that more complex thought processes play a fundamental role in serial learning.

Indirect but nonetheless impressive evidence for the importance of complex strategies or processes at the level of complete interlist relationships can be gleaned from an examination of the relative magnitude of facilitation and interference deriving from various degrees of change or transformation between the two serial lists, plus the fact that interlist interference has been a more prevalent finding than facilitation. While the literature cited above is virtually devoid of comparisons involving systematic variations in the amount of change from the first to the second list, some comparisons that can be made across experiments suggest very strongly that it may be sheer magnitude rather than particular kind of interlist change that represents the basic determinant of serial-to-serial transfer. In other words, the degree to which sequential as opposed to positional arrangements are maintained across the two lists appears far less important than the number of first-list items that are changed or remain unchanged in the second list. The results of Battig and Lawrence (1967), particularly under the serial-recall procedure, are clearly suggestive of such a systematic relationship between transfer performance on a second serial list and amount of change from the first-list serial order. More clear-cut evidence derives from another recent study using a serial-recall procedure (Battig, 1966b), in which subjects received, on alternate trials, two different serial orders of the same list of items, so that, in effect, the subject simultaneously learns two serial lists. These results showed performance to be determined almost entirely by the degree to which the two serial orders differed from one another. Systematic variations as to the location in the list and/or adjacency of the items maintaining the same positions in both serial orders, on the other hand, produced no significant effects upon performance in this experiment.

These results, while somewhat puzzling on the basis of an interpretation restricted only to sequential and position associations, become quite sensible if the subject is conceded sufficient powers of thought to be able to detect and attempt to use orderly relationships between two serial lists as a basis for learning the second list. Since the interlist relationships in the serial-to-serial transfer studies typically have been both incomplete and highly complex, the predominance of interference emerging therefrom should come as no surprise. Rather this can be taken as indicative of the persistence of the subjects' tendency to think in this situation, and to search for some consistent relationship between the two lists even when learning of the second list is significantly retarded thereby.

Comparison of ends and middle of serial list. The dearth of evidence for intertask facilitation between serial learning and either a related serial or paired-associate task offers, at best, indirect evidence for the operation of complex thought processes through the exclusion of alternative sequential or positional associative processes. The results discussed thus far could equally well be interpreted as demonstrating merely the insensitivity of the tasks and/or procedures employed therein for the detection and evaluation of either sequential or positional associations, as is suggested elsewhere (Battig and Lawrence, 1967). Differences between learning and transfer effects localized at the ends as compared with the middle of the serial list, however, represent a remarkably consistent finding emerging from both types of transfer comparisons that cannot readily be explained away on the basis of methodological inadequacies.

Young and his associates appear to have been the first to note differential transfer at the ends and the middle of the list, arguing that sequential associations operate at the beginning and end of the list, whereas position associations predominate in learning the middle of the list (e.g., Young, 1962; Young, Patterson, and Benson, 1963). Ebenholtz (1963), and later Keppel and Saufley (1964), reached the opposite conclusion; i.e., that positional associations operate at the ends of the list and sequential associations at the middle. Still a third ends versus middle distinction was proposed by Battig *et al.* (1964); namely that both position and sequential associations were involved primarily at the ends of a serial list, whereas more complex multiple-item associative (e.g., thought) processes operated in the middle of the list. A similar position has subsequently been taken by Young (1968), on the basis of studies of transfer from serial to paired-associate lists wherein the serial items were paired with numerical or spatial representations of their serial positions (Jensen and Rohwer, 1965; Young *et al.*, 1967). Such studies, in agreement with evaluations of transfer to paired-associate pairs of adjacent items from the serial list, have consistently shown transfer effects to be limited to the ends of the list and virtually absent in the middle. Young (1968) also describes some evidence for significant negative transfer for either sequential or position associations from the middle of the serial list. This result, combined with the evidence of Battig *et al.* (1964) for greater second-list facilitation on clusters of three adjacent first-list items when these are taken from the middle rather than the beginning of the first list, clearly points to the importance of complex, multiple-item associative or thought processes in learning the middle of a serial list. While the exact nature of these complex thought processes remains to be assessed, the necessity of their invocation appears incontrovertible.

Sequential Learning as a Prerequisite to Thought

Thus far, our discussion has been limited to concurrent relationships between sequential learning and thought, such that both are assumed to take place at the same time. Alternatively, as has been most cogently expressed by Mandler (1962, 1965), sequential learning may be conceived of as a necessary prerequisite to the development of symbolic representations, the covert manipulation of which constitutes human thinking. Mandler argues that the complex symbolic structures employed in thought develop through extensive overlearning of interitem associations. Such overlearning results in the integration of these items into a single functional unit existing at a symbolic level independent of the actual overt occurrence of the component individual associations. As a consequence of this integration, the sequential occurrence of the component items proceeds quasi-automatically upon activation of the symbolic structural representation. Jensen's (1962, 1965) analysis of serial learning appears to lead to the same end result—a single, integrated, sequentially ordered, symbolic representation which (according to Mandler), after sufficient overlearning, would become a structure capable of symbolic manipulation.

Whatever the mechanism whereby the initial associations are formed (and we have already seen that this remains a matter of considerable dispute), there can be little argument with the view that many of the symbols basic to human thinking represent combinations of several elements upon which a particular sequential order has been imposed, presumably through sequential learning. Words, numbers, descriptive phrases, and various forms of complex motor activity all illustrate the development of symbols out of sequential learning, and one may be hard-pressed even to find an instance of human thought where the symbols involved are completely devoid of sequentiality.

As has been pointed out previously (e.g., Underwood and Schulz, 1960), the process of response learning or integration that is widely accepted as a necessary first stage preceding the development of associations involving these responses both in serial and paired-associate learning can itself be conceived as a rudimentary form of sequential learning. With nonsense syllables, for example, response learning requires primarily that the subject form a single verbal unit by learning a particular sequential order of three previously learned letter elements. Thus, even so-called paired-associate learning can be conceived of as dependent upon the prior occurrence of sequential learning of the individual stimulus and response elements to be associated together. It has been argued elsewhere (Battig, 1966a) that subsequent learning in the paired-associate task consists largely of complex thought processes. Thus, the notion of sequential learning as a prerequisite to thought emerges either from an associationistic or cognitive orientation toward the analysis of complex learning.

This view of sequential learning as a prerequisite to thought and other complex associative structures should not be taken to imply that the learning of sequential order represents one of the first learning processes to occur. Lashley's (1951) view that sequential ordering is determined by a generalized, central, integrative process that is largely independent of and is imposed upon the specific acts or elements to be ordered appears to imply a relatively late appearance of sequential ordering in the total learning process. Similarly, on the basis of his findings that variations in conditional probability between adjacent items in his probabilistic serial-learning task produced significant effects only with longer lists and at later stages of learning, Voss (1966) has postulated that learning of the sequential ordering of items in a serial list is the last of four mechanisms to occur during serial learning, being preceded not only by short-term serial memory and item or response learning, but also by an item-placement process whereby the items become associated with their general location if not their specific serial positions in the list. However, there appears to be no fundamental inconsistency of such a conception of serial ordering as independent of and/or preceded by basic item-learning processes with Mandler's position that sequential learning represents a prerequisite for cognitive structure. Not only is it quite plausible, but also entirely consistent with both viewpoints, to assume that the overlearning which produces cognitive structures (according to Mandler) consists primarily of the imposition of a consistent sequential order upon the multiple individual elements constituting the sequential learning task, as suggested by Lashley and Voss.

While the view that sequential association precedes cognitive structure has yet to deliver its full impact upon sequential-learning research, there is nonetheless some evidence from the few serial-learning experiments involving variations in amount of practice on a serial list prior to the introduction of a serial-transfer task that is entirely consistent therewith. The interesting discrepancy has already been noted between findings of nearly complete positive transfer to the same sequential order with a changed starting point after the list had been learned to a high criterion (Bernstein, 1964; Rehula, 1960), and the repeated demonstration (e.g., Ebenholtz, 1963) that consistent variation of the starting point over all serial-learning trials produces considerable interference in serial learning. This becomes readily explicable in terms of the late development in serial learning of an overall sequential structure which is strong enough to carry over to starting-point variations, whereas the latter produces considerable disruption during the early stages of learning before this sequential structure has become fully developed. Rehula's (1960) additional finding that transfer to the varied starting point was considerably less for a low (6/13) first-list criterion offers further support for this interpretation. So also does Keppel's (1965) finding that the disruptive effects of starting-point variation are eliminated on the second of two successively learned serial lists.

The manipulations of degree of first-list learning in the Battig et al. (1964) experiment also yielded evidence that overlearning of a serial list produced increased second-list facilitation on the last item of a three-item cluster of adjacent items from the first list, when these appeared in the middle of the second list. This increasing dependence of performance following high levels of first-list practice upon the second-list maintenance of a sequence of two preceding items is clearly indicative of the gradual development during serial learning of unitary multiple-item structural units which ultimately may encompass the entire serial list.

Merely to point out how sequential learning may be a prerequisite to the development of the cognitive structures employed in thought tells us little or nothing about how or why this relationship between sequential learning and thought develops. We may speculate, however, that the specification of the temporal or spatial sequence in which constituent elements follow one another represents a necessary property of effective thinking activity, and that this is basically what is accomplished through sequential learning. Moreover, the sequential-learning task, and most instances of thinking, also have in common the requirement that the sequence be unidirectional rather than readily amenable to reversals in directionality. This question concerning unidirectionality is raised here in part to elicit a reaction from Leonard Horowitz, the discussant of this paper, who was one of the first and foremost to be deceived into believing that directionality is not a basic property of verbal associations, and that associative symmetry is the rule (e.g., Horowitz, Norman, and Day, 1966). Hopefully, his own data (Horowitz and Izawa, 1963) will force him to concede that unidirectionality rather than symmetry is the rule in sequential learning, wherein the crutch of differential item availability can hardly be invoked to account either for the common-sense observation that it is much easier to say the alphabet forward than backward, or the experimental finding of considerable difficulty in learning the reversed or backward order of a previously learned serial list (e.g., Young *et al.*, 1963).

Thought as a Prerequisite to Sequential Learning

The preceding discussion of the inapplicability of associative symmetry to sequential learning renders it appropriate to conclude with an exploration of the applicability of this principle to the organization of the present paper, inasmuch as the preceding three sections have been entitled "The role of sequential learning in thought"; "The role of thought in sequential learning"; and "Sequential learning as a prerequisite to thought." While there is little if any research directly bearing upon the question of whether thought is a necessary prerequisite to sequential learning, both the intransitivity of the "prerequisite" relationship and the conclusion of the preceding section would seem to imply that it is not.

Nonetheless, there seems little doubt that adult human subjects do engage in a considerable amount of thinking prior to their actual learning of serial lists in the laboratory. If so, we might be able to learn a good deal about both sequential learning and thought merely by accepting this possibility and attempting to find out just what subjects are thinking about before the experiment begins, particularly during the interval between the preliminary instructions and the first sequential-learning trial. I wish that I were as convinced that experimenters in serial learning (*not* excluding myself) have either engaged themselves in a sufficient amount of thinking activity, or devoted proper attention to such capabilities of their subjects, in planning, performing, and interpreting their experiments. Certainly we should require no further convincing that simple associations of items with preceding and following items or with their serial positions, either alone or in combinations, are totally inadequate to account for sequential learning, and require immediate supplementation if not replacement by more complex thought processes. And however unpalatable such a notion may be to serial-learning experimenters, I suspect it would come as no surprise to the serial-learners themselves.

REFERENCES

Anderson, N. H. Effect of first-order conditional probability in a two-choice learning situation. *J. exp. Psychol.*, 1960, 59, 73-93.

Battig, W. F. Evidence for coding processes in 'rote' paired-associate learning. *J. verb. Learn. verb. Behav.*, 1966, 5, 177-181. (a)

Battig, W. F. Investigation of serial-learning processes through a serial-recall procedure. Paper read at Psychonomic Society. St. Louis, 1966. (b)

Battig, W. F., Brown, S. C., and Schild, M. E. Serial position and sequential associations in serial learning. *J. exp. Psychol.*, 1964, 67, 449-457.

Battig, W. F., and Lawrence, P. S. The greater sensitivity of the serial recall than anticipation procedure to variations in serial order. *J. exp. Psychol.*, 1967, 73, 172-178.

Bernstein, D. A. Serial learning of lists differing in associative relationships among items. Unpublished master's thesis, University of Virginia, 1964.

Bourne, L. E., Jr., and Battig, W. F. Complex processes. In J. B. Sidowski (Ed.), *Experimental methods and instrumentation in psychology.* New York: McGraw-Hill, 1966. Pp. 541-576.

Bourne, L. E., Jr., and Parker, B. K. Interitem relationships, list structure, and verbal learning. *Canad. J. Psychol.*, 1964, *18*, 52-61.

Diethorn, J., and Voss, J. F. Serial learning as a function of locus of chained associations. *J. exp. Psychol.*, 1967, *73*, 411-418.

Ebbinghaus, H. *Memory: A contribution to experimental psychology.* (Translated by H. A. Ruger and C. E. Bussenius) New York: Teachers College, Columbia University, 1913.

Ebenholtz, S. M. Serial learning: Position learning and sequential associations. *J. exp. Psychol.*, 1963, *66*, 353-362.

Epstein, W. The influence of syntactical structure on learning. *Amer. J. Psychol.*, 1961, *74*, 80-85.

Epstein, W. A further study of the influence of syntactical structure on learning. *Amer. J. Psychol.*, 1962, *75*, 121-126.

Horowitz, L. M., and Izawa, C. Comparison of serial and paired-associate learning. *J. exp. Psychol.*, 1963, *65*, 352-361.

Horowitz, L. M., Norman, S. D., and Day, R. S. Availability and associative symmetry. *Psychol. Rev.*, 1966, *73*, 1-15.

Hovland, C. I. Experimental studies in rote-learning theory: I. Reminiscence following learning by massed and distributed practice. *J. exp. Psychol.*, 1938, *22*, 201-214.

Hull, C. L., *et al. Mathematico-deductive theory of rote learning: A study in scientific methodology.* New Haven: Yale University Press, 1940.

Jarvik, M. E. Probability learning and a negative recency effect in the serial anticipation of alternative symbols. *J. exp. Psychol.*, 1951, *41*, 291-297.

Jensen, A. R. Transfer between serial and paired-associate learning. *J. verb. Learn. verb. Behav.*, 1962, *1*, 269-280.

Jensen, A. R., and Rohwer, W. D., Jr. What is learned in serial learning? *J. verb. Learn. verb. Behav.*, 1965, *4*, 62-72.

Keppel, G. Retroactive inhibition of serial lists as a function of the presence or absence of positional cues. *J. verb. Learn. verb. Behav.*, 1964, *3*, 511-517.

Keppel, G., and Saufley, W. A., Jr. Serial position as a stimulus in serial learning. *J. verb. Learn. verb. Behav.*, 1964, *3*, 335-343.

Lashley, K. S. The problem of serial order in behavior. In L. A. Jeffress (Ed.), *Cerebral mechanisms in behavior.* New York: Wiley, 1951. Pp. 112-136.

Leuba, H. R. Symmetry in paired associates. *J. exp. Psychol.*, 1966, *72*, 287-293.

McGeoch, J. A., and Irion, A. L. *The psychology of human learning.* New York: Longmans, Green, 1952.

Mandler, G. From association to structure. *Psychol. Rev.*, 1962, *69*, 415-427.

Mandler, G. Subjects do think: A reply to Jung's comments. *Psychol. Rev.*, 1965, *72*, 323-326.

Mandler, G., and Mandler, J. M. Serial position effects in sentences. *J. verb. Learn. verb. Behav.*, 1964, *3*, 195-202.

Miller, G. A., and Selfridge, J. O. Verbal context and the recall of meaningful material. *Amer. J. Psychol.*, 1950, *63*, 176-185.

Noble, C. E. The role of stimulus meaning (*m*) in serial verbal learning. *J. exp. Psychol.*, 1952, *43*, 437-446.

Postman, L., and Stark, K. Studies of learning to learn: IV. Transfer from serial to paired-associate learning. *J. verb. Learn. verb. Behav.*, 1967, *6*, 339-353.

Primoff, E. Backward and forward association as an organizing act in serial and in paired-associate learning. *J. Psychol.*, 1938, *5*, 375-395.

Rehula, R. J. A test of two alternative hypotheses of the associations that develop in serial verbal learning. Unpublished doctoral dissertation, Northwestern University, 1960.

Runquist, W. N. Verbal behavior. In J. B. Sidowski (Ed.), *Experimental methods and instrumentation in psychology*, New York: McGraw-Hill, 1966. Pp. 487-540.

Shuell, T. J., and Keppel, G. A further test of the chaining hypothesis of serial learning. *J. verb. Learn. verb. Behav.*, 1967, *6*, 439-445.

Underwood, B. J., and Schulz, R. W. *Meaningfulness and verbal learning.* Philadelphia: Lippincott, 1960.

Voss, J. F. Serial acquisition as a function of item probability and sequential probability. *J. exp. Psychol.*, 1966, *71*, 304-313.

Wallas, G. *The art of thought.* New York: Harcourt, Brace, 1926.

Young, R. K. A comparison of two methods of learning serial associations. *Amer. J. Psychol.*, 1959, 72, 554-559.

Young, R. K. Tests of three hypotheses about the effective stimulus in serial learning. *J. exp. Psychol.*, 1962, 63, 307-313.

Young, R. K. Serial learning. In T. R. Dixon and D. L. Horton (Eds.), *Verbal behavior theory and its relation to general S-R behavior theory.* Englewood Cliffs, New Jersey: Prentice-Hall, 1968. Pp. 122-148.

Young, R. K., and Casey, M. Transfer from serial to paired-associate learning. *J. exp. Psychol.*, 1964, 67, 594-595.

Young, R. K., Hakes, D. T., and Hicks, R. Y. Ordinal position number as a cue in serial learning. *J. exp. Psychol.*, 1967, 73, 427-438.

Young, R. K., Patterson, J., and Benson, W. M. Backward serial learning. *J. verb. Learn. verb. Behav.*, 1963, 1, 335-338.

SEQUENTIAL LEARNING, ASSOCIATIVE SYMMETRY, AND THOUGHT[1]

LEONARD M. HOROWITZ

Stanford University

I should like to thank Professor Battig for his very thorough paper. Speaking as one who has been "deceived" by associative symmetry, I now invite you to join in my illusion. I would like to re-assemble the data that Professor Battig has reviewed into a slightly different sequential presentation and try to re-create my illusion for you.

Of all the possible tasks that Ebbinghaus might have used to study memory, why did he happen to choose the serial method? Historians do not seem to comment on this rather odd choice, but they do repeatedly stress how experimental psychology grew largely out of British empiricism. Surely Ebbinghaus' method must have reflected this philosophical spirit of his times. The philosophy from Hobbes and Locke to Wundt and Ebbinghaus claimed that sensations left ideas in the mind: Contiguous ideas became associated, and thinking was viewed as a succession of ideas. Ebbinghaus must have meant for serial learning to simulate this characteristic of everyday thinking. Each of Ebbinghaus' nonsense syllables left an idea in the mind, and adjacent ideas of this kind became associated. Just as happens in the grander

[1] The preparation of this paper and the unpublished research that it cites were supported by Grant GB-4561 of the National Science Foundation to the author.

process of thinking, so it apparently happened in the miniature process of serial learning: one idea came to elicit the next idea which, in turn, came to elicit the next. This chaining interpretation of serial learning corresponded nicely with the chaining interpretation of thinking.

However, as Professor Battig has reported, this view of serial learning is wrong: after a subject has learned the serial list A-B-C-D-E, he does not show much positive transfer to the paired-associate task which contains the pairs A-B, B-C, C-D, D-E (Primoff, 1938; Young, 1959). *Thinking* may still involve chains—this we simply don't know at the present—but remembering a serial list is not a chain. On this point we can all agree.

Then what is the point of searching for the stimulus of a serial task? Is serial learning so important theoretically? Or is serial learning of such *practical* significance? Probably not. I think we would like to identify the stimulus that elicits, say, Item D in the serial list, because this stimulus may have the same form as many stimuli which operate during thought. "Thought $n - 1$" does not necessarily elicit "Thought n"; instead, some more subtle stimulus, like the stimulus of a serial task, may be operating.

What kinds of stimuli, then, might be operating? Professor Battig has referred to two classes of hypotheses. One class assumes that the stimulus lies within the serial list itself. According to this hypothesis, the stimulus is *internal* to the list. For example, consider the cluster hypothesis. The cluster hypothesis claims that the stimulus for an item is the cluster of items that precedes it. In the serial sequence A-B-C-D-E, the cluster BCD might come to elicit Item E. BCD might work as a unit which elicits Item E, or possibly B and C form a context for D to elicit E. In either case, the stimulus would lie entirely within the sequence. We now know, as Professor Battig has remarked, that a simple interpretation of the cluster hypothesis is not valid (Young, 1962). However, the size of the cluster has not been specified, and the hypothesis has not really been fully explored. Surely some form of this hypothesis must be relevant to thought: the stimulus *man* in the context of *evil, sinister, devil* produces different associations from *man* in some other context (cf. Howes and Osgood, 1954).

The other class of hypothesis claims that the stimulus during serial learning is *external* to the list. Every adult human subject has already overlearned certain sequences—the ordinal numbers, the letters of the alphabet, ordered physical locations, and so on. One of these external sequences can serve as stimuli for serial items that the subject has to learn. The numbers from 1 to n, for example, can be aligned with the serial items. Thus, the external sequence could be viewed as a set of pegs for the serial items to hang on. The position hypothesis is one example: the item's spatial location in the list is the peg that the item hangs on. This position hypothesis has been supported in several studies (Ebenholtz, 1963ab; Young 1962).

If *this* kind of hypothesis fully accounts for serial learning, then serial learning only has the most superficial resemblance to thinking. If the stimuli are all external to the list, then serial learning is really not very interesting psychologically, since it could not teach us anything about thought. The serial task would not have any particular implications for other mental processes.

In fact, let us pause for a moment and consider what kind of results we are looking for in this research, anyway. What would please an investigator whose subject was transferring from a serial task to some related paired-associate task? Suppose the subject mastered the serial task and then transferred *perfectly* to the paired-associate task; assume he showed maximum positive transfer. That experimenter would seem to have analyzed the serial task correctly, and the case would be closed. So far, however, no experimenter has come close to that ideal.

Many experimenters, though, have found *some* positive transfer. Does this mean that the stimulus has been *partially* identified? Or might it mean simply that a subject *can* use higher mental processes to apply what he learned in serial learning to facilitate a subsequent paired-associate task? For example, suppose a subject learned the sequence A-B-C-D-E through any strategy imaginable. Then suppose he was asked to learn the pairs 1-A, 2-B, 3-C, 4-D, 5-E. This subject might note the connection between tasks and, perhaps, even verbalize the relationship to himself. Then he would learn the paired-associate task faster. People are always discovering new properties and relationships in tasks they have once learned. Thus, the positive transfer does not necessarily clarify the nature of serial learning. Hence, the results of these transfer studies are always somewhat ambiguous.

For this reason, other approaches should also be used to help understand the serial task. I think we may be insisting too rigidly on a stimulus-response analysis *where each serial item is a discrete response.*

I would like to propose an alternate approach to the serial task. Let us consider a very simple sequence—the sequence of letters in a word. This miniature serial sequence has two interesting characteristics. And these characteristics could not be understood through traditional methods alone.

Consider a sequence of letters forming a word—say, "expect." When this sequence is shown to a subject with some fragment missing, the subject can think of the *entire word* faster than he can think of the missing fragment. When a subject is shown e x p e _ t, he can say "expect" nearly twice as fast as he can say "c," the missing letter. This result holds up as well for nonsense words like "neglan" after the subject has used the nonsense word enough: "n e _ l a n" would make the subject think of "neglan" faster than it would make him think of the missing letter "g." Apparently, to think of the missing letter, the subject thinks of the whole word first.

Furthermore, the sequence has a second important property: the different parts of the whole word seem to vary in their importance. Various techniques have shown, for example, that the middle of a word is less important for identifying that word than other parts. The beginning, on the other hand, is the most important part. Miller and Friedman (1957) asked subjects to supply a deleted letter from the body of a word. The subject performed best when the middle letter was the one missing. As the missing letter moved to either end of the word, the subject's performance got progressively worse. This result can be explained in informational terms (Carson, 1961; Garner, 1957, 1958, 1962; Garner and Carson, 1960): letters which are adjacent in a word are correlated more highly than letters which are one or more characters apart. Therefore, the best predictor of a missing letter in a word is the letter which lies next to it. Now, a letter which is missing from the middle of a word has *two* best predictors—one on either side. But a letter which is missing from the end of a word only has one.

For this reason, a typographical error in the middle of a word is not very disruptive. Bruner and O'Dowd (1958) tachistoscopically presented words which had an error in the beginning, in the middle, or in the end. The subject had to identify the word as fast as he could, and his latencies were measured. The data showed that typographical errors at the beginning of a word are the most disruptive; and those in the middle are the least disruptive.

Results as the above suggest why subjects probably tend to examine the ends of a word during a very brief exposure. Haslerud and Clark (1957) rapidly exposed nine-letter words to subjects, and the subjects reported whatever they saw. According to the data, the subjects identified the end letters best, and their performance got worse and worse for letters nearer the middle. Apparently a subject spends less time looking at the middle since the middle is less informative (more redundant). A similar result also holds for children (Marchbanks and Levin, 1965).

We have found (Horowitz, White, and Atwood, 1968) that some parts of a word are better cues than others for making the subject think of the whole word. The beginning of a word is the best; it elicits the whole word very fast. If you want a subject to think of the word "figure," show him f i _ _ _ _. The middle of the word is a very poor cue; the subject will not think of the word as often, and if he does, he will respond rather slowly. The end of the word is an intermediate cue. Therefore, the fragment "_ _ g u _ _" would be a very poor cue for "figure" while the fragment "_ _ _ _ r e" would be intermediate.

All of this research can be summarized this way: the series of letters in a word has a characteristic organization. Some parts of the series are more important than others. The more important parts elicit the whole series faster than they elicit other parts.

This kind of organization may also hold for a serial list of nonsense syllables. Meyer (1939) performed a study with very simple serial lists. He presented nonsense-syllable triplets to the subject; for example, the series BEK-JAF-LUN along with other such triplets. Let us denote a set of syllables as ABC. The subject studied the triplets for 10 trials. Then he was shown one syllable of the series and he had to report whatever came to mind.

Meyer's data yielded two interesting results. First Item B, the middle one, was more apt to elicit Item A than it was to elicit Item C. Thus, in this miniature serial task, the "backward" association B-A seemed to be stronger than the "forward" association B-C. Second, Item C, the final item, was more apt to elicit Item A than it was to elicit Item B. Thus, the "remote backward" association C-A seemed to be stronger than the "adjacent backward" association C-B.

These results, of course, are further evidence against the chaining hypothesis of serial learning. More interesting, though, they show a tendency for B and C both to elicit A. Apparently A has a greater salience in the unit as a whole; the subject is always readier to emit A. Müller and Pilzecker (1900) called this tendency the *initial reproducing tendency*; it is probably a subject's first step toward recalling the entire complex.

Likewise, in a longer serial task, a group of items—say, F, G, and H—may form a unit within the larger list. G or H, then, would tend to elicit F. The whole unit, FGH, might then elicit some other large unit —say IJKL; but IJKL would also have its own internal organization of elements. And the details of organization, of course, might vary from one subject to the next.

Research on grammar has taught us not to look for simple, linear S-R relationships. Perhaps now is the time to apply this lesson to serial learning.

Professor Battig has also raised the issue of associative symmetry, so I might say a word about that. As he points out, remembering a serial list is clearly directional. Does that prove, though, that *simple associa-*

tions are directional? We have already agreed that C is not the stimulus for D in a serial list. Therefore, we certainly cannot conclude from the serial task that the C-D association is directional (p. 127, par. 2). Papers on associative symmetry have already noted that the alphabet is easier to recite forwards than backwards (Horowitz, Norman, and Day, 1966), but that is no reason to infer that an association exists from K to L and not backwards. We cannot draw any inferences about simple associations from serial learning. When the letter "f" elicits the word "figure," the phonemes are emitted in sequence, but this result says nothing about simple letter associations.

It *is* ironic, though, that the most interesting evidence for associative symmetry comes from studies of serial learning. Imagine a subject who has learned the serial task A-B-C-D and now learns the pairs A-B, B-C, C-D. This paired-associate task is perhaps the hardest learning task we have every devised. Why is it so hard? The subject's errors tell us why. Say a subject is learning this paired-associate task and the stimulus C appears. The subject has an overwhelming tendency to respond with "B" instead of with "D." His major error is to give a backward association instead of the correct forward association. (Apparently B grows as available as D, so the backward association C-B is about as strong as the forward association C-D.) This is the phenomenon which first convinced me that associative symmetry should not be dismissed too readily.

But actually, if all data that exist are taken together, I think forward associations *are* slightly stronger than backward associations. Often, the difference does not reach statistical significance, but still the forward association does show a consistent advantage. Does this mean that A elicits B more strongly than B elicits A? Not necessarily. Suppose two nonsense syllables, A and B, united into a six-letter sequence. We can call the compound AB. Now A and B are fragments of the whole. The syllable A is an initial fragment so it elicits the whole more readily. We could explain directionalities, then, this way: "Forward recall" would mean that A elicits AB and from AB the subject selects B as his response. "Backward recall" would mean that B elicits AB and from AB the subject selects A as his response. Thus, forward or backward recall would require A or B to elicit the whole unit AB. And since A elicits AB better than B does, forward recall would seem superior. Here again is a relationship where the part elicits the whole.

I might conclude these remarks, then, by agreeing with Professor Battig: Yes, "more complex thought processes play a fundamental role in serial learning." This statement is surely true. Thought and serial learning can go hand in hand, so diverse approaches suitable to one may help us better understand the other.

REFERENCES

Bruner, J. S., and O'Dowd, D. A note on the informativeness of parts of words. *Lang. & Speech,* 1958, *1,* 98-101.

Carson, D. H. Letter constraints within words in printed English. *Kybernetik,* 1961, *1,* 46-54.

Ebenholtz, S. M. Position mediated transfer between serial learning and spatial discrimination task. *J. exp. Psychol.,* 1963, *65,* 603-608. (a)

Ebenholtz, S. M. Serial Learning: Position learning and sequential associations. *J. exp. Psychol.,* 1963, *66,* 353-362. (b)

Garner, W. R. Symmetric uncertainty analysis and redundancy of printed English. *Proceedings of the Fifteenth International Congress on Psychology,* Brussels, 1957, 104-110.

Garner, W. R. Symmetric uncertainty analysis and its implications for psychology. *Psychol. Rev.,* 1958, *65,* 183-196.

Garner, W. R. *Uncertainty and structure as psychological concepts.* New York: Wiley, 1962.

Garner, W. R., and Carson, D. H. A multivariate solution of the redundancy of printed English. *Psychol. Rep.,* 1960, *6,* 123-141.

Haslerud, G. M., and Clark, R. E. On the redintegrative perception of words. *Amer. J. Psychol.,* 1957, *70,* 97-101.

Horowitz, L. M., Norman, S. A., and Day, R. S. Availability and associative symmetry. *Psychol. Rev.,* 1966, *73,* 1-15.

Horowitz, L., White, M. A., and Atwood, D. Word fragments as aids to recall: The organization of a word. *J. exp. Psychol.,* 1968, *76,* 219-226.

Howes, D., and Osgood, C. On the combination of probabilities in linguistic contexts. *Amer. J. Psychol.,* 1954, *67,* 241-258.

Marchbanks, G., and Levin., H. Cues by which children recognize words. *J. ed. Psychol.,* 1965, *56,* 57-61.

Meyer, G. Temporal organization and the initial reproductive tendency. *J. Psychol.,* 1939, *7,* 269-282.

Miller, G. A., and Friedman, E. A. The reconstruction of multilated English texts. *Inf. & Control,* 1957, *1,* 38-55.

Müller, G. E., and Pilzecker, A. Experimentelle Beitrage zur Lehre vom Gedächtnis. *Z. Psychol.*, 1900, Ergbd. 1.

Primoff, E. Backward and forward associations as an organizing act in serial and in paired-associate learning. *J. Psychol.*, 1938, 5, 375-395.

Young, R. K. A comparison of two methods of learning serial associations. *Amer. J. Psychol.*, 1959, 72, 554-559.

Young, R. K. Tests of three hypotheses about the effective stimulus in serial learning. *J. exp. Psychol.*, 1962, 63, 307-313.

GENERAL DISCUSSION

HABER mentioned a study in which the letters of a word were presented serially to the same spot on the retina. At a slow rate; i.e., 100 msec/letter with 100 msec between each pair of letters, the subject could spell or name the word immediately. As rate increased, however, the following effects were noted in order: (1) the subject could recite the letters, but naming the word was difficult; (2) errors were made in the order of recalling the letters; (3) some of the letters were missed. These results, HABER pointed out, seem to indicate that there may be independent registration processes for the item, the order, and the meaning.

HOROWITZ commented that the apparent separation of registration functions may be an artifact in that the task forces the subject to recognize the material in an unusual manner.

ANDERSON commented that although Dr. Battig speaks of radical changes in his area of study, his research is tied to quite traditional methods. Hovland, ANDERSON pointed out, apparently attempted to constrain the subjects so that they would learn by associating. Why, ANDERSON inquired of Battig, don't you design studies which will force subjects to use complex thought processes if that is what you want to know?

BATTIG replied that subjects persist in invoking thought processes even when attempts are made to prevent them from doing so, and this provides evidence for the general importance of complex processes. It was further commented that it is better to study what happens when subjects are given a task than to try to force a particular strategy.

SIMON commented that Gregg is attempting to do what Anderson suggested by studying the sequential learning of patterns. Gregg employs conditions, it was pointed out, which will either encourage or discourage the subject's chances of discovering the structure of the pattern.

ATKINSON asked what the impact of EPAM has been upon the area of serial learning.

140

BATTIG replied that insofar as the question of functional stimulus is concerned, EPAM has had little or no influence.

SIMON pointed out that EPAM stores images and uses anchor points, and that EPAM explains why beginning and end items are overlearned before the middle items are learned, and why items adjacent to the anchor points are picked up more readily.

BATTIG indicated that a study involving the transfer of clusters of three items from one serial list to a second serial list produced results opposed to those expected by an EPAM position.

It was mentioned that transfer designs may not be the most trustworthy or fruitful way to study the problem of functional stimulus. Moreover, it was pointed out that 100 per cent transfer from serial to PA learning would not be conclusive evidence for stating that the serial list was learned as a chain of successive associations, because the associations may have been developed late in serial learning and other processes were used earlier in the serial task.

JENKINS stated that trying to study the role of complex processes in serial learning constitutes too mild a revolution. There are many ways to store and retrieve, he commented, and the traditional methods are too limited with regard to input processes.

5

MATHEMATICAL MODELS AND THOUGHT: A SEARCH FOR STAGES

FRANK RESTLE
Indiana University

A single step in thinking is a search, and the search terminates with a discovery. The discovery is new in the sense that it was not available during the search, though it may often be a thought that others have expressed and may be found to be familiar to the thinker himself.

The idea that thinking is a process of search is beautifully expressed in Donald Campbell's paper, "Blind Variation and Selective Retention." Campbell states that the essential characteristic of true search is that the searcher is "blind"; i.e., his search process is not conditional upon what the correct answer actually is. A homelier statement of the same theory is George Miller's allusion to the Junk-Box theory, that thinking may be analogous to searching through a junkbox in the shop looking for a particular wood screw. Miller says that he chose this name for the theory so as to keep the idea to himself. However, like a beauty queen in a cotton dress, this theory shows its good points however plainly presented.

Theory of the One-Stage Search

The subject has a set, S, of hypotheses, of which a subset, C, will lead to correct solution of the problem, and F lead to failure. In simple searches there are no in-between hypotheses, so that:

$$S = C \cup F$$

The subject begins by sampling at random from S. If his hypothesis is in C, the problem is solved. If the hypothesis is in F, the subject suffers a failure, and resamples from S. The process of failing and resampling continues until it happens that an hypothesis from C is chosen.

1. Performance is all-or-none. After each failure, the subject again resamples from S and, hence, has the same probability of success he had at the beginning. There is no partial progress.

2. The probability of suffering exactly n failures forms a geometric distribution and depends upon the proportion of correct hypotheses, c. That is, P $(n$ failures$) = (1 - c)^n c$.

Corollaries:
Mean total failures, $E(T) = (1 - c)/c$
Variance of total failures, $V(T) = (1/c)/c^2$
Standard deviation, $\sigma(T) = \sqrt{1 - c}/c$
which is slightly above the mean if c is small.

3. The speed of solution depends upon the probability of choosing a correct hypothesis. As c increases, mean failures, $E(T)$, decreases. It is natural to use $E(T)$ as an index of difficulty.

4. If A is any set of hypotheses, let $m(A)$ be the measure of A, the tendency for the subject, when he samples from a set, S, containing A, to choose his hypothesis from A. Since $S = C \cup F$, and no hypothesis is in both C and F, it follows that:

$$m(S) = M(C) + m(F)$$
$$c = m(C)/[m(C) + m(F)]$$

5. The speed of solving a problem can be increased by adding alternative correct hypotheses.

6. The speed of solving a problem can be increased by reducing distractions, if this reduces hypotheses in F.

7. The mean total errors increases proportionally with the measure of wrong hypotheses, F.

Proof:

$$E(T) = (1 - c)/c$$
$$= \frac{1}{c} - 1 = \frac{m(C) + m(F)}{m(C)} - 1 = \frac{m(F)}{\overline{M}(C)}$$

8. The speed of solving can be increased by emphasizing the correct hypothesis, by instruction, pointing out the solution, etc. This corresponds to changing the measure or probability of such hypotheses.

9. Transfer of training from one problem to another is all-or-none. If the same hypotheses, selected in the first search, also solve the second problem, transfer is perfect. Otherwise, the subject must begin searching the second problem, and transfer is nil.

10. Let C_1 and C_2 be the sets of correct hypotheses in problems 1 and 2. A subject solves problem 1. The probability that he transfers to problem 2, called t_{12}, is given by:

$$t_{12} = m(C_1 \cap C_2)/m(C_1)$$

11. If a problem is made easy by adding extraneous correct hypotheses (see point 5) then this increases $m(C_1)$. If problem 2 cannot be solved using these extraneous hypotheses, then $m(C_1 \cap C_2)$ is not increased, and the probability of transfer, t_{12}, is correspondingly decreased.

Multiple-Stage Theory

The simple search model does not correspond to most thought processes because it has only one stage and most problems have more than one. James H. Davis at Miami University, with some help from me in the early stages, has studied multi-stage problem-solving.

Some problems clearly require more than one stage. For example, consider the following logic-twister:

> If the puzzle you solved before you solved this one was harder than the puzzle you solved after you solved the puzzle you solved before you solved this one, was the puzzle you solved before you solved this one harder than this one?

This problem seems to require more than one stage: after the subject has read it, he must find three pairs of mutually-defeating sentences and cancel them. He can then arrive at the correct answer that the statement is logically true.

Suppose that the subject performs an all-or-none search until he finds the first part of the solution, then begins a second all-or-none search, and so forth. The time to each stage of solution has a geometric distribution. It is well known to mathematical statisticians that if we go to continuous time, the geometric distribution turns into the exponential. Furthermore, the sum of several exponential distributed variables has a "generalized gamma distribution." If all the stages of the problem are equally difficult, then the distribution of times will be described by a gamma distribution.

The gamma distribution has two parameters; namely, the number of stages added together and the difficulty, assumed the same for each stage. It is possible to estimate the two parameters separately. The same mean time can arise either from one difficult stage or many easy stages; but in the first case we have a skew distribution with large variance, and in the second case we have a more nearly normal distribution with relatively small variance.

Restle and Davis, (1962) have shown, in several experiments, that the distribution of solution-times in various problems is well described by the gamma distribution and that the number of stages, as estimated, agrees quite well with apparent number of stages in the problem. More precise experiments, constructing new problems with given distributions of response time, have apparently not yet succeeded.

The one-stage search process can be characterized by the following model:

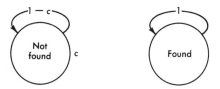

The system remains in the "not-found" stage for a random duration when the subject fails to give the correct answer. Once the answer is found, the system goes into the second state and remains there.

The Restle-Davis model, in its simple form, is a chain as follows:

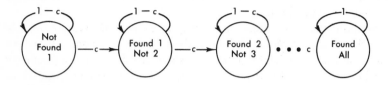

These stages are passed, one at a time and in sequence.

Obviously, if there are several stages preceding final solution, they can be arranged in more intricate designs. Thus, complex thought process may be like a computer program. A simple program consists of two classes of instructions: decisions (branch points) and operations. The Restle-Davis theory has a sequence of operations but no decisions and no branches. An introduction to the theory of branching psychological processes was given by Miller, Galanter, and Pribram (1960). Their unit of "plans" was a sequence, TEST-OPERATE-TEST-EXIT.

In a computer program, there is usually no fixed sequence of calculations, but rather tests that determine which operation will follow. With the use of tests, it is possible to repeat the same operation over and over an indefinite number of times, yet have the process well defined and finite. Consider, for example, adding a column of numbers using an algorithm like FORTRAN (Fig.5-1).

In a program of this general sort, the operations may be replaced by sub-programs of various sorts, and the logic may be relatively complicated with many decision branches and operations. It appears that the form of this "program" depends, mainly, upon the structure of the problem given. This, in turn, is worked out by procedures such as those used by Newell and Simon (1963) and others using list-handling languages. Until this group of computer-handlers appeared, psychologists had no detailed idea of the inner structure of some "simple" problems, and were mostly unprepared to deal with complexity.

The computer models have not, until very recently, included any deep probabilistic elements. The result is that such models believe everything the subject says and does and take no account of the fact (or is it only a possibility?) that the same subject might just as well have done something quite different. The human subject, performing a calculation, does not use "IF" statements, but instead makes choices and discriminations. It is an essential, as well as unavoidable, characteristic of the human that he is not perfectly predictable at those choices.

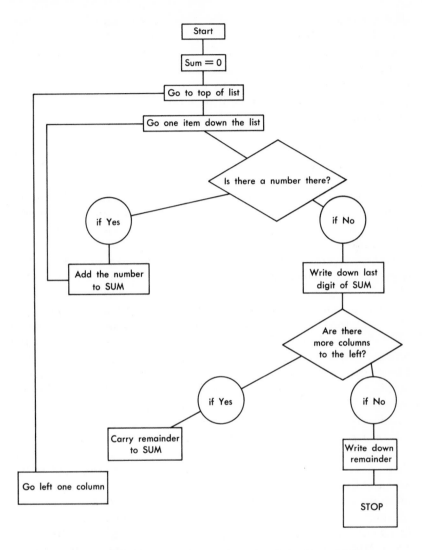

Figure 5-1. **FORTRAN program: example of number addition.**

If, instead of determinate choices, we introduce search processes, the "program" begins to produce outcomes that resemble the data from a typical psychological experiment.

One may argue that humans, despite all appearances, are not random. They always make decisions for good reasons, but we do not know all the reasons perfectly. If it is to represent reality, a model should be more like a computer program and contain little or no random elements. I have no argument here, for I do not observe randomness. However, it is not enough to write a program, then run a subject, and then show that the two protocols resemble one another. We need real experimental tests that tell us when we must change theory, and this requires models that bear, first, a formal resemblance to experimental data.

Higher-Order Control

A subject will continue even a simple search only if he believes that there is a solution to be found. In real-life problems, and sometimes in the laboratory, people quit. Their overall strategy does not maintain searching.

When a problem requires a subject to perform several separate searches, and find several component ideas, grave statistical difficulties may arise. Suppose a problem requires five sub-answers. Does the subject first search all single answers, and exhaust all such possibilities? He might then try all possible pairs of simple hypotheses. At some point dimly seen in the future, he might start on sets of five, and if the total set of possibilities is small enough, he might hit upon the solution. The process would ordinarily be very slow. Consider, for example, a problem having ten possible hypotheses, and a set of five needed for solution. The subject would have to search through between 385 and 637 possible solutions, depending upon how early, in his search of subsets of five, he happened to hit upon the correct combination. This is calculated by realizing that there are ten single hypotheses to try first; then $\binom{10}{2} = (10 \cdot 9)/2 = 45$ pairs of hypotheses. When the subject has exhausted all pairs, he must try all combinations of ten hypotheses taken three at a time: $(10 \cdot 9 \cdot 8)/(2 \cdot 3) = 120$ in number, then all combinations of ten hypotheses taken four at a time: $(10 \cdot 9 \cdot 8 \cdot 7)/(2 \cdot 3 \cdot 4) = 210$. Therefore, he must get through at least $10 + 45 + 120 + 210 = 385$ attempts before even trying a solution with five components. There are 252 groupings of ten hypotheses taken five at a time, and somewhere during his search through set, the subject would hit upon the correct solution. The above values are conservative, for they assume that the subject searches systematically, never repeating a combination of ideas; this would certainly require a remarkable memory.

What is needed to make the solution reasonably easy is that the subject find the first strategy (one of ten) and then *hold* it while he searches for the second, etc. This requires that the subject know whether or not he has a correct part of the solution, when he does not have the whole solution. Usually, certain objective information is forthcoming only when the whole problem is solved. Therefore, to hold a partial solution, the subject must have some concept of what the total solution will look like and be able to fill in that scheme gradually and with a certain confidence. The computer programs, and our verbal descriptions of the problem, usually proceed step by step through a schema of the solution to the problem, thereby implicitly assuming that the subject has such a schema and can store partial successes. What our theories do not say is how does the subject evaluate and handle partial solutions?

The recent experiments by Lyle Bourne and his associates in concept-formation have brought this problem to the attention of the psychological community in an interesting way. Bourne found, as had other experimenters, that he could not teach subjects simple disjunctive or biconditional concepts by the usual discrimination-learning techniques used in the laboratory. When the subjects were to push a certain button when the stimulus was either green or square, they apparently experienced great difficulty in finding the solutions, and could not achieve success in the usual hour's work. In order to study the identification of compound concepts, Bourne had to separate "rule learning" from instance learning. If subjects knew that the solution would be a simple disjunction, and were practiced at that problem, and did not know what dimensions were to be used—they could solve the problem. On the other hand, if they knew the dimensions through instruction and practice, and expected that color and form would control the answer, but did not know the form of the compound—they had a fair chance of inducing the rule.

At Indiana University, Peter G. Polson has done a dissertation on verbal concept-formation by the Hull method in which subjects learn successive lists of paired-associates. The same responses are used in each list, and all the stimuli paired with a given response are connected by a meaningful concept. In one part of his studies, Polson used the Underwood-Richardson "sense-impression" concepts, in which (for example) words like milk, ivory, and snow are grouped together under the heading "white." These concepts do not seem entirely natural to the students, for the words within a category often have very different practical meanings. Polson's mathematical model of this process is interesting in structure; first, when the subject does not have the concept, he learns a new paired-associate item by an all-or-none process. When he has the concept, he of course performs perfectly on the new items within that concept as soon as they appear. The particular concept is learned all-or-none; subjects either look just like control subjects whose words do not form concepts, or they shift into perfect performance. However, the subject does not learn all the concepts independently. Instead, for some (variable) number of lists, the experimental, concept-learning subject looks just like a non-concept control subject. Then the experimental subject hits upon his first concept, and from then on he learns the rest of the concepts in a relatively rapid manner. What has happened? Polson's interpretation is that when the subject first hits on one concept, he begins to look for such concepts in the other items, and his search process, having a narrower field, is successful much more rapidly. This study, somewhat different from Bourne's, shows the importance of higher-order rules and works in the details of how the learning of such structures can be analyzed by mathematical methods.

General Characteristics of the Theory

Problem solving is a search process rather than a process of forming new connections or associations. This idea reflects back into learning —concept-formation experiments, paired-associates learning, and arithmetic may be studied using the idea that the subject is solving problems on those tasks. Thus, there is a close integration between experiments on learning and experiments on thought.

The notion of compound search processes, as briefly discussed here, can be worked out in much greater detail. Each individual problem or task can be analyzed into (a) the component searches to be made, (b) the fields of possible ideas within which each search is made, (c) the general strategy governing the search process, and (d) the structure of the "program" connecting the several search processes. This may seem overly ambitious and, at the same time, too time-consuming and laborious to be interesting. However, both to satisfy our scientific curiosity and to perform our applied duties to education, I think we must make these detailed analyses. Computer programs, automated laboratories, computerized data analysis, and the kinds of higher-order simplifications made possible by mathematical analysis of the process—all of these reduce the labor of detailed analysis to the level of feasibility.

I do not, therefore, end with any glowing generality. I have here sketched a picture of the way in which I believe we can make a real contribution to the psychology of thought. If I am right, from now on general principles, interesting analogies, and research programs will have to prove themselves by working out the details of what people think when doing specific problems.

REFERENCES

Campbell, D. T. Blind variation and selective retention in creative thought as in other knowledge processes. *Psychol. Rev.*, 1960, *67*, 380-400.

Miller, G. A., Galanter, E. H., and Pribram, H. H. *Plans and the structure of behavior.* New York: Holt, 1960.

Newell, A., and Simon, H. A. Computers in Psychology. In R. D. Luce, R. R. Bush, and E. H. Galanter (Eds.), *Handbook of Mathematical Psychology*, Vol. 1. New York: Wiley, 1963. Pp. 368-421.

Restle, F., and Davis, J. H. Success and speed of problem solving by individuals and groups. *Psychol. Rev.*, 1962, *69*, 520-536.

A SEARCH TASK[1]

NORMAN H. ANDERSON
University of California, San Diego

The uses and problems of mathematical models often show up most clearly in specific applications. I wish to begin, therefore, by considering the analysis that Restle gives of the logic-twister:

> If the puzzle you solved before you solved this one was harder than the puzzle you solved after you solved the puzzle you solved before you solved this one, was the puzzle you solved before you solved this one harder than this one?

An ordinary attack on this problem might begin by asking subjects to verbalize their thoughts, to be sure, for lack of a better idea. Davis and Restle (1963) measure only the time that the subject uses to solve the problem. From these bare latencies, they deduce, with the aid of their model, that the subject proceeds through three distinct, independent, all-or-none stages in solving the problem.

Such deduction illustrates that mathematical models can be a tool of remarkable potential to delineate covert mental operations. Moreover, if the interpretation is correct, it constitutes a striking substantive contribution to the psychology of thinking.

Of course, careful evaluation of the analysis, and of the data, is necessary to determine what credence may be placed on the substantive interpretation. Since this discussion is more concerned with the general usefulness of the model approach than with the validity of this particular application, only an overview of the relevant considerations will be given.

---

[1] Preparation of this paper was facilitated by NSF Grant, GB-3913.

For the logic-twister itself, we need first to ask what information the model might provide. To say that the subject is searching for a solution, or that the thought process follows a temporal sequence, is no more than common sense. I take it, therefore, that the special contribution of the model lies in its claim that the temporal sequence is of a particular type: that subjects solve the problem by progressing through a certain number of discrete, independent stages in an all-or-none manner. It is this claim of the model, that the thought process has this form, that will now be considered.

The Restle-Davis Stage Analysis

In any model-data analysis, two classes of assumption require consideration. One class pertains primarily to the model, the other primarily to the data. These two classes of assumption will be considered here for the model that Davis and Restle apply to the logic-twister.

In the model, it is assumed that subjects progress to the solution through a fixed sequence of discrete stages. Within each stage, progress is all-or-none; the subject is assumed to sample hypotheses randomly with replacement; and each stage is completed when the correct hypothesis is sampled. The successive stages are assumed to be independent and of equal difficulty. Thus, in particular, success on one stage does not make solution of the later stages easier or harder. The number of stages is taken as an unknown to be estimated from the data. For the logic-twister, the estimated number of stages was 3.0. For the easier and harder problems, the estimated number of stages had the near-integer values of 1.3 and 5.0.

Restle argues that since there do seem to be three logical stages in the logic-twister, subjects presumably solve the problem by finding and cancelling successive pairs of mutually-defeating clauses. But if this is so, one would question the assumption that the stages are independent and of equal difficulty. One alternative, among many, is that there is a difficult first stage, in which the subject gets the idea of cancelling mutually-defeating clauses, followed by easy stages in which the actual cancellations occur.

Such alternative models could also be applied, and it seems likely that they would fit the data equally well. Indeed, Davis and Restle, emphasizing that their application is tentative, remark that any set of latency data could be fit by various combinations of stages and difficulty levels. Accordingly, the conclusion that there are three discrete stages of equal difficulty cannot, even as an approximation, be considered to be on firm ground.

Of course, the assumption of equally difficult stages is not basic and need be no more than a first approximation. It would certainly be possible to extend the analysis by allowing for stages of unequal difficulty (McGill, 1963; McGill and Gibbon, 1965). A very large experimental program would probably be required, however, and it would be largely irrelevant and wasted if the more basic assumptions about the thought process were wrong. Thus, the assumption that the solution is reached by a sequence of distinct independent steps is basic. So also is the assumption that disallows gradual progress within a stage. The estimate of the number of stages, which the model analysis will always supply, may be an irrelevant number if these last two assumptions are seriously false.

The second class of assumptions, which pertain primarily to the data, requires only brief mention since the difficulties are largely technical. In the data analysis, subjects who did not solve the problem within the allowed time were necessarily eliminated, a procedure that is not unreasonable within the given context (Restle and Davis, 1962). At the same time, it was assumed that the remaining subjects were "identical," having equal skill and ability on the problem, and the same values of the model parameters. However, individual differences just in the speed of solving a stage would bias the estimated number of stages downward. It was further assumed that no subject simply guessed the answer, and a correction for the time required to read the problem was also made. Although this correction may be justified in principle, the actual procedure is questionable since the correction was made by subtracting from each subject's score the mean reading time for a sample of subjects at a different school. This also could bias the estimate of the number of stages. How serious these biases might be is not known.

After having gone through this assessment of the Restle-Davis work, my own feeling is that the substantive implications that were drawn from the model analysis have slight support. These implications may be true, but the evidence is uncertain and tenuous. This may seem like cavalier treatment of a quantitative fit to the distribution of latencies, but fitting the distribution was not exacting. Moreover, previous experience has shown that good predictions can be obtained from models that were later found incorrect when subjected to more detailed and careful tests on the same data (e.g., Anderson, 1964; Suppes and Ginsberg, 1963). Good initial predictions in such cases testify against the practical usefulness of the mathematical-model approach.

Some of the present reservations about the analysis of the logic-twister data could be resolved by more extensive model analysis. For instance, it would be possible to test whether or not individual differences introduce a serious bias. Similarly, it would be possible to determine whether the simplest alternative models would fit the data. In the present state of development of mathematical models, such effort might be expected as a matter of course, much as control groups are used in more empirical research. These additional analyses are often tedious, but without them it may not be possible to say much.

The above difficulties are common among mathematical models and, in general, they seem to get distinctly less attention than they need. Criticism of Restle's paper should not obscure the very definite value of his attack on thought processes; however, at the same time, the difficulties in using mathematical analyses are real, and resolving them will often be difficult or impossible. Consequently, an alternative approach would be desirable.

A Search Task

The task to be described was designed to avoid the difficulties in the mathematical-model analysis. It provides a direct experimental test of the search model described in Restle's paper; whether or not the Restle model is correct will appear directly in the data. Moreover, the task provides similar tests of a wider class of search models.

The task itself is a descendant of the word production problems employed by Bousfield and Sedgewick (1944), and in its simplest version it is quite similar to a task employed by Sternberg (1966) to study memory scanning. The general spirit of the present approach is also similar to that of Sternberg (e.g., Sternberg, 1963).

In the search task, the subject first memorizes a set of N words. The following short list will be used for illustration:

pig   cat   dog   hen   cow   hog

Once the set is thoroughly memorized, various types of questions may be asked. Two such question-types are particularly relevant; the first may be exemplified as follows:

Which one word has as its middle letter: *e*?

To answer this question, the subject must search through the words in his memory storage. His search would then end when "hen" is found and recognized to be correct. In most of this discussion, it will be assumed that the subject selects and tests one word at a time from memory. It will also be assumed that the words are equal in ease of sampling and testing.

Just this sort of situation is envisaged in the one-stage search discussed by Restle, at least if the words are taken as "hypotheses." To apply the Restle-Davis model, only the further assumption is required that the words are selected randomly, with replacement. This last proviso means that the subject has no effective memory for previous words tested so that, for instance, "cat" could be sampled and tested several times in succession.

The data would be the response latencies, and the Restle-Davis analysis could be applied directly to estimate parameters and test goodness of fit, though some allowance might be needed for input-output time. Compared to the logic-twister problem, there would be fewer difficulties in evaluating the results, partly because the "hypotheses" are under experimental control, and partly because it would be feasible to control intersubject differences.

The second question type is much more powerful. It may be exemplified as follows:

Which three words end in: g?

Let t_1 be the time from specification of the search cue to the first response, and let t_2 and t_3 be the respective times from the first to the second, and from the second to the third response. The first response time, t_1, will be ignored for reasons given below. However, Restle's model implies that the mean value of t_3 is twice that of t_2: $E(t_3) = 2E(t_2)$. This relationship may be tested directly in the raw data.

The given relation between the means of the second and third interresponse times depends upon the existence of exactly three words that end in g. For the second response, there then remain two correct words, and for the third response, only one. Since sampling is random with replacement, each word sampled in the second stage has two chances in N of being correct and, similarly, each word sampled in the third stage has one chance in N of being correct. The given relation then follows at once from the assumption that each word requires equal time to process. More generally, if there are K correct answers, and i is a particular correct response, the above relation on the i th response becomes:

$$[K - i + 1]\,[E(t_i)] = [K - i]\,[E(t_{i+1})]$$

Strictly speaking, the above derivation requires that the model be augmented by a mechanism that recognizes and rejects sampled words that are correct but have already been given. This addition should not complicate the model, and it is known that subjects do act that way. In this form, the model is an example of the "extinction chains" discussed by McGill (1963).

The test of the model based on the second question is markedly superior to the model analysis based on the first. The test of fit is made on the raw data. No parameters need be estimated, and each subject serves as his own control.

A finding that t_2 and t_3 had the specified relation would testify directly to the correctness of the assumption that sampling is random with replacement. From its other assumptions, the Restle-Davis model would predict that both t_2 and t_3 are exponentially distributed, and this could be easily checked. McGill (1963) gives expressions for the distribution of $t_2 + t_3$, and similar statistics.

If the model survives the above tests, application of the formal model analysis would be superfluous. It might be desirable to do, however, to evaluate the statistical properties of the model analysis. Such information could be very useful for comparison when the model was applied to other tasks in which the hypotheses were not experimentally controlled.

It is also possible that the model would fail the experimental test. Two main possibilities need comment.

First, the model might fail because of inadequate experimental technique. In this regard, a number of obvious precautions might be mentioned. For most purposes, considerable practice both with the set of words and with the questions would seem desirable. Such practice would tend to make the various words equally available in memory, although some care might be needed to avoid instilling a fixed serial search order. Thus, one could get $E(t_3)$ greater than $E(t_2)$ simply because the third response was less available. Fortunately, many similar questions can be asked about a given list, and interspersed repetitions of the same question might prove feasible and interesting.

If response emission required a time comparable to that of the search itself, the interresponse times might not represent the search process very well. On this basis, relatively large interresponse times would be desirable so that moderately large sets of words may be most generally useful, and questions harder than one-letter identifications may be needed. One-letter identifications could themselves be made harder, of course, by using longer words. Of course, it would ordinarily be desirable to use a homogeneous list to help ensure that the words were equally easy to sample and test.

More generally, one would need to keep in mind the possible role of input and output times (Anderson, 1959; McGill and Gibbon, 1965). In the second of the above questions, for instance, a certain time is required for g to reach the brain. This input time will add onto the search time for the first, but not for the second or later responses. It was for this reason that t_1 was ignored in the critical test.

Failure of the model to fit the data could also mean that the model was at fault, and not the data. Since it seems clear that the task does require search, failure to fit would presumably mean that the nature of the search process is different from that assumed by Restle.

Other modes of search may also be considered. For instance, sampling of the words could be without rather than with replacement. It is then easy to show that $E(t_2) = E(t_3)$. More generally, if there are K words that are correct, then the expected number of words that must be sampled and tested between any two successive responses is $1 + (N - K)/(K + 1)$. Thus, all mean interresponse times would be equal, the first being excepted as before. In addition, the interresponse time intercorrelations would be negative under sampling without replacement, whereas they would be zero if sampling were with replacement.

The possibility that the search is nonrandom must be carefully considered. The extreme case that the subject searched the list in fixed serial order could easily be tested. It would only be necessary to construct a list in which two different questions had each the same two answers, and observe whether the answers were given in the same order in each case. With more labor, a partial tendency to search in a certain order could be detected, and distinguished from random sampling with unequal probabilities. These possibilities would need early testing since deviations from simple random sampling would cause discrepancies from the above predictions. In certain cases, at least, these could be avoided with due forethought in designing the experiment.

Parallel search is also a possibility. In its simplest form, of course, it would imply that response time for a one-answer question would be independent of set size. On the other hand, most of the above discussion would apply even if the subject sampled several items at a time, given a small sample size relative to list length.

Now, each mode of search represents a model of the process that underlies the behavior. These models may easily be cast in mathematical form, at least for the simpler modes of search. From these assumptions, it would then be straightforward to elaborate the deductive consequences. This, indeed, is what Restle and Davis have done for one particular mode of search.

However, if the search follows any simple mode, this will be visible in the raw data, with only modest ingenuity required in constructing the search question. In this task, therefore, one could hope that the nature of the search process would be almost an empirical matter, not requiring an elaborate chain of assumptional and statistical inference. And if the search process is not simple, this would probably become clear from the experimental analysis far sooner than from the mathematical-model analysis.

Of course, it should be explicitly realized that the search process in the logic-twister may be different from that in the present word-search task. The model used by Restle and Davis could succeed in the one task and fail in the other. Nevertheless, the word-search data could hardly fail to afford helpful hints about the model analysis of more complex thought problems. And in any case, it should not be difficult to extend the search task in such a way that the answers require thought comparable to that in the problems employed by Restle and Davis.

Extensions of the Search Task

The original purpose in constructing the search task was to get a firm test of the Restle-Davis model as outlined in the previous section. However, the task seems to have intrinsic interest so that a few possible extensions will be mentioned briefly. One direction of extension would be toward search lists of sentences or ideas, rather than single words. Here however, the extension will be toward more complex search questions, based on a list of simple words as before. Three main problems will be noted.

Whether retrieval from memory is random or ordered arose as a methodological question in the previous section. For many purposes, the assumption of random retrieval is convenient and worth some experimental effort to ensure if possible. Ordered retrieval is not less plausible, however, and the nature of the retrieval concerns the theory of both the storage and search mechanisms. For more detailed consideration, a distinction may be needed between order in the search and order in the memory storage. Random search will necessarily produce random output. However, order in the output may reflect order in the search or order in both search and memory.

The most direct attack on this question would have the subject memorize the words in fixed serial order. If the search were then made in that order, response times to single-answered questions would vary directly with the list position of the answer. A random search might yield a bowed serial curve, since it would be difficult to ensure equal memory strength of all items of a serial list. The use of two-answered questions, as noted in the previous section, could disclose serial ordering other than of the serial list. In general, other questions need not yield the same output order as that which asks for reproduction of the serial list.

Order could also be in terms of class membership in which variety of list-question combinations are possible. For example, the list could consist of names of mammals and birds, and the search question could be a letter-identification with two or more answers. Shorter interresponse times with all answers in one rather than both classes would be one indication of ordering in terms of class membership. With multi-answered questions, categorical clustering in recall (Bousfield and Sedgewick, 1944) would be an even more direct indicator.

The second problem concerns the more detailed specification of the search process. It would appear that there are actually two forms of search that occur: a search that produces words from list memory, and a search associated with each separate word. Thus, with the conjunctive question:

Which words have as first and fourth letters: b and a?

or even with the disjunctive question:

Which words contain: b?

the subject presumably searches through memory word by word, and searches through each word in some possibly serial way.

The within-word search involves some recognition or comparison process. In the second of the above questions, recognition of b would presumably be of the direct perceptual kind mentioned by Haber and by Posner in their papers. In the first question, some short-term storage would also be required unless the within-word search were simple parallel.

Search questions based on meaning rather than on form would require a more complex recognition process. For instance, with the illustrative list used previously, one could ask, "Which one is the bird?" or equivalently, "Which one has no teeth?"

The most important theoretical problem for these last questions concerns the way in which the attributes or aspects of a concept are stored in and retrieved from memory. Presumably, the various attributes of hens are stored in some more-or-less unified way, but even so it is doubtful that thinking of a hen evokes a retrieval from memory of all those attributes. Indeed, the attribute of "no teeth" may pertain to birds and apply to hen only by mediation. It may be possible to construct search questions that will yield a more precise formulation of this problem. However, this begins to pass the scope of the present discussion to the more cognitive aspects of thought.

All questions that have been considered so far have had single words as answers, even though some questions have had several answers. It is worth noting, therefore, that there are questions for which the answer is a subset of words that are interrelated in some way. Such questions would be especially appropriate for the study of thought, since thought usually involves, not simply a search, but more importantly, a construction of parts into a whole.

One of the simplest such questions, based on the previous list, would be: "Which two words rhyme?" This is another search question, of course, although one in which the search cue is not explicitly given.

A simple model would assume that the subject compares two words at a time until the hog-dog comparison ends the search. From a list of N words, random sampling with replacement would require an average of $N(N - 1)/2$ comparisons. Random sampling without replacement, the most efficient method, would still require $[N(N - 1) + 2]/4$ comparisons on the average. In either case, solution time would be quadratic in list length if all comparisons took equal time. Further information about the search process could be obtained from using several words with the same rhyme. The last case has additional interest since it involves the buildup of partial solutions mentioned by Restle. Once the subject has found two words that rhyme, the remaining words will no doubt require very little extra time. Of course, recognition of a partial solution is particularly easy in this question, and Restle is undoubtedly correct in thinking that the analysis of the problem will be highly task-specific.

Finally, it may be noted that these search questions are in many ways well suited for analysis by computer-program theories of behavior. As has been remarked by Restle in his paper, and by Carterette (1967), computerized symbol-processing models have had very light contact with serious data. In part, this seems to have come about because they have been applied to behavior that is not only complex but complicated. The present search task may be at once simple and complex enough to provide a common ground on which to compare mathematical models with computer-simulation techniques.

Concluding Remarks

The main argument of this discussion is simply summarized. If the psychological processes that underly the search behavior are the same as those assumed by Restle, then they will be immediately visible in the raw data of the experiments that have been suggested. Furthermore, if the processes are of certain other simple forms, they also will be seen immediately in the data. Thus, the search task gives a strong, direct test of the theoretical notions, while avoiding the difficulties and uncertainties found in the mathematical-model analysis. For the question at issue, therefore, it seems fair to say that experimental analysis is both more powerful and more general than mathematical-model analysis.

The conclusion from this example holds, I suspect, more generally. No doubt there is a natural tendency for model-theoretic preoccupation to lead to a neglect of the relevant behavior (e.g., Anderson, 1964). Beyond that, however, I wish to suggest that for any problem that allows a model analysis, a more efficient experimental analysis can usually be found.

This does not imply that we should try to do without mathematical models or without theory. Involvement with underlying processes can certainly be treacherous, but contrary to the position taken by Bourne in his paper (Chap. 6), I believe that process notions are often legitimate. Behavior is often of interest per se, and attribution of process may then be unnecessary, not to say gratuitous (Skinner, 1950). More often, however, experimental work will be more cogent the more closely it attempts to delineate the psychological processes that underly the behavior. Most of the experiments suggested here have just such purpose, and would otherwise be rather uninteresting. Thus, if certain simple relationships were found in the observed latency data, a fairly immediate and compelling inference about the nature and existence of the unobserved search process could be made. Thus, one could identify simple search with or without replacement, even though the observed behavior does not simply reflect the structure of the underlying process. It is optimistic, of course, to think that any simple process will explain behavior in the search task, but for the present point it is sufficient that this could happen.

Mathematical models, themselves, have various virtues, not the least of which is that of evoking more detailed and exacting conceptual analyses. That the model predictions fit the data, however, is ordinarily of value only insofar as it helps reveal the processes that underly the behavior. Too often, this is difficult to assess, as has been illustrated here. The locus of the difficulty, it should be noted, was less in the model itself than in the way it was tested. Indeed, the recommended experimental analysis was also designed to test the model, though more generally to elucidate the processes that would constitute the basis of any model. Perhaps it could be argued that the main value of mathematical elaboration lies in suggesting more incisive experimental planning, and that one could almost hope to obtain experiments that would be viable, independent of any particular model. As a practical guideline, I consider this view to be quite attractive, although the problem is not one that can be resolved by all-or-none slogans, however attractive they may be.

I wish to conclude with two apologies. Frank Restle, whose insight and imagination I admire, has been but ill-repaid in these remarks for his pioneering work in the mathematical analysis of thought. What value they may have owes much to him. And from the reader, I ask forbearance for considering so many possible experiments with no data at all. I believe, however, that a potentially good experimental task—one that would hold the mirror up to nature—deserves discussion as much as any theory.

REFERENCES

Anderson, N. H. Temporal properties of response evocation. In P. R. Bush and W. K. Estes (Eds.), *Studies in mathematical learning theory.* Stanford: Stanford University Press, 1959. Pp. 248-264.

Anderson, N. H. An evaluation of stimulus sampling theory: comments on Professor Estes' paper. In A. W. Melton (Ed.), *Categories of human learning.* New York: Academic Press, 1964. Pp. 129-144.

Bousfield, W. A., and Sedgewick, C. H. W. An analysis of sequences of restricted associative responses. *J. gen. Psychol.,* 1944, *30,* 149-165.

Carterette, E. C. Calculo ergo cogito ergo sum. *Contemp. Psychol.,* 1967, *12,* 16-17.

Davis, J. H., and Restle, F. The analysis of problems and prediction of group problem solving. *J. abnorm. soc. Psychol.,* 1963, *66,* 103-116.

McGill, W. J. Stochastic latency mechanisms. In R. D. Luce, R. R. Bush, and E. Galanter (Eds.), *Handbook of mathematical psychology,* Vol. I. New York: Wiley, 1963. Pp. 309-360.

McGill, W. J., and Gibbon, J. The general-gamma distribution and re-action times. *J. math. Psychol.,* 1965, *2,* 1-18.

Restle, F., and Davis, J. H. Success and speed of problem solving by individuals and groups. *Psychol. Rev.,* 1962, *69,* 520-536.

Skinner, B. F. Are theories of learning necessary? *Psychol. Rev.,* 1950, *57,* 193-216.

Sternberg, S. Stochastic learning theory. In R. D. Luce, R. R. Bush, and E. Galanter (Eds.), *Handbook of mathematical psychology,* Vol. II. New York: Wiley, 1963. Pp. 1-120.

Sternberg, S. High-speed scanning in human memory. *Science*, 1966, *153*, 652-654.

Suppes, P., and Ginsberg, R. A fundamental property of all-or-none models. *Psychol. Rev.*, 1963, *70*, 139-161.

GENERAL DISCUSSION

RESTLE commented that the task of the experimenter is to illustrate the relevance of a model to a given type of task. He further maintained that it is unfair to take a model designed to explain one type of task and test its fit to a different type of task. RESTLE indicated, moreover, that he felt Anderson's task would be so simple that the process would become complex because the subject would be free to use any number of self-imposed processes beyond the experimenter's control. RESTLE added that Davis' problem constrains the subject's resources so that he must stick to the task.

It was mentioned by SIMON that an alternative to a random search model is some type of feedback model, and the problem becomes one of determining what type of feedback is used. SIMON also raised the question of why Restle was puzzled about the subject's ability to limit the searchable space, for subjects tend to search in this manner; e.g., a chess player.

RESTLE replied by stating that Simon assumes general understanding and heuristic applications, with one serving as evidence for the presence of the other. The problem, RESTLE indicated, is to establish independently that the subject does have the general knowledge and that he may be able to use heuristics.

REITMAN indicated that it is not unfair to assume both the understanding and the heuristics, for to make such an assumption is to say that the subjects must know the rules and know when to use them.

RESTLE stated that one can find all kinds of heuristics that the subject has used. The problem, he maintained, is to determine where the heuristics come from.

NEWELL observed that he conducted an experiment in which one subject took 20 minutes and another took 1 1/2 minutes to solve the same problem, which could be interpreted as the use of radically different methods (i.e., heuristics).

RESTLE indicated that such variability probably could be eliminated by proper use of instructions with which a hierarchy of heuristics would be established.

NEWELL then asked Restle whether he really wasn't proposing that sampling from the hierarchy takes place without replacement.

REITMAN commented that one implication of Restle's position is that generality of models across problems is poor; the subject, in other words, may "cook up" his own model for each specific case. However, REITMAN continued, the problem that a general theory must answer is how the subject goes about choosing his strategy.

RESTLE indicated that he agreed with Reitman's comment regarding the aim of a general theory. The strategic "outs" for one who holds this position, he pointed out, are, first, to speak of a class of experiments which involve some strategy, and second, to find out why models do not transfer from one class of experiments to another.

It was observed by REITMAN that failure to generalize across tasks may lead to an infinite proliferation of special-purpose models.

ATKINSON commented that he was more concerned about the other extreme; i.e., providing a model of complexity such as the General Problem Solver. He further commented that what is needed is a structure to define tasks and models.

6

CONCEPT LEARNING AND THOUGHT: BEHAVIOR, NOT PROCESS[1]

LYLE E. BOURNE, JR.

University of Colorado

The alleged purpose of this paper is to show how theoretical and empirical research on human conceptual behavior has or might contribute to an understanding of thought. The task is formidable for many reasons, not the least of which is a lack of any substantial agreement about the primary subject matter, thinking. Unless there is an acceptable (albeit incomplete) answer to the question of what thinking is, there is no obvious *way* to proceed. But perhaps the more basic question is, Would everyone recognize the correct answer if there were

[1] This paper is publication number 97 of the Institute of Behavioral Science, University of Colorado. Its preparation and some of the research reported were facilitated by grants GB-3404, National Science Foundation, and MH-08315, National Institute of Mental Health, U. S. Public Health Service. A preliminary draft was written during the summer, 1966, while the author was a visitor in the Research and Development Center for Learning and Re-education, University of Wisconsin. The author is grateful to members of the Center for their assistance and for the use of their facilities.

The author is indebted also to Peter G. Ossorio, Maynard Shelly, Keith E. Davis, Arthur W. Staats, and Gary A. Davis, who read and commented critically on an earlier version of the manuscript. Many of the ideas reported here emerged from a series of discussions with Ossorio and K. Davis. Their many contributions are acknowledged with appreciation and gratitude.

one and it were given? If the answer to that is No, there is no point to proceeding.

The fact that we have a dilemma is disheartening, but that hasn't stopped many of us from talking about thinking, or from positing "thought processes" as the mechanisms which permit or enable organisms to do the complex things they do. And it is largely because of this that there is something to discuss in this paper.

The plan is as follows: First, a summary of some of the current theoretical work in the area of concept formation will be presented. Detailed accounts are available in a number of sources (Hunt, 1962; Kleinmuntz, 1966; Bourne, 1966a,b) so the descriptions will be brief. Emphasis will be placed upon what might be described as the representation of thinking in theory, though there is no hope that the respective theorists would agree entirely with this interpretation of their work. Second, there will be an examination of the logic which relates thinking, as it is embodied in the theories, to behavior. Given that there might be certain inadequacies in these formulations, the next step will be to suggest an alternative which has implications not only for theory but also for the analysis of behavior. Some illustrative research will then be discussed in order to point up the possible uses of an alternative approach. Finally, the paper will return briefly to "thinking" and its place as a concept in psychology.

Theories of Conceptual Behavior

Many contemporary theories about conceptual behavior are special cases of learning theory. While there is considerable variation, most of them are recognized easily as one of two main types.

S-R associational theories. Theories based on the principle of association formation describe a concept as a set of connections between some response and certain attributes or cues in stimulus patterns (Kendler, 1961). These S-R associations are assumed to gain strength gradually as a function of repeated and (relatively) consistent reinforcement of the correct response in the presence of the relevant stimulus attributes. Eventually, associative strength becomes maximal and the concept is said to be formed. The associations are assumed to exist between only certain attributes of the stimuli and the response, so that these are the effective determiners of response. Irrelevant or unimportant attributes—those which vary from one instance of the concept to another—fail to develop any significant associative strength. Indeed, some variants of this description (Bourne and Restle, 1959) propose a process of adaptation, concurrent with the development of associations, which results in the suppression of irrelevant cues (in a sense, the subject learns to ignore them). The proper associations develop in such a way that whenever the defining attributes occur, even in the context of a new stimulus pattern, the conceptual response will be elicited.

In most basic form, theories of this type make no assumptions about processes within the organism, except for those which concern the establishment of associations and the possibility of persistent memory traces. Behavior is a consequence of external stimulus conditions and no assertions are made about intervening, autonomous thought processes. Concept formation, like other forms of learning, is the more or less mechanical connecting up of stimulus and response. No distinction in theory is made between concept formation—the original association of any response with the defining stimulus attributes of a concept—and concept utilization—the reflection of these associations in some different, secondary task such as the identification or discovery of one among several known concepts. Presumably, the principles of transfer of training, especially those concerned with stimulus and response similarity variables, are sufficient for an adequate interpretation of "utilization" problems.

"Hypothesis" theories. Hypothesis-testing or process (Kleinmuntz, 1966) theories (no rubric is entirely satisfactory), in contrast to associational theories, typically characterize the concept as some internal, cognitive representation of objective events or relationships among events. Behavior is largely a by-product of selecting a concept as an hypothesis from the available repertoire (from among those concepts which the subject knows) and acting upon it. The selected concept (hypothesis) is often said to "govern" or to control overt behavior. In a problematic situation, the subject always entertains at least one hypothesis. Each stimulus pattern encountered provides a test of the selected hypothesis—leading to its rejection, revision, or acceptance as a solution. Assumedly, the repertoire of available hypotheses at any given time is a function of nativistic factors and past experience. In theory, new concepts are learned or, better, constructed by putting old concepts together in novel ways. When the problem requires the utilization of a known concept, the task is simply to select or identify which of the available concepts is correct.

Unlike their associational counterparts, hypothesis theories often attribute important internal monitoring and processing functions to the organism. He receives incoming information, makes some kind of consistency check with his current hypothesis, and undertakes decision processes which result in a modification of the hypothesis and, only secondarily, in an overt act of behavior. Further, reinforcement or informative feedback is presumed to operate not directly on behavior but rather on the implicit processes which control behavior (Levine, 1966). These internal activities could, obviously, be construed as the sum and substance of thinking. It might be noted that, although these processes are nonobservable, they are described in terms ("reacting to," "comparing," "selecting and revising," "acting upon") much like those used to characterize overt behavior. In some cases, hypothesis theories seem to embody the notion of implicit rehearsal of action, prior to action itself.

Internalized behavior and the mediational response. What is the origin of an implicit hypothesis or process? Knowing what we do about behavior, the answer (if there is one) should lie at least partly in learning. Surely the individual can internalize only those behaviors which come naturally (e.g., reflexes) or which have been acquired in overt form. Hypothesis-testing and more complicated behaviors are characteristic of sophisticated organisms and depend on a backlog of training and experience which is transferable to new situations.

The mechanics of converting an overt behavior into an internal analog have been the subject of considerable speculation. A popular and intuitively reasonable argument is the mediation hypothesis, first adumbrated by early Behaviorists, later formalized by Hull (1930), and more recently elaborated in the interpretation of a wide range of behaviors by contemporary S-R theorists (e.g., Goss, 1961; Kendler and Kendler, 1962; Osgood, 1953; Staats and Staats, 1964). The general idea is that, in the course of associating external stimuli with overt responses, some representation of behavior becomes anticipatory, producing self-stimulation that has a covert, cognitive, or symbolic cue function. The anticipatory behavior might or might not be a full replica of the overt responses associated with the stimulus. It is said to be mediational in the sense that the self-stimulation it produces can become associated with other overt responses as might be appropriate in a subsequent learning situation.

Insofar as conceptual behavior is concerned, the notion of verbal mediators seems to be particularly important. Kendler and Kendler (1962), as well as Kendler (1960, 1961), have argued in effect that language, first acquired in the form of overt responses serving primarily a communicative function, becomes the means of regulating other overt actions. As a child matures and learns, his activity is mediated through words. This developmental process is represented theoretically by the transition from a single-unit S-R system to a double- (or multi-) unit system, involving verbal mediational components. The Kendlers' analysis of the change in relative difficulty of reversal and nonreversal shifts in the solution of simple conceptual problems in terms of this transition is well known. Goss (1961) and Staats (1961; Staats and Staats, 1964) have extended the mechanism of verbal mediation in an attempt to describe information processing, hypotheses, strategies and other implicit activities often assumed to occur in conceptual problems.

Somewhat different is a proposal by Mandler (1962). He agrees that the basic form of learning is associational—external S with external R or external R_1 with external R_2 probably mediated by stimuli produced by R_1. With practice (training) the correct response or response sequence becomes stable, able to be run off quickly and without error. In the case of inter-associations between two or more responses, the entire sequence comes to function as a unit, much as the individual response elements prior to training. Once associated (or integrated), the new response unit generates (how is unclear) an internal structural representation or analog, which functions independently of the overt behavior it represents.

Analogic structures and mediational processes, being the "substance" of covert activity, are two contemporary, associational vehicles of thought. They are said to provide for cognitive control of behavior. Many mediators or structures might be elicited in a given stimulus situation—this depends on the history and abilities of the subject. Overt behaviors are guided by one or another of these internal processes as determined, perhaps, by their relative strengths, generalization, and other variables. Incorrect or inadequate implicit activities, among those available to the subject, are rejected (suppressed or extinguished) on the basis of events consequent to overt behavior. Eventually, the correct implicit process will become dominant, relative to others; will be reinforced; and, thus, will control the characteristics of the subject's outward performance.

Contrasts and comparisons. It is treacherous to make general statements here, for the individual theorists do not always agree in detail. However, there appear to be few substantive differences among the concepts of mediational process, analogic structure, and hypothesis. With respect to the analog and the mediator, two issues arise. First, mediators in general are thought to be associated with overt behaviors, leading directly to the occurrence of those behaviors. There is no implication of similarity in form between the mediational response and the overt response with which it might become associated. Structures, on the other hand, presumably can occur independently of overt behavior and are not associated in the usual sense with a consequent action. However, the analog (as the name implies) does reflect faithfully and completely some explicit response sequence, to which it leads under the right conditions. Second, the unit mediator seems rather more limited (better defined?) than the unit analog. Whereas the mediator is described in terms of separable response elements; e.g., attending or naming, the analog is any functional response unit including those comprised of several integrated sub-units and takes on, though not explicitly, the character of a rule for organizing sub-units, rather than the peculiar mechanics of the units themselves. But this latter difference might be illusory, for Goss (1961) has argued that mediators too can be interpreted as complex self-instructions which tell the organism what to do in an "organized" way.

The hypothesis idea has some of the character of both mediators and analogs. It seems to contribute little in the way of additional insight into covert activity, although the various forms of hypothesis theory might generate unique expectations of data. In general, however, hypotheses are internal representations of external events and/or potential action which very well might arise from the acquisition of behavior in overt form via associational processes. The all-or-none character of concept learning implied by some hypothesis theories (e.g., Bower and Trabasso, 1963), which is said to be a consequence of hypothesis-testing, could just as conceivably reflect the shifting of mediators or analogs.

Criticism and an Alternative

Mediating stimuli and responses, symbolic analogs, hypotheses— these are some of the modern counterparts of the older elements of the mind, like ideas, images, and feelings. This is the stuff of which thoughts are made and on which thinking (thought processes?) works its magic—at least so some contemporary theorizing might suggest. Once all the intricate, internal, covert, or hypothetical processes have run their course—out comes behavior. Behavior gets subordinated to the underlying process(es) and begins to take on all the earmarks of a rather trivial, almost unessential thing.

Comment. There is no question about the reality of certain private experiences or events such as subvocal speech and visual images. When the concept of thinking is limited to these covert activities, it takes a weak form and, like other behavior, is something that a researcher might seek to find out about through experiments. When these (or other hypothetical) covert activities are further endowed with the special properties of antecedence, control, and causation of overt behavior, the concept takes the stronger form found in at least some theoretical systems.

Why the underlying process? The necessity for assumptions about internal, regulating processes seems to arise from widespread disbelief that overt responses fully reflect all that the subject has learned or knows. We observe the organism classifying complex, multidimensional stimulus patterns in a conceptual task and it is tempting to ask, What lies behind it? How did he figure out how to do it? What are the underlying bases of his classification? There are problems, moreover, with analyzing certain empirical outcomes, such as the relative difficulty of reversal and nonreversal shifts (Kendler and Kendler, 1962), in terms of the establishment of discriminative responses to some specifiable, recurrent set of physical stimuli, and so it seems obligatory to assume the existence of preparatory internal activities and to ascribe responses to some sort of covert, computational mechanism involving mediators, hypotheses, response generators, or what not. And this is thinking.

Criticism. Such theorizing makes for interesting (sometimes exciting) prose; but its contribution to an understanding of thinking and behavior is not always clear. *Assertions* about underlying processes, and correlative ascriptions of behavior, *are not harmless*, if they are taken seriously and literally. *They demand careful examination* and a defense based on necessity, lest the theorist be accused of "explaining away" (not accounting for) important empirical problems and of asserting too much. Theories of conceptual behavior which embody assumptions about underlying processes are questionable on at least three points.

First, underlying processes are commonly described in behavioral terms; e.g., a process which selects and revises hypotheses or compares items of information. The process often sounds suspiciously like behavior gone underground. Moreover, once there it gains the property of control over its outward counterpart. But, as stated, it would seem that the internal process can do nothing a man himself cannot do, publically and overtly. So the task of accounting for human behavior remains. A process description of what organisms do or can do is sensible. After all, behavior is indeed a process. But the theoretical description of a (nonbehavioral) process *which controls behavior* is another matter and requires an entirely different kind of evidence.

Second, such a theory seems to impose the necessity to study invisible processes—processes which might not exist and for which there is no extra-behavioral description (certainly not physiological) which permits recognition when and if they did occur. There is the familiar argument, of course, that internal processes are hypothetical, and that it really does not make any difference how they are characterized. One is free to make any plausible identifications between formal parameters of the model and behavioral events. What counts is how well the theory describes the data. But if that is so, where is the need for process-talk? Nothing apparently hinges on the processes, and it should be possible to describe (and in that sense account for) the behavior of interest; viz., what people can do, in a direct rather than roundabout fashion. If one insists on a theory of a process, he must be prepared to show what difference having the process makes.

Third, the theoretical underlying process seems often to be an invention—an invented answer to the question, What has the subject learned that enabled him to respond as he did? The subject's responses are obviously systematic and organized. Something seems to be needed to do the coordinating. A mechanism working on those coordinating principles is invented, and the invention then is said to "explain" the subject's behavior. There is some redundancy in this reasoning which is illustrated in what follows. But the more basic question is whether there is any need to be concerned about a psychological enabling mechanism that permits behavior to be what it is.

None of this should be taken to impugn attempts to describe (or redescribe) conceptual behavior within a particular classification scheme or quantitative model. It is of considerable interest and importance to determine whether performances may be described by a small set of strategies, to plot performance changes over trials, to search for rules which characterize response sequences, and to compute the fine-grain statistics of data. Whenever empirical information can be summarized and adequately described in a general formulation, it is evidence of genuine progress. These devices provide a handle on behavior—a means for distinguishing behaviors, of recognizing equivalent behaviors, and of identifying new behaviors. They help to show and to explain how the subject solved the conceptual problem.

But there is a difference between saying that the organism's behavior can be described and accounted for satisfactorily in a particular way, and saying that the subject learned something which allowed or enabled a particular description or account to be satisfied. For example, it has become routine for mathematical models to give precise and detailed quantitative accounts of learning data. It is largely for this reason that models are of great use and value in experimental psychology. But, as has been said by others, a model can be right for the wrong reasons (e.g., Anderson, 1964). Its description can be accurate while, at the same time, untenable psychological properties are assigned to its formal parameters and rules. Neither the conceptual development, nor the use of the model in the analysis of experiments, is in any way dependent on these identifications (Bush and Mosteller, 1955). And its value in providing an account of behavior is neither lessened nor enhanced by its psychological "embellishments." Thus, just because the individual's behavior is accurately "predicted" by some rationally derived equation is no evidence that any underlying control processes said to be signified, represented, or identified with the model exist or occur. There are straightforward, objective criteria for deciding whether a model fits the data. But there seem to be no useful criteria for deciding which, if any, underlying processes enabled the data—the subject's behavior—to satisfy the model and the description it provides.

Similarly, while empirical findings might be nicely summarized in terms of the rules of performance that are learned, as matters now stand there are no obvious gains to be had by asking what *psychological process* enabled the individual to follow the rules. Indeed, the question almost forces regression to an invention. Another answer that makes sense, considering the derivation of rules, classification systems, models, and underlying processes from behavior, has already been given; subjects learn to solve conceptual problems in certain systematic ways. The system can be stated as a set of rules, and it is possible to determine the adequacy with which these rules describe or reproduce behavior, or predict behavior on historically different occasions. The rules are principles of behavior, not principles of a mechanism which in turn produces behavior. Finding an answer to the further question about an enabling mechanism (if there is one) is not a necessary condition for understanding or explaining the fact that the subject did what he did.

Thinking and behavior. It would be dead wrong to draw the conclusion from this discussion that people do not think, or that the phenomena of thinking are not complex. What this treatment means to suggest is that many of the complexities are behavioral complexities; they reside in what people do or can do, and, as things stand, are not fruitfully relegated to a governing position interior to the organism and antecedent to behavior. The task of psychology is to ascertain which objective factors in the past and present states of the organism and his environment make a difference in how he behaves, so that behavior can be described and predicted rather than merely attributed to another process.

How is it possible to say that the complexities lie in the subject's behavior when in fact all the organism might be observed to do in the course of solving a conceptual problem is press buttons or sort out cards? These are rather humdrum, everyday-type responses—easily within the capacities of even some quite stupid organisms. Surely when a human being forms a concept, he learns more than button-pressing responses; and it seems fair to ask, What's behind it?

A significant part of the problem is that this description is built on an arbitrary and limiting definition of response and of what constitutes a behavior. The button-press (or whatever is required on each trial) is typically cited as the functional behavioral unit. References are made to changes in its probability of occurrence and to the possibility of its being reinforceable in a unitary fashion, as if it were *the* response being learned or associated in a conceptual problem. But there is nothing natural about this; it follows more from experimental procedure than from empirical evidence. The selection of a workable unit of analysis or description does not guarantee that it is the proper, most meaningful, or most useful one. Neither does it carry any implications about the structure of behavior or about what is learned. The bounds marking one response from another are often unspecifiable. It is clear that any particular unit; e.g., a button-press, can be redescribed in terms of more elementary components. And, if that is the case, it must also be the case that any such response might, itself, be conceptualized as a component of an even larger unit. Clearly, there are various modes of description and classification of behavior which are not necessarily commensurable, and the whole idea of response units—meaningful as separate and isolated entities—bears careful examination.

But that is not at issue here. The point to be made is that many of the complexities commonly identified with thinking might very well find their representation in behavior—not in underlying, antedating mechanisms—and might very well be describable and understandable if behavior itself were viewed not as movements or as a collection of individual, operationally separate (though perhaps inter-associated) units, but rather as an ongoing rule-following *process*.

Rules of behavior. Psychology has been deluged in the last few ears (e.g., Chomsky, 1957; Miller, Galanter and Pribram, 1960; Smith, 1966) with demonstrations of the seemingly obvious fact that human beings have an almost unlimited capacity for new, yet systematic behaviors. Actions are so highly organized, even in novel situations, as to defy interpretation based on the prior acquisition of individual, inter-element associations. A common example is the apparent ability shared by all normal people to speak or write such an astronomical number of sentences that it would be impossible in a lifetime to hear them all even once. But almost any example, such as solving arithmetic problems, improvising music, or playing basketball, would be equally good. Any definition of learning in terms of associations and arbitrarily small response units gets into trouble with these examples. Such a system does not seem to permit the organism to behave in ways in which we know in fact, he can.

What is needed is a description of behavior which allows for its obvious generative and recursive character, which is to say the capacity of organisms to behave flexibly in new situations, unbounded by stimulus and response elements common (or similar) to those encountered in the past. Such a description might well begin by allowing the possibility that what organisms learn are rules, and that behavior is a rule-following enterprise. No assumption about conscious awareness or the verbalizability of a rule is necessary (but neither is that possibility rejected); nor is there any *need for* a commitment to rule mechanisms as an antecedent condition for overt behavior. What is implied is that *any particular behavior* (response or response sequence) committed by the organism *is recognizably consistent with* and *instantiates a rule.* An adequate rule description makes no reference to muscle twitches, and would probably ignore the difference between sorting cards, pushing buttons, and saying "positive" or "negative" instance in a conceptual task. What is important is that, as long as the subject is capable of responding to the task requirements, behavior is regular.

With further elaboration, these statements would surely be classified as "cognitive," for they admit to the possibility that organisms learn, can know, and can understand how to behave. They permit, moreover, the notion that one individual might recognize the rule (or rules) exemplified in the behavior of another person. But they do not depend on the existence of underlying and/or antedating *psychological* processes which are said to control, govern, or regulate responses. Neither are they explainable or reducible to *physiology*, for we already know one crucial fact about physiological mechanisms—they *must* be consistent with the behavior we observe. There is no physiological mechanism from which one *could sensibly conclude* that the behavior which we regularly observe is really impossible. But then, conversely, how could any such mechanism be what *makes* behavior possible?

Physiological or other underlying processes are correlatives of behavior, not enabling mechanisms. The control and regulation of behavior is provided by objective conditions in the situation and by the abilities and skills of the organism.

Related Research

Whether a description of behavior in terms of rules is a viable possibility is something which cannot be settled by any single experiment or perhaps even by *all* the hard facts that we now have at our disposal. There are, however, a few empirical results which merit attention.

Solution shifts. It is an accepted fact that nonreversal shifts in the solution of discrimination learning and simple conceptual problems are more difficult than reversal shifts for human adults, but that reversals are more difficult for preverbal and infra-human organisms. This finding is commonly taken as evidence of the capacity for mediational processes (antedating overt behavior) in the verbal organism. This finding, however, is not as stable as might be hoped. For example, if the adult subject's attention is drawn by instructions to the various stimulus dimensions, with the admonishment that any one but only one is correlated with the correct category responses, the difference in difficulty vanishes; the two types of shift are accomplished with equal rapidity (Johnson, Fishkin, and Bourne, 1966). Moreover, with repeated shifts, in a learning-set paradigm, the initial difference in difficulty is eliminated. Both types of shift are made in a minimal number of trials; and this finding holds regardless of whether the subject is an adult human being (for whom the reversal is easier to begin with), a young child (for whom the nonreversal is initially easier)[2], or a member of some subhuman species (Dufort, Guttman, and Kimble, 1954; Schusterman, 1964). What are recorded in these experiments are the individual, trial-by-trial (category) responses of subjects; and it is natural to think of the responses as being learned (or associated) and to deal with them as the data to be "explained." The general findings, however, might suggest that these responses merely reflect what has been learned—that the subject has learned to behave, within the physical limits and requirements of the task, in accord with a rule. Adult human beings often can state that rule verbally—and when the solution changes, they find

---

[2] This conclusion is based on data collected by P. J. Johnson and J. Wadsworth at the University of Colorado.

a new stimulus characteristic which is correlated with correct responses. Often, there will be enough information provided on a single-error trial to determine the new solution. But the ability to verbalize is no condition for using the rule. The rule is a way of describing and identifying what the subject is doing, and of predicting what he might do later. The rule, thus, is neither a cause of nor a regulator of behavior. Why there is a transition from nonreversals to reversals as the easier of the two tasks when no pretraining or instructions are given is more difficult to account for. It is an interesting, though fragile, empirical fact, that this result may have something to do with the prior learning of stimulus dimensions (Riley, McKee, and Hadley, 1964), the concept of opposites (Bogartz, 1965; Kroll and Schvaneveldt, 1965), or some other peculiar characteristic of the history of human beings.

Learning simple logic. More to the point, perhaps, is some recent research on the learning of relatively simple logical operations. Class concepts can be defined by a variety of operators, among which are the conjunctive, "x and y," the disjunctive, "x and/or y," the conditional, "if x then y," and the biconditional, "x if and only if y," where x and y are any two unique stimulus attributes. In these experiments, the subjects learned a variety of class concepts within a task format similar to the conventional concept-learning paradigm. Specifically, the subjects learned or discovered how to sort stimulus patterns into categories (positive and negative instances of some unknown concept) by observing the proper placement of a series of examples. The problems were of two types: (a) The subject might be required to learn the defining relationship between the relevant attributes of a concept; under these circumstances, the attributes were named at the outset and the subject determined how they were combined, "$x \; ? \; y$"; i.e., to specify the concept. (b) Alternatively, the subject's task might be to identify the relevant attributes; here the relationship was given (through instructions and pretraining, if necessary) and the problem had the form "$? \; Q \; ?$," where Q was some chosen connective, such as conjunction.

Connective learning. A number of experiments contrasting attribute and connective learning problems and comparing the various connectives for difficulty have been conducted (some of which are reported elsewhere; e.g., Bourne, 1967, Haygood and Bourne, 1965). The subject's behavior exhibited some interesting and unique features which are best shown by means of illustrative results. Without any pretraining, some subjects were given the task of learning to sort geometrical designs in accord with the concept "$x \; ? \; y$," where the blank, unknown to the subject, was *if and only if*. There were a total of 81 geometrical designs, the population being generated by four dimensions (color, form, number, and size of figures), each with three values. As a concrete example, let x and y be the attributes redness and triangularity, respectively. The concept then, "red if and only if triangle," required that all patterns which were red and triangular and all patterns which were neither red nor triangular; e.g., blue circles or green squares, be sorted into the class of positive instances, and that all red nontriangles and all nonred triangles be labeled negative instances. The required arrangement is shown in Table 1.

On the average, naïve, but relatively intelligent human beings, took about 60-70 trials to solve such a problem. Over the course of these trials, they responded to and observed the correct placement of several patterns of each type; i.e., red triangles, nonred triangles, etc. The probability of an incorrect response by the subject on these trials is shown in Table 1—under the heading, Problem 1—for all four types of instances. A more detailed breakdown shows these probabilities for the first and second (or first through fourth) examples of each type. (We limit ourselves here to different examples, of which there were only two for nonred triangles [green and blue triangles] and only four for nonred nontriangles, as shown in Table 1.)

Errors; i.e., misplacements by the subject, were distributed unevenly over the various types of patterns; subjects made fewest errors (both proportionately and in absolute number) on red trianglar patterns (the subject had been told that redness and triangularity were the relevant attributes) and most errors on nonred nontriangles (which, like red triangles, were positive instances). Probability of error showed a small but reliable decrease from the first to the second (or fourth) example of each type of pattern.

Another group of subjects was given precisely the same task after a pretraining routine during which they solved a series of six connective learning problems. Each pair of pretraining problems involved a different connective; i.e., two conjunctives, two inclusive disjunctives, and two conditionals—but of course none of these was identical to the test connective, a biconditional. And, of course, the two relevant attributes were different for all seven problems. The order of connectives during pretraining was counterbalanced within the group.

On the average, these subjects required 5.5 trials to attain solution; i.e., to achieve errorless performance on the biconditional problem. Mean error probabilities for the various stimulus patterns are shown in Table 1, under the heading Problem 7. Several features of the data are notable. First, the majority of subjects (77 per cent) solved the

TABLE 1

DESCRIPTION OF THE STIMULUS PATTERNS, THE STIMULUS CLASSES
AND THE RESULTS OF A CONNECTIVE-LEARNING EXPERIMENT

Stimulus Classes	Illustrative Description	Response Class	Overall Error Rate	Problem 1		Problem 7	
				Ordinal Position	Individual Error Rate	Ordinal Position	Individual Error Rate
TT	RTr	+	0.22	—	—	—	0.11
TF	$\overline{RTr}$	−	0.43	1st	0.51	1st	0.51
	(RC, RS)			2nd	0.44	2nd	0.00
FT	$\overline{R}Tr$	−	0.39	1st	0.48	1st	0.48
	(GTr, BTr)			2nd	0.40	2nd	0.12
FF	$\overline{RTr}$	+	0.68	1st	0.82	1st	0.49
	(GC, GS,			2nd	0.77	2nd	0.17
	BC, BS)			3rd	0.69	3rd	0.00
				4th	0.73	4th	0.00

Note: The following abbreviations are used: T, true (or present); F, false (or absent); R, red; C, green; B, blue; S, square; Tr, triangle; and C, circle.

problem with at most one error on each of the four types of instances. This result precludes the computation of meaningful error rates for the four types of patterns. It can be seen, however, that the probability of an error on the first example of each type was about the same—0.5. One can safely ignore red triangles, for those instances containing both relevant attributes were positive under all the connectives considered here; thus, the subject was likely to guess positive for red triangles in Problem 7. The difficulty associated with placing nonred nontriangles in the positive category (along with red triangles with which they share no common attributes) was all but eliminated with pretraining. Finally, the probability of error on the second example (it had at least some different stimulus attributes) of any type was virtually zero. On the third example, and all thereafter, it *was* zero.

These data imply that behavior with training comes to be organized in a particular way. It is as if the subjects learned an algorithm: in any problem of this type, observe the correct placement of an example of each of four classes of patterns distinguished by the presence or absence of the two given attributes; then classify all subsequent examples according to these four observations. One could go further to say that the subject's behavior looks as though it is mediated, generated or controlled by something akin to a truth table. The designations TT, TF, FT, and FF for the four stimulus classes are used in Table 1 purposefully to emphasize this possibility. Clearly, proposition "x ? y" is fully determined by establishing the truth value of xy, $x\bar{y}$, $\bar{x}y$, and $\bar{x}\bar{y}$ (or of TT, TF, FT, and FF instances). Perhaps, what the subject has acquired is an internal deductive device operating on the principles of elementary logic, which *enables* the overt performance.

The subject does behave in accord with "truth-table" rules. This is not only an adequate description of the subject's performance, but also achieves cross-situational generality by providing explicit (and quantitative) expectations about behavior in other problems. It accomplishes this without the assertion that behavior is antedated or controlled by an implicit truth table (or any representation thereof). Subjects in these experiments do not report any systematic prior rehearsal of the truth table. While they can describe what they are doing, characteristically they find it impossible to verbalize the structure of any correlative implicit process. Subjects behave as they were trained to behave. The complexities of their action seem to reside in the behavior itself, in the manner in which it occurs, and not (at least not necessarily) in any preliminary covert representation of behavior. The subjects were trained to solve connective problems, and solve them they do when the necessity arises. What they have learned is a complex behavior which can be described as following a certain sort of rule. There seems to be no point to a deeper psychological mechanism that enables the subject to follow the rule.

Remark. Some of the "fine-grain" features of category responses might be noted in passing. It is tempting to say that, on Problem 1, the subjects seemed to be learning gradually. Correct response probabilities increased over successive presentations of instances of the same class, as might be expected if associations were being formed. On the other hand, the learning in Problem 7 looks all-or-none. The error rate is roughly 0.5 until the subject makes his last error, after which it drops to zero. Which set of assumptions about underlying processes—incremental association formation or all-or-none hypothesis testing—gains the greater support from these data? It is difficult to decide. Still, the subject's behavior makes sense if one looks not only at the response on each trial but also considers the way in which these responses fit in as a part of the subject's ongoing, rule-following behavior.

Attribute identification. All (or nearly all) subjects learn, with training, to solve conceptual problems in an efficient way in which the connective is unknown. There is additional evidence of a similar behavioral "strategy" in attribute identification tasks. With experience in solving these problems (rule given, attribute unknown), the subjects act as if they know and understand the truth table (not really a surprising result), and can identify the unknown attributes in exactly four instances if these instances are chosen properly to represent the four stimulus classes. While familiar enough to academic-types, the problem-solving process is relatively complex. Yet, the complexity is there in the subject's behavior which is open and visible to the public, and not hidden away in some implicit form.

Logic pretraining. One other experiment might be summarized. The results so far suggest that preliminary instructions (or alternatively, practice) in constructing truth tables ought to facilitate the learning of class concepts. Desiring not to be quite so direct about it, Haygood and Kielhbach (1965) pretrained subjects to sort geometric designs into four categories defined by the presence or absence of two named attributes. For example, given redness and triangularity as the attributes, the subject learned to place red triangles (TT) in one category, nonred triangles (FT) in a second, red nontriangles (TF) in a third, and nonred nontriangles (FF) in a fourth. Four sorts of this type were required (each with a different pair of attributes) after which the subject solved one experimental problem of the connective-learning variety. For different subjects, the unknown connective was conjunctive, disjunctive, conditional, or biconditional. Other subjects solved the same problems without this form of pretraining. Mean trials to solution required by pretrained subjects were 6, 6, 11, and 22 for the four connectives in the order given above. For non-pretrained subjects, the comparable means were 12, 29, 32, and 51. The difference was highly reliable. These results take on added significance if it is understood that sufficient information to solve each problem is given in the first six trials (on the average). Thus, subjects pretrained to categorize in accord with the rows of a bidimensional truth table solved conjunctive and disjunctive problems with maximal efficiency. The apparent difficulty with conditionals and biconditionals can be assigned with some confidence to conflicting extra-experimental experience; both connectives require, for example, that FF patterns be grouped with TT patterns as positive instances.

In passing, it might be noted that related results have been obtained from children, ranging in age from 4.5 to 7 years. This study was limited to conjunctions and disjunctions, on the assumption that young people might find the other connectives too difficult. As it turns out, this was probably a miscalculation. Again, there was a marked facilitative effect of experience with the four-class sorting task. The effect interacted with age, with 4.5- to 5-year-olds seeming to benefit only slightly (about 17 per cent reduction in trials to solution with pretraining), while 5.5- to 6-year-olds (about 60 per cent reduction) and 6.5- to 7-year-olds (about 77 per cent reduction) derived considerable benefit. The oldest subjects displayed near maximally efficient problem solving on both conjunctions and disjunctions, their data being quite similar to those of college students.[3]

Thought and Conceptual Behavior

The main question seems to have been lost. What *does* research on conceptual behavior tell us about thinking? What has been said up to now might be taken as a denial of thoughts and thinking altogether. Since that was not the intent, some attempt at clarification is necessary.

People do have thoughts. Moreover, people do engage in implicit activities, like subvocal speech. These things seem self-evident; at least

---

[3] These results are drawn from a study conducted by P. J. Johnson and Anne Fishkin at the University of Colorado.

nothing that has been said heretofore was meant to question them. What has been questioned is the notion that implicit action regulates, or that thinking "explains" behavior. Both implicit and explicit behavior (and thoughts, too, for that matter) are conceived to be part of human skills and abilities, to be described and understood as performances. The assumption that one, as a hidden computing process, regulates and results in the other is doubtful. Nothing seems to hinge on that assumption. As things now stand, the net difference between making that assumption and not making it seems to be zero.

Saying this, of course, does not make the job of understanding thought and behavior any easier. At the most, it can only help to see why theory and research in concept attainment is unlikely to make any special contribution to this understanding. Nothing changes the fact that thought (as a psychological concept), whatever else is involved, is intangible, private, and without substance. This is what makes description difficult, allows speculation to flourish, and generates a good deal of confusion.

What is thought? There is no universally satisfying concept of thought. About the only thing that can be said with any confidence is that thoughts are a kind of event. Like all events, they are datable and locatable (i.e., they occur in time and to a person) and they reflect change. The object of change is, of course, the person to whom the thought occurs; but the more penetrating question is, Can anything precise be said about the difference in his state before and after the thought? Several answers might be attempted. But about the thought itself, only one answer seems to satisfy all sensible cases: the thought is a change in the individual's position with respect to other things; i.e., persons, objects, events, etc., which he can sense and detect. In a word, it is a change in the individual's possibilities (or potential) for behaving (Ossorio, 1966).

To illustrate, if I think of a solution, or a possible solution to a problem, my relation to that part of the world has surely changed. I can now perform; i.e., solve the problem or attempt to solve it, whereas before I could not.

A thought is said to be a change in state. The resulting state is a position from which the individual *might* undertake action; and when he does, the thought seems naturally a part of that action. It must be clear that behavioral sequelae can be either explicit (an overt attempt at proper performance), or implicit (as, for example, in subvocal speech). But to recognize implicit behavior is not to endow it with the special property of control over overt attempts. Note also that a thought might have no explicit behavioral consequences if, for example, one change of state follows rapidly upon another.

The statement that thought is a change of state is like saying that blue is a color. Of course, not all state changes are thoughts; thus, it would be helpful to specify the attributes of thought further. But this, like determining the correlates of blue, is an empirical matter. As the differences that thought makes, in behavior, in physiology, and maybe elsewhere, become known, a detailed understanding of the concept will develop.

One final comment: if thoughts are events, must not thinking be a process—a mental process buried away in the deep structure of the organism? If behaviors such as subvocal speech are classified as thinking, then thinking is a process. But this process seems to be one that follows from rather than one that produces thought. More commonly, the underlying and controlling thought process is imagined to be something which has as its outcome a thought and/or behavior. Whether there is some such process is indeterminate. No matter what else might be said, it is easy to see that the issue here is hardly the same concept of process fruitfully used in other sciences, for *psychological* processes which *produce* thoughts do not occupy any definite time interval, nor are they identifiable independently of an initial state or an outcome (Ossorio, 1966). Examples of scientifically useful processes are plentiful —flow of water, heat transfer, growth in plants, and so on. But having a thought, making a decision, selecting an hypothesis, or forming an association, as processes, lack determinable time characteristics and descriptions which are independent of initial condition and outcome. (For example, what would it be like to be halfway through the process of making a decision? Any decision is likely to have a history, but a process which literally *is* the making of the decision or the determiner of the decision has yet to be observed or described. Anyone who claims to be able to say what it is like to be partially through the process of deciding will characteristically describe some portion of the events or behaviors temporally prior to the decision. These steps can easily be seen as possible antecedents of the decision but, only with great difficulty, as necessary and sufficient antecedents or determiners of the decision.) The problem can further be characterized by saying that it is not so much a matter of lacking information or of being unable to observe the process, as it is simply not knowing what to look for. It is a search for something only rumored to exist, but so indescribable that we cannot even tell when one occurs.

The upshot of these comments is that there might not be anything missing in an account of behavior which fails to mention underlying psychological processes. There are physiological processes, which hopefully can be related empirically to thinking and behavior; and there are behavioral processes, including thoughts as changes in potential for action. These things can be described. Is there anything more? Are there real questions that can be asked about thinking and behavior whose answers depend, in addition, on the discovery of an underlying, psychological controlling process? Real questions exist only when there is a way to recognize the right answer. And questions about thinking can probably be answered cogently and recognizably in terms of describable experience, ability, and performance.

Postscript

Partly because of the heavy emphasis on behavior and description, the foregoing remarks might be misconstrued and assimilated to something resembling Watsonian positivism or some form of movement (muscle-twitch) psychology. Once that leap is made, it becomes easy to assert that the position expressed here is antitheoretical, is based on some fear of mentalism, and is a personal, not a general problem. Such a conclusion is exactly wrong and reflects a fundamental misunderstanding. First, the arguments presented are positive in intent: they are not antitheoretical but omnitheoretical; they admit to *all* possibilities and they ask that each be judged as to its merits on the basis of the evidence and good logic. Second, the position given here might arise from fear, but if so, it is more a fear of mechanism than of mentalism— a fear of assertions that to understand and explain behavior one *must* find a mechanism capable of controlling and producing it, or that to have a nonsterile theory of behavior, one *must* talk of nonbehavioral processes. Third, while it might be agreed that our main business is empirical, no one's hands are completely clean of theory. Thus, the problems raised here belong to psychology and are not the private embarrassment of any individual or group.

Psychological and physiological processes. Nothing said in these pages was intended as a denial of the utility of process descriptions and explanations in psychology. Things that people do, while sometimes lacking the continuity usually implied by the term, are clearly good approximations to process. Likewise, it is easily shown that physiological activities are often correlated with stimulus inputs and behavior. But it should be noted that it is logically impossible for an animal to lack the physiological capability to behave in ways that he is observed to behave. Either physiological description and explanation conforms to behavior or it is false; and if it must so conform, how can it make sense to say that physiology determines behavior?

The point might be expressed differently. Some processes are real, demonstrable, and not to be ignored. But does anything we know about physiology and behavior compel, or even suggest that (a) physiology determines behavior? or (b) physiology explains behavior? Given the available or foreseeable correlational evidence, does it make any less sense to assert that behavior controls physiology? One might contend that, once the facts are all in, he will be able to create a particular behavior by appropriate artificial production of a certain nerve impulse configuration in a certain cerebral locus. Might he not equally well expect that neural configuration to result by artificial production of a certain behavior?

Reductionism. It is sometimes contended that explanations of events at one level of discourse or description are best sought at a more primitive or "basic" level. Thus, the interactions of chemical elements are explained by recourse to the more "basic" principles of physics. This mode of explanation is called reductionism. By analogy, we seek the explanation of behavior by recourse to the principles of physiology.

One purpose of this paper has been to show that there is nothing natural or compelling in this view and that there are quite adequate and philosophically defensible, nonreductionistic explanations for scientific phenomena (Silverstein, 1966). In fact, it has convincingly been argued that the only adequate explanations of specific events; e.g., behaviors, are nonreductionistic (Boden, 1962; Dodwell, 1960; Ryle, 1949), though there is neither space nor necessity to develop that point of view completely here.

The function and utility of reductionism and its companion concept, the hierarchy and unity of the sciences, is as a way of summarizing data. *It can hardly be accepted as legislation as to what explanation must be like.* While it would be nice and tidy if the structure of science did conform, there is little currently in the picture that gives much hope that the data of science will order themselves neatly in some hierarchical arrangement. But, in any case, that is an empirical matter and much remains to be found out.

Controlling processes. The primary interest of psychologists lies in what organisms do. The idea is to be able to explain why organisms behave as they do. If we proceed on the premise that all explanation is reductionistic, it is natural to search for some controlling process in physiology. But given the unavailability of much in the way of evidence on physiological correlates of behavior, not to mention physiological determiners of behavior, it is not too extreme to say that, until now, this approach to explanation has been uniformly unsuccessful. However, if one is convinced that the determiners are there and eventually will be found, he might plug the empirical gap with hypothetical underlying processes until the necessary evidence is uncovered. This commonly has been the procedure in psychological theory.

This approach has considerable utility. Its foremost representatives are able to provide good accounts of available behavioral evidence and to predict outcomes yet to be tested. The general idea is to describe a certain process or set of processes consistent with known behavioral facts. One then proceeds inductively to new situations where the same process is assumed to take place. Knowing the principles of the process and the relevant features of the new situation, one can compute the expected output. Expectations are compared with real data and the theory is evaluated on this comparison. This is good science, for it increases our knowledge of and abilities to deal with behavioral problems. Moreover, it looks like good reduction, for behavior is explained by reference to some presumably lower-level set of principles.

The process itself. Useful as it is, this way of theorizing is not the only acceptable one, just as reduction can hardly be said to be the only adequate mode of explanation. The success of a process theory is said to depend on the existence of evidence that the process is repeatable on historically different occasions. That is, we are able to observe behavior consistent with the process output at different times and over a variety of tasks. (Note that this is not to say identical behaviors, for the inputs might vary from occasion to occasion and task to task.) The argument is that the process works according to certain invariant rules, and that the behavior observed on various occasions is consistent with that process. But actually, we never have any observations in experiments corresponding to the underlying process. What we have are observations of behavior. Over a series of occasions, we have a series of behavior observations which can be described in the same way; i.e., in accord with the same rule or set of rules. Unless there are independent observations corresponding to the process, the process is strictly an excess, and there is no point to pretending that it does add something. It does not make any difference whether we say it is there or not. There is nothing added to our ability to account for behavior, over a wide variety of circumstances, by saying that the process is really there. One can move inductively from one situation to another and one experiment to another having the same firm expectations and achieving the same degree of explanation with or without the assertion that the process, as an entity, separate and apart from the rules it assumedly obeys, really exists.

It would seem that a theorist who prefers to think in terms of underlying processes might respond in either of two ways to these remarks. One is to say that the underlying process has no observable counterpart; it is simply a calculational device permitting one to translate input statements into output statements about behavior. This response is eminently reasonable. It is like saying that behavior is a rule-governed enterprise, and that by assuming or discovering certain rules, we can calculate and forecast what the subject will do given the circumstances under which he must perform. It is a *process description of behavior, rather than a description of a process* presumed to control behavior.

Another response is to say that underlying processes *are real* and potentially *observable*. While we cannot measure them now, if we look hard enough, we will find them. Once we find the physical embodiment of the process, we will understand behavior better. Just because they are not observable at the moment is no reason to ignore them or not to look. This response is more difficult to contend with. First, it should be clear that there is nothing in the rule-following theory which is incompatible with the *existence* of underlying processes. But neither is the *nonexistence* of a nonobservable underlying process incompatible with its *existence*. With a nonobservable underlying process there is no difference between its really being there and its really not being there. The issue for theorists who say there really are underlying processes is that they see a definite point in using process descriptions. But it would be easy enough to convince even the most determined skeptic that there was a point to using a process description in any particular case. All one has to do is produce some observation corresponding to that process *per se*, as opposed to its behavioral outcome; or, alternatively, one might show that a particular process description allows the user to predict an unexpected (surprising) outcome (preferably one that would not have been predicted using a different description). In the latter case, the point of using the process description is the difference it makes in the understanding, prediction, and control of behavior.

Using process descriptions successfully to predict behavioral outcomes, however, does nothing to insure some additional kind of reality for the process. The theorist might very well discover at some point in time that his process (for which there has never been a corresponding observation) has ceased to yield genuinely new predictions. At that point, he might stop talking about the process as if it existed. But, the reality-oriented theorist would see that the utility of the process description had not been lost, disconfirmed, or reduced, even though now there was no question about the process really existing. The previously established usefulness of the process description *never depended* on the process really existing, any more than, for example, the usefulness of Maxwell's equations depended on the existence of ether (an ethereal process?) or the usefulness of Restle's equations depends on the existence of an hypothesis-selection-and-test apparatus.[4]

To say that nonbehavioral processes *really are there* to control behavior, *as contrasted with* their not being there, is not even an expression of faith, for there is no difference of having faith and not having faith. Without any observation corresponding to such a process or any indication of what that observation would be like, there is no difference between the existence and the nonexistence (of processes) for one to have faith in. *Logically*, there is no way to deny the assertion that the underlying process really exists (to prove the universal negative). Further, there is likely to be no *empirical* evidence acceptable as even a provisional basis for concluding that the process does not exist. Yet, it is still fair to ask what difference asserting the *existence* of the process makes to an explication of behavior.

Rule-following theory. The fact of the matter is that there is no way in present circumstances to demonstrate that underlying processes either do or do not exist. Thus, there is no point to asserting that they really do exist, or that they *must* exist, and the way is left open for other approaches which do not talk about underlying processes. The theory expressed, a rule-following theory of behavior, is in a sense another approach. It is nonreductionistic in the sense that it explains behavior by reference to psychological or behavioral constructs; e.g., experience, memory, motives, abilities, and the like. It recognizes the importance of physiological activities as correlates of behavior but makes no assumptions about logical or causal relations between physiological and psychological processes. It makes no assertions about the existence of half-level, control processes, somewhere between behavior and physiology. It is a theory with as much potential for prediction and

---

[4] Conversely, we can make the existence of an underlying process as secure as logic permits: if a given behavior is correctly described as "doing *x*," then *whatever* physiological processes occurred at the same time may be correctly described as "the process of doing *x*." And if the physiological description of those processes is never the same twice, that will make no difference here whatever.

explanation of behavior as any process theory, for rule descriptions by their nature are generalizable (common) across historically different occasions. Further, one can think just as easily in terms of hypothetical rules and principles of behavior as he can in terms of hypothetical rules and principles of a hypothetical process. The difference between the two sometimes seems mainly a question of whether the regularities and principles we observe in research or postulate in theory are principles of behavior or of some process which, in turn, controls behavior—whether behavior, itself, is lawful and operates systematically on a determinable set of principles or whether it is the process that is lawful and behavior is merely its slave.

In point of fact, however, the rule-following theory is *not* merely *an alternative* to process theory; it is *the general form* of which process notions are a special case. The rule-following theory is general enough to subsume process theories and other coordinate approaches. Any instance of a process description of behavior is an instance of a rule-following description. *The rule-following description is*, in fact, *an explicit statement of how one understands the process to work*. The substance or mechanism of the process (which we have already noted need not even exist) is irrelevant for psychology, if its rules of operation are known or knowable. If the process does exist, it is a neurophysiological fact. While it would be silly to say that neurophysiological facts are uninteresting to the psychologist, or that one ought not to push on toward an understanding of neurophysiology, it is just as silly to say that the reason for pushing on is that neurophysiological facts determine or explain behavior. Neurophysiological facts contribute to an understanding of the organism and how he works. But, neurophysiological facts must be consonant with behavior, or else someone's observations are false.

Thus, whatever a process theory can achieve in psychology, a rule-following theory can achieve also, and with no loss of generality or predictiveness. It is not just an alternative; it is not meant to replace process theories of various sorts. It *is* meant to subsume these possibilities and, at the same time, to emphasize that to be *bound* by these possibilities; e.g., by a faith in "the unity of sciences" or in reductionistic explanation, is to leave unexplored some possibilities that really exist. There seems no present danger that the possibilities afforded by process descriptions will be overlooked. Calling attention, in the present paper, to the general case which both process and nonprocess theories exemplify, is based on the assumption that the progress of our science is best served not by keeping to the safety and comfort provided by paradigms made familiar by other sciences or by our past experience but, rather, by venturing to take all reasonable possibilities *seriously*.

REFERENCES

Anderson, N. H. An evaluation of stimulus sampling theory. In A. W. Milton (Ed.), *Categories of human learning*. New York: Academic Press, 1964. Pp. 129-144.

Boden, M. The paradox of explanation. *Proc. Aristot. Soc.*, 62, 1962.

Bogartz, W. Effects of reversal and nonreversal shifts with CVC stimuli. *J. verb. Learn. verb. Behav.*, 1965, *4*, 484-488.

Bourne, L. E., Jr. *Human conceptual behavior*. Boston: Allyn-Bacon, 1966. (a)

Bourne, L. E., Jr. Concept attainment. *Institute of Behavioral Science Report 81*. Boulder, Colorado: mimeo, 1966. (b)

Bourne, L. E., Jr. Learning and utilization of conceptual rules. In B. Kleinmuntz (Ed.), *Concepts and the structure of memory*. New York: Wiley, 1967. Pp. 1-32.

Bourne, L. E., Jr., and Restle, F. Mathematical theory of concept identification. *Psychol. Rev.*, 1959, *66*, 278-296.

Bower, G. H., and Trabasso, T. Concept identification. In R. C. Atkinson (Ed.), *Studies in mathematical psychology*. Stanford: Stanford University Press, 1963. Pp. 32-94.

Bush, R. R., and Mosteller, F. *Stochastic models for learning*. New York: Wiley, 1955.

Chomsky, N. *Syntactic structures*. The Hague: Mouton, 1957.

Dodwell, P. C. Causes of behavior and explanation in psychology. *Mind*, 1960, 69.

Dufort, R. H., Guttman, N., and Kimble, G. A. One-trial discrimination reversal in the white rat. *J. comp. Physiol. Psychol.*, 1954, *47*, 248-249.

Goss, A. E. Verbal mediating response and concept formation. *Psychol. Rev.*, 1961, *68*, 248-274.

Haygood, R. C., and Bourne, L. E., Jr. Attribute and rule-learning aspects of conceptual behavior. *Psychol. Rev.*, 1965, *72*, 175-195.

Haygood, R. C., and Kielhbauch, J. B. Effects of logical pre-training on concept rule-learning performance. Paper presented at MPA convention, 1965.

Hull, C. L. Knowledge and purpose as habit mechanisms. *Psychol. Rev.*, 1930, *57*, 511-525.

Hunt, E. B. *Concept learning.* New York: Wiley, 1962.

Johnson, P. J., Fishkin, A., and Bourne, L. E., Jr. Effects of procedural variables upon reversal and interdimensional shift performance: II. *Psychon. Sci.*, 1966, *4*, 69-70.

Kendler, H. H., and Kendler, T. S. Vertical and horizontal processes in problem solving. *Psychol. Rev.*, 1962, *69*, 1-16.

Kendler, T. S. Learning development and thinking. In E. Harms (Ed.), Fundamentals of psychology: the psychology of thinking. *Ann. N.Y. Acad. Sci.*, 1960, *91*, 52-56.

Kendler, T. S. Concept formation. *Annu. Rev. Psychol.*, 1961, *12*, 447-472.

Kleinmuntz, B. (Ed.) *Problem solving.* New York: Wiley, 1966.

Kroll, N. E. A., and Schvaneveldt, R. W. Cue associations in concept shifts. Paper presented at MPA convention, 1966.

Levine, M. Hypothesis behavior by humans during discrimination learning. *J. exp. Psychol.*, 1966, *71*, 331-338.

Mandler, G. From association to structure. *Psychol. Rev.*, 1962, *69*, 415-427.

Miller, G. A., Galanter, E., and Pribram, K. *Plans and the structure of behavior.* New York: Holt, 1960.

Osgood, C. *Method and theory in experimental psychology.* New York: Oxford University Press, 1953.

Ossorio, P. G. Persons. *Linguistic Research Institute Report No. 3.* Boulder, Colorado: mimeo, 1966.

Restle, F. The selection of strategies in cue learning. *Psychol. Rev.*, 1962, *69*, 329-343.

Riley, D. A., McKee, J. P., and Hadley, R. W. Prediction of auditory discrimination learning and transposition from childrens' auditory ordering ability. *J. exp. Psychol.*, 1964, *67*, 324-329.

Ryle, G. *The concept of mind.* London: Hutchinson, 1949.

Schusterman, R. J. Successive discrimination-reversal training and multiple discrimination training on one-trial learning by chimpanzees. *J. comp. Physiol. Psychol.*, 1964, *58*, 153-156.

Smith, K. U. Cybernetic theory and analysis of learning. In E. A. Bilodeau (Ed.) *Acquisition of skill.* New York: Academic Press, 1966. Pp. 425-482.

Staats, A. W. Verbal habit families, concepts, and the operant conditioning of word classes. *Psychol. Rev.,* 1961, *68,* 190-204.

Staats, A. W., and Staats, C. K. *Complex human behavior.* New York: Holt, 1964.

THOUGHTS ON THE CONCEPT OF PROCESS[1]

ALLEN NEWELL

Carnegie-Mellon University

Lyle Bourne's paper is an attempt to face the growing interest in describing behavior in terms of underlying processes. He makes use of conceptual behavior in his detailed examples; it is an area in which he has done extensive experimental work. But his analysis is cast much more broadly. His paper can be summed up in one of its headings, "Criticism and an Alternative." The nature of the criticism and the alternative is clearly, forcefully, and repeatedly stated.

First, the criticism is not directed toward the phenomena:

> There is no question about the reality of certain private experiences or events such as subvocal speech or visual images (p. 172).

and Bourne distinguishes his concern with process explanations from his general view about the use of theories:

> None of this should be taken to impugn attempts to describe (or redescribe) conceptual behavior within a particular classification scheme or quantitative model (p. 174).

Rather, Bourne is concerned with the mode of explanation:

> So the task of accounting for human behavior remains [when using process explanations] (p. 173).

---

[1] This work was supported by NIH Research Grant MH 07722-02.

My comments followed upon the initial draft of Bourne's paper, available to me before the conference. His revised paper contains both a lengthy postscript and, so it seems to me, a touch of softening on the unequivocalness of the prose. However, I have chosen to present my reaction in its original form, and have not responded to these modifications, except where necessary to correct the quotations. Page numbers from Bourne's paper refer to this text.

.   .   .   .

. . . such a theory seems to impose the necessity to study invisible processes—processes which might not exist and for which there is no extra-behavioral description (certainly not physiological) which permits recognition when and if they did occur (p. 174).

.   .   .   .

. . . the theoretical underlying process seems often to be an invention—an invented answer to the question, What has the subject learned that enabled him to respond as he did? . . . But the more basic question is whether there is any need to be concerned about a psychological enabling mechanism that permits behavior to be what it is (p. 174).

As background to his alternative, Bourne provides a description of the positive task of psychology:

The task of psychology is to ascertain which objective factors in the past and present states of the organism and his environment make a difference in how he behaves, so that the behavior can be described and predicted rather than merely attributed to another process (pp. 175-176).

And now his alternative:

Such a description might well begin by allowing the possibility what organisms learn are rules, and that behavior is a rule-following enterprise. . . . *any particular behavior* (response or response sequence) committed by the organism *is recognizably consistent with* and *instantiates a rule* (p. 177, italics in original).

This leads him to a final position on the role of process explanations:

There seems to be no point to a deeper psychological mechanism that enables the subject to follow the rule (p. 183).

Or again:

The assumption that one [i.e., thoughts], as a hidden computing process, regulates and results in the other [i.e., behavior] is doubtful (p. 185).

In Bourne's position, we recognize first of all the deeply embedded fear within behavioral psychology of mentalistic notions as pseudo-explanations. Since all you have is the behavior, once you have described it there is nothing more to be gained by going beyond it (behind it, would be more appropriate phrasing). Where Bourne moves out into new territory is in his acceptance of complex rules as permissible descriptions of behavior. His paper attempts to confirm the necessity of moving beyond simple lists of stimuli and their associated response, to rules of (I assume) arbitrary complexity. But once we have the regularity explained, that is enough. No need to ask what mechanism enabled the behavior to be an instance of the rule.

The Nature of Explanation

Psychology has long shown an overconcern with methodological issues—with the logical status of intervening variables versus hypothetical constructs, or the nature of operationalism, or the autonomy of psychology from physiology. Yet, I am forced to dwell for a moment on the basic nature of explanation if Bourne's position is to be understood.

Explanation is basically relative, reductionistic, and incomplete. A theory of X is something that introduces another set of things, $Y_1 \ldots Y_n$, in terms of which X is determined. Some of these "things" may be measurements, some may be laws, some may be logical systems according to which the deductions are to be made. We accept whatever the theorist offers, providing only that information about the Y's can be obtained independently of the features of X about which they provide information. Thus, the explanation of X is relative to the Y's.

Explanation is reductionistic because such explanatory schemes form the basis of our notions of reduction. The hierarchy of the sciences, from physics through chemistry, biology, psychology, and up through sociology, is an empirical thing, based on the notion that laws at each level are sufficient for the next one up. In an actively god-supported world, reduction can run the other way, and one finally understands the nature of basic physics when one can see in it sufficiently the design of the creator. But explanation is still reductionistic.

And explanation is surely incomplete. For the Y's themselves are not explained. Or if explained, their antecedents are not. Even in the god-supported world explanation is not complete for god, himself, is not explained.

Thus, there never is a necessity for carrying an explanation further. At some point, one will rest—if not satisfied, at least immobile for the moment. To come back to Bourne, he has his logical rights. Given description of a regularity, one need not press further. So the question becomes why one would want to press behind the regularity. Given that a man can multiply, why should one want to ask after the processes that enable him to do so?

Some Examples of Resting and Pushing On

Before turning to psychology, it might be well to cite a few less controversial examples.

An almost classic example of a theory in which it has paid to push further is thermodynamics. Beautiful in its regularity at a macroscopic level in terms of pressure, volume, temperature, heat, and entropy, it yielded an even more comprehensive theory when these regularities were derived from the kinetic theory of gases.

Perhaps an example of a theory where one does not press on so hard is the theory of electromagnetism embodied in Maxwell's equations. There are two fields, the electric and the magnetic, and, in addition, charged particles. These are interrelated as the equations say, and one does not ask by what mechanism the electrical field is able to interact with the magnetic field or propagate a wave through empty space to affect a charged particle. In fact, this theory is often cited as an example where an underlying mechanism, the ether, was dropped as superfluous.

An example somewhat closer to home is the theory of the gene. Clearly "just" a regularity without supporting mechanisms for many years, it has finally yielded to understanding in molecular terms. Here, clearly, pushing on, even though it took several decades and the striking development of molecular biology to finally provide the explanation, has proved fruitful indeed.

One more example, still closer home and still active, is the concept of the sodium pump in the theory of nerve conduction. Given appropriate changes in the concentrations of sodium and potassium ions in the environment of an axon, one can construct highly satisfactory theories of how the nerve impulse travels down the axon. One can measure the input and output variables of such an hypothesized mechanism, and describe its properties in some detail. Does one push on to discover the molecular mechanism behind this? Of course!

From these examples, let me suggest that the reason one searches for the mechanisms behind a regularity is that they are usually there, waiting to be found. And when found, they usually provide a theory with vastly increased scope. And the reasons one does not push on are all tactical—that one does not have any good ideas about where the next level of explanation is coming from.

These assertions are not meant to be philosophic statements, no matter how much they may sound like a realist as opposed to a positivistic philosophic position. Rather, they are meant to be simple, empirical inductions from the practice of science over a vast range of phenomena. One can find a mechanism for producing the light that shines from the stars. One can find a mechanism for photosynthesis. One can find a mechanism for sickle-cell anemia. One can find a mechanism for inflation. And one can expect to find a mechanism that enables an organism to follow learned complex rules. So let me now turn to the case of psychology.

Why Should Psychological Mechanisms Exist?

There are two reasons, somewhat different in nature, for expecting expect a set of processes behind the complex behavior exhibited by a human—behind, say, concept learning, or to use the more general framework provided by Bourne, behind "having a thought, making a decision, selecting an hypothesis, or forming an association (p. 186)." The first is that the physiological mechanisms are there, confronting us. If we were ingenious enough, they would yield up their secrets. And these secrets would surely take the form of a set of processes in terms of which a human's behavior can be explained.

It should hardly be necessary to document how closely physiology is hovering in the background. It is one thing to engage in "inappropriate physiologizing"; it is quite another to ignore that a major function of psychology is to provide as clear a picture as possible of what it is that has to be explained by the underlying physiological mechanisms. Since Hebb, at least, this has been again clear.

However, I cannot resist one example. The quote is taken from Luria (1966) in discussing a brain-damaged patient with a shell wound in the left fronto-tempero-parietal region.

> The operations of oral calculation with his tongue free presented no difficulty to the patient: Addition, subtraction of a two-digit number from another two-digit number, simple multiplication and division were carried out quickly, almost at the normal speed; he easily performed oral arithmetical operations, for example subtraction of 7 from 100, when a complex mental coding takes place. However, this was radically changed when the patient did arith-

metical operations with his tongue held. The time taken for calculation was increased six to eight times, and the whole range of
arithmetical operations performed equally easily by the patient
in normal conditions could be subdivided into two groups: Some
continued to be performed, although very slowly, while others either became completely impossible or performed by different and
unaccustomed methods (p. 324).

For example, with his tongue free, the patient easily understood
the sentence "To the school where Mary was a pupil, a lady came
from the factory to give a talk," and, after repeating it several
times answered the control questions: "Who gave the talk? Where
was the talk?" and so on. However, with his tongue held, this task
was impossible and after a long delay (2 minutes) he declared: "It
is very long. . . . I cannot say what is what. . . . I cannot collect
my thoughts" (p. 323).

Here is a man with a lesion that produces highly specific and repro-
ducible effects on complex behavior—roughly speaking (if the total
description by Luria is considered), prohibiting the execution of an organized sequence while not prohibiting the components of which the
sequence is composed. Surely, the response to this is *not* "describe the
regularity, but don't look for the mechanism." Surely this behavior
reaches beyond itself to indicate a mechanism consisting of parts in
interaction, such that the lesion is affecting these parts differentially.
To propose, as Bourne does, that the proper strategy of research as to
push no further than the external regularity, is to miss a chance. That
the indicators may be too weak, is clearly possible. Clinical data from
brain lesions are messy. So tactically, one may leave it alone. But
Bourne is proposing more than tactics.

The second, somewhat different, reason for expecting mechanisms
is a concern with what in cognitive simulation circles is sometimes
called *sufficiency analysis* (Newell and Simon, 1965a). Suppose we observe a subject performing a complex task; e.g., multiplying two several
digit numbers together. We ask of any theory for explaining this behavior that it provide a sufficient set of processes for carrying out the behavior. The more elementary processes and underlying structures are,
of course, unexplained, although presumably simpler and in accord
with whatever general evidence exists. For simple behaviors, there may
be little difficulty in proposing sufficient mechanisms, and a sufficiency
analysis may be of no use. But for more complex behaviors, it may be
extraordinarily difficult to specify any mechanism that does the task.
To be particular, in our case of the mental multiplication, there is no

known way to multiply two numbers (given as sets of digits) without a rather complex, time-ordered process involving memory. This is not to say that a unique process exists—many are known—but rather that some process must exist.

The point is that we have every reason to expect that a system that can multiply two multi-digit numbers has an internal structure and internal processes that accomplish this total behavior. We may be wrong, for it is not necessary. But, given the existing extensive understanding of the mechanisms of multiplication, it is a safe bet that those processes are there. Why should one not want to find them? Even suppose, as may be the case temporarily, that there is little information other than input/output specifications. Why should one be led by that to conclude that one should not try to consider theories that propose an underlying process structure to explain the multiplication?

What Do Process Models Provide?

So far, I have argued that there is no necessity to consider enabling processes, but that, even so, there are pervasive reasons for expecting such processes to exist, both from very general considerations of how complex behaviors come about and from the clearly established physiological localization of complex symbolic behaviors to the brain.

Bourne's concern extends further than this. He seems to feel that, however true the general arguments might be, the processes are exceedingly difficult to find; and even when you find them, they give you nothing more than you had in the description of the behavior. Let us consider an example to see what process models do provide.

Figure 6-1 shows the time that it takes a subject to respond when he has to determine whether a presented digit is a member of a class of digits that has been presented two seconds earlier. The number of digits in the presented class is given as the ordinate; it thus represents the number of symbols the subject must remember in order to accomplish the task. The plus marks are points where the test digit was in the class; the minus marks those where it was not. The data are averaged from eight subjects, with about 95 observations per point.

This example is somewhat simpler than the concept tasks discussed by Bourne. Yet, it can serve to make several points. Here we have a regularity. Should we ask why the subject takes more time with the larger class, and a constant increment at that?

A simple process model is immediately suggested: that each member of the class is compared to the test digit with a constant time per

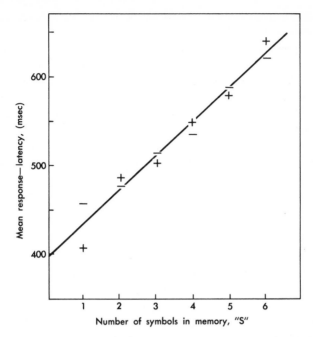

Figure 6-1. Relation between response latency and number of symbols in memory, S. (Adapted from Sternberg, 1966.)

unit act, consisting of obtaining the next member of the set and testing it. This leads to the following analysis by Sternberg:

> On trials requiring negative responses, s comparisons must be made. If positive responses were initiated as soon as a match had occurred (as in a self-terminating search), the mean number of comparisons on positive trials would be $(s + 1)/2$ rather than s. The latency function for positive responses would then have half the slope of the function for negative responses. The equality of the observed slopes shows, instead, that the scanning process is exhaustive: even when a match has occurred, scanning continues through the entire series. This may appear surprising. . . . (p. 653).

Why should one be surprised? Only because one has used a process model to make some calculations that relate various parts of the data. Would it be better not to be surprised; i.e., not to have any expectations of these data?

Sternberg did a second experiment, differing from the first primarily in providing the class of digits at the start of the experiment and testing it repeatedly, rather than repeatedly redefining the set for each trial. There was no change in the slope and slight change in the intercept. Also, the plus and minus points coincided, as in the first experiment. Now the question is, Does one say that one simply has a regularity here? And that the identity of slope (which equals the get-next-and-test time in the process model) is just a coincidence? Should one have had any expectations about these slopes? Perhaps, one could argue that the slopes should be the same on the basis of always expecting the simplest description to hold—the equivalent of "tomorrow is like today" as a baseline assumption in the analysis of economic time series. This would involve no underlying process assumption (which is that we are tapping the behavior of the same process, hence, we can expect the processing times to be commensurate).

The unit times that Sternberg gets are of the order of 40 msec. This, he notes, is four times faster than the maximum rate of silent rehearsal. For example, suppose one has subjects silently count down a highly overlearned list (the alphabet); e.g., start at F, go 11, and say the letter at that point (i.e., Q). Then again one gets response times that are highly linear with the number searched. However, the times per letter are now around 300 msec in practice subjects (Olshavsky, 1965). Should one be surprised at this difference, if one was not surprised at the lack of difference in Sternberg's two examples? It is true that there are differences in the experiment. For instance, in the "go 11" task the subject has more to do (both get next on the alphabet and get next on the integers). But already this assumes a processing model in which the total task is divided into subtasks, each of which is done sequentially. Furthermore, no plausible processing model is apparent that takes unit search times of 40 msec and still takes up to seven units of time to do a slightly more complex task. So there are other differences to be considered, such as the size of the list and its relations to the size of immediate memory (itself a processing notion); and others as well. My interest is not in pursuing the substance, fascinating as Sternberg's results are, but rather in illustrating the way processing considerations come in at every point. That is, the way we achieve intersituational generality is by inducting in one experiment some features of a process model, and then applying this to a second or third experiment.

The assumption that the same processing mechanism that is performing one experiment is performing the other underlies such applications. It is true that in dealing with a complex device, especially one with a very large memory that can contain both data and program, one very often cannot tie two experiments together—they tap aspects of the beast that have too little in common (Newell and Simon, 1967).

But this difficulty should not be mistaken for the notion that the appropriate research strategy is to proceed with a nominalism that seeks for descriptions, each in isolation.

Processing Metaphors and Processing Theories

I have a feeling that Bourne would be unhappy with the arguments I have just given. His unhappiness would stem not from the specific hypotheses used or the derivations attempted in discussing an experiment, but rather from the added freight of assuming that, therefore, the subject *has* any underlying psychological processes that enable him to behave in the way he does, or the way the equations describe. In fact, at this point, there is a haunting possibility that Bourne and I do not mean by psychological process the same thing at all. I find support for this in the following additional quotations from his paper:

> What counts is how well the theory describes the data. But if that is so, where is the need for process-talk? (p. 174).

> Nothing changes the fact that thought (as a psychological concept), whatever else is involved, is intangible, private, and without substance (p. 185).

> More commonly, the underlying and controlling thought process is imagined to be something which has as its outcome a thought and/or behavior. Whether there is some such process is indeterminate. No matter what else might be said, it is easy to see that the issue here is hardly the same concept of process fruitfully used in other sciences, for *psychological* processes which *produce* thoughts do not occupy any definite time interval, nor are they identifiable independently of an initial state or an outcome (Ossorio, 1966). Examples of scientifically useful processes are plentiful—flow of water, heat transfer, growth in plants, and so on. But having a thought, making a decision, selecting an hypothesis, or forming an association, as processes, lack determinable time characteristics and descriptions which are independent of initial condition and outcome. (For example, what would it be like to be halfway through the process of making a decision? . . .) (P. 186, italics in original.)

I read these as saying that psychological processes are something distinct from theory—something that is added to it after the fact—that almost by definition cannot exist in the physical world. Certainly, I have no difficulty assigning "determinable time characteristics" to processes. In Sternberg's case, they take about 40 msec. Certainly, I have no difficulty in knowing what it would be like to be halfway through a decision. In Sternberg's case, it would be to have settled the issue for some, but not all, of the digits in the set. To turn this into an empirical prediction poses problems of experimental technique, surely, since human subjects cannot be "turned off" in tens of milliseconds. The point is, however, that this is a question only of technique, and probably not a very serious question at that. The stream of work represented by Sternberg is based on a very simple, but effective, idea for looking at search times without motor reaction times, and thus represents precisely a separation of processes that to casual consideration appeared welded together.

In my own work, there is no difficulty in saying what it is like to be halfway through a decision on a chess move. The total task takes upwards of fifteen minutes, and we posit and verify many of the intermediate states of information and the state transforming operations of the subject during the course of making the decision (Newell and Simon, 1965b; Newell, 1968).

For me, the attribution of a set of enabling psychological processes to the subject happens in terms of the theory that I build. Some theories are process theories, some are not. A process theory (and for the psychology at hand I want to talk about an information-process theory) has in it terms that refer to memories and their capacities, and to representations of information in these memories. It has terms that refer to processes for encoding and decoding, for storing and retrieving, for communication, and for interpreting structures representing conditional sequential actions. And so on. A theory that has such terms is a processing theory and attributes psychological processes to the subject. It does not ask for measurements of anything except behavior; but that has no bearing on whether it is a process theory or not.

Furthermore, one cannot play the mathematicians' "symbol game" here, and say that this theory is simply a set of equations (or other symbolic expressions) combined according to some formal rules and applied to the empirical data by a set of formal coordinating definitions, without any imputation to the underlying structure of the subject being described. The inadequacy of this view arises precisely at the point where the formal model has to be modified. If the scientist dips into his informal knowledge of information-processing systems and how they operate in order to repair or extend his theory, he has a processing theory indeed.

Again, of course, there is no necessity. Pushed to the extreme, one could admit that a theory formally talks of processes, and that the informal surround, from which the theory emerged and from which it draws its resiliency, is also awash with processing notions, but still maintain that there is no need to attribute any processes to the subject. However, a modern application of Occam's razor would be appropriate —that the nonprocessing assertion is really excess baggage with no remaining operational content.

Summary

Let me summarize my reaction to Bourne's alternative that we can consider humans as rule-followers without asking after the processes that enable these rules to be followed. Bourne is logically justified; there is no necessity. Yet it is a failure to grasp an opportunity, for the processes are there.

My own position is thoroughly pragmatic, based on my interpretation of what has proven to be the way of success in science. In the case of Maxwell's equations, we threw away the scaffolding because it was not needed—because we learned to take the mathematics completely seriously. No other information was to be gained from the underlying process. In the gene, we went first from the abstract theory to an explanation in terms of molecular structure. The gene theory will not revert to an abstract theory with no need to talk about the underlying molecular processes, since they contain orders of magnitude yielding more information. It is possible, of course, that the molecular model will be replaced by something more basic, perhaps a quantum mechanical formalism that makes irrelevant the geometrical "building-block" theory now in use.

The description of complex behavior according to an information-processing model is useful as long as the constraints that seem to affect behavior can be organized and understood in terms of processing assumptions. When more intimate contact with the physiology finally occurs, then such models as have survived with be understandable as the reflection of physiological mechanisms. It is possible, at that time, that the descriptions of physiological processes will be formally so different that they will offer a radically different way of computing the behavior of the complex organism, and one that permits a very large amount of additional detail. If so, the stage of information-processing models will be over. We should look forward to that. But to believe that we should proceed only with descriptions of regularities and avoid any attempt to see in them the processing that is involved seems to me almost a failure of nerve.

REFERENCES

Luria, A. R. Human brain and psychological processes. New York: Harper and Row, 1966 (from the Russian, 1963).

Newell, A. On the analysis of human problem solving protocols. In *Proceedings of the International Symposium on Mathematical and Computational Methods in the Social Sciences,* Rome, Italy: 1968, in press.

Newell, A., and Simon, H. A. Programs as theories of higher mental processes. In R. W. Stack, and B. Waxman (Eds.), *Computers in Biomedical Research.* Vol. II. New York: Academic Press, 1965. Pp. 141-172. (a)

Newell, A., and Simon, H. A. An example of human chess play in the light of chess playing programs. In N. Weiner, and J. P. Schade (Eds.), *Progress in Biocybernetics.* Vol. II. Amsterdam: Elsevier, 1965. Pp. 19-75. (b)

Newell, A., and Simon, H. A. *Memory and process in concept formation.* In B. Kleinmuntz (Ed.), Concept formation and memory. New York: Wiley, 1967. Pp. 241-262.

Olshavsky, W. Reaction time measures of information processing behavior. Unpublished masters dissertation, Carnegie Institute of Technology, 1965.

Sternberg, S. High-speed scanning in human memory. *Science,* 1966, *153,* 652-654.

GENERAL DISCUSSION

ANDERSON asked Bourne why one should be concerned about rules if processes are not a matter of interest.

BOURNE replied that processes *are* matters of interest—both behavioral and nonbehavioral processes. Rules are regularities in behavior; i.e., behavioral processes. Evidence of them is found directly in behavior, and not in mechanisms or nonbehavioral processes assumed by some to control behavior. What are called mechanisms seem better described as correlates of behavior.

REITMAN asked Bourne whether he was objecting the concept of thinking as an antecedent to and the cause of behavior.

BOURNE replied that he was.

REITMAN then asked Bourne whether he accepted rules but opposed the notion of a process to carry out the rule.

BOURNE said that he did accept rules but was opposed to the notion of another kind of process (i.e., nonbehavioral) which regulates rule-governed behavior.

REITMAN then asked where a rule is while the organism is not using it.

BOURNE replied that a rule isn't an "it" at all but rather, a description. He pointed out that one could say, metaphorically, that "it" is probably in memory, but that we wouldn't know for sure until observing whether the person could be characterized as following that rule on some later occasion.

REITMAN said that an organism may be in one state at t_1 and a second state at t_2 and, assuming a deterministic system, the state of thought is a function of the state of the organism at a preceding time. Thus, he argued, attempts to describe the organism prior to the state of overt behavior have a useful purpose.

BOURNE replied that this statement begs a set of questions concerning determinism and whether there is any kind of behavior other than overt. (In the rule-system, there isn't.) He argued that these issues are unresolvable.

HABER indicated that he agreed with Newell since, from an information-processing view, we can try to look at intervening processes which occur between the stimulus and the response. Moreover, he pointed out, probes may be used during this interval in order to study the behavior at the intervening times.

BOURNE asked what a postulated nonbehavioral process adds if you measure the intervening behavior directly, and if what intervenes between stimulus and response is behavior.

HABER replied that measuring a piece of behavior implies an underlying stage which can be extended to other situations.

BOURNE answered that he would settle for any kind of behavior, not just the final response, and that any rule-description is, by its very nature, extendable to other situations. He said that part of the trouble here seems to be in the restrictive use of the term "behavior" only in reference to (gross) bodily movements.

BOURNE, in answer to a question, said that a rule is equivalent to (or a summary of) a set of observations of behavior. In reply to another question, he indicated that a rule may summarize much behavioral data.

NEWELL was asked whether the word "process" is a special term which is applied to unobservables. He answered that a process theory is only a type of theory which attempts to describe how the subject gets from the stimulus to the outcome. Examples, on the other hand, of nonprocess theory, NEWELL pointed out, are utility theory, detection theory, and operant conditioning.

BOURNE indicated that rule-theory is the general case of getting from stimulus to outcome.

ANDERSON observed that Bourne's position implies that a "process" apparently becomes a "rule" and hence scientifically respectable only when data are gathered. However, ANDERSON mentioned, one really cannot refuse to think or talk about some phenomenon only because it is not yet observable.

BOURNE noted that rule-statements depend no more on the availability of data than do process-statements and that, in this connection, the main difference between rule and process is that rule-descriptions carry no implications about the utility of behavioral data as indices of nonbehavioral events and processes.

7

LANGUAGE AND THOUGHT[1]

JAMES J. JENKINS
University of Minnesota

My task, in this paper, is one of awesome magnitude. The attempts to specify the relations between language and thought go back at least to the ancient Greeks and uncounted volumes have been filled with the writings of those who attempted to frame answers. In recent centuries, the problem expanded as it became clear that the terms "language" and "thought" have many meanings, and that most of these meanings are related in some degree. The relations, however, can be highly variable. For example, at one extreme we must think of a particular speech response functioning as an aid to simple problem solving on a particular occasion for some given person—a very concrete instance; at the other extreme we must think of the relation between the code or structure of some natural language and the nature of the thought processes of its speakers—a most abstract instance. Few investigators even claim interest, much less competence, over the entire range. Typically, one's areas of interest and one's convictions are likely to be selected on dis-

[1] Preparation of this paper was supported by grants to the Center for Research in Human Learning, University of Minnesota from the National Institute of Child Health and Human Development (PO 1-HD-01136), the National Science Foundation (GS 541), and the Graduate School of the University.

The ideas expressed were greatly influenced by conversations with Robert Shaw, Donald Foss, John Flavell, and Terry Halwes, to all of whom I acknowledge grateful indebtedness.

ciplinary lines, with the psychologists stressing the effects of speech habits and particularized responses, the linguists and anthropologists stressing the control exercised by the nature of linguistic and social codes, and the philosophers attempting to clarify and criticize one position after another as each appears in the focus of history.

It was asked of the contributors to this text that they "write freely on the issue of what their own area of research may contribute to the understanding of thought processes," but thought processes was not defined so that "definitional issues of interest . . . may emerge . . . ." At this point, my feeling was that I might have a fighting chance at explaining the various things that "language" might be, but that I had little probability of understanding what "thought" might be. I finally decided that I might best serve by surveying the major positions on thought and language that make relatively clear claims about each term and the relationship of the terms. Then, as an epilogue, I could append what seemed to me to be still another view which one might hold (though I think it is not well represented in the literature at the present time).

The major positions on the relations of thought and language can be characterized (or perhaps caricatured) in a series of brief answers to the multiple-choice question: "What is the relation between thought and language?"

1. *Thought is dependent on language.*

2. *Thought is language.*

3. *Language is dependent on thought.*

The fourth answer might be fittingly cast in the devilish mode of the fourth alternative that one uses when he has run out of good responses:

4. *None of the above.* Or perhaps, *All of the above.*

Now let us consider each of the alternative responses. I will try to indicate some of the sources of each view, comment on some of the evidence, and remark on its potential contribution.

Thought Is Dependent on Language

This position throws together several strange bedfellows. It seems to capture the essentials of the position of some of the Russian investigators of the second-signal system and, at the same time, to provide a classification for the radical or "strong" Whorfian position. The heart of the issue is seen to be the dependence of human thinking on language as its very source.

The Russian view has deep roots. To accommodate the great differences which he saw between the lower animals and man, Pavlov postulated that the language system of man constituted a *second-signal system*. Man, like the other animals, is governed by conditioned reflex mechanisms (the first-signal system) but, unlike the other animals, man can signal about the primary signals and, to that extent, he can remove himself from direct contact with reality. The second-signal system, then, represents a higher-control system which is invented chiefly to explain the effects of instruction and other forms of external linguistic control, and the internal use of language by human beings to control their own behavior through "self-instruction."

An illuminating set of experiments concerning the development of the second-signal system is provided by the work of Luria (1961). (See also Jenkins' review, 1961; Hilgard and Bower, 1966; and Brozek, 1964.) Luria presents a series of experiments designed to show that as language develops in the child, the acquisition of other responses is markedly changed from slow acquisition and extinction (typical of the conditioning paradigm) to rapid change, following rules which can be stated verbally and used as behavior control mechanisms. The picture presented is one of a "light-weight" easily controlled system, language, coming to have control over a more ponderous and less flexible behavior system.

The experiments performed by Luria use a very simple apparatus which presents colored lights and forms to the subject. The response apparatus consists of a rubber bulb or ball held by the subject. In very young children (less than 18 months) the problem may consist of having the child squeeze the ball when a light comes on. When this response is obtained, it may be observed that the child keeps on pressing, apparently in response to the stimulus feedback from his own hand. Verbal control is introduced to help him initiate his responses and to respond only the appropriate number of times. (If he is to respond twice, it is helpful for him to say, "Go, go," for example.) Later, negative instructions and negative self-commands will help him withhold responding in the presence of other stimuli and, finally, he will be able to select only certain complex stimuli in response to a combination of external and self-instructions (e.g., "Squeeze three times to the red airplane"). While we might be hesitant to say that the early experiments demand "thought," we would all agree that the later experiments surely require a good deal of information processing and decision. It is assumed that all of this is mediated by language.

Put in its most general terms, this formulation asserts that language first has an activating function. It serves as a start signal for any particular sequence of behavior which is already learned. With further development, language also acquires inhibitory functions and can serve to stop a behavior sequence or delay or prevent it altogether. (In the small child this is said to be lacking with the curious outcome that negative instructions tend to set off the behavior they are designed to prevent; e.g., saying "No, no," acts as an activation signal.) When language can both initiate and inhibit other behavior, it becomes an instrument for regulating other behaviors according to rules or instructions. Finally, when the organism has good control of internal language, he is capable of self-regulation.

The experimental work of Luria and many other Russian investigators supplements and details the general Pavlovian view of the importance of language in the case of human behavior. The emphasis on semantic considerations in the writings of Pavlov and his successors and the role assigned to the second-signal system seems to have escaped most American psychologists until recently. Now, however, they are seen to have been clear points of emphasis, and it is easy to understand why Pavlov thought American psychologists were making the case of human behavior much too simple and ignoring its obvious complexity which had required the invention of the second-signal system.

In many ways, the most sweeping statements concerning the second-signal system and the strongest declarations of the importance of its role are to be found in the recently translated book *Thought and Language* by Vygotsky (1962), originally published in 1934. Brozek (1964), aptly chose the following quotation to typify the book:

> Thought and language, which reflect reality in a way different from that of perception, are the key to human consciousness. Words play a central part not only in the development of thought but in the historical growth of consciousness as a whole. A word— the living union between sound and meaning—is a microcosm of human consciousness (p. 153).[2]

---

[2] Obviously Vygotsky's view and the Russian view generally is much more complex than this simplistic rendering. Diebold (1965), for example, stresses the complexity and chooses the following to characterize Vygotsky's developmental theory: ". . . in the speech development of the child, we can with certainty establish a pre-intellectual stage, and in his thought development, a prelinguistic stage . . . . Up to a certain point in time, the two follow different lines, independently of each other . . . . At a certain point these lines meet, whereupon thought becomes verbal and speech rational."

Vygotsky makes word meanings central to thought and turns to semantic analysis (the study of the development and functioning of the meanings of words) as the key to understanding thought and consciousness. Language is seen to have internal roles in thinking and to serve as a means of communication.

Surely, much of this Russian point of view can be captured in the notions that man is conscious because he has language, and that the behavior of man which is strikingly different from that of the lower animals is attributable to exactly this special behavior capacity.

While these views of human psychology are exciting and of high interest, they seem too extreme to the typical Western psychologist. Acceptance has been further delayed by the fact that attempts to replicate some of the phenomena cited as experimental evidence have not been very successful. (See Jarvis, 1963, for a negative case and Gleitman, 1965, for a positive case.) In all events, this position, though set forth here very crudely, relies on a simple conception of language as sets of words with meanings which can act to control other behavior. It is further asserted that this is the content of human thinking and that consciousness arises from the interaction of the linguistic system and the remainder of the world. Thus, we have a simple conception of language as words and meanings, and a conception of human thinking as verbal regulation by these words. (Consideration of the experimental work suggests that, in practice, language is considered to consist of propositions rather than as collections of words, but linguistic analysis is not found in the writings and no consideration is given to the linguistic code as such.)

The Russian position seems at once both too broad and too specific; the area of application of the second-signal system is almost unlimited and its machinery is never specified in detail. The theory consists of applying the vaguely defined "other way" of learning to the entire range of problems which set human beings, human experience, and human behavior apart from the remainder of the animal kingdom and the principles that govern animal behavior. The machinery of the simple system appears to be, by-and-large, associationistic, and nowhere comes to grips with the problems of organization and structure which form such a prominent feature of language behavior itself. Thus, while the Russian attempt appears to be in the right direction in treating language as a special case of human behavior, it seems not to go far enough in terms of the richness of its formulation or the variety of the theoretical conceptions which it makes possible.

It seems strange to find as the second instance under this same rubric the writings of Benjamin Lee Whorf. Yet, it is clear that the end product of the Russian approach, the control of other behavior by language, is seen in its most sophisticated hypothetical form in Whorf's hypothesis. It is not necessary here to enlarge on Whorf's well-known position that language determines thought. Thanks to Carroll's work, Whorf's writings are readily available and, in addition, many discussions of his hypotheses are in print (Lenneberg, 1953; Brown, 1958; Fishman, 1960; Hoijer, 1954; Osgood and Sebeok, 1954; and Hymes, 1964).

In its strongest form, Whorf's position is that the code that one speaks determines how he perceives the world, hence, the "world view" or *Weltanshauung* label for his claim. This hypothesis asserts that the perceptual givens in the world are a product of the speaker's language, and that these givens provide an analysis of the universe that is different from, and not available to, a speaker of another language. In weaker forms, the hypothesis becomes one concerning the relative availability of different conceptions of the world or different degrees of attention being given to different aspects of the world. In still weaker form, the hypothesis might be only that different vocabularies index the different degrees of importance given in a particular culture to various kinds of items. Finally, in its weakest form, the hypothesis can be seen as a claim that the way a person talks about a situation will suggest what he sees to be its important aspects. Whorf's writings argue for all of these views to varying extents.

The strongest form of the hypothesis asserts that there is no real translation, and that the attempt to learn another's language may be hopeless because one cannot abandon one's own world view and acquire the other's. (See Quine, 1960, for example, on this point.) One must conclude from this that thought patterns are determined in both obvious and extremely subtle ways by the form of the code one first learns to speak. What one sees when he looks at a rainbow; whether one conceives of the world as things and actions or as a continuous flux; whether one has notions of causality, time, and space—are all to be attributed to the language one happens to speak. Surely, this is the strongest claim of the dependence of not only thought but all human psychological functioning on language.

Justification of this radical position has been extremely difficult. Linguists and psychologists are divided among themselves on the degree of confirmation which is to be expected. It seems to this writer, however, that the strong hypothesis is almost surely incorrect. A host of common-sense evidences, such as the existence of thoroughly competent bilinguals in grossly different languages, considerations of the common physical equipment of all mankind and a wealth of evidence concerning the general equality of psychophysical discriminations across language groups, the mastery of western physical science by representatives of every major language family in the world, etc. argue persuasively against it. Indeed, when one looks for hard evidence (as opposed to "funny looking" translations) for the Whorfian hypothesis, it is hard to find any whatsoever. One is much more likely to conclude, in the contrary fashion, that anything that can be said in one language can be said in any other natural language with more or less effort.

In the course of many discussions of this topic, Joseph Greenberg, the distinguished anthropologist-linguist, hazarded the conjecture that any natural language is a meta-language for any language system that human beings can compose. (The converse is obviously not the case; e.g., the language of chess cannot express most of what can be expressed in English, but English can express easily anything that can be said in the chess language.) If this is so, I am strongly inclined to agree with Greenberg; it has important implications for psychological theorizing and important implications for the relationships that we are to establish between language and thought. (This will be treated below in more detail.)

In weaker forms, one finds some confirmation for the Whorfian hypotheses. Carroll and Casagrande (1958) found that obligatory categories in a grammar were used as a basis for sorting "the object that doesn't belong" when no other obvious criteria were present for the decision. Similarly, one suspects that the choice of hypotheses in a concept-formation test might well be a function of what aspects of a situation are noticed first; and there is, in fact, some evidence that this is true. (A very nice example is given by Brown in his discussion "Speech Categories as a Guide to Referent Categories," in particular the experiment with Horowitz on vowel length and categorization, Brown, 1958, pp. 213-216.) To the extent that a particular language provides a vocabulary entry or a construction with just the meaning correspondence needed for a particular problem, one expects the coding of information to be more accurate and better retained by the speaker, as compared to the case where such coding requires a good deal of circumlocution or where the coding categories are so broad as to include many of the competitors in a recognition test. Brown and Lenneberg (1954) showed that retention of color memory was a function of the codability of the color, and Lenneberg and Roberts (1956) showed that differences in such memory were, as predicted, a function of the differences in the zone of applicability of color names from one language to another. Many psychologists have conducted experiments on the effects of labels on the nature of the "memory trace" that subjects are trying to retain over a period of time, and the verbal behavior literature is rich in positive results that have been obtained from such experiments.

Thus, there seems to be a variety of sources of evidence for the "weak" version of the Whorfian hypothesis, leading to the general conclusion that language influences psychological processes such as recognition, recall, problem solving and concept formation, but no real support for the major version of the hypothesis which put it in this category to start with. One is likely to conclude, after studying the evidence, that language *influences* thought processes in a variety of ways, but is unlikely to conclude that language determines thought processes in anything like the fashion that Whorf at one time suspected.

In general, taken from either of the extreme points of view, the claim that language determines thought seems far too strong. The Whorfian view that the code determines what kind of world one knows seems logically to be incorrect and has mustered no supporting evidence. The Russian view that language is necessary for human thought has much more chance of partial corroboration, but currently suffers from an unsophisticated view of what a language is and seems unreasonably restrictive in ignoring other kinds of thinking in which humans must surely engage if one believes introspective accounts at all.

Thought Is Language

Perhaps I should apologize for including this category among the viewpoints being discussed. Certainly, I open myself to the charge that I am creating a straw man to destroy in a heated sham battle. Nevertheless, while no one may wish to hold this position today, it has been held, and it is worth some comment.

In the early part of this century, when behaviorism was displacing the old psychology devoted to the contents of consciousness, it did so with revolutionary zeal and passion. As is common in revolutions, innocent bystanders were sometimes injured or even killed while the new power was being firmly entrenched in the seat of government. One of the victims of the behavioristic revolution was the psychology of thinking. It may well have been that this particular bystander was not in very good health at the time because the older psychologies had been probing him unmercifully in the vain search for accurate identification of images, but it is clear that it was the revolutionaries who disposed of him. In a series of greatly oversimplified attacks directed against mentalism and unobservables in science, images, thoughts, and ideas were all liquidated. What began as a well-motivated desire to find a secure data base for psychology ultimately became a denial of the events of the older science themselves. Mental events were declared to be nonexistent under the laws of the new psychological regime.

Since something had to fill the head once the mind had been disposed of, its place was taken by the "brain as a switchboard." This piece of popular and up-to-date physical equipment was borrowed as the analog of mental machinery which could be linked with a radical peripheralism to produce a "clean" psychology whose data could consist of observable (in principle) stimuli as inputs and observable (again, in principle) responses. Under this model, thinking was seen to be merely covert responding. It might require a good deal of apparatus to detect these responses, but at least they were no longer mentalistic. This preserved the simplicity of the system, took care of disposing of the ghosts, and gave psychologists good reasons to make careful measures of the peripheral equipment of the organism. When the Pavlovian conditioning paradigm was added to this tidy little conception as the "switchboard operator," it appeared that a complete S-R psychology was achieved, or at least promised to be achievable.

The upshot of all of this was that whatever interest in the psychology of thinking survived the revolution was now focused on covert or minimal responses. This was seen to pose new problems, however. It was all very well to have "thinking about picking up a suitcase" represented as muscle tensions in the right arm, but it was not clear how to supply the vast array of peripheral responses that were going to be needed to cover *all* of the things that one could think about. Such responses were indeed difficult to imagine, much less to find and measure. Fortunately, an "escape hatch" was found in language, since anything that could be specified as a thought could be put in words in some fashion for any mental event whatsoever. If, as said previously, natural language is a universal meta-language for all special languages (and all special knowledge), it can always in principle be made to serve whenever one cannot think of an implicit response for the particular "thinking" involved. Perhaps, the only thing that is surprising is that the other muscle twitches were kept as part of the system, since obviously one can tell oneself about "lifting the suitcase" and, thus, save oneself the gross muscle movements which are otherwise required by the theory.

A less devious notion is offered by George Miller when he says (Miller, 1964, p. 29):

> Behaviorists generally try to replace anything subjective by its most tangible, physical manifestation, so they have a long tradition of confusing thought with speech—or with 'verbal behavior' as many prefer to call it.

This paragraph also points up an important aspect of the formulation. Language for the behaviorist *is* speech; it *is* muscle responses. There is no consideration here of language as a system or as a code, and no intention to create any such "mental entities." Presumably, the nature of language is that of acquired word-to-world correspondences via the conditioning paradigm; thinking about the world (when one is not lifting suitcases mentally) is just talking about it subvocally. As Herbert Feigl is fond of characterizing this position, "In short, Watson made up his windpipe that he had no mind!"

But now we must notice a curious consequence of this position. Since *any* stimuli and responses can be associated through contiguity, it is also true that any behavior which goes on while speech goes on can come to "stand for" the word or words being said. This means that it is not always "fair" to look in the language mechanism for thinking, because the subject may be talking to himself with other musculature. Lest it be thought that I am inventing this involuted state of affairs, I recommend that the reader study the little book of readings on thinking that McGuigan (1966) has recently edited. In the opening selection, taken from Watson's chapter, "What is Thinking," found in his book entitled *Behaviorism*, we find the following selections within the space of seven pages:

> *What the psychologists have hitherto called thought is in short, nothing but talking to ourselves* (p. 10, italics in original).

Then,

> The number and variety of habits we form in the speaking of almost every word is thus well-nigh legion . . . . From this circumstance there grows up a complexity of organization which even the psychologist seemingly cannot grasp . . . . Soon *any, and every* bodily response *may become a word substitute* (p. 11, italics in original).

And finally,

. . . one's total organization is brought into the process of thinking
. . . . we could still think in some sort of way even if we had no
words (p. 16).

. . . we can say that *"thinking"* is largely *subvocal talking*—provided
we hasten to explain that it can occur without words (p. 16, italics
in original).

It must have rapidly become clear to the behaviorists, as the difficulties piled up in finding the "right sort" of implicit speech records at
the mouth, tongue, and voice box, that the seemingly objective measures of thought were just as elusive and untrustworthy as the earlier
images. There was first the general escape into language, and then the
escape from language to any sort of bodily activity. There could be,
then, no specific tests of the theory which could conceivably refute it.

For our purposes, we must also note the identification of language
with words and the identification of words with speech acts. The analysis frequently talks about novel utterances as "merely" rearrange-
ments of words. Hear Watson again:

The elements are all old, that is, the words that present themselves
are just our standard vocabulary—it is only the arrangement that
is different (p. 15).

There is, thus, no consideration of structure as such and not even mention of meaning beyond the level of the word.

Thinking is not defined in any useful way except as it is considered
to be subvocal speech or simple trial-and-error learning. In general,
the position has had the effect of stifling research on thinking.

Perhaps the closest that one can come to this position today is to
interpret Skinner's position that "Man Thinking is simply Man Behaving" (Skinner, 1957). Such a position includes all of thinking and all of
verbal behavior under the same rubric, controlled by the same laws,
and inferable from the same kinds of data as any instrumental learned
act. Hence, language, thought, and all other behaviors are "the same
kind of thing." The problems of relating language and thought are
simply defined out of existence.

Language Is Dependent on Thought

The schools of psychological theory that can be classified here represent the most popular middle ground of psychology and, at the same

time, touch both the oldest and the most recent schools of psychological thought, again producing, as in the case of the first categorization, strange bedfellows.

The view that language is in some sense a resultant of thought can be found in the psychology of Wundt where the study of language was recommended to discover those things that were true about the human mind in its most general aspects. Wundt felt that in the study of social products such as language the psychology of the people, "Folk Psychology," was to be found. This idea, which is a sort of reverse Whorfian view, has had many adherents even among psychologists who had thrown out the older psychology (e.g., Dunlap, 1934).

To the best of my knowledge, however, no modern work of this kind has been performed, though perhaps the work of the content and propaganda analysts should be included here. (I shall not so include it since in the social, political, and clinical cases that I know, the objective has been to search for particular pieces of information—solutions for special problems or models for the temporary psychic state of the individual—rather than for *general* relations between thought and language, which is the goal of this paper.)

The current adherents of some form or another of this view constitute the bulk of psychologists at the present time. Piaget seems to feel that children pass through stages of development as far as their cognitive processes are concerned, and that language follows this path as a necessary consequence. Carroll (1964) argues that thought and cognition are presupposed by language, and that speech is due to thought or cognition, even though speech may influence thought.

Osgood in his extensive writings (e.g., Osgood and Sebeok, 1954; Osgood, 1954; Osgood, Suci, and Tannenbaum, 1957) clearly intends for the learner to acquire behavior toward real objects and situations in the real world, and then to learn the verbal labels that are to be attached to the "representational mediators" and manipulated in and by the language. In similar manners, almost all of the current theorists can be seen as depicting the growth of language as an instrument or tool for the experiencing, developing, and thinking child.

The utility of the child's acquisition and the adult's continued use of language is presumably shown by experiments which stress the usefulness of verbal labels for distinguishing stimuli, formulating and attaining concepts, storing items of information in verbally coded form, making certain forms of transfer easy and other forms difficult, etc. By now, there is no lack of studies which illustrate these utilities, though there are some curious failures to show much effect of the supposed variables in experimental situations. (See Jenkins, 1963.)

The most general characterization of this position is that of "interaction" rather than simple "dependency." It is ordinarily assumed that thought and experience precede, and that language follows. It is then supposed, however, that language as a special tool makes possible new extensions of thought and experience and aids and assists thought processes in a variety of ways. It is not usually assumed that language is indispensable to thought and, ordinarily, these theorists suppose that some other instrumental system could serve the role that language customarily plays. It is usually noted that a special virtue accrues to the language system, since it is assumed ordinarily that language has immense social utility and that elaborate forms of language behavior are shaped and molded in the context of skilled speakers and special situational requirements. Thus, one may learn a great deal about "putting his thoughts into language" under the right training and rewarding circumstances, even though the thoughts, themselves, may not be readily available for manipulation.

The curious thing about the American version of this view is that it has tended to fixate on the word as the unit of meaning, that it has given itself no explanatory power by exploiting linguistic advances, and that it confines itself to very weak theoretical notions which prevent extension of the point of view to cover anything more complex than simple serial behaviors.

The encouraging aspect of all versions of this view is that they seem amenable to development and change and seem to be in a favorable and reasonable position with respect to both thought and language to make certain kinds of change possible. A new climate is beginning to prevail with respect to the development of cognitive processes in the child. The work of Piaget is having a serious influence on the kind of research pursued by American psychologists and on the kinds of constructs that they will entertain. The notion that the thought of the child follows a definite sequence is a most encouraging sign for investigators who have entertained the fear that all thinking might turn out to be unique, unsystematized, and anarchistic. The kinds of conceptions that Piagetians find useful are important influences in eroding the doctrines that *simple* stimulus and response units form the building blocks of thinking. The great robustness of the "conservation" experiments and their many replications, for example, have been important in impressing psychologists on this side of the ocean with the fact that "unusual" constructs may nonetheless have "hard-nosed" empirical consequences.

With respect to the adult (and the more traditional pursuit of the psychology of the college sophomore), one sees further encouragement in the emergence of research in concept formation which goes beyond the simplest class of identical stimulus elements, through the class of concepts which draws on identical responses, to the class of concepts that is identified by rule structures (see Jenkins, 1966), and experimentation (such as that of Bourne, 1968) which attempts the separation of stimulus-element detection from rules of combination in the discovery of concepts.

The major problem of this kind of approach, as I see it at this moment, is to rid itself of the conception of language as merely a system of labels for experience. There are all sorts of signs that conceptions of thinking are broadening and taking interesting and creative turns, but no one seems to know quite what to do with the relationship between thinking and language while language is still tied to a simple associationism that limits its role severely.

All of the Above

Given the limits of the responses criticized above, it is clear that I must turn to the option "All of the Above." Obviously, I should now suggest how the three points of view all contain elements of the correct solution but show how, in itself, each is wrong because it is too limited. I should then go on to show that a clever synthesis of the three views emerges with a balanced conception approaching the truth. While I think there are aspects of all three points of view that are correct, I think that the tidy solution to the problem is, nevertheless, going to escape us. Perhaps we must recognize that the other all-purpose alternative to a multiple-choice item, "None of the Above," also applies. It seems to me, that our conceptions of language and thinking both need further explication before we can move toward an appreciably better solution to the question of their relationship.

At this point, I blush to confess that all I can offer is a proposal—not a new specification of the relationship between thinking and language. The proposal is that we accept the approach of the modern linguists with respect to language and that we try to treat thinking in an analogous fashion, using the same methodological tools the linguists are using with such success today. This brings us to two thorny questions: Have we learned enough from the linguists' procedures in their analysis of language so that we can apply the analogous technique to the analysis of thought? Given that we *are* knowledgeable, is it possible to apply the analogous procedures to these subtle and complicated mental activities?

If one looks at the great surge of excitement in psychology in the last decade with respect to psycholinguistics and, especially, the fervor and zeal with which the young psycholinguists have attacked new problems suggested by the generative approach to language, one must grant respect to the influence of the "descriptive" approach (and especially its generative version) as a beginning for psychological effort. If we are to explain thought and thinking, it will surely be helpful to know *what* it is that we are supposed to explain. Just as the current description of language has radically altered the psychologist's account of the acquisition of language (see McNeill, 1966) and has suggested entirely new problems and new dimensions of problems to him, so we may expect that a better description of thinking will show some of our old views to be untenable and will, at the same time, suggest radical ways to approach the further analysis of this phenomenon.

As I see the work of the current linguists, it consists of a series of steps calculated to lead to a grammar or a theory of the phenomena which were observed at the outset. In an oversimplified version, this activity can be seen as a series of three general types of procedures. The first of these is the collection of "clear cases." Here, one studies the phenomena of the subject matter that are available in their least ambiguous form and asks what kinds of events and relationships need to be described; that is, what the specific items are to be accounted for. At this point, one makes use of all the knowledge of the subject matter that he has personally, as well as all of the suggestions and decisions of predecessors who have studied these problems. In the case of language, for example, one knows that he will have to deal with a phonological system consisting of a small number of elements; with a morphological level which is further characterized by classes of entries that are employed in different fashions and have different privileges; and with a syntactic level that must yield at least phrase structures, etc. no matter what kind of linguist one is or what kind of grammar he sets out to write. These are simply part of the heritage of valuable discriminations. If one goes on from there to include phenomena not previously accounted for, such as intersentential relationships, ambiguity, and the like, he is obviously claiming that an even more powerful analysis is possible and the field is thereby advanced to the extent that he is successful.

When one has collected his "clear cases" and set forth the equivalences and differences with which he is to deal and the entities that he will use in the description, he must proceed to *invent* logical systems which can produce the desired similarities and differences at just the levels desired and in just the right way. The importance of this step is clear when one considers the ineffectiveness of a point of view which simply locates clear cases and exhibits them as demonstrations without ever developing the systematic support which makes clear the import of the demonstration. Gestalt psychology seems to have stagnated at exactly this point. Much of the work of the Gestalters appears to have been directed at confounding the associationists by pointing to phenomena (interestingly enough, phenomena of unexpected equivalences and ambiguities, just as in the language case) and saying, "There! Try to explain that!" But watching a reversible figure is a far cry from being able to give an account of it which makes clear *why* it reverses. In short, demonstrating a phenomenon is not explicating it. It only sets the problem—it does not solve it.

Finally, all of the inventions of the theorist must be combined in an overall logical device (or system of rules) which is tested for its capacity to generate all the clear cases it was designed to explain, while at the same time *not* generating ungrammatical strings (impossible outcomes). Notice, in the case of linguists, that the device is not a speaker of the language. It has nothing to say, does not operate in real time, is not constrained by psychological limitations, etc. It is a device whose purpose is to make clear the kinds of operations and entities that are minimally required to show in detail just the way things that are supposed to be alike *are* alike, and the way things that are supposed to be different *are* different.

This model, then, can be considered to set out in detail the "competence" required of the speaker of the language. The competence model can then become the target for the psychologist. It tells him in precise and economical form what it is that he must account for as he attempts to build a description of the human machine which can perform these or equivalent operations and achieve these relationships, in real time, with finite memory, etc.

It must be objected that there is no guarantee that we can make any headway with this proposal when we turn to thought. After all, language must be explicit to play its interpersonal role and thought is under no such constraint. Language is conventionalized, standardized, and systematized; thought may be none of these. Language (at least as represented in the performances of speech and writing) is readily recordable and may be saved for analysis and study; thought appears to be evanescent and fleeting. Language, with all of these advantages, has only slowly and grudgingly yielded up its secrets over some 2000 years of study, and it is possible that the major part of the work is yet to be done; surely thought will be even more intractable at the very best.

But while all these considerations are valid reasons for depression, I feel that there are some grounds for optimism. The first of these is the parallel that we can see between the rapid and consistent development of language under all sorts of scraps and bits and pieces of language stimulation and the consistent sequential pattern in stages of thinking discovered by the Piagetians. If, in fact, thought has the potential of being idiosyncratic, unsystematic, and potentially unmodelable, it is surely odd that it fails to show these characteristics when we ask the right kinds of questions of the thinking processes of the child.

The second ground for optimism is the growing emphasis on the role of innate processes in the child's acquisition of language. If language is systematic only because we have arranged careful reinforcement contingencies and "shaped" the child's behavior in just the right ways, then it is perhaps reasonable to think that language will be radically different from thought because thought processes have never been particularly available for "shaping." If, on the other hand, the language mechanisms *by their very nature* make possible only certain kinds of entities, operations, and rules for any natural language, the role of learning has a much less disturbing effect, and one is encouraged to think that thought, too, is constrained as to its entities and operations.

While it may be difficult to imagine how society manages to "shape" unseen and unobservable mental events, it is not particularly difficult to see how evolution might have accomplished this same standardization. A million years of evolution may well have acted to set the stage for our research.

One might imagine that the organism is constrained by his biological mental equipment to respond in given ways of thinking when he is confronted with the world. This is, after all, merely an extention of the notion that there are built-in perceptual constancies and equivalences and built-in output constancies, regularities, and sequences. (The latter are, perhaps, better seen in the lower animals.) Our further bet is simply that the organism is patterned in some similar way (in process not in content) between these patterned input and patterned output events.

If we are willing to make these optimistic assumptions, we can at least consider moving ahead with the problem. Our next step is obviously to steep ourselves in the phenomena of thinking in search of "clear cases." This will entail a rereading of the philosophers of thought (and, one would assume, reading Kant with a vengeance), reflecting on the phenomena of thought in all aspects, observing instances in any favorable setting we can find, and searching persistently for pervasive examples of the analogs of equivalence, ambiguity, and the like. Fortunately, for our purposes, we can turn immediately to the work of Piaget which is expressly aimed at finding equivalences in mental operations (e.g., in the conservation studies) and which, at the higher levels, is devoted to the examination of formal operations. This work contains insights into important phenomena which could serve as the first targets for the generative theorists of thinking. Further, while Piaget's works are rich in suggesting beginnings for the attack on some types of thinking, the mental machinery that he provides in the "equilibration" model is clearly in need of precisely the kind of work that we said ought to follow. *Assimilation* and *accommodation* are presently gross terms with which to talk about adjustments in, and transitions between, grossly described competencies of the developing human being. The need for precise description and careful explication is apparent.

A problem which currently confronts workers in this area is that of specifying the areas of application of abstract conceptual developments. "Conservation of volume," for example, covers an infinity of concrete instances over particulars of many kinds (liquids, plastics, and solids in various shapes, divisions, and arrangements). The bold and powerful conceptions of Piaget are assertions about abstract equivalences; they are necessarily couched in abstract language. The exercise of building grammars, for instance, of these equivalences requires the mapping of these abstractions (non-terminal vocabulary items) into specific, particular terminal vocabulary items for every domain of application. It seems to me that this is precisely the degree of specificity that is now required.

It would be ideal if I could now present a complete instance of the development of appropriate, tight, generative models and the experimentation that signaled their confirmation or led to their modification. Unfortunately, however, I am unable to do so. At present, we have only part of such a project which is in progress. I hope that it will serve for illustrative purposes.

In the laboratories of the Center for Research in Human Learning at the University of Minnesota, Drs. Robert Shaw and Peter Pufall are studying children's behavior with the Piagetian "diagrammatic layout." (See Piaget and Inhelder, 1956, and Pufall, 1966.) The problem for the child, serving as the subject, consists of mimicking the behavior of the experimenter. In front of the experimenter and in front of the child is a three-dimensional diagrammatic layout or "landscape" with highly-differentiated quadrants, different geometrical objects present in the quadrants, etc. The experimenter places an object (such as a cow) in a given orientation in a given position on the diagram and encourages the child to do "the same" with his object and his diagram. The child's move is recorded and corrected and the experimenter proceeds to the next move. The board of the experimenter and the child may be side by side, or the board of the experimenter may be across from the child, or the boards may be systematically transformed, rotated, etc.

Piaget recognizes three relatively distinct stages of development from the children's performance on this task. The initial stage is observed in children younger than four years of age. This stage is characterized by an absence of even a limited recognition of a coordinate system, and also by an inability to honor changes in perspective; i.e., the child does not demonstrate an understanding of the effects of rotation. However, the child does seem to operate on certain topological features such as "proximities," "enclosures," etc. Hence an object is recognized as "next to" a distinctive feature on the board but not as fixed in a locus of features. The second stage is highlighted by the child's apparent ability to coordinate two or three features of the board as well as imposing a reference system. But this system is an egocentric referencing of locations in space. While the four- to seven-year-old child at this stage can recognize an object's position among a locus of display features, he does not honor a rotation of the layout as he places the object to *his* left or right or near or far *from him* within this locus. The third stage is achieved around seven years of age when the child apparently can coordinate more features than before (logically multiply relations according to Piaget) and also honor changes in perspective (rotation), no longer demonstrating an egocentric reference system.

Research has generally been done with children who are chronologically beyond the first stage, and it has supported, in general, the arguments put forward by Piaget. However accurate Piaget's appraisal of these stages of development, it remains descriptively difficult to formulate and organize a set of spatial relations with which the child may be working at any stage or while moving through a stage. For example, the pervasiveness of an "egocentric reference system" has not been clearly demonstrated. Does it determine the positioning of the object in toto? Or only in part? Nor is it clear what consistencies can be observed and formulated in the "transitional" child.

Shaw and Pufall conceived of the situation as follows: The diagram may be regarded as a physical locus on which the position and the orientation of a piece may be physically specified to any desired degree of accuracy, far beyond the accuracy with which the psychological organism is expected to function. The problem of understanding the conceptual apparatus of the child is the problem of mapping, from this fine-grained display, information into the child's response categorizations and vice versa. The "grammar" of the child's cognitive apparatus (its generative set of rules) should specify the many-to-one mapping for the positions of the board which result in equivalent responses on the part of the child, and the one-to-many mapping for the position on the board which is multiply mapped in the responses of the child.

Rather than preparing a set of grammars that strictly reflected the cognitive levels cited by Piaget, Shaw and Pufall devised a set of grammars defined over different independent bases (e.g., an egocentric base, an object-proximity base, etc.). It was recognized that what would be discovered would be a "mixture" of these grammars, but it was reasoned that an initial specification of the same behavior by independent grammars would indicate most clearly what task conditions would be needed to force the child to operate within one or another of these systems. This meant, in turn, that they could specify test operations in which placements on the board, neutralization of specific features of the board, rotations of the board, transpositions of the board, etc., would yield contrasts between different grammars. Thus, "mixing" of grammars could be detected and dominance of one mode of attack over another could be appraised.

Preliminary findings show this approach to be quite fruitful. It is apparent that children as young as four years of age can coordinate physically distinct board features such as colored objects of discriminable forms; but that not until age ten can the child organize the board structure when features are neutralized; i.e., when objects are all white and forms are all of the same shape. Secondly, it has been observed that not only do children at age six and ten appear to use an egocentric reference system as described by Piaget, but that also they employ a system whereby quadrants of the board are translocated; i.e., one quadrant is mapped on top of another. The latter accounts for responses which are only subtly distinct responses from the former but which represent obviously distinct psychological processing. What may be the case is that the egocentric reference system is used *to the neglect of* rotational effects whereas translocation is used *to account for* rotational effects. Looking at the grammatical analysis in more detail, it appears that a combination of an egocentric reference system with a grammar generating locations in terms of distinctive board features accounts for a high proportion of the errors of the six-year-old group and a much smaller proportion in the ten-year-old group. This result is, in part, to be expected from Piaget's analyses, except for the fact that the ten-year-olds still employ the egocentric system whereas Piaget found no child beyond age seven who did so.

While much more remains to be done here, it is clear that the investigators are on a profitable track and that they will succeed in specifying to a much greater degree of detail the behavior of children as they confront this spatial orientation task and the changes in that behavior developmentally.

The second thing that one would do if the situation were ideal would be to project into the future and show how the extended examination of thinking and the extended examination of language will relate. While my confidence as a prognosticator is very low, I do have some intimations of what that relationship might look like. Let me speculate for a moment.

Begin with two notions, one attributable to Walter Reitman and one to Robert Shaw. Recently, Reitman suggested that the human being with an unlimited amount of paper, armed with a pencil and an eraser, is a Turing machine as long as he lives. That is to say he has all the resources of the universal Turing machine and, hence, can compute anything that is computable. (What he lacks, of course, is unlimited time.) Yet, psychologists lose sight of this enormous capacity of the human being when they begin with a particular model of psychological functioning which restricts the human being (or "the machine") to operating as if he were some particular device of limited power. Let us at this point decide to treat man as a universal or quasi-universal machine.

Let us now add the notion that Shaw has been working on recently; namely, that man is a mimicking device. Given a piece of behavior, Shaw conjectures that man mimicks the least powerful machine which can perform that behavior. This, then, means that we begin with a very powerful device, essentially a Turing machine, but that the way in which we use it depends on the task to which it is set—certainly a reasonable assumption. We now arrange the situation so that the organism finds out through instruction and experience what behavior he is to produce. (During the interval in which he is finding out, we may expect him to "overpower" and "underpower" the task as he guesses what its essential nature is and as he gains experience with it.) Finally, he reconstructs his "internal machinery" to do the task with the least amount of power required. That is, he now mimicks the weakest machine which can produce the correct sort of behavioral output.

It can be seen that this kind of approach makes sense out of the studies of "set" and "learning to learn." Presumably, the human being, going through a series of experiments, learns to behave as a particular kind of machine on particular kinds of data within the experimental situation. Even though, under different conditions, the subject might process a stimulus in a different fashion, we can, perhaps, constrain him to process it in only one way. Alternatively, stimuli which might be hard to organize in some given fashion may yield readily after he has been organizing all his inputs in a given way.

There is some evidence from the work of Shaw and Pufall on the diagrammatic layout problem that this characterization of the organism is a useful one. They examined children at ages six and ten under two conditions: with the board features fully coded (with color, form, etc.) or with one set of features reduced or neutralized. The reduced board required that the child function at a higher level (in terms of power of the automation required) in order to be successful. The groups with full information did best on the first task series, of course. Then the children were given another task with *all* of the board features neutralized. None of the six-year-old children could perform adequately on this task, but the ten-year-olds who had been given a partial reduction on the first task showed a *decrease* in errors from the first to the second task, while the ten-year-olds who had had full information on the first task showed a marked *increase* in errors and a poorer absolute level of performance. Two days later, when the second task was repeated, the ten-year-old groups were equal in performance. What these data imply is that the older children worked at a simpler level when the task conditions permitted, even though they were capable of the higher level. When the task was changed, they floundered a good deal adapting to the new level which, however, they achieved in time. This concept of adaptive functioning may, in part, explain developmental adaptation as the six-year-old appears not to be able to change his power easily, never adapting to the reduced cues task. To make a bold analogy, this conception seems highly significant in understanding the U-shaped developmental curves which imply similarities among highly separated age groups at the "surface" levels where there is no reason to suppose the groups are similar at "deeper" levels (cf. Wier, 1965).

This view suggests some important alterations in our conceptions of the capacities of men and animals; specifically, it argues that man is a *fundamentally different* machine from animals because he possesses response repertories of a different sort (e.g., language) which animals do not possess. It further argues dramatically that man plus paper and pencil is a radically different machine in capabilities from man prior to paper and pencil. It suggests that an organism and his special resources (both inside and outside his skin) must be considered in relation to the task *and* his experience on the task in determining what kind of machine he is at a particular moment in time. It also suggests that different organisms with different resources may perform the "same task" in different fashions in their efforts to function most efficiently as the kinds of machines that they can be.

In order for these to be fruitful suggestions, we must find ways to evaluate the capacities of organisms, in terms of the power of the rules they can use for given kinds of tasks. This implies that we must have "capacity experiments" from which we can make inferences concerning minimal levels at which the organism can operate. The "capacity" of an organism is, of course, not directly available to us, but experiments modeled after the one sketched above may permit us to make estimates if we are insightful, inventive, and clever. If we find a task which requires a certain complexity of computation, we can then assert with respect to that domain that the organism performs at least at the level of such and such a machine. He may, of course, be a much more complex machine than this, and he may also have special properties in some domains which let him perform as a highly sophisticated machine in one area when he is capable of performing as a machine of only limited power in some other area.

We have presumed throughout that the organism has some sort of "principle of least effort," and that the machine ultimately comes to function in the simplest way that it can. (We must remember, of course, that we have no idea what the cost functions are of the various portions of the operations and that "simplest," "least cost" and "least effort" are still metaphorical.) If the organism can become a "through put" machine with one output mapped onto one input, we presume that he will stay at that level. That is, if he can handle his task with a simple list relating behaviors one-to-one to features of the situation, he will build such a list and behave in that fashion. We suspect, however, that at some limit of list length, the "cost" of storage of the list becomes excessive and the organism examines whether there are other ways of "computing" the behaviors which would be more efficient. We expect that the organism tries more and more powerful analyses as the need for an alternative solution increases. If there is no more powerful approach, he simply has to make a list or give up the task. It appears, for example, that list building is the only basic solution to the problem of the lexicon. While some computation and analysis is possible (e.g., most of us can make nouns of verbs, adjectives of nouns, etc.), in the main, the lexicon is arbitrary. One makes and stores lists of enormous size. Our needs, however, are still greater, so we augment our internal lists with external lists; we write and use dictionaries. On the other hand, with respect to syntax, the problem of storage is overwhelming. Rather than storing sentence forms, it appears that for most purposes we compute sentences for output and analyze sentences we get as inputs. While we do not know how we perform either of these tasks, a generative grammar shows that the syntax is, in principle, computable. This is, after all, a major assertion to make and represents an enormous advance over the notion that syntactic orders are simply stored one after another. Generative grammars may even suggest how the computations have been done, although they need not.

Our best hope for the future is that there are some basic general rules which govern the kinds of moves that the organism makes as he tries to generate solutions of varying degrees of power for the tasks that he finds before him. We assume that he is predisposed to make certain kinds of attacks on the problems that all men have previously faced (e.g., that he has special language mechanisms, visual mechanisms, kinesthetic mechanisms, etc.). The data on perceptual development currently available indicate very strongly that he is predisposed to certain kinds of perceptions or, indeed, that he comes "prewired" for certain elaborate perceptual integrations. Our most general bet is that the organism is a collection of specific machines which have partially overlapping functions. An additional hope is that they may, at the base, rest on some universals of the operation of the mind.

Though one can only at this moment extend the most vague, promissory note concerning the future, one can at least catch the vision of a psychology of thinking that has as its explanatory device a deep set of universal rules of thought, supplemented in each special domain by the rule systems of the components, with language featuring heavily as one of the components but by no means as the single component. One sees dimly other subsystems which are, in principle, different kinds of machines, perhaps, servo-mechanisms for balance and motor skills, finite state devices akin to simple lists for point-to-point correspondences, complex geometries for visual perception, etc.

One suspects that some of these components will be incompatible in their rule structures so that direct translatability will not be possible (say from a motor skill to a verbal description of it), but the most generally useful meta-language will prove to be that of natural language which, in the very long run, will be found to have the essential features necessary to express the functioning of the other systems.

Thus, the point of this paper is a proposal to capture, by this new, partially sketched mode of investigation of thinking and language, all the elements of truth that have persuaded other investigators to make the claims of the first three categories.

Thought *does* depend on language to the extent that it uses that subsystem of its much more extensive and complex machinery.

Thought *is* language to the extent that natural language is a universal meta-language that can, in principle, capture any nuance of thought in any domain whatsoever.

Language *does* depend on thought to the extent that it is one manifestation of the general universal rule system that governs all thought, and to the extent that it uses inputs and constructs from all other systems operating under the general guidance of the universal system.

To the multiple choice question:

What is the relationship between thought and language?

the correct answer is:

All of the above.

REFERENCES

Bourne, L. Concept Attainment. In T. R. Dixon and D. L. Horton, *Verbal behavior and general behavior theory.* Englewood Cliffs, N.J.: Prentice-Hall, 1968. Pp. 230-253.

Brown, R. W. *Words and things.* Glencoe, Ill.: The Free Press, 1958.

Brown, R. W., and Lenneberg, E. H. A study in language and cognition. *J. abnorm. soc. Psychol.*, 1954, *49*, 454-462.

Brozek, J. Recent developments in Soviet psychology. *Annu. Rev. of Psychol.*, 1964, *15*, 493-594. Palo Alto, Calif.: Annual Reviews, Inc.

Carroll, J. B. (Ed.) *Language, thought and reality: Selected writings of Benjamin Lee Whorf.* Cambridge, Mass.: M.I.T. Press, 1956.

Carroll, J. B. *Language and thought.* Englewood Cliffs, N.J.: Prentice-Hall, 1964.

Carroll, J. B., and Casagrande, J. B. The function of language classifications in behavior. In E. E. Maccoby, T. M. Newcomb, and E. L. Hartley (Eds.), *Readings in social psychology.* New York: Holt, 1958. Pp. 18-31.

Diebold, A. R., Jr. A survey of psycholinguistic research, 1954-1964. In C. E. Osgood and T. A. Sebeok (Eds.), *Psycholinguistics: A survey of theory and research problems.* Bloomington: University of Indiana Press, 1965.

Dunlap, K. *Civilized life*. Baltimore: Williams and Wilkins, 1934.

Fishman, J. A. A systematization of the Whorfian hypothesis. *Behav. Sci.*, 1960, 5, No. 4, 323-339.

Gleitman, L. R. A study of the acquisition of syntactic structure. (Presented at Linguistic Circle, New York, 1965.)

Hilgard, E. R., and Bower, G. H. *Theories of learning*. (3rd ed.) New York: Appleton-Century-Crofts, 1966.

Hoijer, H. (Ed.) *Language in culture*. Chicago: University of Chicago Press, 1954.

Hymes, D. H. (Ed.) *Language in culture and society*, New York: Harper and Row, 1964.

Jarvis, P. E. The effect of self-administered verbal instructions or simple sensory-motor performance in children. Unpublished Ph.D. thesis, University of Rochester, 1963.

Jenkins, J. J. Review of "The Role of Speech in the Regulation of Normal and Abnormal Behavior" by A. R. Luria. *Science*, 1961, *134*, 1063.

Jenkins, J. J. Mediated associations: Paradigms and situations. In C. N. Cofer, and B. S. Musgrave (Eds.), *Verbal behavior and learning*. New York: McGraw-Hill, 1963. Pp. 210-244.

Jenkins, J. J. The challenge to psychological theorists. In T. R. Dixon and D. L. Horton (Eds.), *Verbal behavior and general behavior theory*. Englewood Cliffs, N.J.: Prentice-Hall, 1968. Pp. 538-549.

Lenneberg, E. H. Cognition and ethnolinguistics. *Language*, 1953, *29*, 463-471.

Lenneberg, E. H., and Roberts, J. M. The language of experience. Mem. 13, *Indiana University Publications in Anthropology and Linguistics*, 1956.

Luria, A. R. *The role of speech in the regulation of normal and abnormal behavior*. Oxford: Pergamon Press, 1961.

McGuigan, F. J. *Thinking: Studies of covert language processes*. New York: Appleton-Century-Crofts, 1966.

McNeill, D. Developmental psycholinguistics. In F. Smith and G. A. Miller (Eds.) *The genesis of language*. Cambridge, Mass.: M.I.T. Press, 1966.

Miller, G. A. The psycholinguists. *Encounter*, 1964, *23*, 29-37.

Osgood, C. E. *Method and theory in experimental psychology*. New York: Oxford, 1953.

Osgood, C. E., and Sebeok, T. A. Psycholinguistics: A survey of theory and research problems. Mem. 13, *Indiana University Publications in Anthropology and Linguistics*, 1954.

Osgood, C. E., Suci, G. J., and Tannenbaum, P. H. *The measurement of meaning.* Urbana, Ill.: University of Illinois Press, 1957.

Piaget, J., and Inhelder, B. *The child's conception of space.* London: Routledge and Kagan Paul, 1956.

Pufall, P. B. Acquisition and generalization of spatial order conservation in young children. Unpublished Ph.D. thesis, Catholic University, Washington, D. C., 1966.

Quine, W. V. *Word and object.* Cambridge, Massachusetts: M.I.T. Press, 1960.

Skinner, B. F. *Verbal behavior.* New York: Appleton-Century-Crofts, 1957.

Vygotsky, L. S. *Thought and language.* (Transl. by E. Hanfmann and G. Vakar) Cambridge, Massachusetts: M.I.T. Press, 1962.

Weir, M. W. Developmental changes in problem-solving strategies. *Psychol., Rev.*, 1964, *71*, 473-490.

REFLECTIONS ON LANGUAGE AND THOUGHT

JOHN B. CARROLL
Educational Testing Service, Princeton, New Jersey

It is almost impossible to disagree with the conclusion reached by Jenkins; namely, that there is merit in all three of the possible positions he sets forth concerning the relation of language and thought. But this is hardly saying much, because none of the three positions is stated precisely enough with respect to the kinds of thinking processes or language behaviors it deals with. I think I know something about how to classify language behaviors, but I know very little about how to classify or even to identify thinking processes. Even before reading Jenkins' paper, I had decided that at least one prerequisite to making any headway with the language-thought problem would be some reasonably cogent taxonomy of thinking processes. To my surprise, Jenkins presented nothing of the sort. I fail to see how we can usefully talk about language-thought relationships unless we specify what we mean by these terms. Clearly, not all of what we ordinarily think of as thought has any immediate relation to language. As an erstwhile musician and amateur composer, I am tempted to assert that there is a whole realm of covert behavior that deals with notes, chords, timbres, melodies, or even symphonies. None of this behavior, which is phenomenologically very real to me, has to do with language. I am sure that persons who are expert in the visual and plastic arts, or with the dance, would make parallel remarks about the "thinking" in which they plan their work in these fields. Thus, I believe we must immediately revise the first position about language and thought stated by Jenkins to read, not that "thought does depend upon language, etc." but rather that "thought *can* be dependent upon language to the extent that it happens to use the machinery of that particular communicative system." Of course, if we redefine language to include the systems in which music, art, the dance, and similar activities may be codified, we might revert to something more nearly like Jenkins' original statement, but, to me, such redefinition stretches things too much.

Likewise, I would suggest revising Jenkins' second position to read: "Thought *can* be identical to language, or at least closely parallel to language, to the extent that it uses the apparatus of the language system in dealing with universal or special categories of thought." Even with such a revision, I would want to define terms more carefully or to substitute new terms in the statement. To identify thought with language seems to confuse a process or an activity with a system that governs that process or activity. In de Saussure's terms, it is analogous to a confusion between *la parole* and *la langue*, or in more contemporary terms, it is analogous to a confusion between *performance* and *competence*. Since it seems to be agreed that thought is a process or activity, if we want to identify thought with language, we must redefine language to refer to an activity. Usually, the word *speech* is used to refer to the activity that is governed by a language system. The proposition we might want to consider is that *thought and speech may be identical, or at least closely parallel*. This seems to me to be an attractive proposition. Whenever an individual creates an utterance that is in any sense novel, the resulting utterance can be said to be, in some sense, a record of the cognitive processes that lay behind it, and it could be asserted that the utterance is merely "overt thought" and, therefore, identical with thought. Similarly, the comprehension of speech utterances ordinarily entails a cognitive activity of some sort on the part of the hearer —*not only* the construing of its grammatical structure, but also the understanding of its semantics—"what it is about." It is not trivial, I think, to say that a sentence is a program for generating or at least influencing the cognitive activity of the hearer. We tend to lose sight of this rather remarkable property of language stimuli because language is so much a part of our ordinary experience. I do not have time to argue this position in detail; I hope it is self-evident.

But in this connection, I would also draw attention to the possibility that the grammar of sentences may provide an important clue to the organization of thought. (There must be some sense in which it is true, as English teachers tell their students, that a sentence is a "complete thought.") The idea that grammars of various languages are at least more similar than they are different (in the fact that they incorporate certain language universals) opens the door to this possibility. That is, if we study the concepts embodied in such universals as noun phrases, verb phrases, modifiers, etc., we can see the operation of universal categories of thought. This is a matter that needs much further investigation and experimentation.

At any rate, I would not be too hasty in dismissing Jenkins' second position. As he dealt with it, he seemed to identify it with the traditional behavioristic position that thought is "nothing more" than some reduced form of *peripheral* activity but, that no matter how far reduced, it is still peripheral. But the line of reasoning I have followed above would suggest that "thinking" could be completely central, yet identical or parallel to language behavior at any level of overtness. In saying that thinking and (covert) language behavior could be identical or parallel, we would be saying that one never occurs without the other and, thus, that they are indistinguishable.

Implicit also in the second position is the notion that there is at least some kind of thinking that is always formulated in terms of language, perhaps not in completely well-formed sentences, but rather in the deep abstract structures that the transformationalists believe underlie well-formed sentences.

Since Jenkins has cited me as one who favors the third possible position—that language depends on thought, it would be ungracious of me to reject this position. But as before, I would demand a clearer statement of the position; one may note, incidentally, that my exact words were "*speech* is a consequence of some kind of thought or cognition, even though language structure may channel or influence thought" (italics added). The notion that language behavior depends on thought suggests that one should consider the different kinds of thinking processes that can be embodied in language. Actually, this is the basis of a long tradition that starts at least as early as Leibniz, and was continued by Kant, Cassirer, Heinz Werner, the British analytical philosophers, and others who have studied the manifestations of thought categories in language.

Let me say a word about Whorf and linguistic relativity. Although I was once a student of Whorf, I must assert that I have always been more interested, just as Sapir was, in the universal categories of language than in the special quirks that turn up in certain languages. As a matter of fact, I now tend to view the special quirks in particular languages as merely chanceful evolutions of optional categories into obligatory ones. Some obligatory categories occur rarely—like the shape categories in a certain sector of Navaho grammar—while others, being presumably more widely useful and functional in communication, are distributed more widely—like the plural category that occurs as a mandatory category in most languages (nearly all I know about, in fact, except Chinese). Whorf drew our attention to the differences between languages with respect to such matters, and for a decade (in the 1950's) psychologists were much intrigued with the possibility that such differences might affect cognitive processes. As Jenkins points out, a few ripples of influence were suggested by some of the evidence, but I think it is now time to realize that languages are more similar than they are different, so far as their cognitive structures are concerned. I am quite deliberate in choosing this phraseology, for I think languages *do* embody cognitive structures. Both in their lexicons and their grammars they embody thousands of concepts of our experience, in ways that we are only beginning to understand. Thus, it is clear that it will be more profitable to approach the study of language-thought relationships by focusing attention on universal characteristics of languages and their counterparts in universal categories of thought.

GENERAL DISCUSSION

It was observed that a taxonomy is needed for the higher mental processes and that the difficulty encountered in trying to devise a taxonomy for total computer programs may be analogous. CARROLL observed that programs vary in the degree to which they reduce to basic processes and added that he would like to see a taxonomy developed without resorting to computers. It also was pointed out that the choice of the basic processes may provide the basis of the taxonomic system.

SIMON observed that a number of situations have been studied in which thought and language processing are assumed to exist. He added that the important feature of such analysis is not devising names for the processes involved in such situations, but is isolating important situations and constructing models to account for problem solution in these situations.

CARROLL commented that classification, however, may be needed to isolate the important situations and problems.

SIMON replied that the primary question is how people solve problems, not how problems are alike.

JENKINS was asked whether language may be considered as communication of meaning across structures. He replied that language can be defined in such a broad manner that the definition becomes meaningless. He indicated that it may be preferable to study the development of operations in a child rather than to try to isolate such processes in the more complex adult in a complex situation.

CARROLL pointed out that, as the child learns the concept of conservation of volume, the language; i.e., words and structure, does not change, but the way in which the language is used changes.

8

INFORMATION-PROCESSING MODELS, COMPUTER SIMULATION, AND THE PSYCHOLOGY OF THINKING [1]

WALTER REITMAN
University of Michigan

For six weeks during the summer of 1965, Professor Robert Glaser and I were instructors at a research conference on Learning and the Educational Process organized by Lee Cronbach at Stanford. (See Chap. 10 for Glaser's paper.) Glaser was billed as an advocate of S-R and reinforcement concepts in educational technology and I was there to explicate the latest developments in information-processing models and computer simulation. Our initial dealings with one another tended to be correct, though with touches of approach-avoidance conflict. We

[1] Preparation of this paper was supported in part by U.S. Public Health Service grants MH 12160-01 and MH 08607-03.

Though those named here will no doubt disagree with some of my interpretations and conclusions, it is a pleasure to acknowledge their contributions to them. Jerry Fodor and David McNeill patiently clarified many points of fundamental importance in the work of Chomsky and his associates. A number of the main ideas developed here also were borrowed from or worked out with Fodor. George Baylor sat in on one another's courses, raised questions and made comments, but neither of us appeared about to become a convert to the other's way of thinking.

Then one afternoon Glaser invited me for a swim in the pool of the luxurious establishment he had taken for the summer, and after several poolside cocktails confessed that he had once been a swimming coach. My daughter Anne, who was with us that afternoon, was in the throes of learning to swim. She would push off, float with her head in the water, and thrash with her arms until her breath ran out. Then she would gasp, touch bottom, and reload. It seemed an ideal occasion to take advantage of our host's professional experience.

He got down into the pool with her. "First, Anne," he told her, "I want you to put your head in the water and blow bubbles." Anne put her head in the water and blew bubbles. "Very good," he said, reinforcing her. "Now I want you to put your head in the water, then turn it out to the side, and take a deep breath." He showed her what he meant, and she did it. "Very good," he said again. "Now put your head in the water, blow bubbles and when you have no more air, turn your head out to the side and take a deep breath." She did, and of course he reinforced her once again. Next he asked her to "do the same thing, and after you have taken the deep breath, put your head back in the water and blow bubbles again, and so on." She did. After scarcely more than ten minutes of this he had her swimming. I was very impressed. "Congratulations," I said. "I'm glad to see that all the talk about information processing and heirarchies of subroutines has had some effect on you." Glaser looked stunned. "What do you mean?" he said, "I'm simply reinforcing stimulus-response sequences."

The examination of specific instances of everyday experience may not be the only way to discover what someone who doesn't use your concepts is talking about, but it helps. And it is well to avoid premature conclusions about the adequacy of conceptual systems other than one's own.

No doubt it would be instructive to compare systematically information processing and S-R treatments of a range of specific complex

---

made many valuable suggestions, as did James Jenkins and those associated with him at the Center for Research on Human Learning at Minnesota. I am deeply grateful in particular to Terry Halwes, Henry Lackner, Robin Ladd, and Robert Shaw. The very important contributions of Peter Reich and of Richard Sauvain, my colleagues at Michigan, are evident throughout the paper. I have also made use of suggestions by Sydney Lamb and by Leonard Uhr, as well as others by Donald Foss, Stuart Kanter, Judith Lerner, Robert Litke, Walter Stolz, and Daniel Wheeler.

behaviors. Uhr (personal communication, 1966) has raised questions about how one might analyze the formation of new units, as in the pattern-recognition program described below, in S-R terms. It would be interesting to see how matching as dealt with in Posner's paper (pp. 32-34) would be handled in S-R language. To what extent are differences between S-R and information-processing treatments matters of semantics? or of the concepts used? or of the questions asked? or of implicit preferences for particular ways of phrasing and answering these questions?

Problems of this sort call for careful joint effort. The present paper, though it may be relevant to such questions, takes on a more limited assignment. It attempts to clarify the concepts and techniques information-processing psychologists use in their work. Impressed as I am with Glaser's ability to teach complex skills using S-R theory to guide him, I myself find information-processing concepts and the associated analytic and simulation techniques by far the most effective ways I know of for studying the complex activities we classify as thinking, reasoning, and skilled performance. What follows is intended to give some idea of how information-processing models may come about, what their advantages are, how the work is carried on, and what it all adds up to. Since such an assessment of the state of our knowledge or lack of it is very much a matter of individual interpretation, it must be emphasized that the discussion gives my own opinions and in no sense represents a consensus among those working in the field.

The events of that day in Glaser's pool suggest that a paper intended mainly for those not thoroughly conversant with information-processing research should be shaped in terms of a small number of examples. We will consider three, each displaying a somewhat different use of information-processing concepts and techniques. The first example is taken from Gregg and Simon (1967). These investigators have designed a set of models to account for learning in the kind of experimental situations studied by Bower and Trabasso (1964). Their work illustrates the uses of information-processing models to provide experimentally verifiable accounts of standard laboratory behaviors. The second illustration is a model of pattern recognition which shows how these techniques may be used to specify and explore quite complex process systems cutting across the boundaries defined by the chapter headings of our psychology textbooks. The third model, at a much earlier stage of development, illustrates the application of information-processing techniques to the study of language behavior, and also suggests how these techniques may be used to explore what I take to be

fundamental questions about the underlying organization of psychological activity—questions at the level of those with which Lashley
(1951) was concerned in his famous paper on the problem of serial
order. In the process of examining these models, the paper also considers several related issues: the evaluation of information-processing
models; the relation of information-processing models to current work
by linguists on generative grammars; and the relation of analyses of
psychological processes to taxonomies of the tasks these processes deal
with.

A few general remarks about information-processing models may
be useful before we turn to specific cases. Quite typically, these models
express psychological propositions in terms of individual operations for
matching, generating, transforming, and retrieving information. These
operations are knit together to form systems of complexly organized
structures and processes. Since the structures and processes are represented explicitly, such models enable us to go beyond measures of the
quantifiable and statistical properties of behavior to investigations of
the specific sequences of stimuli and responses involved. Programmed
models may be run on the computer, and so we lose no objectivity or
precision when we concern ourselves in this way with the microstructure of behavior. By comparing model-generated behavior with data
from humans, we can decide unambiguously whether the model is
sufficient to account for the phenomena we are investigating. Concerned as they are with the microstructure of behavior, information-
processing psychologists often prefer to work with extensive sequential
data from individual subjects. They may be inclined to think of intelligence not as a distinct variable, but rather as a term referring to global
properties of the systems of structures and processes they work with.
Finally, because an information-processing model that accounts for
some class of behaviors does so by generating those behaviors, there is
a continuing interplay between the modeling of human intellectual
processes and the construction of artificial intelligences of various sorts.
Each of these points will be illustrated in detail.

This description is intended only as a rough guide. Particular instances of information-processing work will vary from it in one or more
respects. There is no single Simulation Way in psychology. Individuals
working within the area share a common knowledge and experience
with the work that has been done. But each selects his own concepts,
techniques, and research goals. In particular, formal information-processing languages and the use of the computer to generate streams of
behavior implied by a model both are theoretically neutral. You can be

a Hullian, a Lewinian, or a Freudian. You are free, if you prefer, to analyze a problem such as teaching a child to swim in terms of reinforcing the correct S-R sequences. All that matters, if you want to write a model and test its sufficiency by simulation, is to set down the ideas involved clearly and precisely enough. Then, regardless of the theory they embody, the computer will show you just what they do or do not imply.

Those without prior background in this area may find Newell and Simon (1965) or Reitman (1965; Chaps. 1-3) useful. Newell and Simon are largely responsible for the introduction and development of information-processing models in psychology, and so the cited article, an excellent statement of their current views, will be of particular interest. Reitman (1965) is a more detailed general introduction to the design and uses of simulation models and also includes an evaluation of the place of such models in psychology. Other valuable discussions, each from a somewhat different viewpoint, may be found in Abelson (in press) and Hunt, Marin, and Stone (1966).

It is a sign of the coming of age of information-processing research that it has developed a rather healthy critical literature, much of which also will be of benefit to those interested in obtaining a balanced view of the area as it stands today. Baylor (1965) and de Groot (1966), for example, discuss certain aspects of perceptual selectivity that do not seem well represented in current models. Neisser (1963) points out certain motivational, effective, and organizational aspects of these models he believes inadequate. Newell (e.g., 1962) has given us several excellent discussions of basic problems in programming problem-solving systems. And a fairly detailed evaluation of some characteristic examples of information-processing research against the backdrop of the kinds of questions psychologists are accustomed to asking about psychological theories may be found in Reitman (1965, 1966, 1967). Also available are some excellent critical discussions of specific information processing models, for example, Wynn's (1966) very fine analysis of the Feigenbaum (1961) EPAM program, a model of verbal learning.

I should note, finally, before passing on to the first of our examples, that the term "thinking" is used throughout our discussion in its everyday sense rather than as a technical term. It refers to the sorts of things involved in working out this paper or in reading it. For our purposes, there is no need to restrict statements to "thinking" as opposed to "cognition," "perception," or "learning." The points to be made here apply over the full range of psychological activities encompassed by this set of terms as a whole.

Information-Processing Models as Experimentally Verifiable Theories

Hilgard and Bower (1966, p. 418) have observed that the best known information-processing models, such as Newell, Shaw, and Simon's (1960) General Problem Solver (GPS), are theories of much more complex forms of behavior than those typically studied in learning laboratories. The first example to be considered here, a family of learning models proposed by Gregg and Simon (1967), is something of a departure from that tradition. The example is especially appropriate for our present purposes for several reasons. The work concerns learning. It provides an excellent demonstration of the ways in which information-processing concepts may be applied in the development of an experimentally testable model. It is directly comparable with other models of the behavior investigated (and indeed one of Gregg and Simon's main aims is to demonstrate the advantages of this approach over other alternatives). Finally, its small size makes it relatively easy to explain and to understand. Many psychologists may find that in contrast to the more cumbersome information-processing theories Hilgard and Bower discuss, the Gregg and Simon models are compact enough to fit in easily with the rest of their professional equipment.

In their paper, Gregg and Simon construct a class of information-processing models for the concept attainment experiment previously studied by Bower and Trabasso (1964). They then proceed to demonstrate how the stochastic theory presented by Bower and Trabasso may be derived from the information-processing models, and furthermore how these models, with fewer degrees of freedom, may be made to generate more specific predictions over a wider range of experiments than the stochastic theory. They also compare the process descriptions formally contained in their models with the informal process descriptions Bower and Trabasso use in attempting to account for some of their own findings and, in so doing, are able to point out a number of inconsistencies and unstated assumptions in the original analysis.

The point to be emphasized here is that in models such as those worked out by Gregg and Simon, assumptions about the structures and processes underlying psychological activity may be introduced and evaluated directly within the formalism of the model. Thus, if one believes that these kinds of constructs are the appropriate bases for psychological theories of learning, it becomes possible in situations of the sort encompassed by the Gregg and Simon model to enjoy all of the advantages; e.g., precise statements and strict deduction of consequences, even while casting one's theory directly in terms of these constructs.

Before considering the advantages Gregg and Simon claim for their models, let us see how the models are constructed and, in particular, how the models' propositions are stated directly in process terms. The data the models are designed to account for come from experiments employing n-dimensional stimuli, each dimension taking one of two possible values. The concepts to be attained are simple in the sense that each is defined by a value on a single dimension. On each trial, subjects are given a positive or negative instance. They respond "positive" or "negative" and are then told whether they are right or wrong.

Gregg and Simon begin by stating the basic assumptions of Bower and Trabasso's theory:

1. On each trial, the subject is in one of two states. If he is in state K, he knows the correct concept and will always make the correct response. If he is in state $\bar{K}$, he does not know the correct concept and will make an incorrect response with probability p.

2. If he responds correctly, the subject remains in his previous state. If he responds incorrectly, he shifts from state $\bar{K}$ to state K with probability π.

According to Gregg and Simon, the only strong psychological predictions of this theory that are critically tested by the empirical data are those having to do with the stationarity and independence of p from trial to trial. Documenting their case with quotations from Bower and Trabasso, Gregg and Simon next assert that the theory just described actually is derived from an informal theory of the processes subjects use in responding to the experimental stimuli. Furthermore, the derived theory does not distinguish among the alternative processes subjects might be using. Why translate and weaken the initial process model, Gregg and Simon ask, when it can be stated and evaluated directly? In a very aggregative sense, Bower and Trabasso's theory may be regarded as a process model of their subjects' behavior. But the theory says nothing about the subjects' processes that generate the probabilities. The Gregg and Simon models are alternative formulations incorporating somewhat more detailed assumptions about these processes. As my colleague Daniel Wheeler has observed, they may therefore be regarded, if we prefer, as alternative stochastic models—models making stronger and better differentiated predictions than those possible with the Bower and Trabasso theory.

Gregg and Simon begin by defining a small set of variables (e.g., "instance," "current hypothesis," "tally"); constants ("positive," "right," etc.); and processes. An instance, for example, is represented as a list of values such as "large" or "square," one value for each of the n dimensions. The set of possible hypotheses is a list of the $2n$-dimension values. Each of their models takes some eight processes to specify. Five of these eight processes specify the experimental situation. The differences between the models are explicit in the replacement of this or that process from one model to the next. The three processes specifying the subjects' behavior in the first of their models, for example, are these:

1. If the current hypothesis is satisfied by the instance presented, then respond "positive," and otherwise respond "negative."

2. If feedback from the experimenter is "wrong," then generate a current hypothesis by process 3.

3. Generate a new hypothesis by sampling randomly from the set of possible hypotheses. Set the current hypothesis equal to this new hypothesis.

The variant models are obtained by replacing process 3 in the above model. For example, a model in which it is assumed that a subject selects an hypothesis from among those consistent with the last instance presented to him is specified by processes 1, 2, and 3a.

3a. Generate a new hypothesis by sampling randomly from the set of possible hypotheses. If the new hypothesis is satisfied by the last instance, sample again. Otherwise set the current hypothesis equal to this new hypothesis.

The overall course of the simulated activity is organized by the main experimental process, defined as follows:

> *Main experimental process.* Do first experimental process, then first subject process, then second experimental process. If feedback from the experimenter is "right," set the value of the tally variable to the previous value plus 1. Otherwise set the value of the tally variable to 0. If the value of the tally variable is k (some preset number of correct trials defining attainment of the concept), then halt. Otherwise do subject process 2. Then do the main experimental process.

Each such process may be given by a set of instructions in a list-processing language for a computer (e.g., IPL-V; Newell *et al.*, 1964). The set of variables, constants, and processes completely specifies a particular model in the sense that the model may be run on a computer (or followed out by hand) and its predictions generated with all the precision and objectivity of a mathematical model.

With the Gregg and Simon models in mind as a concrete case, we may now remark a few general properties of information-processing models. They are specified as systems of operations. Each of the three subject processes is such an operation or function. The overall operation of the model or program is defined by these functions and their interrelations. Functions may be defined to consist of integrated systems of simpler functions. The main experimental process, for example, includes as subprocesses the first two experimental processes and the first two subject processes. Note also that the main experimental process concludes by calling upon itself. Thus it forms one big loop. The program as a whole is thus a recursive system in that it includes processes that call upon themselves. The program includes branches, which take into account the match between inputs and certain stimulus or internal conditions. These allow it to respond in varied ways depending upon feedback about the state of the environment or internal conditions. The whole system is a dynamic model in the sense that it generates a temporal sequence of behaviors. Any particular behavioral act is a function not only of the present stimulus situation, but also of the states through which the system has passed. If we like, we may treat such a model, or those of its subcomponents representing the subject, as a representation of the mediating processes determining his response to a stimulus. But it is a completely explicit and objective representation, leaving nothing to the imagination. Each of its assertions corresponds to a psychological assumption. Though much more limited than systems such as GPS, the Gregg and Simon models are typical in asserting that overt psychologic activity is mediated by complex dynamic systems of recursive processes matching, retrieving, and transforming information.

Some advantages of the Gregg and Simon approach. Gregg and Simon devote a substantial part of their paper to comparisons of the Bower and Trabasso model with theirs. They point out that their models require fewer free parameters and clearly distinguish those aspects of the theory that have to do with the experimental situation from those representing the structures and processes ascribed to subjects in the situation. Given this sharp separation, it is much easier to represent diverse psychological assumptions; e.g., about the extent of a subject's short-term memory and the use he makes of it, directly in the model. Furthermore, changes in the experimental design that do not affect subjects' response strategies are easily mirrored by modifications in the experimental processes and input constants of the model. Given these modifications, the model will generate predictions for the new experimental conditions without introducing additional degrees of freedom into the system. Since all such changes in psychological assumptions and experimental conditions are represented explicitly, Gregg and Simon have no need of the informal arguments Bower and Trabasso fall back upon and, consequently, there is no possibility that errors or inconsistencies may be introduced in the course of such informal arguments. If, for example, we believe that a variation in the length of time the stimulus is exposed may influence subjects' strategies, we may introduce a strategy-selection process to make the dependence explicit and to specify how strategy selection is assumed to interact with the rest of subjects' activity in the experimental situation. Finally, the information-processing model generates more psychologically significant predictions than does the Bower and Trabasso model. Hence, it is more falsifiable, stronger, and more useful in suggesting directions for further experiments. The bases for each of these conclusions are developed in the Gregg and Simon paper in detail. Even this brief summary, however, should convey the main import of their assertions concerning the advantages of information-processing models for psychological research.

Gregg and Simon conclude their paper with a penetrating discussion of some problems in choosing among theories, dealing in particular with the notions of strength, verifiability, and flexibility in the context of information-processing models. One may wonder about the extrapolation of their conclusions to models such as GPS which are a great deal more complex than those examined in detail in their paper. The problem here is less a matter of theory type than of the utility of theories of any sort at that order of complexity (for discussion see Reitman 1965, Chap. 2; 1966; 1967). This question aside, however, the Gregg and Simon paper provides a superb example of the uses of an information-processing approach in the context of laboratory experimentation.

Studying Interacting Systems of Structures and Processes

One of the purposes of this text is to examine relations between learning and thinking. The form that examination takes depends upon the content subsumed under those heads. Gagné (1964), for example, favors a definition of learning so general that it includes problem solving as a subcategory, and Melton in informal presentations has defined a learning process as any process which results in a relatively permanent change in the organism. By the same token, a motivation theorist might define a motivation process as one involving persisting and directed activity (Hebb, 1949); an emotion theorist might consider an emotional process as anything involving activity of the autonomic nervous system; and so on. A particular human process might very well satisfy all of these conditions, and most probably do. If that is the case, then the interactions among the psychological processes underlying behavior are fundamentally important. Most psychologists may subscribe to that view in principle, even though considering it a practical necessity to focus upon one or another isolated process. The history of experimental psychology may be read as a sequence of attempts to define and characterize the properties of such isolatable factors or units underlying behavior—so far with indifferent success.

Note that even if we stay within a single psychological domain, the set of processes involved may easily exceed the reach of the isolated units approach. Haber, for example, speaks in his paper of block diagrams and feedback loops as the crux of information-processing analysis (see Chap. 1). But beyond a very modest level of complexity, the block diagrams and feedback loops become impossible to understand simply by looking at them. Within psychological domains as well as across them, we need tools enabling us to understand behavior as the product of complexly organized systems of psychological processes. The advantage of information-processing models and computer-simulation techniques is that they enable us to represent and study the implications of such systems directly. Furthermore, in contrast to the first case we considered, for problems of the sort described below, information-processing models constitute the only candidates available for the job.

Recalling the events in Glaser's pool, we once again develop the point by means of a concrete example. The program to be described originated as part of Leonard Uhr's general plan of research in pattern recognition and was written in collaboration with Richard Sauvain, a graduate student at the University of Michigan. The discussion that follows is based upon an excellent working paper by Sauvain (1966).

We may begin by noting that when we recognize an object, we generally can do more than classify it as an instance of some percept or concept. Usually, we also can describe the object and the structure of its parts. At times, in fact, our recognition of the object *depends* upon our recognition of subparts and our knowledge of the structures into

which those subparts enter. How are we to think of the system of structures and processes in the human head that mediates these accomplishments? The pattern-recognition program to be described is typical of
many information-processing investigations in that, to the extent that
it is viewed as relevant to the psychological question, it translates or
replaces that question by another: How can we design a system *sufficient* to display phenomena corresponding to the observed behavioral
capabilities of humans?

The program is typical of many information-processing studies in
another respect as well, since it is as much an exploration of some problems of artifiicial intelligence (how can we design a system to do it?)
as a psychological theory (how do people do it?). A good many information processing models; e.g., Gregg and Simon (1967) or Simon and
Kotovsky (1963) are, as we have seen, explicitly constructed purely for
psychological purposes. Nonetheless, the mixture of aims and aspirations reflected in the present work is characteristic of many other investigations. See, for example, Newell (1962) for an excellent discussion
of the ways in which these mixed interests may interact in the course
of constructing a complex system.

Note that if such a design attempt succeeds, it becomes no more
than a candidate psychological theory. We still must determine
whether this possible account of human activity is to be regarded as
anything more than that. But for many of the phenomena we are concerned with, we lack anything resembling a candidate theory. Thus,
such work, by providing us with possibilities whose sufficiency is objectively demonstrable, often gives us ways of thinking about how we
might fill these gaps.

Program operation. The program learns to recognize line drawings
and to describe them in terms of the subparts of the drawings and the
interrelations among them. A drawing is taken to be a collection of elemental strokes (lines differing in slope, length, and curvature). The
program tries to construct an internal representation ("percept,"
"schema," "visual concept") from such basic elements and from previously learned patterns. It also accepts descriptions from a trainer and
extracts information from this kind of tutorial feedback that may enable
it to improve its subsequent performance. In other words, it can in
several interesting ways learn from experience.

The program also displays a number of other noteworthy properties.
For example, it gives a structural description of the patterns presented
to it. This ability is especially significant in the light of the emphasis
given corresponding human capabilities by those exploring the perception and production of the sentence patterns of natural language.

To grasp more concretely the kinds of things the program does, consider Fig. 8-1, a very simple example of an interaction between the program and its trainer.

Input pattern to the program:

Program: "THERE IS A (SMALL SEMICIRCLE TO THE LEFT OF A SMALL SEMICIRCLE) ABOVE A LONG STRAIGHT LINE"

Trainer: "CIRCLE ABOVE LONG STRAIGHT LINE"

Program: "THERE IS A CIRCLE (CONSISTING OF A SMALL SEMICIRCLE TO THE LEFT OF A SMALL SEMI-CIRCLE) ABOVE A LONG STRAIGHT LINE"

Trainer: "CIRCLE ABOVE STRING"

Program: "THERE IS A CIRCLE ABOVE A STRING"

Trainer: "BALLOON"

Program: "THERE IS A BALLOON (CONSISTING OF A CIRCLE ABOVE A STRING)"

Figure 8-1. Interaction between pattern-recognition program and trainer. From Sauvain (1966).

Basic to the structure of the program is the way in which it forms and uses "inferences"—schemas "inferred" from the patterns and sub-patterns presented to the program and employed to organize inductive explorations of new patterns presented to it. These inferences, each consisting of a pair of objects and some relation between them, allow the program to identify objects in terms of either their surrounding context or their substructure. Thus, input patterns are recognized by searching for inferences involving stored subcomponent patterns having features satisfied by subparts of the novel input pattern.

The set of features, properties, and known patterns the program uses can grow indefinitely. Furthermore, they may be applied selectively, under the guidance of feedback obtained during the ongoing recognition process. In this respect, the program goes a good way beyond the organization of the categorization processes found in such important pattern-recognition programs as that of Uhr and Vossler (1963). The program handles various kinds of quite complex patterns, including patterns consisting of several noncontiguous objects. It has some ability to learn and generalize spatial relations among objects. And, as Fig. 1 indicates, it also can produce and analyze limited natural language descriptions of line drawings.

Any system, natural or artificial, that is to recognize and exploit regularities in its environment must store and use information about that environment. One reason the working out of such a program is of interest, is precisely because it confronts us with all the problems of human memory and its use in situations of the sort the program investigates. The present program may be regarded as an integrated system of conjectured solutions to those problems. It is a system of hypotheses so well specified that it is capable of generating observable behavior, thus making explicit the implications of the conjectures. As the program performs, it invites us to compare its structures and operations with whatever we know of those the human organism has evolved. In what ways are they similar? At what points do they differ in the observable behaviors they generate? To what extent can we use the system of mechanisms embedded in the program as a framework for thinking about the corresponding human functions? At what points does program behavior deviate so radically from our experience with human performance as to suggest the need for radically different concepts or structures? And as the need for such structures and processes becomes evident from the behavioral divergences, we once more enter the modeling cycle, asking how these new mechanisms might work. How might they be organized? How might we represent them explicitly? How might we formulate our ideas about them sharply enough to embed them in a computer program and see whether they generate behaviors more closely approximating those we see in man?

How, in fact, does the present program store acquired knowledge of its environment? Figure 8-2 illustrates the memory structures set up as the program examines an input pattern. Concepts or percepts are represented in multi-relational graph structures. The nodes in the graph represent the elemental lines, subpatterns, and patterns. The edges linking them indicate part-whole relations, contiguity relations, and spatial relations. Information about previously examined patterns is stored by associating with each object the program has come across a special pair of lists. The first list gives the inferences leading to that object, the second those leading from it.

The embedding of this scheme in the program enables us to explore its possibilities as a way of thinking about the problems of human stor-

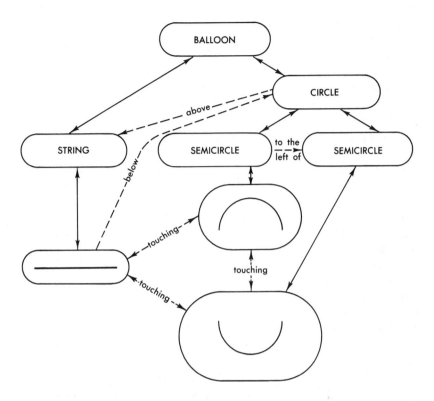

Figure 8-2. Example of representation of a visual concept by a multi-relational, hierarchical graph structure. Solid lines indicate naming and part-whole relationships, dashed lines indicate spatial relationships. From Sauvain (1966).

age and use of information in the context of a system of interacting perceptual, learning, and decision processes. By running experiments with the operating program we realize some of these possibilities, and as we observe the results, we learn something about what happens when this form of memory representation is employed in this context. Once again, we may ask about the extent to which the operating consequences of this scheme parallel our observations of human information processing. To the extent they do so, the program may serve as an explicit and well-specified framework in terms of which we now may turn to related problems; e.g., those having to do with the development and use of semantic or cognitive structures.

As a further example of the sense in which information-processing models facilitate analysis of the interactions among the psychological processes they postulate, thus enabling us to examine questions about individual functions in a larger operating context, consider the sorts of decision problems that arise in the present program. For example, it may come up with several alternate hypotheses about an input pattern, each corresponding to a possible interpretation or structural description of the pattern. If this occurs, it now must choose one of these possibilities.

Several questions appear at this point. When, for example, should the system stop generating hypotheses about the pattern and take its decision? Should it select one hypothesis and then look for information which would allow it to reject that hypothesis? Or should it follow the classical model, generating all possible hypotheses and then choosing among them? In the present program, when an inference matches some portion of the input pattern, the resulting subpattern becomes the focus of attention. In other words, if the program succeeds in putting two semicircles together to make a circle, it will continue by searching for things it can make or do with a circle. Thus, it tends to continue working in an area in which it is having success. Note again the departure from such earlier pattern recognition schemes as the Uhr and Vossler (1963) programs, in which recognition strategies are independent of the pattern. In such programs, a certain number of features of the input pattern is determined regardless of the structure of the pattern. In the present program, the pattern itself, together with the system's knowledge of previous patterns, is a principal determinant of the directions the recognition—and decision—processes take. In this respect, there is some resemblance to the EPAM programs of Feigenbaum (e.g., 1961), but the actual mechanisms used appear to be more flexible.

The main thing to observe here is that the problem of decision making in the context of such a system requires of us not just a choice among alternate decision-making rules in isolation, but also an analysis of the ways in which the taking of decisions is to be organized and integrated into the system as a whole as it perceives, analyzes, makes inferences about, and communicates with its environment. We may sympathize with efforts such as Haber's to define a separable perceptual process amenable to analysis more or less independently of the rest of our information-processing capabilities. But if the present program is on the right track, it implies that perceptual acts, far from being isolatable in any simple sense, in many cases depend upon and make use of a whole collection of other processes not specific to perception that analyze and organize the processing of information.

Program evaluation. Several times, we have alluded to advantages simulation models afford insofar as the computer enables us to generate and study their behavioral implications. For models such as those of Gregg and Simon, explicitly constructed to account for some body of experimental data, the evaluation of the model can follow the standard rules of the game. But how do we evaluate systems such as the pattern recognition program we have been considering? In what sense do we benefit from having constructed and run a program of this sort?

Quillian's (1966) observations in the context of his own work are relevant here. As he suggests:

> . . . developing a simulation program is not an unrestricted guessing game, but a completely empirical investigation into how some psychological process can *and cannot* operate in order to produce some given kind of results.
>
> First, the experimenter with a theory to formalize into a program will typically find that he must persist through a rather lengthy phase of compromising, rethinking, and "debugging" before he ever gets his theory to run as a program at all. Then a cycle of incremental improvements such as the one outlined above may begin. However, for a long while each of the small improvements he attempts is likely to cause the program's performance to break down completely, because of various subtle interdependencies in the program that he inevitably will overlook. After finding and correcting these problems the experimenter can again proceed to look for other shortcomings in the program's performance. But after a number of such patch-like changes have accumulated in some particular section of the program, the experimenter will discover that he can no longer understand *what* the program is doing in that section. By now, however, he is likely to think he knows how the whole section *should* have been conceived and written initially, so that he can tear up and redo the whole section. This may result in anything from a great leap ahead in conceptual clarity and in the generality of the processing capability—and hence, to further cycles through the improvement cycle—to a decision that programming the theory was not such a good idea after all.
>
> In practice, therefore, developing a program to simulate some particular human behavior is a continuous grappling with the empirical problem of how to formulate, in the completely literal language that is a computer program, a model of the factors underlying that behavior that is detailed and complete enough to recreate it to a degree that will satisfy the experimenter. Besides the steps above, the serious simulator will almost certainly be led at some points to review or conduct traditional psychological studies, but his work in this regard will be strongly directed by the need to discover facts that are *functionally* relevant to the psychological processing he is interested in.

Though they substantially extend our ability to represent and explore the complexities of psychological activity, programmed theories like other forms of theorizing, necessarily involve simplifications and abstractions. In evaluating a given program, we first must become aware of the key simplifications and then must decide their significance. Any simplification defines a limitation of the model in which it occurs. But some models appear capable of extension and generalization because the simplifications are temporary and remediable expedients. In others, the simplifications are basic and the models, themselves, dead ends.

On occasion, we may substitute a clearly artificial function in a program to carry the load of a human function we do not yet comprehend or else prefer not to tackle in the context of a particular program. Like the artificial kidneys used to remove wastes from the bloodstream, the substitute does the job but is not to be taken as a model for the human function involved. The artificial function may parallel the human process at the input-output level, but differences between them in such things as processing organization and side effects make it unlikely that the functional correspondence is maintained at a more molecular level. The psychological consequences of this limitation may remain local, given that the machine function is taken as a bridge across the input-output gap at that point in the program rather than as a model of the corresponding human function. The limitation becomes a great deal more significant in those cases in which the machine function imposes constraints upon the overall program design. In the extreme case, the constraints imposed may amount to flaws so fundamental that the model as a whole loses its value as a psychological tool.

Some kinds of evaluation often may be carried out to a rough first approximation by appropriate gedanken experiments. In effect, what one does here is to jiggle the input, process, and structure parameters of a model a bit, in order to observe the consequences. We may, for example, imagine changing the inputs to a concept-inducing program like that of Simon and Kotovsky (1963) in order to discover what modifications it would take to get it to work given the change (Reitman, 1966). Or we may imagine taking a component from one program and swapping it with the corresponding component in a related program to observe the effects. One discovers a good deal about the limitations of the EPAM models, for example, by imagining them operating with tests of the sort Uhr and Vossler (1963) use. This kind of game presumes a good knowledge of the program being evaluated as well as a reasonably explicit idea of the underlying problems involved in the psychological functions it models. But the effort frequently more than pays for itself in terms of the insights one derives both into the program and also into the psychological functions modeled. In any case, evaluation of a program of the sort we are considering requires that we first ask not only what the program does, but also what it does *not* do, and next that we evaluate the sins of omission and commission against some criteria that permit us to differentiate the trivial from the critical.

Limitations of the pattern-recognition program. Sauvain's (1966) own description of the research is a model discussion with respect to the evaluation problem since he himself provides a detailed listing of the many ways in which the program deviates from what most of us would take to be characteristic of human functioning. He notes, for example, that it aways looks in detail at all of the input pattern. People almost certainly very often notice and attend only to selected cues. Then, too, the program now matches patterns on an all-or-none basis. People can make near matches and, more important, can and do take note of the points of mismatch with respect to the patterns they already know (see Woodworth's [1938] notion of schema plus correction). Finally, the program as it now stands is unable to acquire or use the properties (e.g., transitivity) of the relations it functions in terms of.

Sauvain lists many other limitations in addition to these. Note that for the most part each such shortcoming is readily established by comparison with human performance even in the absence of strict laboratory evidence. Simulation models do not do away with the need for solid experimental data. On the contrary, there is a pressing need for development and exploration of better experimental techniques to test these models and to exploit the richness of the hypotheses about the temporal course of complex behavior we may derive from them. But as Sauvain's discussion makes evident, analysis of the consequences of an integrated system of psychological propositions may proceed a good ways even in the absence of the kinds of data we ideally would like to have.

Programming a computer model of this sort has many of the characteristics of a conversation with a detached but sympathetic adviser. Do you want to know how people might learn to recognize patterns? or what mediates human ability to generalize from previous experience and to transfer previous training appropriately? Do you want to understand better how perceptual patterns might be categorized? how new categories might be constructed? and how functionally effective associations among them might be formed and used? Do you think you know how inputs are matched to stored templates? or how the phenomena of set and attention interact with perecptual categorization and are influenced, in turn, by feedback about the accuracy of the subject's response to the perceptual stimulus? Can you formulate clearly your ideas of just how the processes of categorization relate to those involved in the making of other sorts of decisions? Good. Try setting them down and see. If your formulation is incomplete, or inconsistent, or undefined at some points, the running of your program will so inform you. Your next remarks may make things clearer. If not, your program will gently but firmly tell you so. Even though it remains limited at some points and incorrect at others, as the program we have been discussing surely is, your program, nevertheless, gradually comes to be a useful embodiment of your present concepts and a powerful tool for developing better ones.

Psychological Organization

As de Groot (1965) so ably demonstrates, the conceptualization of thinking as an activity generated by a system of quite specific operations is an intellectual achievement anteceding computer models by at least a generation, notably in the work of Selz (see de Groot, 1965, pp. 52-76). It remained for Newell, Shaw, and Simon (e.g., 1957, 1960) to develop and demonstrate the potentialities of such a treatment by designing information-processing programs and showing what they could account for. Largely as a result of their work, this general conceptual paradigm is now accorded serious consideration even among those, e.g., Hilgard and Bower (1966), whose roots are deep in the rather different traditions of the experimental psychology of learning. Working within this paradigm, the psychologist who wishes to investigate the strategies involved in some information-processing activity now has available concepts and techniques generally adequate to the task. He may face technical barriers, notably in getting adequate data from his subjects. Yet, even here, progress is being made both in the art of protocol analysis (de Groot, 1965, Chap. 9; Newell and Simon, 1964; Newell, 1966; Reitman, 1965, pp. 33-37) and also in the integration of experimental verification procedures with information-processing models (de Groot and Jongman, 1966; Gregg and Simon, 1966; Reitman, 1966; Tikhomirov, 1966).

We ought not to underestimate the difficulties that remain in these regards. My point is rather that the conception of human information processing as a recursive activity mediated by systems of operators, now is well understood; the already extant models; e.g., the General

Problem Solver (Newell, Shaw, and Simon, 1960) can serve as frameworks for thinking in these terms and for extending the analysis. In this respect, the situation in psychology parallels that of linguistics. There, Chomsky (e.g., 1957, 1965) and his associates have developed a somewhat similar conception of the grammar for a language, which they regard as a recursive system of rules sufficient to generate the sentences of that language.

The parallel is not exact, in part because the linguists also are attempting to develop a general theory of language which is to incorporate whatever is universal to all languages, thus separating the theory of grammar from the specifics of a particular language. Information-processing theorists have constructed general programs, notably the General Problem Solver, in which certain core aspects of problem solving are separated from the specifics of particular problem tasks. But there remains a substantial difference between such efforts and a theory of the universals of human-information processing activity.

The consensus in linguistics regarding universal terms and propositions probably falls short of that to be found, say, in economics, and occasionally it seems less a matter of fundamental agreement than of a desire to avoid moving the conceptual furniture around too often. Still, there is substantially more consensus there than in information-processing psychology, where we have yet to discover how to move beyond the growing collections of specifics embedded in our programs. Carroll's mention of the need for cognitive taxonomies in his paper in this volume, and efforts by Jenkins and his associates to utilize the categories of automata theory for taxonomic purposes, are evidence of concern about the problem among psychologists. At present, however, the strategy system embedded in information-processing models are often best regarded as detailed accounts of how to do it and sometimes of how people do it. They are useful, as are textbooks, as guides in our thinking and in empirical studies, but they do not in general satisfy our traditional concept of theories as parsimonious sytems of widely applicable laws (see Reitman, 1965, pp. 42-47; 1967).

None of this detracts from their utility as paradigms for thinking about human information processing. Their great advantage over ordinary textbooks is that they are *generative* in Chomsky's sense. They are *sufficient* though not necessarily correct or unique accounts which can be made to *produce* the phenomena they are designed to account for.

The problem of development. Even if we accept this assessment of the status of the information-processing conception of human behavior, however, at least two fundamental psychological problems remain open. The first concerns development. We can think of the human perceiver, language user, and problem solver as a recursive rule-using system, but we know almost nothing about how he gets that way or what he starts from. Fodor (1966a) has discussed the question in terms of empiricist versus nativist positions, contrasting the idea that everything is somehow or other learned, with the view of Chomsky (1965) and his associates, who prefer to assume, at least in the case of language, that the child is born with a highly sophisticated, innate language capacity and only thereby succeeds in selecting from among all possible grammatical rules the particular subset underlying his native tongue.

Most psychologists regard such complex motor skills as walking as having substantial innate determinants, and the work of such investigators as Hubel (see Thompson's paper in this volume) suggest substantial innate determination in perception as well. Given this collateral information, and in the absence of working models that might account for the development of a recursive rule-using system given only a general ability to form associations, it would seem that we have no compelling reason to insist on what Fodor terms the radical empiricist view. I would suggest that the more interesting issues now before us have to do with the breadth and generality of the innate capabilities we assume. Is language learning capability, as Chomsky sometimes seems to believe, really a unique function separate from whatever mediates perceptual and cognitive development? Or is it less a totally special case than a phylogenetically novel use of some more general capacities for inducing certain kinds of regularities from the environment?

The MIT group appears to believe it highly unlikely that a child ever could induce the grammar of his language unless he began with an innate knowledge of such linguistic universals as the basic categories and the forms of the rules. Perhaps that is so if the child is regarded as having nothing more than an ability to form simple associations to work with. These are hardly the only two possibilities with respect to innate linguistic endowment, however. We may, for example, suppose that the child is born with whatever abilities it takes to develop the recursive context- and feedback-sensitive strategies he later uses in perceiving and thinking about his environment. If so, it is not at all clear how much else he would need in order to induce the grammar of his language.

The functional organization of the human-information processing system. The second wide-open psychological problem becomes apparent, somewhat paradoxically, through the very success of the approach taken by Newell, Simon, and others. It was natural for Selz to regard an adequate account of the system of operations humans use as the goal to be attained in his studies of thinking. Once we had the Logic Theorist (Newell, Shaw, and Simon, 1957) or the General Problem Solver, however, the very fact that such operations could be incorporated into computer programs made it evident that there was nothing uniquely human about them. In itself, this is at most mildly deflating. If we can represent any human strategy in some computer language, it means only that this aspect of our psychology is a special case of a more general information-processing science, much as those aspects of anatomy that deal with the operation of our bone and muscle systems form a special case of the science of mechanics. Far from presenting difficulty, it is one of the advantages of the information-processing approach that it encourages us to think in these more general terms and to discover the structural and functional similarities that exist between men, machines, and other complex information-processing organizations—both natural and artificial. Nonetheless, we can run these strategy systems on the computer with little or no modification of its underlying process organization. Consequently, they involve nothing specific to the human nervous system. Since both man and computer are able to realize them, it must be the case that they involve nothing reflecting the peculiarities of human information-processing organization or the ways in which that organization differs from the functional organization of a digital computer. We know that humans and computers are elements of the subclass of information-processing systems that can use such rule systems to solve problems, classify patterns, or produce and evaluate the sentences of a language—at least to some extent. But that fact does not enable us to distinguish between information-processing systems differing as widely in the logical organization of their components as people and computers presumably do. Thus, even if we satisfy ourselves that we have analyzed adequately the strategies humans use in a variety of domains, the question of the logical structure of the human system remains an open problem for psychology.

Note that we are not raising questions about hardware of physiology. As Newell, Shaw, and Simon (1958) note, one may embed identical functional organizations in fundamentally different electronic systems, or even in a mechanical or hydraulic computer for that matter. Present computers, for example, have substantially similar functional organizations. Each involves something serving as a passive respository for information—an active process that retrieves and stores information in that memory—something analogous to an accumulator, and so on. But what about the human information-processing system? Is it organized the same way? Opinions differ. My own feeling is that is is not, and that our progress in the study of human information-processing strategies ought not blind us to the still unsolved psychological problems of human functional organization.

The bases for this view are of two sorts. In the first place, efforts to program information-processing systems that can parallel human cognitive, perceptual, and linguistic capabilities themselves appear to suggest some fundamental inadequacy in our conceptions of human information-processing organization. The problem has been recognized in one form or another for some time (de Groot, 1964; Neisser, 1963; Newell, 1962; Reitman, 1965; Reitman, Grove, and Shoup, 1964; Zvegintzov, 1963). Probably the most general statement will be found in Dreyfus (1965), who examines computer programs for playing games, solving problems, language translation, and pattern recognition and concludes that each of these areas suffers from a common set of limitations.

Evaluation of Dreyfus' analysis is sometimes difficult because he is deeply hostile to the whole artificial intelligence endeavor, and his discussion is anything but detached. On the whole, however, I think many of those working in these areas would agree that the problems he cites do exist. Much of Dreyfus' argument is, in fact, based on quotations from the primary investigators themselves.

What is the difficulty? It shows up as a search problem in game-playing, pattern-recognition, and problem-solving programs. There are too many alternatives to evaluate, and humans notice things more quickly than we can account for in terms of our current conceptions of search strategies. In language translation, it appears as a question of semantics: the human knows and is able to use more than we are prepared to encompass in our programs. I prefer to think of it as a problem in the organization and use of human memory. That is equivalent to the formulation in terms of search if we assume that memory is a passive storehouse of information, waiting to be interrogated by retrieval processes under the guidance of some search heuristics. But the problem looks very different if we assume instead that human memory is active, as Hebb (1949) suggests. Then, our task is not so much to develop new and better search strategies as to devise explicit models of how such a memory might be organized and operate. Dreyfus' view is simply that humans possess a unique capacity, which he labels "fringe consciousness." Since he provides no account of how this fringe consciousness is achieved, the term is actually just another label for the problem. Dreyfus' main concern, in fact, seems to be to keep this uniquely human capacity and to forestall efforts to comprehend it or to provide an explicit account of the structures and processes mediating it.

My own view falls between Dreyfus', on the one hand, and that of some of my colleagues who would dispute the very existence of the problem on the other. The problem may prove insurmountable, but I don't think Dreyfus proves that point. And someone right now may be putting the final touches on a model which solves it. If so, it will come as a most welcome surprise.

A second difficulty in taking the digital computer as a model for human functional organization is the biological evidence to the contrary. Recent work on cell genetics, for example, reveals an astounding amount of independent local activity even at a molecular level. Witkin (1966) discusses cellular subsystems apparently capable of patching up damage to genes caused by ultraviolet radiation. Lwoff (1966) describes how the fate of individual cells infected by virus particles depends upon complex mechanisms determining "whether a repressor or the key enzyme responsible for autonomous multiplication is formed first." "An organism," he writes, "is a molecular society and biological order is a kind of social order." Jacob (1966) discusses research designed to discover "how molecules find each other, recognize each other, . . . transmit the signals which modify the activity of their neighbors," and he writes of genetic material as containing "not only the plans for the architecture of the cell, but also a program to coordinate the synthetic processes, as well as the means of insuring its execution." All of this, note, is attended to well below the level of individual cells. At every higher level, the story is the same. The firing of sensory cells is determined by events within them and at their boundaries. The heart beats, food is digested, and wounds are repaired all without the intervention of some omnipresent central processor. In fact, as Eliza Doolittle might have observed to Henry Higgins, most everything within us seems to go on quite nicely without our willing it.

There seems no reason to believe that the activity of our billions of neurons or of the information-processing components they form is organized differently. Simon's (1962) own discussion of the organization of activity in complex systems evolved or assembled from simpler subsystems would seem to lead to a similar conclusion. In fact, if the functional organization of the human information-processing system roughly parallels that of a digital computer, with its passive repositories of information and its single central processor mediating all activity, then the great unsolved problem is how, out of the local changes in our billions of neurons, that form of organization is achieved. In any case, if current programs fall short in the ways Dreyfus claims, it may well be because, almost without exception, they embed the strategy systems inferred from human behavior in functional organizations very different from those the biological evidence suggests mediate such behaviors in man. The corollary is that it is alternative forms of functional organization we ought to be investigating in our programs.

Dreyfus' conclusions to the contrary, the limitations of present programs do not necessarily imply a fundamental flaw in the information-processing approach or even in the modeling languages now available. The problem is rather the inadequacy of our concepts of functional organization. As the program to be considered next demonstrates, it is quite feasible to simulate other modes of organization using current computer hardware. True, for example, that hardware operates serially and utilizes a passive memory. But just as we may represent three-dimensional objects in two dimensions, by means of conventions for interpreting the relations among the lines on our sheet of paper, so we may specify conventions allowing us to simulate parallel systems with serial machines. The difficulty is not one of hardware or of the limits of our computer languages, but rather of ideas: we don't know what so say. The program described below is of interest precisely because it is part of a search for what we are now most in need of: some good ideas about the functional organization of the mind as an information-processing device.

Trotski's real name. The problem of the functional organization of memory may be illustrated by the following example. X and Y were lunching together and conversing after the usual academic fashion, about Russian names. There are no Russian names, Y asserted, that have two syllables and end in *i*. "What about Trotski?" X objected. "Trotski is a pseudonym," Y replied, "and doesn't count." X at this point became preoccupied. What was Trotski's real name? He reports that he may have felt it began with *br*. He is fairly sure that Tito's pseudonym, Broz, occurred to him.

Two days later X and Y lunched together again. During an idle moment, X's eyes fell upon an old newspaper. He was not reading it carefully as evidenced by the fact that he completely misconstrued the sentence containing the word that stopped him. The word was Bronson. Immediately, X remembered the Trotski problem. Trotski's real name was Bronson, he said to Y. Both agreed that wasn't quite right, however. But then after a moment's concentrating, X said "Bronstein." Bronstein is right.

Since X happened to be interested in the vagaries of human memory, he stopped at that point to document the situation. There were strong context effects that might have been at work, notably a second lunch with Y and a second conversation about eastern European topics. Were X a clinician, he might have described himself as ego-involved in the problem. He was sure the Trotski question had not come up during the intervening two days.

Had the paper contained the word *Trotski*, we would need only assume that X's memory was organized so as to interrupt ongoing processing upon coming across an element marked in some way as a result of previous incomplete processing (a variant of the Zeigarnik phenomenon, if you like). But the interrupting word could not itself have been marked, and it does not seem reasonable to assume that the letters *br* were so marked since X did not recall any previous interruption, although he certainly must have seen and heard many words with *br* during the intervening two days. Though it is not necessary to do so, it is tempting to assume that X has a memory consisting of elements capable of activating those related to them without first interrupting and securing the intervention of a central processor. Were that the case, we might imagine that some cognitive element, perhaps that representing the sound or syllable *bron*, was activated by the word. Furthermore, we might assume that this element had been activated previously in the course of the search for Trotski's pseudonym, not enough to bring *Bronstein* up, but enough so that this additional activation now was sufficient to do so.

X's report is anything but solid data, and the account just given is far from an adequate description of a mechanism capable of mediating phenomena of this sort. But this example is easy to think of in these terms, and it is possible to specify functional memories built of active elements as precisely as any other sort (see Reitman, 1965, Chap. 8). The model we consider next is defined in such terms and demonstrates how one may use information-processing and computer-simulation techniques to explore theories of psychological organization very different in their functioning from the hardware of the computers upon which they are simulated.

Competence and Performance

Our final example of information-processing research deals with the use and comprehension of language. The investigation is to some extent a reaction to the approach to language the MIT group has taken, and we may find it useful to begin by noting the relevant features of that approach. Central to the MIT group's strategy is the distinction between linguistic *competence*, what a speaker of a language in some sense knows about it, and linguistic *performance*, his use of that knowledge in comprehending and speaking sentences of that language. The distinction has several advantages. In particular, it enables the linguist to study individual languages, and language generally, without necessarily considering problems having to do with the ways in which humans use language in real time. To say that a human is competent in a language is simply to say that, were he given samples of sentences and non-sentences in that language, he could decide which were which and, furthermore, could assign the sentences their correct structural descriptions.[2] Were we clever enough to be able to program a computer to do the same thing, the computer could be said to be equally competent in the language. The notion of competence, in other words, involves only what is known, not how what is known is stored or processed. Competence implies nothing about the information-processing functions or functional organization required for effective use of linguistic knowledge by a human or a machine. The linguist may agree that humans often speak ungrammatically, and that in grasping one another's statements they frequently use not only their knowledge of the language but also extralinguistic information derived from experience with the objects of discourse and with the intents, attitudes, and abilities of the speaker. But these aspects of communication are outside the concept of language competence.

The work of the MIT group is related to psychological research on human communication and thought in several ways. The formalization

---

[2] The significance of structural descriptions comes out in the following informal comments by Fodor (1966b) apropos his own present interpretation of the competence-performance distinction and its psychological implications: ". . . while it is far from clear what sort of claims ought to be made about the relation of the grammatical rules to the rules in one's head, and . . . still less clear what ought to be said about the relation between the grammatical operations involved in recursively enumerating the set of sentences and the psychological operations involved in either producing or understanding particular sentences, yet it *is* clear that psychological claims can (must) be made for the structural descriptions grammars assign. And it has characteristically been the correctness of structural descriptions that the psychological experiments [concerned with the MIT work] have been testing. . . . In short, the grammar does make one type of "psychological" claim, that it provides markings for whatever grammatical relations are recovered in understanding a sentence. This claim had better be true since if it isn't the grammar is simply false. Where the grammar makes no claims (so far as I can see) is in the area of the rules it uses to specify those relations or of the operations involved in applying these rules in grammatical derivations."

of a language competence in a grammar provides the psychologist with a representation of what the language-user knows. It need not be psychologically reasonable, only isomorphic to some representation in our heads that is. The collection of grammatical rules is not subject to whatever constraints might be implied by a theory of the psychological mechanisms necessary to utilize the rules in actual discourse. That is a performance problem. Competence is a matter of what "in some sense" is known, not of the specific representation and use of the knowledge. The concern is with adequate formal or logical representation of language knowledge. Note that the theory of competence does provide the psychologist with a well-defined framework related to his thinking about the behavior of the language-user. Thus, it generates psychological questions and casts doubt upon psychological conceptions incapable of accounting for man's ability to acquire and use generative grammars. Coupled with hypotheses about the ways in which language knowledge is stored and processed, it leads to empirically testable propositions about human behavior. Then, too, the linguist's study of linguistic universals bears directly upon such problems as the extent of innate determination of linguistic ability. Finally, though they are not a part of formal linguistic theory, one finds in such sources as Chomsky (1965) many fascinating suggestions about possible psychological mechanisms mediating linguistic and intellectual functioning generally.

In sum, the MIT approach, by segmenting out the question of competence, has enabled its practitioners to make substantial progress in understanding the formal structure of language. It has served as a powerful stimulus for research in psycholinguistics. It even provides a suggestive paradigm for the study of other sorts of competence; e.g., those underlying perceptual or problem-solving ability. Taken by itself, however, it is not a direct attack upon the information processing underlying communication. It does not deal extensively with the cognitive, perceptual, and problem-solving skills that enter together with our linguistic capabilities into production and comprehension of utterances (Lindsay, 1964; Reitman, 1965, Chap. 9). The members of the MIT group do not presume that language necessarily is a self-contained system sufficient for communication in and of itself, but they tend to study it as if it were. Consequently, it should be useful to consider concurrently lines of exploration outside the framework of the competence-performance dichotomy, particularly by those taking real-time discourse as their central focus.

Reich's work: general setting. With these remarks as background, we turn to our last case history in information-processing research, a model of language processing developed by Peter Reich, a graduate student at the University of Michigan. The investigation, like the pattern-recognition program, may be approached from several vantage points. Based mainly on conversations with Reich, the present description of it is intended to illustrate a use of information-processing models somewhat different from the two considered previously.

Reich's program is a concrete implementation of a linguistic theory being developed by Lamb (1966b). In contrast to the MIT work, Lamb's theory does not sharply segregate the problems of linguistic knowledge from the processes involved in producing and comprehending discourse. According to Lamb (personal communication, 1966a), the theory treats linguistic structure not in terms of discrete rules such as those employed in Chomsky's theory of syntax, for example, but rather as a system or network of relationships. "The network of relationships is what the speaker of a language has stored in his brain, not rules," Lamb writes. "Rules are at best a rather inefficient means of representing relationships in the network." In this respect, Lamb's approach is very similar to that taken by Quillian (1966, 1967), who treats concepts not as discrete elements, but rather as nodes or entry points in a network of relations.

Since the information-processing activity in Reich's networks is treated as a property of the networks themselves, the work also is of interest from a psychological viewpoint, as an attempt to provide a viable alternative to conceptions of psychological activity cast in terms of search and transformation routines operating upon passive stores of knowledge. Should these efforts prove successful, the model may prove useful in accounting for some of the organizational problems of human information processing discussed above.

Though his more immediate goal is a model generating some of the regularities and abnormalities of human language use, the eventual scope of Reich's work is still more ambitious: he wants to specify a model of human functional organization able to serve as a substratum for treatments of cognition, perception, and problem solving as well as a point of departue for a theory of development—an account of how the adult gets that way. These long-range aspirations seem presumptuous when set down in print so early in the game, but they are valuable as guides constraining the otherwise ad hoc and unrestricted guessing game Quillian speaks of, and they help the model-builder avoid dead-end models and theoretical cul-de-sacs.

It is a very long way from such vague, universal aspirations to a program. How does the real work begin? Gregg and Simon started from a body of data and an already extant model they considered inadequate. Sauvain and Uhr began in the context of an ongoing line of research by Uhr. The programming of the pattern-recognition model proceeded from a fairly detailed memoir specifying mechanisms for relating, in a flexible fashion, current input to previously acquired knowledge. Reich begins by specializing his problem. Developmental questions are put aside for the time being, and rather than thinking in terms of higher mental processes generally, he focuses upon a single area—language processing—thus taking advantage of the very considerable structure already provided by research in linguistics. Furthermore, he works in detail only with a limited subset of linguistic processes—those involving the use of syntactic information. Thus, the immediate programming problem gradually takes shape.

Reich now uses for grist a small number of assumptions about basic human information-processing mechanisms and their organization and then sets out to see whether these assumptions, with an appropriate grammar, will generate sentences in a psychologically reasonable way. Both the information-processing assumptions and the grammatical formulations he uses are drawn from Lamb's (1966b) linguistic theory. This is not the place to debate the merits of Lamb's grammar or its relation to other formulations; e.g., those of the MIT group. These are matters for linguistic theory—and there does not seem to be much consensus about them among linguists. Reich works with Lamb's formulation because of what he takes to be its advantages in a psychological context: it does not involve a competence-performance distinction, and it represents grammatical knowledge in informational networks whose operations may be simulated to determine their behavioral and psychological implications.

Operation of the model. Grammatical knowledge is embedded in a network illustrated by the fragment shown in Fig. 8-3, p. 276. The network consists of interconnected nodes of several types. Five of these node types are specified in the key to the figure. The key feature of this active-memory model is that each node becomes active whenever its input conditions are met. Each node is an operator or function just as the routines of the Gregg and Simon models are. But, in a passive memory, such operations are carried out one after another by a central processor. Here, functions anywhere in the system go into effect directly, as soon as the appropriate inputs are present. The system is a parallel processor in that many nodes normally will be active at any given time in the course of language processing. Becoming active, a node propagates a message to each node it, in turn, connects to. Thus, each node is a function or operator that carries out its information-processing activity whenever it receives the pattern of input information appropriate to nodes of its type. This is the sense in which the network is not only a storehouse of information but also the processor of that information. This is why I have referred to the memory employed in the model as consisting of active elements rather than being a passive store of information operated upon by an external central processor coming in to retrieve or make transformations upon the information stored.

Just as one works out the details of a projected building in a two-dimensional blueprint, one studies such an active-element memory model, at least at present, by simulating it using a digital computer. The digital computer is very different in the logical organization of its components from the model we wish to study. As is the case with blueprints, we have to work out details of the model in a medium that lacks properties postulated in the model. In both cases, the representation of the model in that medium requires systematic transformations of the relations modeled (spatial relations in the blueprint, temporal relations in the computer simulation). Furthermore, we must, in most practice, settle for an approximation when we model an active-element memory on a serial computer. But the transformations are regular, and the approximation can be as fine as we think necessary. Thus, simulation with the computer in no sense limits us to "computer-like" models.

Since we can approximate the active-memory model in a digital computer representation, however, evidently there is at least a rough equivalence between the active and passive conceptions of memory. Given this equivalence, one might agree that the active-memory model can be simulated but now find oneself wondering whether the active-passive distinction is really so very fundamental after all.

Such an interpretation of the correspondence seems to me to miss the point. In principle, if only we were persistent enough and could afford it, we could simulate all of the information processing that goes on in our bodies on a serially processing digital computer. But there is no obvious reason to think of our bodily activities in this way, and to do so is to risk ignoring fundamental questions about the means by which the simultaneous multilevel activities of our cells and organs are coordinated and integrated. The same applies to memory. We can simulate an active-element memory on a serial computer. But the simulation is motivated by a desire to be able to think about problems of integration, coordination, and control that do not arise in a serial system. As Newell (1962) notes, the problems of an active-element system have a certain Alice-in-Wonderland quality about them. Unless we really believe that croquet mallets occasionally turn into flamingos and wander off the field, we are not likely to worry about organizing a game under those circumstances.

The Reich model postulates that the same networks are used in producing and comprehending language. In the case of language production, we can think of the system as embedded in a much larger structure realizing our perceptual, problem-solving, and other cognitive capabilities. The sentences to be produced by the language network may originate, for example, from a desire to communicate something about a problem we are working on, or perhaps from a need for additional information related to that problem. Alternately, the language network may be producing the sentences of a description of some object we are seeing, or of something we have seen and now are recalling or reconstructing from memory. Thus, one might view the Reich model as treating, in a vastly more powerful and sophisticated way, the language functions of the pattern-recognition program described previously. These remarks are intended only to locate the psychological activities under investigation in Reich's work in a larger context of ongoing human activity. None of these interrelations has been investigated and, indeed, it is hard at this point to characterize exactly the inputs to the language network in the production mode. For that reason, we cannot really evaluate the adequacy of the model at this stage of its development. The example to be discussed is presented purely to provide a more concrete grasp of the way in which this particular active-element model actually processes information.

Let us look at the portion of a grammar depicted in Fig. 8-3. This fragment realizes certain syntactic relations (or lexotactic relations in Lamb's terms) involved in grasping and creating sentences, specifically those combining, at node 23, a main clause with preceding or succeeding subordinate clauses of various sorts. This portion of the net would be involved for example in realizing the sentence "If I don't go soon, I won't go at all" from the preceding *if* clause and main clause components. The net both represents and processes in accordance with the condition that every sentence have at least a main clause. This is achieved by an arrangement of the nodes such that the path through nodes 1, 2, 11, 20, 23, and 28 always is active. The other paths are optional possibilities. Let us follow out some of the details to see how this is achieved, and to get some general idea of how such an active-memory net actually uses the relations it embeds and the information it receives from other nodes in the network.

Consider, for instance, how it would produce a sentence involving a main clause preceded by a subordinate clause that begins with the word *although*. We start somewhere in the middle of the process, with

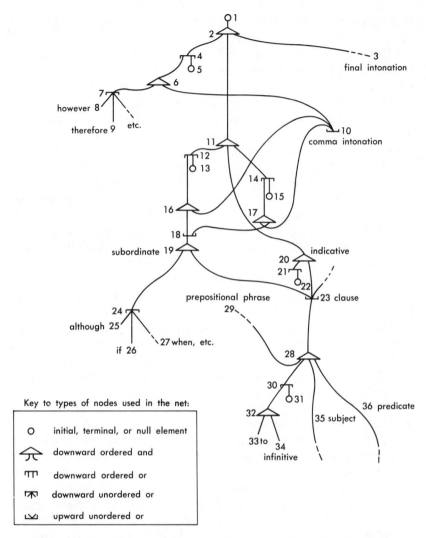

Figure 8-3. **Fragment of a network grammar (based on discussions with Reich). Numbers are placed next to each node in the diagram only for purposes of reference in the text.**

a number of inputs from other portions of the net given as specified in what follows. There is a signal into node 24 from the *although*. Node 24, as the key indicates, is of the *downward unordered or* type. It is *unordered* in that the signals to it are not subject to any sequence constraint. It is an *or* node in that activity from any one source into it, in this case from the *although*, is sufficient to generate a signal from it up to the next node, node 19, which is of the *downward ordered and* type. Any *and* element requires signals from *all* of its sources before it will propagate a signal onward. Node 19 is an *ordered and*, and this means that there is a sequence constraint upon it as well. With reference to the figure, such sequence constraints are represented as a requirement that the input signals necessary to activate an *ordered* node arrive in temporal order from left to right. Thus, node 19 will propagate activity to node 18 only if the *although* is going to precede a main clause (signaled by activity from node 23 to the right side of node 19).

Node 18, an *upward unordered or*, simply permits the signal from node 19 to propagate simultaneously over several paths in the net. Considering only the path through node 16, we see that activity will be maintained upwards past that node only if the *although* subordinate clause is followed by comma-intonation activity signaled from node 10. In that case, the left path through node 12 will be taken. Otherwise, node 12 will propagate activity from null node 13 (null elements are defined to be active-signal sources at all times), thus making it possible for activity to propagate upwards from node 11, given that the other paths to it are active in sequence, even in the absence of the optional subordinate clause. The path from the null element will be followed only if no signal is present at the left input to node 12, since an *ordered or* is activated by and continues the path associated with the leftmost signal received at a particular time. In the case of our example, the *although* subordinate clause, followed by sequenced signals through the center (main clause) and right branches of node 11, will propagate activity to node 2. Given that this signal is one of three properly sequenced signals at that node, activity will propagate to node 1, the null terminal node. At that point in the total activity of the net, the grammatical relations embedded in this fragment will have been satisfied by the sentence being processed.

Had the activity in the net not succeeded in finding some path through to node 1, this would mean that no sentence could be produced satisfying both the grammatical relations of this fragment and also the other language and cognitive constraints imposed by the rest of the total (hypothetical) network. In terms of behavior, the speaker, perhaps, would break off and pause while trying to recast what he was trying to say in such a way as to lead to the production of an acceptable sentence. The example illustrates the sense in which the network not only stores information but also mediates, via that information, the creating and evaluating of language outputs.

As another example, take the chain branching off at the top left in the diagram. If an introductory word (e.g., *however* or *therefore*) and a comma intonation are signaled in order from nodes 7 and 10, node 6

will activate node 4. Node 4, an *ordered or*, gives first preference to the
left path if it is active. If either the introductory word or the comma
intonation is not signalled, or the signals are not in sequence, node 6
will not activate node 4. Node 4 will then, however, be activated
through the path from node 5, a null element. Thus, just as there
always is a signal from node 12 to node 11, there always is a signal
from node 4 to node 2. This is necessary if node 2 is to propagate
activity in all those cases in which no introductory word is involved.
Note the kinds of patterns this arrangement precludes. The comma
intonation path (node 10 to node 6) will be active whenever a comma
is required for any purpose at all. But because node 6 is an *ordered and*
element, the *system* of paths from *both* nodes 7 *and* 10 together
through node 6 to node 2 will be active if *and only if* the comma signal
is immediately preceded by an introductory word signal.

The five types of nodal-processing elements used in this portion of
the net give some idea of what gets accomplished by the full set of
nine or ten distinct element types that Reich, largely following Lamb,
presently employs. Where, we may well ask, do these elements come
from? They are, after all, the basic structure and process assumptions
underlying the entire effort. How do we know they are the right ones?

We don't. All one can say is that they work over the portions of
grammar described so far in terms of them. They emerged through a
long evolutionary process, in the course of which other formulations
were tried, found to lead to difficulties, and modified or discarded. The
evolutionary process here, so well described by Quillian in the remarks
quoted earlier, no doubt will continue. Next year's diagram for this
portion of the network will be somewhat different. Playing the model-
building game requires a high tolerance for uncertainty. It may help
to remember that, at this stage, we are only constructing surrogates—
candidates for psychological theories. Reich's first problem is to get the
thing to work. When and if he gets past that stage and is able to account for an adequately interesting corpus of sentences, he then can
turn to the analysis of behavioral data in an attempt to evaluate the
usefulness of his model as a psychological theory. The chances of success are obviously very small, but as the most cursory review of the
last one hundred years of psychological theory seems to suggest, the
chances for all psychological theories are small; what we are, after all,
trying to understand is the structure and function of perhaps the most
complexly organized matter in existence. The relative advantage of the
strategy Reich has chosen is that grammatical rules and the corpus of
language constitute a system of objective facts that can be used to
guide and constrain his constructions. Only a perennial optimist will
expect unconditional success in the enterprise. Nonetheless, like blind

men grateful for the one-eyed king, those of us who see the problem of search, semantic organization, the structure and use of human memory, or fringe consciousness to be fundamental and pressing will be grateful for something far short of success. The General Problem Solver and other passive-memory systems are also, at best, limited successes, but we understand their possibilities as psychological explanations immeasurably better now for the decade of experience we have had in thinking about psychological problems in terms of them. If active-memory models look to be a source of concepts that might help us to account for the organizational problems we have discussed, then all the experience we can get with them is to the good. Reich's work is preliminary. He has written an algorithm (Reich, 1966) which approximates such networks on a digital computer, thereby providing another concrete demonstration of the extent to which computer models can go beyond the organizational concepts underlying present computer hardware. Now there is a year or two of work ahead before we can begin to draw some general conclusions about what, if any, explanatory power active-memory conceptions of human information-processing organization can add to those we already have.

Psychological models: theories of functional organization and theories of the environment. Selz, we noted, took an adequate account of the systems of operations humans use as the goal to be attained in his studies of thinking. We have seen, however, that it is possible to give an accurate description of strategies for carrying out some complex activity without necessarily specifying, for the system under investigation, the actual functional organization of the processes realizing such strategies. The distinction is fundamental and must always be considered in evaluating a particular psychological model. Fitts (1964, p. 249), discussing an early artificial intelligence system, the autopilot, notes that "it is more than a coincidence that the pilot's job, in many respects, corresponds to that of an autopilot, and that the variables which are considered by the design engineer in perfecting an automatic control system are analogous in many respects to the task variables which affect the . . . pilot." The autopilot embeds a theory of the environment in which the pilot operates. If both pilot and autopilot cope with that environment successfully, the strategies of the two systems may be similar at many points. But that is not to say that the autopilot necessarily is a good model of the process organization of the pilot as he behaves in that environment.

Many of our models of cognitive processes are substantially models of the environment. Peterson and Beach (1967) provide a particularly striking example. They review the experimental literature on human judgments of the statistical properties of various sorts of stimulus distributions and demonstrate that, to a very substantial extent, the human information processor carries out strategies functionally equivalent to those embedded in standard statistical measures. But, once again, there is no reason to conclude that humans do so by carrying out computations in their heads paralleling in their organization those we carry out with a desk calculator or on a computer. Perhaps, the most fully developed theory of the environment is one we considered earlier: the competence theory of the MIT group. Here is a theory that explicitly excludes psychological functions from its domain. It is an analysis of the formal properties of language, which is, perhaps, the single most important feature of the environment of the human information processor.

What about information-processing models? Elsewhere (1966, 1967), I have tried to show that typically they do not make explicit the distinction we are concerned with here. Often, they are excellent representations of the strategies people use, but to a substantial extent those strategies mainly reflect internalized properties of the environments upon which they operate. We have much less reason to assert that the processing organization embedded in passive-memory models necessarily corresponds to human functional organization.

Psychology cannot do without theories of the environment. If we are studying the behavior of rats solving a maze, we need information about the maze they are trying to solve. If we know nothing of the number and arrangement of paths or the location of cues and rewards, we cannot expect to grasp what the rats' behavior depends upon, regardless of what their gross performance turns out to be. Similarly, if we are trying to understand how people solve problems of some sort, it is necessary to have a good grasp of the structure of the problems they undertake. This will be true whether we are interested in models to simulate the performance, or in experimental designs intended to tease out the conditions upon which particular sorts of performance depend. But we must, as the MIT group does so clearly, distinguish questions about environment from questions about process organization, particularly since the models we are concerned with normally deal with both at the same time.

Strict observation of the distinction yields one very important further advantage in connection with the taxonomizing of complex behaviors. There are various bases for such taxonomies. Conventional textbook chapter headings give us one sort, the limitations of which we noted earlier. One may try to taxonomize by distinuishing certain key features of gross classes of cognitive operations. Thus, one might distinguish between categorization processes (perceptual, conceptual, or otherwise) and comprehension processes on the basis of the presence or absence of a fixed set of categories into which inputs to the process are coded. Language processing, for example, would generally fall under the second head, since language rules are generative and permit us to construct indefinitely many output classes. One may postulate a set of elementary operations, as Newell, Shaw, and Simon (1958) do. One may taxonomize at the level of higher-order classes of operations, as is done in the General Problem Solver by the system of goal types. One may taxonomize with respect to some external scheme, as Jenkins and his associates do using the categories of automata theory. The main advantage following from the environment-processing organization distinction is that it allows us to ask about a presumably finite set of process components without worrying about classifying the tremendously complex set of strategies the system of components carries out. Though we have no very adequate taxonomy of computer programs, any manufacturer can give a precise description of the components of his computer and of their properties. We are very far from being able to do the same with the human information processor, but it is at least a reasonably clear taxonomic goal. And after all, that is precisely the form in which the rest of our knowledge of the organism takes. We do not categorize the forms of human activity. We consider the components of the system, heart, lungs, skin, etc., and study their properties and their interactions. Reich's work may or may not be a step in the direction of a taxonomy of human information-processing functions, but at least it should serve to help clear the distinction between process organizations and the strategies they embed.

Recapitulation

Given the details and divagations of the preceding discussion, it may be useful to conclude by trying to review just where we have been. As Berlyne and Glaser have demonstrated, in book (1965) and pool, information-processing concepts and techniques have no exclusive rights in the domain of skills, learning, thinking, and higher mental processes generally. They do have significant advantages, however. They permit precise statements directly in terms of complex structure and process systems, and they allow strict tests of the sufficiency and the implications of our models.

In one fundamental sense, we are all associationists—all S-R psychologists. Information-processing models simply enable those of us who use them to specify and evaluate particular systems of associations and S-R mechanisms and to ask about the logical structure of the components that, taken together with the associations, habits, and strategies they embed, generate the behavior we study. The advantages of information-processing models may be put to work for us in various ways. Gregg and Simon build and test a model in the classical sense of experimental psychology. The pattern-recognition program and Reich's work use them in constructing tools for thought—key concepts and organizing ideas for posing questions about the intricate systems underlying complex human accomplishments in language, perception, problem solving, and learning.

The information-processing approach has its methodological problems (Reitman, 1965, Chap. 2; 1966; 1967), and in common with all other psychology, it has yet to provide convincing accounts of human intellectual development and of the ways in which men use what they know in seeing, speaking, and thinking. Just as some theologians see man as intrinsically good, others as intrinsically bad, and still others as a mixture of both, so do interpretations of information-processing achievements and prospects vary from those on the left, who see nothing wrong that the next program can't handle, to those on the right, like Dreyfus, who sees so great a discontinuity between what has been done and what remains before us that he compares information-processing claims of progress to the progress of a man trying to get to the moon by first climbing to the top of a tree. The view set forth in this paper might be characterized as right revisionism. In more theological terms, programs are ultimately perfectable but it will take work. The difficulties before us seem great, but not unresolvable. I would hope that this account conveys some sense both of the problems and of some of the ways in which those who use information-processing concepts are attempting to resolve them.

REFERENCES

Abelson, R. P. Simulation of social behavior. In G. Lindzey and E. Aronson (Eds.), *Handbook of social psychology.* Vol. 2. Reading, Massachusetts: Addison-Wesley, (in press).

Baylor, G. W. Report on a mating combination program. Santa Monica, California: System Development Corporation, 1965 (mimeo).

Berlyne, D. E. *Structure and direction in thinking.* New York: Wiley, 1965.

Bower, G. H., and Trabasso, T. R. Concept identification. In R. C. Atkinson (Ed.), *Studies in mathematical psychology.* Stanford: Stanford University Press, 1964. Pp. 32-94.

Chomsky, N. *Syntactic structures.* The Hague: Mouton, 1957.

Chomsky, N. *Aspects of the theory of syntax.* Cambridge, Massachusetts: M. I. T. Press, 1965.

de Groot, A. D. Chess playing programs. *Proc. Koninkl. Nederl. Akademie van Wetenschappen-Amsterdam,* 1964, Series A, 67, and *Indag. Math., 26,* 385-398.

de Groot, A. D. *Thought and choice in chess.* The Hague: Mouton, 1965.

de Groot, A. D., and Jongman, W. Heuristics in perceptual processes: an investigation of chess perception. In A. de Groot, and W. Reitman (Eds.), *Heuristic processes in thinking.* Moscow: "Nauka" (Science) Publishing House, 1966. Pp. 15-24.

Dreyfus, H. L. Alchemy and artificial intelligence. Santa Monica, California: Rand Corporation, 1965 (mimeo).

Feigenbaum, E. A. The simulation of verbal learning behavior. *Proceedings of the Western Joint Computer Conference,* 1961, *19,* 121-132.

Fitts, P. M. Perceptual-motor skill learning. In A. W. Melton (Ed.), *Categories of human learning.* New York: Academic Press, 1964. Pp. 243-285.

Fodor, J. Some trends in cognitive psychology. Paper read at the Summer Lecture Series, University of Minnesota, July, 1966. (a)

Fodor, J. Personal communication. October 16, 1966. (b)

Gagné, R. M. Problem solving. In A. W. Melton (Ed.), *Categories of human learning.* New York: Academic Press, 1964. Pp. 293-317.

Gregg, L. W., and Simon, H. A. Process models and stochastic theories of simple concept formation. *J. math. Psychol.,* 1967, *4,* 246-276.

Hebb, D. O. *The organization of behavior.* New York: Wiley, 1949.

Hilgard, E. R., and Bower, G. H. *Theories of learning.* (3rd ed.) New York: Appleton-Century-Crofts, 1966.

Hunt, E. G., Marin, J., and Stone, P. J. *Experiments in induction.* New York: Academic Press, 1966.

Jacob, F. Genetics of the bacterial cell. *Science,* 1966, *152,* 1470-1478.

Lamb, S. M. Personal communication. October 21, 1966. (a)

Lamb, S. M. *Stratificational grammar.* Washington, D. C.: Georgetown University Press, 1966. (b)

Lashley, K. S. The problem of serial order in behavior. In L. A. Jeffress (Ed.), *Cerebral mechanisms in behavior: the Hixon symposium.* New York: Wiley, 1951. Pp. 112-146.

Lindsay, R. K. A heuristic parsing procedure for a language learning program. Information Processing Reports 12 and 13. Austin, Texas: University of Texas, 1964 (mimeo).

Lwoff, A. Interaction among virus cell and organism. *Science,* 1966, *152,* 1216-1220.

Melton, A. W. (Ed.) *Categories of human learning.* New York: Academic Press, 1964.

Neisser, U. The imitation of man by machine. *Science,* 1963, *139,* 193-197.

Newell, A. Some problems of basic organization in problem-solving programs. In M. C. Yovits, G. T. Jacobi, and G. D. Goldstein (Eds.), *Self-organizing systems,* 1962, Washington, D. C.: Spartan Books, 1962.

Newell, A. On the analysis of human problem solving protocols. Paper read at the International Symposium on Mathematical and Computational Methods in the Social Sciences. Rome, Italy: July, 1966.

Newell, A., *et al. Information processing language-V manual.* Englewood Cliffs, New Jersey: Prentice-Hall, 1964.

Newell, A., Shaw, J. C., and Simon, H. A. Empirical explorations of the logic theory machine. *Proceedings of the Western Joint Computer Conference,* 1957, *11,* 218-230.

Newell, A., Shaw, J. C., and Simon, H. A. Elements of a theory of human problem solving. *Psychol. Rev.,* 1958, *65,* 151-166.

Newell, A., Shaw, J. C., and Simon, H. A. Report on a general problem-solving program. *Proceedings of the International Conference on Information Processing.* Paris, France: UNESCO, 1960, 256-264.

Newell, A., and Simon, H. A. An example of human chess play in the light of chess playing programs. Unpublished manuscript, Carnegie Institute of Technology, 1964 (mimeo).

Newell, A., and Simon, H. A. Programs as theories of higher mental processes. In R. W. Stacy, and B. Waxman (Eds.), *Computers in biomedical research.* Vol. II. New York: Academic Press, 1965. Pp. 141-172.

Peterson, C. R., and Beach, L. R. Man as an intuitive satistician. *Psychol. Bull.*, 1967, *68*, 29-46.

Quillian, M. R. Semantic memory. Unpublished doctoral dissertation, Carnegie Institute of Technology, 1966.

Quillian, R. Word concepts: a theory and simulation of some basic semantic capabilities. *Behav. Sci.*, 1967, *12*, 410-430.

Reich, P. A. An algorithm which executes a network of finite automata used by stratificational grammar. Information Processing working paper 6. University of Michigan, 1966 (dittoed).

Reitman, W. R. *Cognition and thought.* New York: Wiley, 1965.

Reitman, W. R. The study of heuristics. In A. de Groot and W. Reitman (Eds.), *Heuristic processes in thinking.* Moscow: "Nauka" (Science) Publishing House, 1966. Pp. 44-53.

Reitman, W. R. Modeling the formation and use of concepts, precepts, and rules. In L. M. LeCain and J. Neyman (Eds.), *Proceedings of the Fifth Berkeley Symposium on Mathematical Statistics and Probability.* Berkeley: University of California Press, 1967.

Reitman, W. R., Grove, R. B., and Shoup, R. G. Argus: An information-processing model of thinking. *Behav. Sci.*, 1964, *9*, 270-281.

Sauvain, R. W. An adaptive pattern description program. Information Processing working paper 5. University of Michigan, 1966 (dittoed).

Simon, H. A. The architecture of complexity. *Proceedings of the American Philosophical Society,* 1962, *106*, 467-482.

Simon, H. A., and Kotovsky, K. Human acquisition of concepts for sequential patterns. *Psychol. Rev.*, 1963, *70*, 534-546.

Tikhomirov, O. K. Experimental analysis of heuristics. In A. de Groot and W. Reitman (Eds.), *Heuristic processes in thinking.* Moscow: "Nauka" (Science) Publishing House, 1966. Pp. 33-43.

Uhr, L. Personal communication. October 6, 1966.

Uhr, L., and Vossler, C. A pattern-recognition program that generates, evaluates, and adjusts its own operators. In E. A. Feigenbaum and J. Feldman (Eds.), *Computers and thought.* New York: McGraw-Hill, 1963. Pp. 251-268.

Witkin, Evelyn M. Radiation-induced mutations and their repair. *Science,* 1966, *152*, 1345-1353.

Woodworth, R. S. *Experimental psychology.* New York: Holt, 1938.

Wynn, W. H. An information processing model of certain aspects of paired associate learning. Unpublished doctoral dissertation, University of Texas, 1966.

Zvegintzov, N. On killing the bugs. Center for Research in Management Science working paper 75. Berkeley: University of California, 1963 (dittoed).

COMPUTER "SIMULATIONS" OF THINKING ARE JUST (WORKING, COMPLETE, BIG, COMPLEX, POWERFUL, MESSY) THEORETICAL MODELS

LEONARD UHR

University of Wisconsin

There is a small, but rather vocal, underground clique whose members go around with the computer, like an elephant gun, in hip pockets. We brandish our weapon rather frequently, and we get quite a bang describing the havoc that results when the thing goes off.

The computer is, indeed, a uniquely powerful weapon. But it is time we stopped pointing it at the defenseless psychologist who feels slightly guilty and out of things for not knowing how to use it, or slightly hostile because he doesn't know why he should use it, and more than slightly scared to get near one anyway. For the computer, if it is anything, is a tool for all of us. If it is an elephant gun, it should be used not against skeptical psychologists, but against elephants—the scientific problems that all of us are trying to solve.

As a member of the computer clique, I would like to make absolutely clear, once and for all, what the computer is, and what it is not.

Virtues and Vices of Computer-Programmed Models

The computer, in truth, will do certain things a million, or even a billion, times as fast as the human being. And the things it will do include all describable procedures. Our big problem lies in making an adequate, complete description. But, potentially, we can now specify any mechanism, or put any set of rules or processes into the computer, and it will turn this into a *working* mechanism that grinds out its behavioral consequences at least a million times faster than the best and most diligent human research assistant could do. The computer gives every one of us the power of a million, or a billion, graduate research assistants.

This is certainly exciting; but let's stop for a moment to consider it. What would each of us do with a million graduate research assistants? So much potential power quickly becomes an appalling prospect. I have trouble enough handling five assistants, or two, or even handling myself.

Very simply, the computer puts incredible potential power at our disposal. But just because of the enormity of this increment in power, it is extremely difficult to know how to use it.

The computer is a completely general thing. It is not like a particular mathematical system such as the calculus or group theory; nor is it like mathematics as a whole. It is more like a piece of paper of virtually infinite size, plus the power to write any kind of mathematical or English language statement, or statements in any other language system that we may devise, *plus* the built-in mechanism that will explore the meaning and the consequences of these statements. The computer is thus, basically, a substrate on which we can write our theories. It is a very unusual, very active substrate, for it is the pencil and the research technician as well as the piece of paper.

But the computer is simply the substrate on which we write our working models, and we would be far better off if we stopped bragging about the computer, emphasizing its mysteries and cult-aspects, and began to admit that a "computer model" is simply a model, and nothing more. That is, we are doing nothing more, when we write a computer program that attempts to model some phenomenon of interest to psychology, than any other psychologists do when they build working models. We have a far more powerful tool; we have the possibility of building far more complex and more powerful models. Mathematical models, verbal models, and all other types of models that have been built to date could be rewritten in the form of computer programs, and they would form an infinitessimal and trivially simple subset of the models that can now be written, because we have the computer. It is just as silly to call these new models "computer models" as to call our old models "paper-and-pencil models" because the mathematician would not have been able to work out his proofs, or to solve his equations, if he had been forced to keep everything in his head.

This is not to say that there is not a new thrust. We do indeed have this new opportunity to build more powerful models—to begin to theorize about the more difficult, heartland problems of psychology that we have been forced to ignore for so long, for lack of tools of appropriate power. For the first time, we have built-in touchstones that absolutely force us to be precise and self-consistent; otherwise our programs will simply not get written at all, and will not run. Once our programs have run, they are there for all to observe (the fact that they are usually far too complicated for anyone to understand makes this observation rather difficult, and leads to a very real and upsetting set of problems, but it is not relevant here; for the important point for the scientific method is that, *in principle*, the work is public and duplicable).

So we are, I believe for the first time, actually in a position, using the computer as our tool, to develop working theoretical models, to use them to predict empirical data, which data will tend to confirm, infirm, and modify our theory, and so on. That is, we are on the verge of making psychology a hypothetico-deductive, as opposed to an empirical, science.

State of the Art of Scientific Theory-Building

What we have actually accomplished to date is another matter. The potentialities are enormous, and the work that has been done, by a small handful of people over the very short span of five or ten years, is, I would assert, not only impressive in its diligence (for a running computer program is the fruit of an enormous amount of drudgery), but also brilliant. But we have been like little children romping and playing around in a strange new world, so overwhelming in its richness that it is still hard to distinguish the glitter from the gold. We are still on one of the plateaus of learning, where we must simply explore, tear apart, and reintegrate, before we can consolidate in the right direction.

Or, I should say that it is not really very clear whether we have accomplished an enormous amount or very little; whether the powerful, precise, and general theories that we will certainly have at some future date will look very similar to or very different from the programmed models that we have today. I personally think that they will not be very long in coming, and that they will not look very different. But it should not be treated by us as a heresy when someone has a very different opinion. It is far more important to give people a feeling for the range of powerful models that can now be built, than to assert that any particular model of today is, itself, the answer. Our propaganda is merely an unfortunate reflection of the insecurities and doubts on our side of the elephant gun. The beauty of scientific evidence is that it compels assent among rational men. To the extent that we try to sell our models (as I am afraid I and others have done) we advertise our own doubts. The scientific method itself carries all of the baggage that we need, or want, to test out and assert the worth of a model.

So let me turn our elephant gun, which is at bottom the hypothetico-deductive method, enormously augmented, at the computer modelers, and especially at myself, and assert that what we have today is a handful of bad models—for pattern recognition, for concept formation, for problem solving. Rather, I should say *better* models. For there can be no absolute standards, ever, in judging a model. All that we can ever assert is that one model is better or worse than another. We never have a "perfect" or a "correct" model; and our greatest hope when we build a new model—one that is better than the models built to date—is that it will stimulate the scientific community to come up with infirming evidence that will reveal where the model is *wrong*, and thus lead to a still better model.

Thus, though we might be disposed, for relatively vague, intuitive, and therefore necessarily fallible, reasons to assert that our present computer-programmed models are bad models, they are at the same time for all but the very simplest cognitive processes, quite clearly, the *best* models that we have. Mr. Reitman points out that the Gregg-Simon model for concept formation is clearly better in just about every way than the Bower-Trabasso model, but then he makes the mistake of suggesting that the Newell-Simon chess player is not a model at all, apparently because no psychologist has even tried to tackle the problem of chess at the level of precision needed to build a working scientific model. Thus, the computer-programmed models for such things as chess playing, theorem proving, and pattern recognition are in the position of being better models because they are better than nothing— the situation that existed before they were programmed. I hope that it is clear that I am not denigrating the importance of these models (and also that I am of the model-builders I am discussing). For the jump between nothing and something is probably the most important, the most significant, and the most difficult jump that can be made.

But I find it very strange—except as a sign of one's own vanity, insecurity, and defensiveness (and I am as guilty as anyone else in these respects)—to see people who are building real models—for the first time carrying psychology over the brink to being a hypothetico-deductive, as opposed to a purely empirical, science—adulterating their models by expanding the claims for what these models do, and in other ways trying to protect them. Our model is just the last thing that we should want to protect, for we built it exactly so that it would lead to its own downfall, and thus to further knowledge and a better model. We have seen far too often in psychology the blight that comes from such cultish impulses. The Freudians have defended myriad positions by broadening and qualifying their constructs to the point where those constructs take on any form that may be desirable, no longer containing any meaning in themselves. There seem to be far too many papers in this text (possibly inevitable from those who have been trained in the naïve scientific prejudices of a behaviorism that is still uncomfortable about private minds but now begins to examine such private matters as thinking and complex learning) which seek to broaden the word "behavior" to the point where it encompasses everything, so that a thought or a dream or a nerve firing across a synapse must be thought of as a piece of "covert behavior."

Learning and Remembering

It is a very pleasant experience to be in the position of discussing a paper written about your own work and that of your students. It's difficult to resist agreeing when some aspect of a model is described as a step forward, even when it has already been done elsewhere; and I won't. But I'd like to point out, without being able to take the time to document this statement, that a great deal of research has been done, especially in developing models of pattern recognition, and these models contain a rich variety of ideas. Psychologists still do not seem to be aware of this literature, and those that have looked into it are too prone to dismiss it as "engineering"—chiefly, I fear, because the jargon and the union card are not of our club.

It is more difficult not to comment on aspects of the described research that seem especially pertinent to the theme of this text. These are the mechanisms for learning a usable memory structure that these and other recent computer-programmed models employ.

Programs such as the one discussed in Reitman's Figs. 8-1 and 8-2 are, I think, first approximations toward the goal of building up, through learning experiences with an interacting environment, what we have called a "semantic" or "cognitive" "map" or "model" or "representation" or "memory structure." This memory structure must further be usable by the program or organism that contains it, and must further help and even direct.

The memory structure sketched out in Fig. 8-2 (Reitman) actually illustrates four different types of learning mechanisms that had to be embodied into the computer program that builds the structure as a function of its experiences with a human trainer. Several other mechanisms have been incorporated into other programs. I will briefly sketch out this set here, in order to clarify what we might mean by the term "learning," and to make apparent exactly what the program by Sauvain and me that Reitman described does and doesn't do.

Discovering

1) Each entity in Fig. 8-2 (e.g., the straight horizontal line, "BALLOON") is a "thing" or "chunk" or "characteristic" that the program had to *discover* and *define*. In this program, the discovery problem has been pretty well trivialized, for the program is shown just one new thing at a time. But there are several learning programs that discover the pertinent, meaningful chunks in more sophisticated ways. (For reprints and discussions see Uhr, 1964, 1966, 1967.)

Naming

2) When an entity like "STRING" is connected to an entity like the straight line, a *naming* relation is formed; it must now be interpreted by the program as signifying "when this name is recognized, it signifies that thing."

Compounding

3) Chunks are compounded into higher-levels chunks. Thus (in Reitman's Fig. 8-2), Circle = (Semicircle) to the left of (Semicircle). This program builds up n-place relations by successively compounding 2-place relations, and it insists that the compounding statement stored in memory be satisfied completely and exactly before the program will recognize. We have coded other models that handle n-place relations directly, and allow a good bit of flexibility in accepting partial and distorted matches.

Connecting and reweighting

4) Each line connecting two boxes is a connection, and attached to each of these connections is a number, signifying its strength. These

numbers can be thought of as associational strength, and are, I think, what we usually study in the psychology of conditioning and verbal learning.

There are several additional types of learning mechanisms that have been embodied in programmed models. They were clearly needed in order to improve performance and handle problems that human beings can handle; and they clearly exist and have meaning, in that they are running routines in computer programs. These include:

5) *Classifying.* Several things can be put into the same class when they act similarly in certain situations. Now we have a new relation of "belonging" between a thing and its class. The model uses this relation in order to see whether these things might act like, or take the place of, each other when a problem arises.

6) *Generalizing.* When a class has been established, a program that is capable of discovering characteristics of its inputs can now try to discover characteristics that are common among the members of the same class. Now, rather than describe a class by the cumbersome method of enumeration, the program can use a more general set of characterizations.

7) *Integrating and differentiating.* When a compound has been represented in memory, it is frequently nice to refine this representation, differentiating out the accidentals and the inessentials, adding on pertinent parts, and, in general, more sensitively delineating its structure. We still have only the most roughshod ways of doing this; but compounding plus unlearning and refining methods are a beginning.

8) *Contextual interacting.* The parts of a compound in a trivial sense interact, as context to one another, to form the new whole. Less trivially, we must have a program or organism that can learn that although something usually implies one thing, under certain circumstances and in certain contexts it may imply something else. This necessitates a whole new level of statements in a program's memory, in which, when there are ambiguities and alternate possibilities of action, information about contextual interaction is stored and used. Contextual interaction statements can become quite general and powerful when they are about *classes* rather than about individual things.

9) *Transforming.* In a trivial sense, when STRING and CIRCLE equal BALLOON we have a transformation. But this was built into the

program discussed by Reitman. We are beginning to have programmed models that *learn* how to distinguish which of *several possible* transformations is appropriate. These programs must use context in order to make these distinctions, and they must learn what is the operative context, and what *it* signifies.

The above is a rather haphazard list that tries to enumerate *some* of the features of programmed models for complex learning of highly structured information like patterns in objects, natural language sentences, or sequences of configurations and moves in a game. The points I want to emphasize are: a) Connecting and conditioning are not enough; they don't get us very far and they are grossly inefficient. b) Other mechanisms can be and have been specified, and they markedly improve performance. c) These mechanisms are internal, look like a first approximation to something like a "cognitive map" or set of "ideas," and are perfectly precise in that they are running computer routines, and perfectly open to observation in that we can have our program and, like a guaranteed perfect introspectionist, trace out any of its internal processes to any detail desired.

Verbal Salads

Whatever people seem to mean by words such as "rule," "mechanism," or "transformation," the computer program is capable of embodying them. I take a *set of rules* to be the specification of a *mechanism;* when this mechanism runs, a *set of transformations* is effected in some proper sequence, and this is what we mean by *"information processing."*

What is the value of arguing about the meanings of the words above, or other terms like "gestalt," "image," "fringe consciousness," or "active memory"? Or choosing up sides where we purport to believe in one as opposed to the others? or asserting that the ones we believe in cannot be programmed onto a computer? Unless we merely enjoy the game of debate, we must make our ideas clear. The burden is on the person who trots out his favorite term and chides us that computer programs can't do *that* to give us some inkling of what he is talking about. Let's assume that a computer program has exhibited every behavior and function of a human being. How would we then react to a psychologist who rushed in screaming "I've discovered that people do gluck, and gluck is one thing that computers can't possibly do!"?

At some point, each of us must face his own gluck, and describe it well enough so that others can recognize it independently. Computer programs are entirely satisfactory languages for such descriptions, probably the best. What other clear languages are there? Psychology need no longer be satisfied with vague feelings of dissatisfaction, or distaste, at half-grasped ideas. On the other hand, people who program the computer should not claim deep meanings for trivial processes; and we should try to capture, rather than explain away, the richness of the mind.

Active Memories

Reitman's term "active memory" appears to refer to a mixture of three things: a) parallel processing, b) the memory itself deciding what to do next, and c) the memory knowing what to do next. I find it hard to determine what Reitman takes to be the desiderata, the necessaries, and the sufficiencies, of an "active memory." Such a situation is fine; we can only proceed to more appropriate and more powerful constructs by grappling with such vague and ambiguous matters. But there is a great danger in prematurely deciding that one is satisfied with an embodiment of his construct—unless one is absolutely sure. I am afraid, therefore, that I must defend the concept of "active memory" from Reitman's premature attempts to define it. Let's keep it vague and ambiguous, like a beautiful moorish body of flowing robe and veil, and, if it is an inspiration for Reitman and others, let's encourage them to weave their dreams around its image.

"Parallel" is a concept that relativity theory has shown to be pertinent only with respect to a particular point of view. Reitman is upset by the fact that the digital computer does everything sequentially; for example transforming all of the symbols in a matrix one at a time in order to transform the matrix. But, from the point of view of matrix manipulation, it is equally just, and far more pertinent, to say that all of the points in the matrix were transformed in parallel. Now any parallel machine; e.g., the TV camera or a matrix of photo-cell scanners, has something in its design—in the relations between its parts—that coordinates the separate elements—keeping them parallel on the one hand and, at some point, making appropriate combinations and transformations of their outputs. The digital computer's sequential embodiment of a process that would be performed in parallel by a nerve net or some other machine must have a far more explicit mechanism to transform the parallel operations into a sequence of steps. The weakest of such mechanisms are the random sampler and the sequential processor; e.g., the scan of the TV camera which is, itself, serial at a micro-time level. That is, any procedure for going through the set of processes that *would* have been done in parallel by the parallel machine, such that no matter what particular order was actually taken, the results were guaranteed to be the same, should be thought of as a parallel process. Put another way, the scope of a sequence of processes in which there is no decision rule that actually influences this sequence of processes can be thought of as a parallel operation with respect to the larger model as a whole. Put another way, a subroutine is a black box within nested black boxes; so long as our function has been well specified and the subroutine has been coded to effect a correct mapping in all cues, it is pointless to ask, "How does it do it? Is it sequential or parallel?" unless we are interested in looking at a question another level down: What are the workings of this reduced black box?

Now there can be more rigid and less rigid processes. Reitman seems to be bothered more, if I understand him, by the rigidity of the situation that leaves a program out on the limb of one unsuccessful operation that invalidates a lot of tentatively held hypotheses that got it farther and farther out on this unfortunate limb. Reitman would like the model, as all of us would, to be able, at such a point, to forget about all the things that led it astray and jump back to the main trunk of essentials. This is easily dreamed, but less easily done. Doing things in parallel may, superfiically, seem to be the answer. But, in the context of this problem, "parallel" simply means that at any moment in time the program will be out on several limbs—not just one—so that if one limb crumbles, it can continue its explorations from another.

Reitman is bothered by the typical method for handling a set of processes that take one out onto the limbs of such programs as the Newell-Shaw-Simon Chess Player and General Problem Solver. Essentially, these programs climb farther and farther out onto limbs in the way Theseus wandered through his maze in hunt of the Minotaur—by keeping track of where he had just come from (at which point he would be told from what previous point he had come from, and so on). I agree with Reitman—and I am sure that Newell and Simon do too—that once an hypothesis has been proved bad, it is better to take as much information as possible into account to decide which hypothesis to pursue next, rather than be forced to backtrack to whatever hypothesis happens to have been the last one previously entertained. But this is routinely done in any program that stores these hypotheses and asks for a re-assessment as to which is most likely each time that the likelihood of any particular hypothesis changes.

Conclusions

It's perfectly fine to use loose words, and to use words loosely. It provokes thought and keeps the richness of the ambiguous predicament we are in. But such a situation is the ground from which the weeds of jargon, and undefined and nonexistent distinctions too easily grow. That is, the danger lies more in taking pregnantly vague words and prematurely narrowing them or, even worse, implying that they have taken on a definite meaning without making that meaning absolutely clear.

We have a healthy share of these consequences in Reitman's paper, and in the whole movement of simulation modeling. I would like to re-establish our claims to ignorance. There is nothing more dreary than an argument about the distinctions between two undefined jargon terms. There is nothing sadder than the broadening and crumbling of a previously well-defined term, because it can no longer be defended as it stands, to the point where, for the dubious advantage of having eliminated its lacunae in universality, it has lost all of its meaning and import. Particular definitions of such terms as "behavior," "mechanisms," "rules," and "information processing" seem increasingly slippery when we try to point out exactly what they mean, and don't mean, with a structure as precise, real, and open as a computer program.

On the other hand, the computer program allows us to specify, with complete precision, complex models that certainly embody what we are vaguely pointing to with these words. We can then, as with the concepts "active memory" and "learning" briefly discussed here, study our models to get a better idea of what we have been talking about.

The computer is just a powerful tool for clearly specifying rules that mechanisms must follow in carrying out procedures that process information.

REFERENCES

Uhr, L. Pattern-string learning programs. *Behav. Sci.*, 1964, 9, 258-270.

Uhr, L. (Ed.) *Pattern Recognition.* New York: Wiley, 1966.

Uhr, L. *Pattern Recognition, Concept Formation and Learning.* New York: Wiley, 1967.

GENERAL DISCUSSION

NEWELL observed that with respect to the *active*-memory notion, if awareness is not accepted as a response to a stimulus, then we must assume constant awareness. However, if this is assumed, then there is no real value to the active over the passive notion of recognition memory.

NEWELL also pointed out that the Trotski problem does not require the assumption of an active memory, but instead a discrimination net could handle the problem.

9

CONCERNING PARALLELS BETWEEN ADAPTIVE PROCESSES IN THINKING AND SELF-INSTRUCTION[1]

ERNST Z. ROTHKOPF
Bell Telephone Laboratories, Incorporated

One function of thinking is that it yields products which are stored in memory and which can be characterized as knowledges. I plan to discuss some apparent parallels between thought as a knowledge-producing process and what humans do when they study written instructional discourse. The particular class of activities I shall emphasize is that which I have called mathemagenic behaviors.

Experimental results are described that indicate that the complexity, variety, and persistence of mathemagenic behavior is determined by test-like events and other similar environmental contingencies. It

---

[1] I wrote this paper because Professor Voss asked me to discuss relationships between instruction and thought. It is difficult to write on this topic without constant recourse to guess and speculation. Under these circumstances, caution and modesty, those homely virtues of science, bid one to remain silent. The paper was written in spite of these considerations, because Professor Voss encouraged me not to be unduly impeded by virtue and to speculate freely. I took this as license.

will be argued that thinking is an adaptive process and that the complexity and variety of its products, as well as the persistence of their production, should also be alterable by test-like events. This view has some practical implications for how instructional dialogue shapes thinking, and I plan to pursue these implications to some degree.

Mathemagenic Behavior

The concept of mathemagenic behavior (Rothkopf, 1965) is a weakly defined notion that has been useful in trying to understand how humans learn from written material. It also seems applicable to other learning situations. The roots of this small lexical conceit are Greek. They are the word *mathema*, which means that which is to be learned, and the word *gignesthai*, which means to give birth.

Mathemagenic behaviors are all overt and covert activities of a subject that occur in a given instructional or experimental situation and help to produce the learned consequences of this situation. In other words, mathemagenic behaviors are activities that can give birth to learning. It is not necessary, however, to assume that mathemagenic behaviors have to be consistent with the attainment of instructional objectives. On the contrary, some mathemagenic activities may interfere with instructional objectives or will result in learned performances that are different from what the instructional goals demand.

Mathemagenic behaviors bear some functional resemblance to the interesting concept of epistemic curiosity that has been proposed by Berlyne (1963). However, mathemagenic activities are conceived to be habit-like (Hull, 1943, pp. 102-123) and readily modified by environmental contingencies, while epistemic curiosity has drive-like characters. Some of the activities that have been described as mathemagenic (Rothkopf, 1965) have been referred to as attention, concentration, orientation, inspection behavior, learning set, and so on.

The textbooks of the last three decades often have described the learning process as if it depended almost exclusively on the impact of environmental particles upon the organism. The assumptions underlying mathemagenic behavior differ from this position. It is recognized that the character of the effective stimuli in many learning situations depends critically on some activity of the subject. In a sense, mathemagenic activity can be perceived as the key regulator of the relationship between nominal and effective stimulation. It plays a particularly important role in learning from written material because, in those situations, the gap between nominal and the effective stimuli is wide. The subject must engage in prolonged and skilled activity; namely reading, if desired instructional objectives are to be achieved. However, reading skill; i.e., the ability to translate the alphabetic symbols into speech sounds, is not enough to master the subject matter contained in the book. This fact is very clear from brief observation of a student who is confronted by a difficult and boring textbook.

In learning situations involving written materials, it is expedient to endow mathemagenic behaviors with certain potential functions. These are translation, segmentation, and processing. Each of these functions has topography, including some attention-like characteristics, stimulus controls, and persistence.

Translation involves scanning the page and translating the alphabetic display into the sound of words or their subvocal surrogates. Segmentation refers to activities that break the stimulus string into syntactic and other unit components. The rationale for the segmentation function of mathemagenic behavior is discussed is somewhat greater detail elsewhere (Rothkopf, 1965). Its theoretical need stems from attempts to account for the kind of data about sentence learning with which Thorndike (1931) was trying to deal in his *Law of Belonging*. One way of conceptualizing the segmentation function is to think of it as activities that have their overt vocal accompaniment in speech intonation and pauses.

The third important aspect of mathemagenic behavior is processing. I mean to include here a variety of activities including review, the invention of mnemonic devices, problem solving, as well as other activities that resemble thinking.

The three functions that I have just described do not exhaust all mathemagenic behaviors. On the contrary, they are but a small part of the totality of such behaviors. They have been singled out for discussion here because these functions play a critically important role in determining whether instructional objectives are attained through study of written documents. Actually, the great bulk of mathemagenic behaviors produces learning states that are unrelated or inconsistent with instructional objectives and may be, from the view of the instructor, quite undesirable. Examples of such behaviors are some cases of skipping and page turning, yawning, daydreaming, and doodling in the margins.

Mathemagenic behavior is often observed to deteriorate (from the instructional point of view) during the course of study. Such deterioration bears some resemblance to the phenomena of experimental extinction. In general, mathemagenic activities appear to deteriorate in reverse order from their nearness to the human periphery. First, proc-

essing becomes instructionally ineffective, then segmentation deterio-
rates, and finally the translation and scanning process. Many of you
have, I am sure, observed aspects of the extinction-like deterioration of
mathemagenic behavior. One of the more dramatic forms is finding that
one has reached the bottom of a printed page without having "read"
anything.

The study of mathemagenic behavior is handicapped to some degree by crude experimental methods. Adequate measurement of visual
scanning during prolonged reading is difficult with available instrumentation. Some observations of eye movements have been made, but
there are many difficulties. However, there is some hope that new and
more sophisticated observational techniques which are now being
evolved will provide better understanding of the scanning and translation process. Physiological measures such as blood volume also may
turn out to be a workable indicator of attention-like states. But little
progress has been made in applying physiological techniques to the
study of mathemagenic activities.

We sometimes have used inspection time as a measure. But, in the
main, we have restricted ourselves to measurement of the consequences
of mathemagenic behavior; i.e., of what has been learned. This is an
unusually crude measure. It permits one to infer only two stages for the
mathemagenic behavior that has taken place. These are: (a) that they
were consistent with the test objectives, or (b) that they were not consistent with the test objectives. This outcome is inconvenient. We are,
however, beginning to make a little progress on new techniques for
measuring mathemagenic activity.

In summary then, mathemagenic behaviors are covert activities that
are studied through physiological correlates and behavioral consequences. They influence what is learned by determining the effective
stimulation that produces learning.

A View on Thought

The ghostly concept of "thought" has haunted experimental psychology throughout its short and disappointing history. Neither the
bold sallies of behaviorism nor the "new" theory of meaning of the
Vienna Circle has exorcised this specter. The present text testifies to
the fact that interest in "thought" processes is, if anything, on the
upswing today.

The undiminished vitality of interest in "thought" is undoubtedly
largely due to the universality and vividness of conscious thinking in

human experience. Thought plays the center ring for all of us, and many are reluctant to deny such a salient aspect of private experience the public status of a scientific construct.

In the contemporary dialogue about thought, there seems to be an emerging consensus that thought processes can be analyzed into components. The components include some kind of display, some transactions, and some products.

The displays are generally thought of as two kinds: (a) those that are the immediate consequences of environmental stimulation, and (b) those from memory. Memory content can be separated further into (1) some vicarious, partial, and not necessary faithful representation of the world; and (2) routines for processing direct external stimulation and memory displays. The transactions that are performed with or through the displays yield, according to this view, some kinds of results that are at times stored in memory, or perhaps only sometimes storable. The great bulk of results are discarded. In any case, some of the consequences of these mental transactions are retained in memory and/or result in some overt act. The parallel with a computer memory that holds both data and stored program is obvious, and it is clear that knowledge about the internal plumbing of digital computers have shaped these conceptions to some degree. I find this ironic because, in the recent past, those concerned with the explication of thought processes usually have been identified with the humanistic wing of the psychological parliament. Those who denied "thought" a place in their psychologies were often labeled mechanistic. Yet the recent renaissance of interest in thought and the conception described above, very likely received its strongest stimulation from the ascent of a machine—the digital computer.

It is very unlikely that the model described above can be experimentally tested in any detail. But the gross end products of thought are observable. I shall concern myself mainly with these consequences of thought that are retained in memory and can be characterized as knowledges.

One model of thought that considers the genesis of such knowledge was proposed by Campbell (1960). He calls it the blind-variation-selective-retention model. Campbell's conception of thought posits that thought can generate more knowledge; i.e., that learning is a sometime consequence of thinking. Basically, Campbell's position (Campbell, 1960, p. 380) is that "a blind-variation-and-selective-retention process is fundamental to all achievements, to all genuine increases in knowledge, and to all increases in fit of system to environment. The many processes that shortcut a more full blind-variation-and-selective-retention process are in themselves inductive achievements containing wisdom about the environment achieved originally by blind-variation-and-selective-retention." The model for creative thought involves persistent blind variation at (probably) the display and certainly at the transactional level. The author implies that blind variation resembles overt "trial-and-error" activities in problem solving. Some results of the blind-variation process are retained and stored. This happens because they meet some environmental demand.

Inductive or creative thought, as seen here, resembles the model of natural selection that has been proposed for organic evolution. Whether the results from the blind-variation process are discarded or retained has been to some degree determined by the environment and, therefore, the retained results of thinking tend to approximate relationships among the entities in the world that surrounds the thinker. This is a very interesting general conception although, perhaps, unduly restricted in scope by Campbell's insistence on blind variation as the basic source for transactions.[2]

In summary, under certain circumstances, unobservable thinking events take place. These tend to result in behaviors that occur either immediately, or are learned and can occur later. The behaviors that result from these processes are different in some distinguishable way from what was previously in the thinker's repertoire. Such behaviors, therefore, become ipso facto evidence that thinking has occurred. Thought-generated behaviors also tend to approximate the satisfaction of some environmental demand on the thinker.

Mathemagenic Behavior and Thought

The concept of mathemagenic behavior and the conception of thought that I have described are at present unduly plastic. This does not please me but cannot really be helped at this time. It seems clear,

---

[2] "Blindness" in variations has three properties according to Campbell. These are: (1) the variation emitted be independent of the environmental conditions of the occasion of their occurrence; (2) the occurrence of trials individually be uncorrelated with the solution, in that specific correct trials are no more likely to occur at any one point in a series of trials than another nor are they more likely to occur than specific incorrect trials; (3) variations evolved on successive trials be independent, at least in the sense that a variation subsequent to an incorrect trial is not a correction of a previous trial, and does not make use of the direction of error of the previous trial. These requirements appear to exclude partial knowledge systems, calculations, and the like. In fairness to Campbell, it must be said that he was addressing himself primarily to the "Eureka" phenomenon.

however, that there are some commonalities between the two constructions. Both result in learning. Mathemagenic behavior tends to be oriented towards external environmental displays, while thought tends to be more inwardly oriented. Further, the processing component of mathemagenic activities appears to involve thought-like elements. It does not seem unduly venturesome to assume that, at times, thinking does take place while a subject is confronted with written instructional material, and that such thinking results in learning. It can be argued, as a matter of fact, that some kind of thought-like transactions are a critical element in effective mathemagenic behavior.

What I would really like to tentatively propose, is that some thought processes are very much like some mathemagenic behaviors in the presence of written material. The function of instructionally useful mathemagenic behavior is to convert environmental events such as printed pages into effective stimuli. The instructionally useful objective of some thinking activities is mainly to convert internal events such as items from memory into effective form. What I am proposing is that such thought has topography, rate, and persistence, and that, in general, the factors which have been found to modify mathemagenic behavior also will shape thought process. This is, admittedly, quite speculative. But it may be possible to explore this speculation experimentally by finding out whether measureable consequences of thought, such as new knowledge, are affected by some of the variables that affect mathemagenic behavior.

Some Factors That Shape Mathemagenic Behavior

It can be demonstrated that mathemagenic behavior has some lability and can be modified by environmental events. These modifications are, in a sense, adaptive, and the conception that we have of this process bears a marked resemblance to the variation-and-selective-retention notion which Campbell proposed for "thought."

Our work during the last four years at the Bell Telephone Laboratories has permitted us to gain some understanding of the way in which mathemagenic behavior becomes adaptive. I will describe to you studies of the effects of test-like events, such as questions, on the shaping of mathemagenic behavior. Questions and similar test-like events are particularly interesting because they are an important form of instructional intercourse. Our work has been aimed at understanding how questions determine both the characteristics and persistence of mathemagenic behavior. As part of this work, we have discovered the fact that mathe-

magenic behavior, because it is adaptive, can at times result in undesirable kinds of learning, or frustrate the attainment of instructional
objectives. In the main, however, the adaptive character of mathemagenic behavior serves the student well.

The general experimental situation is as follows: We are interested
in the effects of questions on mathemagenic activities while confronted
with written instructional material. Mathemagenic behavior is measured by finding out how much the subject has learned. This is done by
administering a test after the completion of study. In effect, we attempt
to measure the effect of test-like events during study on post-study test
performance.

One of the technical problems in this general approach is that questions and similar test-like events have a direct instructive or communicative effect (e.g., Estes, Hopkins, and Crothers, 1960; Levine, Leitenberg, and Richter, 1964). That is, questions are practice-like events, a
fact that users of the anticipation method have put to work in their
experimental studies of rote-learning phenomena. The direct informative effect of questions must be eliminated from the experiment before
inferences about mathemagenic shaping can be made. Consequently,
it is necessary to devise methods by which the direct instructive effect
of questions is neutralized. This was done in the following way: the
experimental materials were long prose passages such as two chapters
from Rachel Carson's book, *The Sea Around Us*.[3] The materials had
strong factual content and were chosen so as to be topically uniform
but of weak sequential structure. As illustrated in Fig. 9-1, a large pool
of short-answer questions was made up for the passage. This pool was
divided into two subsets, A and B, such that there was no direct transfer of training between the knowledges supporting correct performance
on questions of the two subsets. This meant that a subject who could
respond correctly to all questions in subset A might only perform at
chance level on subset B. This relationship was experimentally verified,
and questions in subset A were then used as experimental questions
during study, while questions in subset B were used as the post-training performance test.

Using this technique, we found several interesting facts about how
to produce mathemagenic behaviors that are consistent with high-cri-
terion test performance. First of all, short-answer questions shape the
topography of the mathemagenic activities. This shaping can result in

---

[3] Permission for the experimental use of these copyrighted materials was kindly
granted by the publishers, Oxford University Press, 417 Fifth Avenue, New York,
New York, 10016.

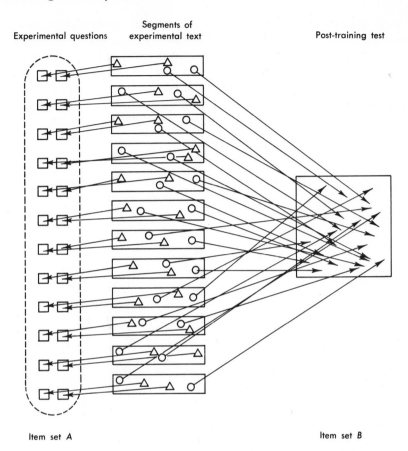

Experimental questions
Segments of experimental text
Post-training test

Item set A

Item set B

Figure 9-1. Scheme for selecting experimental questions. For questions are selected from each of twelve three-page sections of text. Two of these four are assigned to the experimental questions pool (Item set A), while the other two are incorporated into the post-training test (Item set B). The selection is made so as to assure that there was no direct transfer of training between the knowledges underlying set A and those underlying set B.

general facilitation of learning. This was shown by the following experiment (Rothkopf, 1966). Subjects were exposed to a long prose passage. At the end of each three-page segment two written questions were asked of the subjects. The two major experimental treatments differed in whether the questions they saw were relevant to (a) a text segment that they were *about* to read, or (b) a text segment that they had *just* read. A control group was used that saw no questions at all. Treat-

ments were compared on two post-training tests. One of these measured the mathemagenic effects of questions; i.e., whether questions produced study behaviors that were consistent with training objectives.
The second measured the direct instructive effect of questions. (For
further detail see Rothkopf, 1966.) The results are shown in Fig. 9-2.
The data in the left panel indicate that questions administered *after*
the relevant text segments shaped mathemagenic behavior consistent

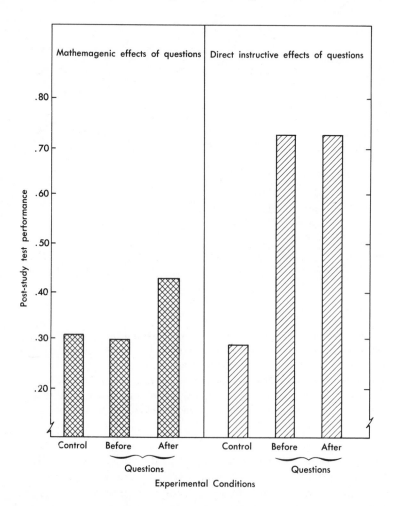

Figure 9-2. Mathemagenic and direct instructive effects of questions administered during reading. Direct instructive effects were
measured by readministering the experimental questions following the
retention test.

with training objectives, while questions administered before the relevant text segment produced about the same results as no questions at all. The two treatments did not differ as far as the direct instructive effect of the question was concerned (see the right panel of Fig. 9-2).

In another experiment (Rothkopf and Bisbicos, 1967), the effect of biasing the questions seen by the subjects during study was investigated. Can biasing the experimental questions shape mathemagenic activity that facilitates test performance on those specific classes of knowledge which reflect the question bias? For example, if the experimental questions uniformly require quantitative answers or proper names, is more knowledge about quantities and names acquired during the course of study? The answer appears to be Yes. The experimental technique was similar to that used in the earlier study. The following procedures were used: High school students $(N = 252)$ were exposed to a 36-page written passage. For each three-page segment, they were asked two questions. Three students saw these questions immediately before seeing each segment and three students immediately after. Some students only saw questions requiring either a measured quantity (a distance, date) or a name for an answer $(SBMN, SAMN)$. Some saw only questions requiring either a common English word or a technical word (e.g., bathyscaphe, photophic) $(SBCT, SACT)$. Others saw a mixture of all question types $(SBMX, SAMX)$. Learning of various categories of text content was measured on a post-training retention test. The results are shown in Fig. 9-3. The right-hand panel is particularly relevant. It indicates that quantitative and name questions on the retention test were answered correctly more often by subjects who had been exposed to this class of questions during study, provided the questions were presented *after* the relevant text segment. These were subjects in the $SAMN$ condition, who saw *only* quantitative and name questions, and those in the $SAMX$ condition who saw a mixture of questions which included quantitative and name questions. This finding occurred without apparent deterioration in the learning of other classes of material within the text.

It should be noted that these results do not lend themselves readily to glib interpretations such as: "Well, you told the subject what you wanted of him and he looked for that kind of information." The experimental effect that I have just described was only obtained when questions *followed* the relevant text segment. As Fig. 9-3 indicates, it was not observed when questions preceded the portions of the text from which they were drawn; i.e., the $SBMN$ and the $SBMX$ treatments. This is, of course, consistent with the findings of the experiment described earlier (Rothkopf, 1966).

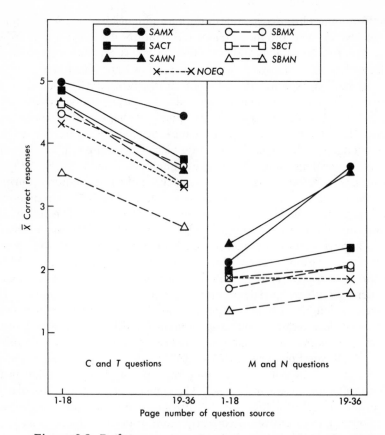

Figure 9-3. Performance on retention test questions of various kinds derived from the first and second half of the instructive text. The treatment designations indicate whether experimental questions are administered shortly before (*SB*) or shortly after (*SA*) the relevant text segment. The suffix *CT* means that only questions requiring common-word (*C*) or technical-word (*T*) answers were required. The suffix (*MN*) indicates that only questions requiring measures (*M*) or *name* (*N*) answers were used. The suffix *MX* means a mixture of the four answer types. The treatment designation *NOEQ* means no experimental questions; i.e., a control group.

The effects of questions on mathemagenic behavior persist for some time after the practice of questioning the subject while reading was halted. However, continued study following the cessation of questions was accompanied by a gradual but fairly rapid deterioration of mathemagenic activities. This was observed in an unpublished study by Bisbicos and myself. Subjects, reading a 36-page experimental text, saw

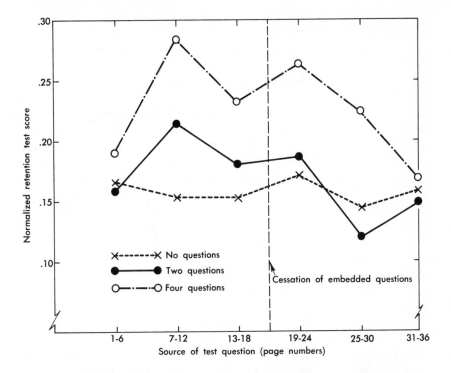

Figure 9-4. Persistence of effective mathemagenic behavior during reading after the cessation of experimental questions embedded in the text. The retention test scores were adjusted to reflect differences in item difficulty.

either two or four questions after each three-page segment. After eighteen pages, this practice was halted and subjects proceeded just as in the control group that had no questions. Retention test performance on items from various text locations is shown in Fig. 9-4. The effects on the four-question group persisted somewhat longer than on the two-question group, although both were at nearly the same level as the control group at the end of the experimental passage. This deterioration of mathemagenic activity was accompanied by decreases in inspection time per page, an effect that we have frequently observed to be associated with deterioration of mathemagenic behavior.

While our results do not exclude other interpretations, they are very nicely fitted by a selective adaptation model. The subjects engage in an unknown variety of mathemagenic activities during study. If performance on the interposed experimental questions is satisfactory, similar mathemagenic behaviors will tend to take place again during the study of the next segment of the written instructional text. If performance on the interposed experimental questions is not satisfactory, mathemagenic behavior is likely to be modified, and this process is likely to continue until mathemagenic behaviors have evolved that produce the knowledges that are required to support satisfactory performance on the experimental question.

Although we hope to refine our experimental procedure to some degree, our results are encouraging. We have been able to show that questions can affect studying behavior so as to increase learning, and also that questions determine to some degree what is learned. Questions also have been found to increase the persistence of studying behavior. We do not know the limits of these experimental manipulations. As a matter of fact, our experiments provide little more than a series of existential proofs. But our experimental manipulations affect fairly complicated activities, some of which have decidedly thought-like components. It is encouraging to note that these experimental manipulations; i.e., composition and arrangement of test-like events, can be readily carried out in many different instructional situations and circumstances.

I do not wish to leave the impression that the use of questions in instruction necessarily has educationally desirable consequences. It has been proposed here that inquiry and thought are adaptive mechanisms that are shaped by questions or the consequences of questions. This does not imply, however, that the knowledges that result from inquiry and thought will necessarily be useful in contexts other than the questioning situation. It seems to me that this is a general point that it is worthwhile to make. The way in which we have conceptualized the usefulness of questions in instruction is based on the assumption that inquiry and thought processes are modified until their products (knowledges) satisfy the demands of the questions. The stability and peculiar characteristic of inquiry and thought processes that are evoked in some particular instructional situation depend, in part, on the homogeneity or stereotypy of questions within some psychologically meaningful dimension. Stereotypy may be there by design, as in the experimental situations previously described. The stereotypy may, however, result from the fact that teacher or textbook writer, for unknown and perhaps unconscious reasons, was a biased question source. There is need for caution here. The instructor should not treat questions to students in a cavalier manner because, in some case, the stereotypy or bias of questions has undesirable educational effects. This finding has been observed in connection with experiments on the effect of the presentation-test interval in learning equivalences from Gruanda (see Rothkopf, 1963a; Rothkopf and Coke, 1963; 1966) materials. In these experiments, it repeatedly was found that post-training performance was depressed if a test-like event followed immediately after the initial presentation of information throughout training, and if the demanded responses belonged to a highly predictable conceptual category. We interpreted this finding to mean that subjects, in fact, learn to make their responses to the test-like events in the training series from the resources of short-term memory. This has as its consequence that subjects do not learn to form the associations that are, within this experimental context, educationally relevant. The resources of short-term memory are, in a sense, enough to satisfy the demands of the test-like events that are administered during training. When subjects are tested after training and under conditions when short-term memory can no longer support performance, their performance is found to be weaker than that of subjects who are tested during training under conditions where short-term memory provides little useful support for performance.

Implications of the Experimental Findings

The results reported in the preceding pages have been based on experimental studies of learning from written materials. We sampled the knowledges that subjects acquired by reading, and tried to find out how the quantity and variety of acquired knowledge was influenced by the questions that we asked the subjects. This experimental paradigm can also be applied to the study of how knowledge is generated by thought and other complex processes. What differs mainly is the task which is set for the subject. The experimental facts that have been obtained in studies of learning from written material therefore allow some speculation about the shaping of thought-like activities both in experimental situations and in broader instructional context.

The first salient fact is that the questioning maneuvers support the persistence of mathemagenic activities. The interesting question is, of course, whether thinking activities that are not so heavily loaded with search-and-translation factors will also be affected by test-like events. It should be noted that Campbell's conceptual scheme for creative thought may, in a certain sense, include a search-and-translation component, since "blind variation" suggests some search activity to me. In any case, it seems clear that any procedure that promises to increase the persistence of thinking and problem-solving activity, perhaps in the face of failure and adversity, would merit systematic study.

The second fact is that there are some factors that result in the deterioration or extinction of mathemagenic activities. It is not clear what these factors are, but we do know that test-like events counteract them to some degree. It does not seem unreasonable to generalize these findings to thinking activities. We commonly speak about degree of persistence in problem solving. It would be interesting to understand how the extinction-like factor in these activities is related to the least-effort principle, and in what ways persistence is related to the character of the experimental task.

The most intriguing finding about the result of questioning is that in some way the character of the questions tends to shape the character of the knowledges that are acquired. This finding is not as obvious as it appears at first glance. The zero-transfer rule, which was imposed in all of the experiments that I have reported so far, should be recalled. In our experiments, the questions shaped knowledges that were related only in a remote and peripheral way to the subject-matter content of the question. It would certainly seem profitable to inquire whether similar relationships between questions and acquired knowledge can be demonstrated for those tasks which require extensive thought-like activities.

The finding that the character of questions determines to some degree what knowledges are acquired, suggests that the character of questions to which students are currently exposed will determine what their thinking will produce. Perhaps, Thorndike (1924) and others should have asked another question in connection with their work on the theory of formal discipline. The main direction of their inquiry was to find out whether Latin and various other academic subjects affected performance on an intelligence test that was administered at the end of the year. This is a common scheme for instructional research. The question that is asked is how earlier training affects later performance. Our findings suggest that a promising line of inquiry may be an investigation of how progress in subject matter *A* is affected by *concurrent* instruction in subject matter *B*, even if subject matter *A* and *B* are relatively unrelated. For example, how do the kind of direct questions to which students are subjected in an English course affect what they learn from a psychology course during that same semester?

It seems fairly clear that test-like events, when they occur in conjunction with other practice events, have a peculiarly potent forcing function. In the psychological economy of students (and for good cause, I suspect, particularly middle-class students), the complexity of the processes of search, inquiry, and thought that lead to learning are determined to some important degree by the test-like events which occur during training. The explanation of this process proposed in this paper is that mathemagenic activities and thought are adaptive processes. Therefore their products reflect utility in some sense, both in terms of environmental contingencies and in terms of cost to the subject.

Questions are the major form of dialogue in instruction. There appears to be substantial evidence that the frequency, timing, and character of questions and other test-like events shape the nature of the student's methods of inquiry and thought in a practically important sense. The character of the stimulus control of these processing activities and their lability is largely terra incognita. Psychological folklore, that Hydra of 1000 predictions, however, seems to favor the view that man can alter his methods of inquiry and thought with very little disturbance as he switches from book to book, from subject to subject, and from task to task. I personally have some serious doubts.

Finally, our findings as well as those of others (e.g., Keislar, 1960) about the shaping of mathemagenic behaviors by questions, suggests a caution for researchers who investigate thought-like processes by interrogating subjects. Something like a psychological Heisenberg principle may be operating here. The questions and other test-like activities that are used to prepare protocols of problem-solving activities, or to make inferences about thought, likely modify the very activities that are being studied.

Summary

I have tried to point out some similarities between thought and the psychological processes that take place during self-instruction and study. Both classes of events result in some products that are either discarded or retained according to a selective process that is adaptive to the demands of the environment. The retained results of thought and study are changes in the organization of behavior that I have simply called knowledge. In instructional situations, questions become an important feature of the environment against which the results of thought and study processes are tested. Mode of questioning during instruction therefore tends to shape the character and persistence of the thought and study processes that produce knowledge.

REFERENCES

Berlyne, D. E. Motivational problems raised by exploratory and epistemic behavior. In S. Koch (Ed.), *Psychology: a study of a science.* Vol. 5. New York: McGraw-Hill, 1963.

Campbell, D. T. Blind variation and selective retention in creative thought as in other knowledges processes. *Psychol. Rev.*, 1960, *67*, 380-400.

Estes, W. K., Hopkins, B. L., and Crothers, E. J. All-or-none and conservation effects in the learning and retention of paired associates. *J. exp. Psychol.*, 1960, *60*, 329-339.

Hull, C. L. *Principles of Behavior.* New York: Appleton-Century-Crofts, 1943.

Keislar, E. R. A descriptive approach to classroom motivation. *J. Teach. Educ.*, 1960, *11*, 310-315.

Levine, M., Leitenberg, H., and Richter, M. The blank trials law. The equivalence of positive reinforcement and nonreinforcement. *Psychol. Rev.*, 1964, *71*, 94-103.

Rothkopf, E. Z. Learning from written sentences: within-sentence order in the acquisition of name-clause equivalences. *J. verb. Learn. verb. Behav.*, 1963, *2*, 470-475. (a)

Rothkopf, E. Z. Some conjectures about inspection behavior in learning from written sentences and the response mode problem in programmed self-instruction. *J. program. Instruc.*, 1963, *2*, 31-46. (b)

Rothkopf, E. Z. Some theoretical and experimental approaches to problems in written instruction. In J. D. Krumboltz (Ed.), *Learning and the Educational Process.* Chicago: Rand McNally, 1965. Pp. 193-221.

Rothkopf, E. Z. Learning from written materials: an exploration of the control of inspection behavior by test-like events. *Amer. educ. Res. J.*, 1966, *3*, 241-249.

Rothkopf, E. Z., and Coke, E. U. Repetition interval and rehearsal method in learning equivalences from written sentences. *J. verb. Learn. verb. Behav.*, 1963, *2*, 406-416.

Rothkopf, E. Z., and Coke, E. U. Variations in phrasing, repetition interval and recall of sentence material. *J. verb. Learn. verb. Behav.*, 1966, *5*, 86-91.

Rothlopf, E. Z., and Bisbicos, E. Selective facilitative effects of interspersed questions on learning from written material. *J. educ. Psychol.*, 1967, *58*, 56-61.

Rothkopf, E. Z., and Bisbicos, E. Persistence of adaptive inspection behavior and frequency of interspersed questions in learning from written material, in preparation.

Thorndike, E. L. Mental discipline in high school studies. *J. educ. Psychol.*, 1924, *15*, 1-22, 83-98.

INNOVATION WITHOUT ANALYSIS

RICHARD C. ATKINSON
Stanford University

My remarks on Rothkopf's paper are going to be brief. First, let me say that I find his program of experimental research to be extremely interesting and one that deserves serious attention. There is no doubt that a major portion of those activities in our society that are typically classified under the general title of "learning" involve the act of reading. Thus, it is surprising that learning theorists have paid so little attention to the reading process or to an examination of experimental variables that might influence it. Rothkopf's paper offers a novel attempt to characterize the reading process. More important, it outlines a set of experimental manipulations that look extremely promising for future research. I was particularly impressed with the results which indicate that post-training performance is depressed when a test-like event follows immediately after the initial presentation of information during training, as compared with a delayed presentation. This result ties in very nicely with much current theorizing about memory, and the observation that successful retrieval from long-term memory has a more pronounced effect on later performance than successful retrieval from short-term memory. If substantial bodies of experimental data of this type can be developed, they undoubtedly will play a central role in future theorizing about information processing in the human organism. I think that it is probably too early to judge the merits of the specific experiments that Rothkopf has reported, but I applaud his efforts, which, from my view, are quite innovative. Even if the research turns out to have only minor implications for psychological theory, the work still will be worthwhile for it has clear, practical applications in the area of instruction.

Obviously, what Rothkopf has called mathemagenic behaviors is very close to those behaviors that most of us have in mind when we talk about thought. In fact, for the sake of argument I, for one, would be willing to defend the position that the thought process and mathemagenic behavior are one and the same, except that the latter is a process operating in part on environmental stimuli, whereas the former operates on memory images. However, to pursue such an argument we would have to be more specific about what we mean by mathemagenic behavior. It is true that Rothkopf has made some general theoretical remarks about mathemagenic behaviors that include a categorization system of translation, segmentation, and processing. His remarks are interesting, but they do not represent a substantial theoretical effort. In fact, the shortcoming of Rothkopf's paper is that although it alludes to a theory, there is no substantial theoretical analysis. Certainly, not a theory that could be used to characterize the types of experimental results that he reports, let alone a theory that could be used to generate predictions for such behavior. In a certain sense, this is not a criticism, for no one has made substantial progress in this direction, but it is important to keep in mind that vague reminiscences of this sort do not take us closer to a theory of the thought process.

Let me summarize my remarks as follows: Rothkopf's paper describes some interesting experimental work on information-processing activities that is clearly part and parcel of what we mean by the thought process, and this work could well turn out to be extremely important in laying the foundations for a general theory of thought. My major criticism is that the paper appears to offer a theoretical framework in which to view this experimental work when, in fact, the ideas are extremely vague and will require much sharpening and further analysis to be useful.

GENERAL DISCUSSION

ROTHKOPF was asked how he could analyze his task into stages. He replied that they tried to use pauses in reading, in order to delimit such segmentation, but that their results did not indicate that pause frequency was a sensitive variable. In response to another question, ROTH-KOPF indicated that asking subjects to outline paragraphs in order to force segmentation would not be fruitful because segmentation likely is limited to smaller units than a paragraph.

ROTHKOPF was asked whether eye fixation is correlated with syntactic breaks. He replied that recording eye movements over long periods of time involves a problem of instrumentation. He did indicate, however, that he has evidence which suggests that segmentation may break down after one-half, thus making time an important variable.

In reply to another question, ROTHKOPF indicated that in short-term delay studies, new material continues to appear between the critical sentence and the question. He also said that studies involving variation in type of question have not yet been conducted.

CONFERENCE COMMENTS

10

CONCERNING THE TEACHING OF THINKING

ROBERT GLASER

University of Pittsburgh

A science of behavior should, among other things, tell us how to teach people to go from unskilled thinkers to skilled thinkers. This involves the development of a behaviorally based technology of education. The development of such a learning technology requires the application of psychological knowledge about thinking, and also the sensitivity of psychologists to the kind of knowledge required for a technology of behavioral change. An attitude of behavioral change in the minds of experimental psychologists can serve to give their observations and descriptions of learning phenomena a predisposition toward a learning technology. This technology can, in turn, provide both a proving ground and a nurturing place for the further elaboration and refinement of learning theory. Psychologists should, to my way of thinking, become excited about changing behavior through instruction, like Restle in his interest in producing perfect transfer in his subjects by directing attention and by managing distractions, and like Jenkins in his concern about the inability to change the behavior of the children in his laboratory.

The development of a technology of learning and education requires something like the following operational schema: (a) analysis of

323

the skilled performance or competence to be taught; (b) specification of the initial, pre-learning state of the organism; and (c) environmental structuring to allow the learner to get from unskilled performance to skilled performance. Each of these can be examined a bit more closely.

Analysis of Skilled Performance

Psychologists have rarely undertaken to precisely describe complex behavior of the kind relevant to educational concerns. In contrast, they have, for the most part, devised special laboratory tasks, and developed theoretical descriptions and experimental approaches based upon relatively simple situations. As a result, there is very little well-developed methodology in experimental psychology for looking at complex behavior as it is given to the psychologist to study (Glaser, 1964). For example, concept-learning experiments rarely deal with the learning of complex subject-matter concepts. When one reviews the psychological studies of concept learning as they are relevant to the teaching of concepts, it is found that the work to date is applicable to a narrow domain of subject matter, and that there is a lack of analyses of a wide variety of conceptual tasks (Glaser, 1967). Some help in the analyses of complex tasks is forthcoming from the work of such people as Piaget, Chomsky, and Simon and Newell, but these are only beginnings. We need to know the nature of skilled performance so that we can be specific about how people learn to attain this performance.

Description of the Initial State of the Learner

It seems irrational to think about behavioral change without initially characterizing the baseline behavioral repertoires from which the change must proceed. A major problem in this regard is the resistence of most theories and formal models of behavior to incorporate parameters of the pre-learning state of the organism and individual difference parameters among organisms. Some help is available here from the methodology of operant conditioning with its procedures for determining base-rate levels of responding, and from recent information-processing approaches like the work of Gregg (1967) in which he describes the different series of information-processing acts and the various alternative representations of a concept that different individuals employ in attaining proficiency in the same conceptual task. In general, current mathematical learning-theory models such as described in

Atkinson, Bower, and Crothers (1965) are less amenable to individual difference and initial-state variables than are information-processing models. For a review of the psychological literature on the problem of learning theory and individual-difference phenomena see Glaser, (1967). For the purpose of learning technology, research in thinking needs to study the interaction between environmental variables and the long-term and short-term response histories of the learner.

Environmental Structuring

In structuring an environment to produce behavioral change, some help is forthcoming from several areas involved in the experimental study of learning. A prominent characteristic of learning in general, and learning to think in particular, is the increasing precision of the subject's performance as he becomes more skillful. In learning complex behavior, initial performance is variable and crude and rarely meets the criteria of skilled competence. Establishing increasingly skilled performance is accomplished by gradually contracting performance tolerances over the course of learning. If competence criteria are available which define skillful thinking in some subject-matter domain, then such skillful performance might be successively approximated by the frequent matching of current skill with the skill to be obtained and by adjusting performance tolerances accordingly. In this regard, work on the control of operant response shaping is of particular interest.

In addition to the increasing precision of response, skillful performance is also characterized by a high degree of stimulus control over these precise responses by appropriate subject-matter components. The pertinent task in teaching is the restructuring of the students' old learning. This involves not only differentiating out and increasing the precision of new forms of response, but also transferring stimulus control so that skillful responses can be employed in response to new stimulus patterns. The transfer of stimulus control seems to be a major process in teaching students to use previously learned skills in response to new stimuli. Conditioning studies should give some help here since they have been involved in attempting to understand this process.

A fundamental characteristic of skilled performance, especially relevant to thinking, is that this performance is self-sustaining and apparently not very dependent on overt environmental control. A skillful thinker may continue to work on a problem for long periods of time without seeming external support and without support from the aids and references that are needed by the novice. This seems to be what

Holland is getting at when he looks at how to use overt behavior to influence and produce covert behavior. The research task in investigating the teaching of thinking is to discover how to use overt environmental manipulations to influence covert behavior, and how to make unskilled overt behavior become increasingly covert and efficient.

Other Considerations

Battig's statement that traditional, typical serial-learning experiments have been conducted under conditions which maximally discourage thinking by the subjects or its detection by the experimenter is to be taken very seriously in the context of my remarks. Battig points to the effect of instructions and experimenter-imposed restrictions which inhibit thinking. This characteristic of most verbal-learning experiments is symptomatic of a deeper neglect referred to earlier, which is the general disregard of the initial state of the subject—disregard of such aspects as the effect of experimental instructions, knowledge of the objectives of the experimental task, available problem-solving heuristics, etc. The neglect of these sorts of pre-learning variables which are characteristic of the learner must certainly obscure their interaction with significant environmental variables. Related to this is the general nonadaptiveness of the traditional psychological experiment. Learning conditions are kept quite rigid so that the experimenter can study the learning process under conventionally accepted conditions. This rigidity (and the frequent necessity to lengthen the acquisition curve by a procedure which results in slow learning so that the learning process can be investigated) presents, in many experiments, a situation in which learning and acquisition is actively prevented and delayed. In contrast, a concern with teaching requires the elimination of an unresponsive learning situation which involves appropriate rigidity for certain kinds of experimental study, but does not attempt to design an environment in order to elicit the behavior to be taught. For the study of the teaching of thinking and for the development of a learning technology in general, a different strategy is required. One kind of experimental investigation which seems most appropriate is measurement of the properties of short-response histories on the basis of which the next learning trial is prescribed in order to optimize learning with respect to a specified criterion.

The observation made by Melton that there is a consistent finding of a lack of transfer in verbal-learning studies is disconcerting because transfer is probably the key dependent variable in education. I would encourage studies concerned with the maximizing of transfer. I believe also that it is regrettable that there is not more concern with the influence of environmental contingencies on learning—the kind of environmental contingencies employed in Rothkopf's attempts to shape mathemagenic behavior and in Holland's concern with using overt behavioral contingencies to shape covert behavior, and that might be operating in Newell's observation that one individual took twenty minutes and another a much shorter time to think through a problem.

A variable that is mentioned a number of times in this text is response latency. In recent literature, the study of response time has become increasingly popular. It is becoming a less difficult variable to measure nowadays, especially with computer-controlled experimentation. Latency may be of special significance in the study of thinking, but so little is known about response latency that many studies are required to find out its parametric properties; i.e., how it is influenced by task properties and individual differences, and how it changes over the course of learning and at learning asymptotes. Changes in response latency as a function of learning raise many interesting questions: What is the nature of the function relating latency to practice early in learning? Do latencies remain constant, or is there a steady increase in response time up to the point at which learning takes place? Do correct response latencies differ from incorrect response latencies during certain stages of learning? Is latency a function of learning rate; i.e., do the more difficult items have longer latencies, and are slow learners also slow responders? Is it a consistent finding, as a few studies report, that a subject's last incorrect response to an item may be exceptionally long before a run of correct responses. Is the first correct response to an item slower if a subject makes subsequent errors on that item? To what extent are latencies related to or indicative of implicit information-processing activities?

Finally, these remarks have been an attempt to ask that psychologists consider what we know in terms of what it means for changing behavior in an educational sense. The experimental study of thinking can become applicable to the teaching of thinking if it undertakes to do the following: analyze the nature of competence in different thinking tasks, carry out experimental studies which are adaptive to response histories, not neglect individual difference-learning process interactions, and develop strong theories of reasonably complex behavior. Such knowledge of thinking should enable us to bring about behavioral change, and as a result, contribute to the education of skilled thinkers.

REFERENCES

Atkinson, R. C., Bower, G. H., and Crothers, E. J. *An introduction to mathematical learning theory.* New York: Wiley, 1965.

Glaser, R. Implications of training research for education. In E. R. Hilgard (Ed.), Theories of Learning and Instruction. *Yearb. nat. Soc. Stud. Educ.*, 1964, *63*, Part I.

Glaser, R. Concept learning and concept teaching. In R. Gagné (Ed.), *Research approaches to school-subject learning.* Itasca, Illinois: Peacock Publishers, 1968.

Glaser, R. Implications of previous work on learning and individual differences. In R. Gagné (Ed.), *Learning and individual differences.* Columbus, Ohio: Merrill, 1967.

Gregg, L. W. Internal representations of sequential concepts. In B. Kleinmuntz (Ed.), *Concepts and the structure of memory.* New York: Wiley, 1967. Pp. 107-142.

11

ADAPTING TO THE NEED TO UNDERSTAND THOUGHT

HERBERT A. SIMON
Carnegie-Mellon University

These comments will avoid or evade the personal methodological problems with which Holland and Bourne are wrestling, and which they feel obliged to resolve. Nor will the comments say much about the rather general models or conceptual schemes considered by Reitman and Jenkins. As a reflection on my own preference, they will be chiefly concerned with the remaining papers—those that receive the closest and most frequent guidance from data.

Some question was raised as to whether we did not all mean different things by "information processing," and whether we should not, therefore, abandon the term. Closer examination of the papers—in particular, Battig's, Haber's, Restle's, and Voss's—does not support these doubts. All these authors are engaged in essentially the same undertaking. Like their fellows in other sciences, they are interested in explaining the phenomena by discovering and testing an underlying system of processes that is capable of producing these phenomena. In cognition, the processes have to do with operations on "symbols" or "patterns." They involve mechanisms that input patterns into the system, store patterns in various kinds of memories, output patterns, perform matching operations to determine whether two patterns are the same or different, copy patterns, and so on. These are the basic information-processing mechanisms, and they turn up—essentially the same ones—whenever and wherever human cognitive processes are studied.

There is a particular kind of difficulty evident in these studies that arises in all research on thinking; indeed, in all research on systems that are adaptive. (For thinking is one of the main processes the human organism uses to bring about its continual adaptation to its environment.) An adaptive system is an elusive object of study. When you pour water into a bowl, it takes on the shape of the bowl. If you then freeze it to retain that shape, you are learning in a way about the properties of the bowl, but not much about water. Thinking (perhaps it should be called "thoughtful behavior") adapts itself to the shape of its task environment much as water adapts itself to a container.

As Restle observed, in research on thinking we are always in danger of building a theory of problem environments—of problem-solving tasks—rather than a theory of human psychological mechanisms and processes. Because thought is adaptive, this is a very real danger, but not necessarily one always to be deplored or avoided. As *part* of a theory of human thinking, a theory of problem environments is needed. In this area, psychology and artificial intelligence research have common concerns, and both have already made significant contributions. A considerable understanding has already been attained of the structures of several task environments: for example, chess, to mention one where the artificial intelligence interest has been strong; and concept formation, a rather different one that has been cultivated effectively by psychology.

What progress has been made toward an understanding of thinking, beyond creating a theory of problem environments? In studying an adaptive system, most of what is learned about it, beyond the nature of its tasks, has to do with the limits that prevent it from being *perfectly* adaptive—completely Protean and characterless. The research on perception reviewed by Haber, for example, answers many crucial questions about the limits of adaptiveness of the human thinking system on the input side. It has produced several specific numbers (including seven, the magic one) that characterize the processing speeds of this system, or that indicate the limits of its channel capacity. It has taught us that channel capacity must be measured in "chunks," not "bits," and has shown how to determine operationally what constitutes a chunk.

The numbers that characterize the perceptual system still need very much to be firmed up, but it is encouraging to be able to talk rather specifically about certain processes that require about 30 milliseconds, others, 500 milliseconds, and to know that a particular effect is maximized at a delay of 50 to 100 milliseconds. When investigators can talk that way about an adaptive system, they know something significant about how far and how fast it can adapt. Moreover, Thompson's paper provides encouragement that, while there is still an enormous gap between our knowledge of cognitive processes from physiological and psychological standpoints, respectively, there are possibilities for finding connections between the "magic numbers" revealed by studies of chemical and electrical processes in the brain, and some of the numbers that have been identified in psychological research as characterizing the thinking behavior of the system.

The surveys of research on serial learning by Battig and associative learning by Voss provide further evidence of a growing understanding of behavior in terms of cognitive processes. It is not terribly important whether verbal agreement has been reached on the nature of the elementary association—if there is such a thing. What is important is that there now exists a considerable body of tested, and to some extent quantitative, knowledge about the conditions under which associations occur and how fast they occur—how and how rapidly this adaptive thinking system can store new information in its several memories and access that information. Though the point has not been much discussed here, relatively general information-processing theories, like EPAM, are now at hand that incorporate and sum up a significant part of this knowledge about the system's mechanisms for memorizing, and make correct quantitative predictions of its behavior.

Restle's and Reitman's papers, because they approach their task in a somewhat different way from those mentioned above, do not provide surveys of exactly the same kind for the areas of problem solving or concept formation; but such surveys are available in the recent literature of those fields, and show the same kind of progress. It is known today, for example, that the limits of short-term memory are a major factor in determining how rapidly adaptive a subject can be solving concept-formation problems posed to him by an experiment. By providing subjects with memory aids, their rates of concept attainment can be greatly and predictably increased. Though Bourne, in his paper, professes to deplore theory, his own very interesting experiments on concept attainment have helped to demonstrate some of these interactions of short-term memory with thinking.

No purpose would be served by going on with this list, which is in large part a survey of what has already been surveyed by the papers in this text. The central point that emerges from the inventory, however, is that we, in fact, know a great deal today about that system of adaptive processes we call thinking (and not only about the task environments in which it occurs), and we are able to make increasingly powerful predictions about the circumstances under which and the degree to which a human organism will meet success in using its thought processes to adapt to a task environment—to solve its problems. Rothkopf's paper illustrates that we even know something about *improving* thought processes.

Of course, data about human cognitive processes has been coming out of psychological laboratories since Ebbinghaus, or before. As long as each piece of data could only be related to a particular laboratory task—rote learning by the serial anticipation method, a particular form of concept-attainment experiment with particular kinds of stimuli, or the like—our knowledge was a mass of factual detail with little order of coherence.

The progress reflected in these papers, and characteristic of the period since World War II, comes not primarily from new facts, although there are a number of those, but rather from a new coherence and ordering of the facts in terms of an underlying set of hypotheses about the processes that produced them. As psychologists have come to talk about the data of cognition more and more in information-processing terms, they have become increasingly aware that only a limited number of elementary information processes are required for the performance of a wide variety of thinking, problem-solving, and learning tasks; and that the main features of these processes, as they affect thinking behavior, can be summed up in a relatively small number of parameters.

The vocabulary and concepts of information processing provide a language and a framework, as operational and as formal as we please, for cumulating the available facts and putting them together into an organized picture. That picture is becoming an increasingly recognizable portrait of cognitive man—of man thinking.

12

A LETTER TO
ART MELTON[1]

GREGORY A. KIMBLE
University of Colorado

DEAR ART:

Since you probably share more of my general prejudices than any [of the contributors to this book], I wonder if you would be willing to listen to my problems in commenting on it and perhaps give me some advice. As a way of stating my main difficulty, one of my nonpsychological colleagues at Duke, Dr. Anne Scott (speaking in a very different context), once gave a talk with a very appealing title, "A Modest Proposal for a Quiet Revolution." I had the feeling that most of the authors [represented in this text] thought that they were making proposals of the type implied by Dr. Scott's title although, of course, some of them were more modest and quieter than others. In any event, I think that what I want to do in my comment is to attempt to relate several of the main themes appearing in the papers to familiar, even old-fashioned, ideas, and to show that they represent natural outgrowths of these ways of thinking. A part of my problem is that I don't know how far to go in this.

---

[1] This discussion was written as a letter to a colleague of Dr. Kimble's, Dr. Arthur W. Melton.

For one thing, if I try to be at all comprehensive, some of my points will be pretty trivial. For example, I wonder whether I should bother to mention again that some of the temporal parameters of simple decision making turn out to be the same as those in classical conditioning under circumstances where the similarity is not surprising; or whether there is any point in calling it to the attention of those who are interested in the storage of visual images that the facts of backward masking were well known to Helmholtz; or what good would come of it were I to remind the group at large that Bryan and Harter, before the turn of the century, described a series of stages in some forms of learning in which the stages were defined by the collection of small individual habits into larger organized units.

Probably, there is no way of avoiding the necessity of noting that Skinnerian progress in the study of thinking consists of a regression to the motor theory of consciousness developed in the twenties by Jacobsen and Max. I agree with Jenkins that this theory is unlikely to give us a complete account of the higher mental processes, and with our physiologically minded brethren that the curare studies provide strong support for such a conclusion. On the other hand, it seems to me that Holland has a point in developing the dimension from vigorous behavior, to delicate behavior, to covert behavior, and then in extrapolating this continuum to include thought. On the basis of this extrapolation, it does not seem unreasonable to me that thinking might be modifiable by some of the same techniques that work with overt acts. In fact, I think that Rothkopf's paper proved that an imaginative extension of a highly similar idea to the study of one aspect of thinking can lead to a very interesting program of research. It could also be argued, on the basis of evidence as old as Perky's results, that a similar relationship holds between the classical study of perception and thinking. For Perky showed that, under certain circumstances, percepts and images are indistinguishable, and sometimes, of course, we talk about having images as a form of thinking.

Obviously, a discussion of this type would lead in a dangerous direction. I would have to worry about the definition of thinking and about a possible taxonomy of thought, if there is more than one kind. This, in turn, would lead to all of the issues once raised by Skinner in his theoretical analysis of the concept of reflex. To paraphrase slightly, "We are proceeding, of course, upon the assumption that there *is* a process of thought, etc., etc., etc." Clearly, it would not be popular in a text about thinking to ask whether there is such a thing. So probably what I should do is just ignore this problem and proceed to discuss thinking as if I and everyone else really knew what I were talking about.

Maybe I could say something like this: Although it is probably too early to perceive the history of the science of thinking, the trends in the papers presented here suggest that future historians will give the credit for the first clear statement of the essential ideas to Sechenov. Sechenov, as you may recall, defined thought as "the first two-thirds of a reflex," or sometimes as "a reflex with an inhibited end." Such a definition, of course, sounds wildly unlike the more elegant statements in some of the papers, but the ideas were really much the same. In the abstract, and reduced to essentials, the Sechenov reflex consisted of four components: an input (or stimulus), a central switching mechanism, and an output (or response). The fourth element was a neural loop that allowed the brain to participate in reflex behavior, specifically by blocking the response. In this way, a reflex could be initiated and the central process could take place without overt reaction. To Sechenov, this suggested that an organism could think about an action without performing it.

In the psychology of learning, as you know, we have given this last idea formal status in the distinction between learning and performance. I hope you were reassured, as I was, to discover that several of our colleagues have retained this distinction. They differentiate, for example, between rules and actions carried out in the service of those rules and, for another example, between competence and performance. In these developments, they have generalized the distinction between learning and performance, I think, appropriately. Actually, we probably have a bigger problem in teaching this distinction to the physiological psychologists. It seems to me that what they say about what is innate and what is learned would be very different if they took the distinction in question as seriously as we in the psychology of learning do.

The big developments that carry the contributors to this text beyond Sechenov have been their powerful analyses of what goes on between input and output and, in various senses, this seems to be what they mean by thought. All that Sechenov had was a serial chaining of reflexes by way of feedback from responses, and the only hint of parallel processing lay in the fact that Sechenov thought that associations were probably formed at several levels in the nervous system. Now we have *mediation, computer routines, information processing, mental transactions*, and Lord knows what else, although it is clear that one thing else is Hull's old concept of Habit-Family-Hierarchy. I do think that the Hullian concept is in good hands with Frank Restle and Ernie Rothkopf. Frank calls the habits "hypotheses," of course, and Ernie calls them "mathemagenic behaviors," and both show that the organization of the hierarchy is uncomfortably complex. Moreover, the reor-

ganization involved in a single problem-solving thought may be as
complex as the whole history of evolution. But the parentage of the
Restle-Rothkopf approach seems clear. (Legitimacy is another matter,
but I, at least, could detect no methodological hanky-panky in these
extensions of Hull's theory of selective learning.)

One thing I find missing from most of the central-processing mechanisms described by our colleagues is anything resembling extinction
or inhibition although I suppose, if I make this criticism in my discussion, I had better say "information rejection" instead. In fact, the situation reminds me more than a little of an interchange between B. F.
Skinner and Clarence Graham in the old days when Skinner almost had
a theory that took the form of a hydraulic model with reflex reserves,
subsidiary reserves, and the like. Graham, who was interested in learning at the time, upon hearing Skinner describe the theory, is reported
to have said, "Fred, you know, what your system needs is a sphincter."
As I say, I don't know whether I'll mention this point in my discussion
at all but, if I do, I hope I have the good taste not to pursue the implications of that metaphor any further.

Probably, I will have to restrict my remarks to a certain length, and
I may not have a chance to deal with some important problems such
as the role of transfer of training in several of the analyses of thinking,
and the dubious worth of additional disproofs of Watsonian Behaviorism. But I do think that I will need to comment on a few matters of
general style. For one thing, the new students of thought seem to have
accepted an outmoded rationalism and intuitionism in their psychology,
although the exact way of applying these approaches has changed.
Whereas Tolman would have tried to answer a theoretical question by
imagining what he would do if he were a rat, the new fashion is to
imagine how you would behave if you were a computer with such and
such a program. A part of these same trends seems to be a relative de-
emphasis of the noncognitive functions in this control of behavior.
Almost nothing has been said about reinforcement, even from the Skin-
nerians; there has been hardly any reference to motivation and none
at all to adaptive value—considerations that we know to be important
in other areas.

It may be, of course, that these omissions are not oversights, but
rather that thinking and problem solving are less affected by these
motivational influences than are simple learning and conditioning. For
this reason, I do not believe that my preceding remarks represent important criticisms, or that those who study thinking have departed in
serious ways from the standard procedures of science. In fact, as most
of this letter has tried to say, my main reaction is quite the opposite.

We have seen a set of familiar ideas taken over, modified, reassembled, and applied to new phenomena—the whole process being greatly aided by the availability of powerful new techniques. It seems to me that this, in essence, is the way that scientific progress comes about. But this reraises my problem, Art. Do our colleagues recognize this? They seem so sure that they are on the verge of something brand new—something, as I suggested at the beginning, that combines certain elements of breakthrough with others of intellectual revolution. Do you think that I should continue to let them think this way? Or shall I show them that if they remove the R's and S's (as several of them seem to want to do) from their several modest proposals for quiet (r)evolution(s) that the true nature of their contributions stands revealed but is not thereby diminished?

Cordially,
Gregory A. Kimble